Theories of Cinema, 1945–1995

THEORIES OF
CINEMA
1 9 4 5 – 1 9 9 5

FRANCESCO CASETTI

Translated by Francesca Chiostri
and Elizabeth Gard Bartolini-Salimbeni
with Thomas Kelso
Revised and updated by the author

UNIVERSITY OF TEXAS PRESS, AUSTIN

Publication of this book was supported by a grant from the Sid Richardson Foundation.

Translated from *Teorie del cinema, 1945–1990* by Francesco Casetti, © 1993 Gruppo Editoriale Fabbri, Bompiani, Sonzogno, Etas S.p.A., Milan, 1993

First edition, 1999

Library of Congress Cataloging-in-Publication Data

Casetti, Francesco.
   [Teorie del cinema. English]
   Theories of cinema : 1945–1995 / Francesco Casetti ; translated by Francesca Chiostri and Elizabeth Gard Bartolini-Salimbeni with Thomas Kelso — 1st ed.
     p.   cm.
   "Revised and updated by the author."
   Includes bibliographical references and index.
   ISBN 0-292-71206-5 (hardcover)
   ISBN 0-292-71207-3 (pbk.)
   1. Motion pictures—Philosophy.   2. Film criticism.   I. Title.
   PN1995 .C36913   1999
   791.43'01—dc21   98-58071

TO MARTA

WATCHING A MOVIE

CONTENTS

Theories of Cinema, 1945–1995

INTRODUCTION

No art has ever become great without theory.
Béla Balász

This book is about theories. It offers a survey of the different ways in which films have been conceived, defined, studied, and observed from the mid-1940s to the mid-1990s.[1] It is meant as an addition to the existing studies, but with specific characteristics of its own. It examines the last fifty years of research, from 1945 to the present. The period of classic theories, to which Canudo, Epstein, Eisenstein, Balász, and Arnheim contributed, is already behind us. The postwar age hails new perspectives and styles, which make this era as interesting as the previous one, and even more complex, while the debates that originate in it are better articulated.

This book also focuses on broad trends more than on isolated contributions. It is true that every theorist's ideas deserve attention, but they need to be placed in the broader context of contemporary, more or less widespread statements, attitudes, and interests. Consequently, the following pages will approach the contributions of each scholar as representative of a specific trend or school of thought.

Another peculiarity of this book is that it develops an idea of film theory that is far from both the abstractions of those who would like to make it what it never was and the complacency of those who find traces of it in any intelligent discourse. Contemporary epistemology, in its effort to redefine the notion of "scientific theory," helps us to avoid this double danger. "Theory" is no longer seen only as a formal device, based on a restricted number of postulates, a well-defined conceptual framework, and rigid modalities for the employment of empirical concepts (Nagel); rather, it is thought of as a conjecture that allows us to try to grasp the meaning or the function of certain phenomena (Popper) or—better yet—as a point of view shared by a scientific community and considered effective (Kuhn). Therefore, a theory need not be an axiomatic construction, but it must at least be shared knowledge with which one tries to explain the world.[2] According to this logic we will characterize *film theory* as a *set of assumptions, more or less organized, explicit, and binding, which serves as a reference for scholars so that they can understand and explain the nature of the phenomenon under investigation.*

Such a definition, although generic, allows further clarification of our aim and the point of view behind it. Over the years film theories have appeared in many different guises. We find general definitions and probing exemplifications ("cinema is . . ."); precise opinions and motivated wishes ("cinema should be . . ."); trend-setting suggestions and official defense ("cinema can only be . . ."); comprehensive investigations and systematic explorations ("cinema seems to be . . ."); personal readings and meticulous evaluations ("cinema claims to be . . ."), etc. What gives these statements "density" is not, however, one form or another, but the ability to express a coherent, evident, and necessary proposal that is above all both shareable and shared by a group of scholars. An assumption acquires a theoretical dimension if, besides expressing *knowledge,* it also succeeds in proposing itself as a *community's heritage.* In other words, it presents itself as a body of knowledge that simultaneously guides the investigation, connects everyone's observations, synthesizes a generally felt impression, reveals recurrent questions, embodies "collective points of view," etc. A theory, in order to be such, must function as both a testing ground and a reason for discussion, and it must be acknowledged and appropriated by a more or less restricted group of scholars. Only then does it become a model of explanation or interpretation for a given phenomenon. This justifies the fact that no specific poetics will be analyzed in the pages that follow (although this choice is certainly open to dispute). We will not focus on those poetics in which authors offer a theory of their work unless they present an image of cinema that goes beyond its origin, one with which others can identify or on which others may base their research.[3] This is also why this work will privilege above all those contributions that "initiated a debate," even if they only did so much later than the moment of their appearance or indirectly. It is the *productivity* of a knowledge that ensures, perhaps more than anything else, its theoretical status.[4] After all, as stated above, this book is focused more on the frameworks of research, on their development and their dynamics, than on isolated contributions.

The definition of theory that we have advanced also allows us to clarify the slant of this work. On the one hand, we will devote a great deal of attention to the content of the various studies. We will see what notion of cinema they express, which aspects and problems they underscore. On the other hand, we will devote even more attention to the ways in which all research is realized. We will study the motivations behind it, the instruments it relies on, the strategies with which it proceeds, the traditions from which it emerges. Thus, on the one hand, "what is said" about film; on the other hand, *how* that content is expressed. Better still, we will examine the *image of cinema* proposed by a group of scholars and the *styles of reflection* adopted by them. In the last analysis it is often the latter that really differentiate one approach from another. As we will try to show, what changes in the postwar age is not the characteristics attributed to cinema by the scholars, but the way in which scholars organize their research. It is quite true that the theoretical underpinning of a discourse does not depend on the "genre" in which it is expressed; but it is also true that this "genre" does more to define the "kind" of theory at play than the statements contained therein.

Given these premises, we hope that this book will be of use to two branches of research that in some ways intersect with ours. First, this book aims to contribute to the history of cinema. For some time, cinematic history has been more than the history of films, evaluated in terms of their aesthetic results, oriented in the world of their filmmaker, and connected to their cultural context. Today the history of cinema deals with three different elements: the industrial "machine" regulating the production and circulation of films; the psychological "machine" regulating their understanding and consumption; and the discursive "machine" regulating their impact and valorization.[5] Together with criticism, theories are an important element in the third sphere: not only because by defining cinema they more or less openly support the films that approximate their conception of the cinema, but also because they sustain the existence of the cinema by making it an object worthy of theorizing. Therefore, mapping the theories of the last fifty years means shedding light on the "ideals" that have punctuated the history of cinema and, through these "ideals," the values to which this medium referred, the tasks it was given, the artistic or communicative events it was compared to, etc. It also means shedding light on the reflections to which the cinema gave birth, which belong to the cinema as much as the production and consumption of films do.

But theory is also a form of social knowledge: it tells what a group of scholars sees in a given phenomenon and, by means of these scholars, what a larger portion of the population is invited to see in it. "Seeing" here has a double meaning, because it is necessary to define both which aspects of a phenomenon are perceived and why. On the one hand, there is the "appearance" with which things present themselves. On the other hand, there are reasons why they catch our attention. It can thus be said that film theories shed light on both the notion of cinema shared by a certain society and the reasons why this society tends to be interested in films, on both the phenomenon's characteristics when it enters the collective scene and the awareness of it displayed by the collectivity. Both aspects underscore the *social nature* of the knowledge expounded by a theory. If it is true that the latter defines the way movies are watched (as stated above, by a group of "experts" but, through them, also by larger groups of people), then it is also true that a theory testifies to what is seen in films (the *social perception* of cinema) and the angle from which they are viewed (the *conditions of social existence* that lie behind this phenomenon). Viewed in this light, this book may also offer a useful sociological reflection on culture.

Of course, such goals require some systematic enlargements of perspective. For instance, one should compare the image of cinema as presented by theory with the one shared by society. This means keeping in mind popular magazines and books and reviews in newspapers. One should also compare the image of cinema proposed by theory with the image of other fields more or less related to cinema itself, such as theater, literature, and television. And one should compare the investigative styles developed by film theory with the ways of thinking active in other fields, examining how other theories (including scientific ones) and, more generally, other forms of social knowledge are expressed. Finally, one should compare the practices introduced by film theories with other activities related to cinema: critical practices, the practices of cultural politics, marketing practices, etc. We will attempt to broaden our framework, especially when necessary for a complete understanding of the meaning of our investigation. But it is evident that such an overview exceeds the limits of our investigation (and, if nothing else, those of the author himself).

The scope of this book is clear, in any case: we will return to the theoretical debate of the last fifty years in order to underscore its essential *meaning* and developments; we will reconstruct both the content and modalities of film studies in order to make evident the succession of *images of cinema* presented through time and the corresponding *styles of investigation;* we will concentrate most of all on the *framework of the debate* more than on isolated contributions (which explains why we will deal mostly with Euro-American theories); we will risk an attempt to *map* the development of the various theories both diachronically (and historically) and synchronically (as the expression of a complex typology).

Similarly clear is the role of this book. It will delve into the *tradition of the past* with the *awareness of the present,* as any historical or typological reconstruction requires. We can speak of "tradition" because the theories under examination still influence our age, even if only through distant echoes or through contrast with the present. The way we "talk about cinema" is still defined by them. We can also speak of "awareness of the present" because our analysis belongs to present history, and as such our gaze will not always be neutral and aseptic, if only because of the choices it will be necessary to make.

The epigraph to this introduction is a quotation from Balász, which indicates the necessity and the inevitability of theory, perhaps as an almost unwitting answer to Lumière's prophecy, according to which cinema was "an invention with no future." In the pages that follow we will try to discern how film theory has manifested itself through time and with what consequences. The necessity and inevitability of theory are two principles that, more than any other, will guide us.

This book would never have been written without the support of many friends and colleagues. Among others, this project was discussed with Dudley Andrew, Jacques Aumont, Michel Marie, Roger Odin, Pierre Sorlin, Giorgio Tinazzi, and Marc Vernet, to whom I am grateful for their generosity in sharing ideas. Suggestions and information also came from Rick Altman, David Bordwell, José Luis Fecè, Frank Kessler, Jenaro Talens, and Chris Wagstaff. An essential contribution to the completion of this work was the result of two long periods of study at the Université Paris III, DERCAV, and at the University of Iowa, Department of Communication Studies. I would like to thank Roger Odin and Dudley Andrew for making this possible and the teachers and staff of the two departments (in particular Carol Schrage) for their helpfulness. Some chapters are the result of discussions with experts in the field, and my thanks for their advice go to Alberto Abruzzese, Giuliana Bruno, Lucia Lumbelli, Maria Nadotti, Peppino Ortoleva, and Mauro Wolf. I am also grateful to those who, like Lauren Rabinovitz and Steve Ungar, provided access to otherwise inaccessible material, such as syllabi, research projects, and conference and seminar programs, which was useful for the reconstruction of the sources and developments of the debate. Gian Piero Brunetta, Elena Dagrada, and Giovanna Grignaffini read the manuscript and provided me with insightful suggestions, and I remember our discussions with pleasure and gratitude. Federica Villa and Roberta Lietti checked the manuscript from the point of view of its didactic effectiveness. Therefore, if the exposition of this complex topic has achieved a good degree of clarity, it is also thanks to them. Finally, I am grateful to Christian Metz, Gianfranco Bettetini, and Lino Miccichè for the care and attention with which they followed this whole work.

The American edition of the book has been a good opportunity for me to analyze some important contributions published in the 1990s. The new pages I wrote for this edition have enlarged and renewed the Italian edition. I wish to thank Jim Burr and Carolyn Wylie, whose help was essential to me.

1 POSTWAR FILM THEORIES: THREE PARADIGMS, THREE GENERATIONS

1.1. The Specificity of Film Theory after 1945

World War II does not represent, at least at first sight, a rupture in the history of film theory. Some of the trends that powerfully asserted themselves after 1945, such as the valorization of the realistic dimension, were rooted in experiences and debates that were ongoing between the 1930s and the 1940s; others, which had flourished before the war, like the analysis of film language, became established in the postwar years. Why then should World War II be considered some kind of watershed? Why should it be made into a turning point?

As a matter of fact, behind an apparent continuity of themes, the years around 1945 witnessed a series of unprecedented phenomena, which would slowly change the structure and the meaning of theory.

The first of such phenomena was the now widespread *acceptance* of cinema as a cultural fact. Until 1945 theoretical discourses had often seemed to be guided by the need to promote the new medium. By underscoring its potentials, if only by comparison to the other arts, and by praising its major achievements, these discourses tried to rescue film from its marginal position and to make it into something deserving full respect. In the postwar years cinema no longer needed to be defended. Of course, many perplexities were still shared by those who were used to dealing with the higher spheres of arts and thought and encountered the resistance of the custodians of tradition. Most intellectuals, however, took for granted the legitimacy of the new medium. The reasons for this are twofold: on the one hand, cinema had widely proved its ability to testify to the spirit of an epoch and to express individual creativity. On the other hand, the notion of culture itself was becoming broader, to the point of including all the cultural forms—even the most current ones—that society used to speak about itself, its members, or the world. In this sense the famous letter written by Croce in 1948, in which film was accepted as a work of art, was already behind the times,[1] while the success of filmology, which was born in 1947 with the aim of transforming cinema into a topic for research at the university level, showed the direction in which our interests had already developed.[2]

The second phenomenon that needs to be mentioned is the accentuation of the specialized characteristics of film theory. Before the war, the debate about the new medium appeared to be open to anyone. Directors, scholars, critics, musicologists, and psychologists all found themselves working the same terrain. After the war, more precise areas of expertise began to be defined. Those who intervened in the discussion did so in the name of their specific scholarly background, if not on the basis of their profession. This also happened because the institutions producing theory were changing. They were no longer cultural journals that devoted special issues to the new medium (such as the Italian *Solaria* or *L'Italiano*),[3] but cinema journals, which were engaged in a continuous debate, often free from the task of popularization, and ready to promote research and accept detailed suggestions (in Italy, for example, besides *Bianco e Nero,* which was already active in the prewar period, and *Cinema,* whose "new series" started in the postwar years, *La Rivista del Cinema Italiano, Cinema Nuovo,* and *Filmcritica* emerged). Theory was no longer produced by private clubs, animated by enthusiastic amateurs (remaining in Italy we find, for instance, Ferrieri's *Convegno*), but research groups and pressure groups that became the meeting point of professionals working in the field (the Circolo Romano del Cinema). There were no longer only film schools (the Centro Sperimentale di Cinematografia), but universities (from the early 1960s onward, first Urbino and then Turin and Genoa).

Specialization worked on at least three different levels. First, there was a separation between theoretical and ordinary language. We moved from a common lexicon, scarcely marked by any technical terms ("montage," "close-up," "photogenic quality," etc.), to a real jargon, full of words that defy immediate decoding, at least some of which were borrowed from other fields.

Filmology once again set an example, by explicitly proposing a new vocabulary ("filmofanic," "profilmic," "diegetic," etc.), just as semiotics and psychoanalysis would become exemplary in the 1960s and 1970s by tending toward private lexemes ("syntagmatic," "icon," "suture," etc.). There was, then, a separation between theory and criticism. Instead of a mutually enriching interchange that made theory into a sort of "conscience" of criticism, we observe an increasing mutual indifference. The categories elaborated by one group did not rely immediately on the discourse developed by the other. In this sense, it is significant that some journals appeared that dealt only with theory, such as *Screen, Iris,* and *Hors Cadre.* For them the important thing was no longer discussing films, but discussing the ways in which films can be discussed.[4] Finally, there was a separation between theory and practice. Both the figure of the director–scholar and the old division of roles were disappearing (according to this division, the critic was both a mentor and a prophet, and the filmmaker appeared in the guise of a witness and an explorer); in their place appeared a theater of incommunicability in which the theorists dreamed of a cinema that did not exist, and yet continued to propose it, while the directors made the films they wanted or were able to make, not paying much heed to the suggestions they were given.[5]

The third phenomenon to be taken into account is the *internationalization* of the debate. Before the war, the discussion took place mostly at a local level. Of course, there were also theories that transcended national boundaries (Russian theory comes to mind), as well as fruitful exchanges (e.g., the constant relations between Italian and French intellectuals). But theory was fundamentally autochthonous. After the war, a fragmentation of the national landscapes took place, leaving room for currents of thought that were often indifferent to one another, while the channels of communication between geographically distant groups became stronger. A few facts show how the development of theory stepped beyond national boundaries to operate in a worldwide setting:[6] the way in which the Italian theory of realism took hold abroad; the cooperation among universities that was promoted by filmology; the "coagulative" capacity exercised by semiotics.

Thus, cinema was *accepted* as cultural fact, theory became more *specialized,* and the debate was more *international.* This is of course only a schematization and does not take into account either the slow pace at which some phenomena evolved or the relapses that sometimes took place. Its aim is essentially to record some trends. These trends not only emerged, however, but became a constant presence in the postwar years. Film theory was so influenced by them that it acquired a different profile and a greater importance than before. In this sense, theory after 1945 acquired a *specificity* of its own.

Besides the three phenomena mentioned above, there was also a fourth one, which played an equally relevant role: the *plurality* of the procedures. This does not mean that prewar film theory ever knew real unity; it abounded in diverse themes, interests, and sensibilities. After 1945, however, there was a growing feeling that such differences might also influence the construction of a theory, the motivations behind it, the aims that guide it. Thus, the idea of a possible multiplicity of *paradigms* took shape. This is going to be our field of inquiry.

1.2.   The Research Strategies

In a 1965 essay, in which he focused on the different theories that had developed during the past fifteen years, Christian Metz observed how—besides journalistic essays, historical monographs, and criticism itself—any discourse wanting to deal with cinema as such fits into one of two very different categories: we find an "internal" approach to the phenomenon, which tries to show how cinema belongs to the domain of *art* and, on this basis, attempts to bring to light its intrinsic richness; and we find an "external" approach, which considers cinema an objective *fact:* it is necessary to distinguish its psychological, sociological, and economic (etc.) dimensions and to analyze it through recourse to various sciences.[7] Nineteen years later, in a different cultural context, Dudley Andrew noticed a new split: there are theories that consider cinema a stock of *examples* to which a number of perfectly systematized categories—be they semiotic, psychoanalytical, or ideological—can be applied; and there are theories that see cinema as a site of *questions* that can be brought into accord in order to formulate ever more advanced theoretical criteria.[8]

We could cite more evidence, but Metz and Andrew already suggest the essential point. In fact, they not only offer us concrete proof of how scholars in the field perceive the existence of precise contrasts in the modes of theorizing, but also point out—one for the 1950s and 1960s, the other for the 1970s and 1980s—the nuclei around which such differences are constructed. Let us reconsider the oppositions evoked by Metz and Andrew, respectively, one between a view of cinema as art or as fact and the other between the use of film as a stock of examples or as a site of questions. The line of opposition is clear. It only needs to be described in more detail.

In the 1950s and 1960s there was a conflict between those who considered cinema a means of expression through which personality, ideology, and culture were manifested and those who viewed it as an objective reality, to be examined in its tangible components and in the way it actually works. Thus, we have an *aesthetic* discourse, which in the final analysis is *essentialist,* and a discourse that attempts to be *scientific* and is therefore *methodological.* The former tries to define the nature of cinema in order to exalt its peculiarity; the latter attempts, rather, to derive a series of observations from it, to compare them, and to use them as the basis for further work as well as to verify them through new experiments. Also, the aesthetic discourse tries to perceive cinema in its totality, as if to encompass all its aspects in a single glance; the scientific discourse tries, on the contrary, to distinguish among possible perspectives, each connected with a specific point of view and, consequently, with a specific method of inquiry. Finally, after recognizing the fundamental characteristics of cinema, the former suggests the trends to be followed, whereas the latter derives general laws from the recurrence of certain data and uses them to explain all that happens.

Let us now move on to the 1970s and 1980s. The scientific or methodological approach had taken over, but it had also become cumbersome, so that the need to develop tools for research often prevailed over the analysis of facts themselves. The models to be applied risked becoming more important than the results of their application; cinema was thus reduced to a mere stock of "examples" to be exhibited, as opposed to a field of "inquiry." Thus, we observe the rise of a new border line. Here the conflict was between an *analytical* and an *interpretive* approach. The former proceeds through prospecting, surveys, measurements, polls; the latter through a sort of dialogue between the scholar and the object of study, a dialogue capable of progressively modifying both its protagonists. The former prefers to apply to the cinema research criteria that have already been tested, whose effectiveness does not depend on the kind of phenomenon under investigation; the latter is engaged in experimenting with categories that, without being ad hoc, are still influenced by the particularity of the field of investigation. Finally, the analytical approach aims to offer a picture of the reality observed that is as complete as possible, at least with respect to the chosen perspective; the interpretive approach knows that there is no end to its questions, and yet it continues to formulate them, availing itself of any hint of an answer. In short, the former views cinema as a well-defined field that can be grasped both in its specific and in its more general aspects; the latter, on the contrary, perceives it as an open-ended reality, which cannot be reduced to a fixed formula and may reveal dark zones and unforeseen folds.

There was an opposition between an aesthetic and a scientific discourse and, after the victory of the second, an opposition between an analytical and a hermeneutical discourse. The question to be asked, then, is whether this doubled line of opposition implies differences in the orientation and style of research or something more.

In order to answer this question we need to take a step back and see how a theory is usually structured. It consists of three major components.[9] First, there is the *metaphysical* or *constitutive* component, which legitimizes the assumptions that form the basis of the research (for instance, the status assigned to the object, our idea of knowledge, etc.). It is this part that legitimizes the conceptual foundation of a theory and that determines its intelligibility. Then we have a *systematic* or *regulative* component, which legitimizes the shape of the research and the methodological criteria it obeys (for instance, simplicity vs. elegance, symmetry vs. generality): this is the part that legitimizes the criteria according to which a theory is constructed and that determines its rationality. Finally, there is the *physical* or *inductive component,* which legitimizes the acquisition of empirical data, the methods of their discovery and selection, and their linkage. This part legitimizes the criteria for verifying, or falsifying, the theory itself and determining its factuality. All three components are necessary. A theory is such only insofar as it aligns some basic beliefs with a way to organize data and with the observation of reality. This does not mean that some kinds of reflections cannot emphasize one component more than another, relying on it for support. Thus, we have theories that underscore the importance of the metaphysical dimension, others for which the systematic dimension is fundamental, and still others that give precedence to the role of the physical dimension: rationalism, operationalism, and empiricism could serve as examples.

Film theories do not behave differently. They, too, rely on three components. There is a nucleus of basic ideas that frames the research; there is a network of concepts that establishes the order and the modality of the exposition; and there are several concrete observations that make verification possible. And film theories, while relying on all three dimensions, also underscore one of them. Some prefer conceptual explanations, perhaps in the attempt to define cinema as such. Some emphasize the way in which their own discourse is articulated and work on methods of analysis. Still others rely on direct observation and initiate a dialogue with the field of investigation.

This is exactly what I think happened in the postwar years. The contrast between the aesthetic and the scientific approaches indeed was a clash between those who for the most part challenged general assumptions and those who devoted more effort to the study of analytical tools. The contrast between the analytical and the interpretive approaches was a clash between those who worked on methods of analysis and those who gave more weight to the factual dimension. This means that the dividing lines pointed out by Metz and Andrew do not concern simply the orientations and the styles of the research, but the very structure of the theoretical discourse. They mark the tension between different *paradigms,* that is, between the different models (shared by a scholarly community) according to which research was planned, conducted, and explained.[10] In particular, we observe the demarcation of three areas: the aesthetic–existentialist, the scientific–analytical, and the interpretive. Let us try to assemble the data so far collected and to describe these areas one by one in an organic way.

1.3.   Three Paradigms

The appropriate name for the first paradigm is *ontological theory.* The term recalls André Bazin, and in particular the title of perhaps his most famous essay, as well as the subtitle of the first volume of his work.[11] Why "ontological" theory and not "aesthetic," as we have called it so far? Because, beyond the widespread reference to the typical problems of art, this approach is characterized by the question around which it revolves, formulated by Bazin himself: "What is cinema?"[12] Such a question, with its conciseness, sheds light on two things. On the one hand, it underscores the existence of several preliminary assumptions that provide a foundation for the research, such as the idea that cinema itself is an identifiable object, that it can be grasped directly, etc. Hence the valorization of the theory's conceptual presuppositions, of its core, of its constitutive moment, in short, of what we called the *metaphysical component.* On the other hand, Bazin's question directs our attention to the very nature of the phenomenon under investigation, going beyond its various facets. Hence the attention to the features considered fundamental, to the properties believed to be decisive, in short, to its *essence*. Here the ontological theory finds justification of its name as well as its recurrent features, in the valorization of the metaphysical component and the search for essence.

Other features derive from these. First, the procedures of the ontological theory, more than breaking down or weighing the phenomenon, look for its typical, typifying elements or its key functions; thus, its aim is not simply a collation or a list, but a real *definition* of what lies in front of us. A second feature is the kind of knowledge that is at stake: ontological theory expresses a comprehensive idea of cinema, based on a tacit agreement among assumptions and data and capable of imposing itself with a kind of immediacy. Therefore, it deals with a knowledge of the phenomenon that is, so to speak, *global* (or all-encompassing). Finally, there are the criteria to be followed: by superimposing that which is given empirically and that which is given according to the premises of the theory ("so it is and so it must be"), ontological theory confronts something that it assumes has an intrinsic value. It works on the basis of certainties. It chooses *truth* as its own measure.

These are the principal features of ontological theory. Of course, its specific characteristics may vary. There are approaches that answer the initial question by insisting on the realistic nature of cinema (Bazin, Kracauer); others insist, rather, on the fact that cinema belongs to the realm of the imaginary (Morin); others extol its linguistic or communicative capacities (Della Volpe, Mitry). But, beyond the diversity of these positions, the basic, fundamental question remains, together with the common strategy for answering it. In asking what cinema is, ontological theories always aim to uncover an essence in order to define the phenomenon, to reach a global knowledge, and to measure themselves in terms of a form of truth.

The second paradigm, which we could call that of the *methodological theories,* radically modifies the field. The question behind it, in fact, is no longer "What is cinema as such?" but "From which standpoint should cinema be studied, and what does it look like from such a perspective?" Thus, the attention shifts toward the way in which the research is planned and conducted. What is now emphasized is the need to choose a certain point of view and to model, on this basis, both the gathering and the presentation of the data. Here we focus on the order that underlies the research and on the ensuing report. In short, we focus on the "method" behind the revelation and the writing, and as a result we valorize the theory's *systematic component.* Similarly, what we discover in this way is no longer a set of rules, but a "section" of the phenomenon, which depends on the point of view adopted and which sheds light on some facts, which are given precedence. As a result, it underscores what is *pertinent* rather than what is essential.

The recurrent features of the methodological theory are a privileging of the systematic component and a search for pertinence. It may appear in many guises, which correspond to all those disciplines (sociology, psychology, psychoanalysis, semiotics, etc.) that have approached cinema, applying their point of view to it, making it into an object of research. Beyond the diversities of all these approaches, however, two constant features are the prominence given to structure and the selection of facts on the basis of their pertinence.

From these features derive some behaviors and outcomes of this paradigm. Let us start by considering how methodological theories proceed: because they rely on a specific point of view, their preoccupation is to promote a coherent, complete collection of data more than to shed light on the ultimate nature of the phenomenon; the focus is more on an *analysis* than on a definition. Let us then think of the kind of knowledge supported by the methodological theories: starting from a specific point of view, they mobilize a knowledge that comes directly from the application of certain research tools. Thus, on the one hand, such knowledge appears to be tied to the effectiveness of the method of data collection and as such to be verifiable only by an expert. On the other hand, however, it seems to be able to cover all the chosen objects, thanks to the systematic quality of its samples, the continuous linking of the data, and the final construction of a model. In short, this sort of knowledge may well be termed "perspectival." Let us think, finally, of the criteria adopted by methodological theories as their yardstick. Conscious of their specific point of view, they invoke an assessment more than a certainty, the possibility of proof more than the evidence, the *correctness* of the research more than a specific truth.

Let us now move on to the last paradigm, which we can call that of *field theories*. The question behind it is "Which problems does cinema give rise to, and how does it manage to both shed light on them and receive light from them?" Such a question gives prominence to a sort of dialogue between scholars and the object of their studies, as well as the willingness of the former to open up to events and the ability of the latter to constitute a real field of investigation. In any case, what is being valorized is the theory's inductive, *phenomenal dimension*. Similarly, the aim is to single out the questions that touch on cinema and to notice the exemplary quality of some of its articulations: what emerges is neither essence nor pertinence, but rather a field of questions or a *problem.*

Thus, the two basic features of the third major postwar theoretical paradigm, which give it its name, are the formation of a "field of observation" with the prevalence of the inductive component and the delineation of a "field of questions" with the focus on a problem. The paths actually followed are many. Some scholars approach cinema in order to question its modes of representation (Bellour, feminist film theory, Aumont, Bordwell, etc.); others do it in order to analyze the audience's position and role (Odin, enunciation theory, narratology, etc.), or to question the political validity of the medium (see French, Italian, American, etc., journals of the first half of the 1970s), or even to reconstruct the history of cinema. The field, once explored, gives rise to many different questions, some of which relate directly to it, others only tangentially. Its two fundamental features remain constant, however, and orient the whole sector.

These two features shed light on other properties of this paradigm. Let us consider first of all the way it proceeds. When we privilege a contact and a problem, we try above all to grasp the emerging aspects, rather than the constitutive or relevant ones, of a phenomenon. The dominant feature is the pleasure of *exploration* more than the need for definitions or the will to analyze. Let us consider the kind of knowledge that this implies. Field theory promotes a knowledge that is common only to researchers who share the same preoccupations, and in this sense it may seem limited and localized. Such knowledge, however, is informed by problems that are, so to speak, "in the air," so that it concerns many subjects of study, many groups of scholars, many research methods. As a result, we have a knowledge that is neither global nor focused, but rather transversal. We must not forget to mention the measures that field theory adopts as its own. The criterion that marks an approach as good or bad is no longer tied to the truth of its statements or to the correctness of its research, but to the quality of the question it asks cinema and to the richness of the answers the latter provides. This approach emphasizes such relevant boundaries as the interest of the research, the productivity of the data, the singularity of the observations, in a word, the "pregnancy" of the discourse.

So far we have dealt with the internal, formal features of the three main kinds of postwar film theory, which are summarized in Table 1.1.

Table 1.1

	Ontological Theories	Methodological Theories	Field Theories
Component	metaphysical	systematic	phenomenal
Object	essence	pertinence	problematic
Operation	definition	analysis	exploration
Knowledge	global	focus	transversal
Criterion	truth	correctness	pregnancy

1.4. Three Generations

These three kinds of theory can not only be characterized by their internal structure. As with all paradigms, they also constitute a reference scheme, shared by a number of scholars. They represent a cluster of ideas, procedures, and results that a community confronts. In this sense they are formulas with a high social valence, closely connected to the intellectual profile of scholars, to the motivations behind their work, and to the institutions where such work is done. These formulas, having their roots in society, mark its changes. In fact, they shed light on choices made in each period, on solutions that are rewarded and procedures that are considered appropriate, on groups that are foregrounded, and on openings that are created. A paradigm is a social device and as such it influences (or is influenced by) history.

This allows us to observe that these three kinds of theory characterize the work of three generations of scholars, each with its own needs, resources, environment, tools, and paths. Although we know that from a generation to the next intersections and superimpositions continuously occur, it is still possible to try to define the general contexts in which they operated.

The champions of ontological theories are those critics who are not satisfied with simply reviewing a film but intend to explore the nature of cinema itself, viewing this second task as the foundational and orienting moment of their activity. These scholars form an intellectual group whose homogeneity depends more on the language they use than on a common educational background. This group's professionalization relies more on its ability to intervene in the cinematographic debate than on a precise institutional role. Its tools are essentially essays or lead articles published in trend-setting journals, underscoring both the still extant link between criticism and theory and the different roles and degrees of importance that these two discourses assume. We should add that the purpose that animates these scholars is their need to fully include cinema in the domain of art and culture. In order to do so, however, they no longer rely on a valorizing procedure, which would simply list its merits and results. Rather, they single out the great polarities that characterize the aesthetic or expressive dimension and view the new medium in relation to these. Here we find that logic of acceptance already mentioned at the beginning: theorists no longer appear as generous prophets, but as explorers sent by some East India Company to determine the coordinates of the new territory.

Methodological theories usually have other champions, scholars in precise disciplinary fields, for whom cinema is one of many possible objects of interest and who apply to it research tools that have already been well tested. Such groups are heterogeneous in terms of language and interests, but homogeneous in terms of scholarly background. Sociologists, psychologists, and semiologists follow different research paths, but share a common scientific training and have an overall feeling of the obligations they are supposed to meet. Professionalism here does not depend on the importance acquired by the debate on cinema. Rather, it depends on an institutional role (the profession of the researcher): being a sociologist, a psychologist, a semiologist, etc., means having received training of a certain kind before developing an interest in cinema. It also implies straining to make the transplant of skills painless. The research takes place, obviously, within research institutions, laboratories, and university departments, and the results are published in disciplinary journals, which address themselves more to experts in the field than to film lovers. We should add that these second-generation theorists take for granted the status of the cinema as part of cultural phenomena. Their main concern is supplying cinema with internal coordinates, discovering the laws of its functioning, and measuring their extension and effects. The purpose of the research becomes less generic, but in some ways more general, and the discourse loses its residual evaluative features to become one piece in a large mosaic.

Field theories operate in yet another context. These scholars may be specialists in the field of film who engage in a more general debate. But they may also come from other fields, finding in cinema a crucially interesting

Table 1.2

	Ontological Theories	Methodological Theories	Field Theories
Subjects	film critics	disciplinary scholars	specialists and intellectuals
Environment	journal or group	research institute and university	university of mass media
Unifying factor	common language	intellectual background	convergence of interest
Means of expression	essays or lead articles	scientific paper	study or research
Purpose	cultural	scientific	social

subject. Thus, "technical" background and "all-inclusive" engagement blend: what matters is the clarification of the problem being worked on. This is what assures the homogeneity of the research groups; their professionalism depends both on the fact that they work in specific environments (mostly universities) and on the fact that they become visible on the social scene (think of the roles assigned today to intellectuals, who are seen as experts, witnesses, polemicists, etc.). Their research tools include both disciplinary quality and "lack of discipline"; similarly, the results appear both as essays, perhaps published in a trend-setting journal, and as lectures, reports, newspaper articles, etc. We should add that the emerging trend is, however, to give up strong models, to operate on intersections, peculiarities, lines of flight, black holes. The scientific community becomes a nebula.

Table 1.2 summarizes these observations.

Let us conclude the description of the three great kinds of film theory that developed after World War II here. So far we have offered a general overview of their internal features and external contexts.[13] The following pages will present a more detailed view of this same picture, first showing its internal development. As far as ontological theories are concerned, we will examine the canonical definitions of cinema as reality, as imaginary, and as language. With regard to methodological theories, we will look at the sociological, psychological, semiotic, and psychoanalytic approaches. In dealing with field theories, we will reconstruct the discussion on the ideology, the representation, and the generic identity of the subjects on and beyond the screen, on cinema's ability to become witness to cultural processes, and on the possibility of reconstructing its history. The following pages will offer a detailed analysis of the field by presenting the superimpositions and layerings of cinema theories in such a way that the landscape will emerge as more varied and richer in (sometimes crucial) nuances than we have managed to show so far.

2   CINEMA AND REALITY

2.1.   The Splendor of the Real

"No image is beautiful in itself . . . but because it is the splendor of the real."
With these words Jean-Luc Godard, writing in 1959 for *Cahiers du Cinéma,*
described *India* by Roberto Rossellini. In so doing, he was recalling—albeit
with a touch of irony—some of the concepts around which the question
of cinematic realism had developed. Godard's sentence, in fact, summarized
with the succinctness of a slogan a well-established attitude: on the one hand,
the rejection of an image conceived as "beautiful in itself," thus perfectly self-
sufficient and autonomous (one could call this an image-image); on the other
hand, the return to something that is reproposed and prolonged by the image,
namely, the splendor of the world, the truth of things, in a word, *reality.*

The debate on cinematic realism developed around two central points:
opposition to the image-image and support for the recovery of the splendor
and truth of reality. These cues gave rise to the famous metaphors of cinema
as a window open on the world and of cinema as a mirror of life. Let us try
to deepen our understanding of the various directions and different stages
of this investigation, beyond the most immediate suggestions emerging from
Godard's sentence.

Three preliminary observations are necessary, the first being of a more
general nature than the others. The demand that the cinema deal directly
with reality was of course not a product of the mid-1940s. We can find prior
examples of such a demand, on more than one occasion. It was, however,
only in the immediate postwar years that this still marginal request became a

strong hypothesis, because it was no longer based, as it had been previously, on matters of style or effectiveness, but on an intrinsic necessity. In fact, the idea was that cinema orients itself toward reality because of its "photographic nature." The cinema is disposed to become evidence, a document, because it is constructed to record what lies before the camera. This initiates an intimate—not an occasional and external—bond with reality, a natural bond due to the nature of the medium itself. As a consequence, there was a shift from declarations of poetics or cultural statements to a precise theoretical proposal.

The second observation consists in noting that this theoretical proposal radically overturns a belief that was most common between the wars: the belief that the cinema could not be art insofar as it was merely a reproductive instrument. If it has no aesthetic value, one would say, it is because it *copies* reality, rather than playing with its particular and universal elements, and because it copies it *mechanically,* rather than through the mediation of the "creating" director. Benedetto Croce's position comes immediately to mind, as do, more generally, the positions of many Italian theorists of Idealism in the 1920s and 1930s. Their primary aim was to show the distance between filmic images and filmed reality, as well as the role played by the filmmaker in the reelaboration of the initial material.[1] In the postwar debate, however, the reproductive dimension of cinema became its strong point. By respecting that, and even making it the first priority, cinema found itself. It is not by chance, then, that both among Italian Neorealist scholars (who are mostly free of Croce's influence) and in theoretical contributions such as those of Bazin or Kracauer (whose thought is rooted, respectively, in phenomenology and positivism) the focus is on evaluating the "photographic basis" of cinema. This basis is the starting point of any study. Above all, it is by adjusting to this that a film may reach its true artistic potential.

The third observation is the following. If within the debate everyone extols the close relationship between the reality that lies before the camera and the images that represent it, each theorist thinks of this relationship in different terms. The dividing lines are manifold. For instance, one of the questions is whether this representation should emphasize the singularity of what is reproduced or, rather, should afford us a comprehensive view of the world and, therefore, whether it should have a mainly documentary value or should somehow become interpretive. This is the difference between immediate and critical realism, between empirical and great realism, present throughout the

Italian debate on Neorealist cinema. Furthermore, we should ask ourselves if this representation returns the real to us in all its density and fullness, beyond the form in which it appears, or if, on the contrary, it only provides us with the outlines, perhaps even the most imperceptible ones, but still only outlines. In other words, do films somehow prolong our experience of the world, bringing it to life on the screen, or do they present it as an event complete in itself, merely describing it as best they can? This is the difference between Bazin's existential (so to speak) realism and Kracauer's functional realism.

These dividing lines will become clear through an analysis of some key episodes of the debate. We will begin with those Italian theorists who are closest to the experience of Neorealist cinema; then we will move on to Bazin and Kracauer, who probably represent the moment of greatest clarification of the problems and who lead us to the end of the 1950s. We will end our analysis with the development of theory in the following decades, during which the previous experience reemerged in different contexts, together with methodological (Pasolini) or hermeneutical studies (Deleuze).

2.2.   Cinema as Reappropriation of Reality: The Neorealist Debate

In postwar Italy Neorealism furnished both a strong stimulus and a valuable site for confrontation. Prompted by the works of Rossellini, Visconti, and De Sica, many scholars—both in Italy and abroad—studied the relationship between cinema and reality. Yet the relationship between cinematic practice and theory was not linear. If it is true that Neorealist films allowed some positions to emerge, develop, and progress, it is also true that scholars often stepped beyond concrete evidence to take other motivations into account. More clearly stated, the appearance of a series of films revealed this orientation and brought it to the fore,[2] but wider obligations gave detailed shape to the scholarly reflection.

The Italian debate[3] is a good example of the complexity of the situation, and its beginnings are indicative. In 1954 *Roma città aperta* let the world know of this new school. *Paisà* gave the movement its manifesto in 1946. But Italian theory only started concentrating on Neorealism around 1948–1949. Before this there seems to have been a need to reconnect with the past or to end an earlier discourse that had been left unfinished. We find again, for instance, the reproposal of a theme characteristic of the 1930s, namely, the definition of a "third way" for cinema in the age of sound, examples of which could be found in Eisenstein's *Ivan Groznij,* Carné's *Les enfants du paradis,* and Olivier's *Henry V.*[4] We also find again the attempt to obtain recognition from the "official" (Crocean) aesthetics, which strongly questioned the possibility of cinema as art.[5] Even those critics who, at the beginning of the decade, had hoped for a return to realism (see *Cinema*) were at least partially disoriented. The struggle to recover Giovanni Verga's lesson[6] had prevailed over the idea of a "live" story, which was also dealt with in the journal.[7] Rossellini's two films seemed to upset this hierarchy and started taking a somewhat unexpected path. Thus, Italian scholars were a little slow in realizing the importance of the cinema that was being born. This confirms that theory takes into consideration both contemporary production and its own history and requirements.

We find a similar mixture of different trends when Neorealism received full attention, from 1948–1949 onward. It is enough to think of the reasons that led to this new attitude. Some of them were purely cinematic. First, scholars realized that Italian films received great recognition abroad. Second, two key works, *Ladri di biciclette* and *La terra trema,* were produced. Other reasons transcended cinema itself: the choice to take an active part in the contemporary political situation (because of which, right before the 1948 elections, defending Neorealism against censure and attacks became a sign of one's political engagement); the desire to find a wide ground for comparison (thus, Neorealism was discussed—see the proceedings of the convention held in Perugia in September 1949—as the means to establish connections among scholars coming from different fields).[8] Again, we observe a close intermingling of filmic and more general elements.

These observations allow us to delineate the framework of the debate. First, the terms at stake: theory must deal with its history (going back to and overcoming Croce's philosophy); it responds to social obligations (the presence of a political engagement, the involvement—often a real militancy—with the left); it reconsiders some fundamental themes (Neorealism was seen as a contribution to redefining the cultural identity of a country that had just emerged from a war). On the basis of the observations above we can also attempt a periodization: the phase during which film production was not paralleled by the development of theory (1945–1948) was followed by another, during which films considered essential initiated questions on cinema itself, on its role, its destiny. From 1955 onward, we observe yet another phase, in which theory showed signs of both saturation and renewal. If this is the general framework, it should be added that within it some voices assumed particular significance, because of both their exemplary nature and the complexity of their motivations. The first voice to be taken into account is certainly that of Cesare Zavattini, not only a screenwriter, director, and indefatigable proponent of Neorealism, but also a lucid, perspicacious theorist. It is not easy to offer a synthesis of his innumerable contributions to the ongoing debate, which were often prompted by specific occasions and always quite long (many of the works on Neorealism, collected and edited by Mino Argentieri, are now found in Zavattini 1979), but we will try to single out some of his major points.[9]

Zavattini's starting point is the idea that both the war and the fight for liberation taught everyone—even filmmakers—to appreciate the richness of the real and to discover the importance of current events. Hence the need to bring life and spectacle together until they coincide: "The space between life and spectacle must disappear" (Zavattini 1979: 103).[10] This closeness was achieved in two steps. Initially, real elements were introduced into fiction in order to invent stories as close as possible to reality. But this was not enough: real events themselves were recaptured, to re-create reality as a story. "What we are really attempting is not to invent a story that looks like reality, but to present reality as if it were a story" (103). And again: "It is not a question of making imaginary things become 'reality' (making them look true, real), but of making things as they really are most significant, almost as if they were telling their story by themselves" (97). Thus, life itself must appear on the screen. Naturally, this approach will produce spectacles that no longer have any ties to fiction. It will create stories that are already far from artificiality. Film will emphasize ordinariness, normality; it will discover the importance of what lies before our eyes, things we do not usually notice. In particular, no longer will any event be considered merely a prerequisite to another event, which will in its turn be quickly abandoned. We will "stay" on the scene, because the scene has in itself unlimited density. Nor will the individual frame serve as a simple "bridge" to the next frame, but each one will be equally intense and revealing. "Every moment is infinitely rich. Banality does not exist" (104). Therefore, the terms *spectacle* and *story* will still be used, but we will need to know that we are outside the logic that has so far characterized them in opposition to each other. The mark of this new trend will be that filmmakers will give up predetermined theses, indicated by a happy or a sad ending according to the case at hand. The call of reality is the only voice to be obeyed. In reality, "we are neither good nor bad, neither saints nor devils. We *are*" (56).

But why does this new trend privilege life and its everyday moments, the idea of being simply what one is? There was a moral reason for this, connected with human beings' need to *know each other*. Interpersonal knowledge became a means to achieve solidarity, to realize a real community of intentions that excluded no one. Cinema, thus, was the perfect instrument of knowledge. "No other form of expression shares cinema's original and innate ability to photograph those things that we deem worthy to be shown in their everyday aspects, in their longest, truest duration. . . . No other form of expression has, to the extent that cinema has, the possibility of bringing knowledge to the majority of people" (98). Of course, this vocation was often betrayed: Méliès' fairy-tale world overcame Lumière and his wish to stay close to life. But it is necessary to go back to cinema's original reasons for being, rejecting economic ties and restoring importance to those who work in the world of cinema ("dictatorship of artists" vs. producers). It is necessary to reject the division of labor that cameras impose and to maximize the director's responsibility (the single filmmaker vs. collaboration). It is also necessary to reject preexisting formulas and to open oneself to possibility ("only what we are may be preordained. For this reason, man himself, in his integrity, both ready and disarmed in the face of events, will become the topic [of Neorealism]" [75]). The need is felt to reject books of grammar and rhetoric, allowing things themselves to lead us ("No longer are canons or style rules needed . . . ; form will be dictated only by events, by the thing that happened itself, expressed at once" [68]). Also, there is a need to reject the notion of the saintly actor in favor of real people, with their real first and last names. In a word, we should reject any path except that of analytical documentary and privilege the direct reflection of things, their immediacy, relevance to the present, and duration. "Cinema must tell what is going on. The camera is meant to look at what lies in front of it" (83). Hence the idea of a real *shadowing* of reality: "The time is ripe for throwing away scripts and following men with the camera" (83). This is the lesson of Neorealism, through which the need to give cinema its mission of exploring the world was discovered.

Guido Aristarco's position can be said to be the opposite of Zavattini's. Again, we have before us a wide range of research activity (his reflection on Neorealism, to be found mostly in the reviews of, first, *Cinema* and then *Cinema Nuovo*, was flanked by a systematic reflection on the theoretical status of theoretical discourse, which began with the essay "Urgenza di una revisione dell'attuale indagine critica" and continued with the publication of *Storia delle teoriche del film*).[11] In this range of research it is still possible to discern a precise nucleus of his thought. The idea of a direct encounter between cinema and reality is replaced by the idea of a more complex alignment. The idea of cinema's innate orientation toward life is replaced by the view that this predisposition should be cultivated and directed. The idea of the conquest of reality without any formula is replaced by the idea that, while telling us about the world, cinema can and should take advantage of the previous experience of great literature. In other words, the *aesthetics of shadowing* is replaced by what—as we will see—may well be called an *aesthetics of reconstruction*.

This nucleus of thought slowly emerges through the films reviewed by Aristarco. For instance, he notes how in *La terra trema* Visconti helps Neorealism "become a style," doing exactly what Verga had done for Naturalism. For both Visconti and Verga, truth no longer coincides with an external mirror of things, but "identifies with poetic creation" (Aristarco 1950). In *La terra trema* this shift is signaled, on the one hand, by the search for a dimension broader than the mere description of an ambience, reaching the threshold of a "psychological, spiritual, social analysis of the drama." On the other hand, it emerges through the unusual expressive means "used in connection with the spiritual and human meaning they slowly acquire" (Aristarco 1950). An extremely complex picture is the positive result of this operation. Iconographic and human material is used to reconstruct the exemplary nature of a whole world in its entirety, presented not only in outline, but in detail, with all its logic and deepest reasons.

Aristarco develops this kind of argumentation in all his work, using individual films as a starting point for a discussion of cinema in general. It appears in its most compact form in his famous discussion of Visconti's *Senso,* in which the shift from Neorealism to realism is realized. This shift implies the affirmation of a demand that had been underestimated for a long time. Cinema should not be content simply with recording what happens. Neither should it limit itself to observing and describing. On the contrary, it may even become narration, when this allows one to perceive the design behind the events. Similarly, it is possible to achieve the full participation of facts, when this guarantees the greater significance and persuasiveness of the whole. Therefore, cinema may broaden its range of action, for it has both the ability to do so and the opportunity to profit from it. In fact, the choice to narrate and participate, rather than to observe and describe, allows cinema to step beyond the mere surface of a phenomenon, to grasp its internal mechanisms and hidden reasons. The result is a more complete portrait of reality, in which a list of facts is paired with an understanding of their causes and in which the mere recording of events is supplemented by the perception of their underlying logic.

"There are many degrees of realism, just as there are many degrees of reality (reality as it is perceived) that directors may uncover according to their inclination and capacity for examining it" (Aristarco 1955b). In principle, cinema should aim very high. It is not enough to verify what happens in the world; it is necessary to understand the dynamics and motives. If, to draw such a diagram, it is necessary to rely on a literary structure such as the presence of a plot, this does not constitute an impediment. In fact, it is only because of prejudice that we separate cinema from all other forms of expression. Instead, "the problem of realism in art should be perceived as a single, all-encompassing one, common to literature, figurative arts, theater, film" (Aristarco 1955b). Starting from such a unified background, it becomes possible for different devices to be shared by different areas, if this may help to improve the survey of specific data and broaden the perspective from which they may be observed. Such an exchange is even auspicious when it allows us to give up the simple documentary approach in favor of an all-encompassing perception of phenomena and a complete explanation. This exchange allows the shift "from a documentary, chronicle-like cinema that aims to denounce specific situations . . . to a critical cinema" (Aristarco 1955a). Given this situation, the recovery of plot and also the recovery of character do not constitute a filter or a barrier, but, rather, a useful instrument to make the discourse more exemplary, to give it greater value. Because, it is worth repeating, what is at stake is understanding more about the events represented than their mere occurrence, within a broader frame and in their universality. What is at stake is the effective knowledge of phenomena that the cinema can achieve not by recording facts, but by going deep into them. Thus, in cinematic terms, mirroring the world means both reproducing outward appearances and overlaying them with what has determined them, going beyond mere appearances, grasping the logic behind them, emphasizing a lesson.

Making Neorealism into a style, overcoming appearances, and adopting the instruments of great literature is the credo with which Aristarco seems to answer Zavattini's wish for immediacy and desire to abolish all filters. He is obviously inspired by Lukács and his aesthetics (as well as by Gramsci's *Letteratura e vita nazionale*). In any case, Aristarco opposes a purely descriptive realism with a "critical" one, capable of refracting not only isolated situations, but those that typify a historical and human condition.

Of course, the debate on Neorealism does not consist only of the two positions described here for their general value.[12] There are also other contributions worth mentioning, including, first, the work of two scholars who had already expressed their teachings in the 1930s, Luigi Chiarini and Umberto Barbaro.[13] The former (see in particular Chiarini 1951 and 1952) starts with a clear distinction between *cinematic spectacle* and *film*. The spectacle is a composite area, dominated by scenographic splendor and the will to tell a story, by the audience's pleasure and the fictional game. This is part of the tradition of the theater, for which cinema offers new and greater technical possibilities. Instead, choosing the path of pure film means giving up traditional filters, such as fiction, narration, and mise-en-scène, and establishing a direct relationship with reality. This is the way of Neorealism, which thus takes up Lumière's original lesson. A direct relationship with reality does not, however, imply a lack of mediations. The director's task is still the creative reelaboration of the initial data. He must not betray the photographic basis of the film, which happens when preconceived schemes are superimposed on the shooting of the film. On the contrary, it is necessary to give the camera its true role and to ask for its cooperation in the exploration of the world. In other words, it is necessary to allow the camera itself to observe the events, until it, "in turn, affects man" (Chiarini 1952) and shows how to represent what surrounds him.

After all, the balance of creative reelaboration and respect for the photographic basis of the film is the peculiar element, the distinctive trait, the "specificity" of cinema as compared to all other arts. Against those who believe that the essence of films lies in such elements as editing, Chiarini insists that its fundamental characteristic lies "in the possibility of artistically elaborating, without previous literary and theatrical mediations, a material that is still formless from an aesthetic point of view" (Chiarini 1952). In a word, cinema's fundamental characteristic is its ability to capture reality and shape it without betraying either its spirit or its letter.

Chiarini seems to occupy a position somewhere between the immediacy advocated by Zavattini and the mediations accepted by Aristarco. Barbaro also takes an intermediate position, although he insists more on the presence of the director's imagination as a fundamental element of film and on editing as a principle of aesthetic construction (Barbaro 1953). Younger scholars, such as Fernando Di Giammatteo, give a slightly different meaning to this middle position. If it is true that cinema tends toward the documentary, then it is also true that it cannot exist without language. A film's ability to reflect reality is thus inevitably connected with its ability to "speak" of the world (Di Giammatteo 1950).

Let us conclude this necessarily brief review here.[14] After all, our aim is more the definition of wider frameworks than the compilation of lists. And the overall situation of Neorealism is clear. The basic idea is that cinema should literally "reconquer" reality. We have identified two paths to this end, however: the pursuit of the immediacy with which this medium reflects the world (Zavattini's poetics of shadowing) and the emphasis on the mediations necessary for a complete mirroring (Aristarco's poetics of reconstruction). Within this polarity we find positions supporting a mediation between the photographic basis and poetic re-creation (Chiarini), the role of the director's imagination (Barbaro), or even the complementarity of the documentary and linguistic aspects (Di Giammatteo). Many of these motivations are also part of the credo of two theorists whose activity was very intense during the post-war years, André Bazin and Sigfried Kracauer. Their influence on the debate, the richness of their discourse, and even their relationship with the Neorealist experience differ (to Bazin's advantage). Both allow us to clarify, in an extreme form, the reasons leading to the recognition of cinema's realistic vocation.

2.3.   Cinema as Participation in the World: André Bazin

In its very first pages the essay that opens the collection of Bazin's writings (to 1945) offers an extremely suggestive image: the plastic arts are rooted in the psychoanalytic "complex" of the mummy. Both statues and pictures, in fact, reproduce the features of people and objects, and in so doing they try to achieve the same result as embalming: the preservation of what is doomed to decay. Behind sculpture and painting lies, in other words, the idea of defending oneself against time, which corrupts things and bodies alike, thus defying death. "Artificially preserving a being's corporeal appearance means extracting it from the flux of duration, bringing it back to life" (Bazin 1958:11). From this derives a reproductive obsession that overcomes any aesthetic exigency. Behind the artists' wish to express themselves lies "the totally psychological wish to replace the outside world with its double" or the instinct to "save being through appearances" (11).

Photography supports this deep need, adding an essential trait: its absolute objectivity. In fact, photography affords us "the complete satisfaction of our appetite for illusion through a mechanical reproduction from which man is excluded" (14). Representation thus becomes a purely technical fact without the interference of re-creation. In other words, while "all arts are based on man's presence, only photography allows us to enjoy his absence. It strikes us as a natural phenomenon, like a flower or a snowflake whose beauty is inseparable from its vegetable or telluric origin" (15). As a consequence, on the one hand, "its objectivity gives photography a credibility lacking in any pictorial work" (15). Nobody can alter appearances, for what is reproduced appears before our eyes by itself, in all its evidence and richness. On the other hand, its radical nature allows photography to distance itself from the other plastic arts. "Both liberation and completion, it allows painting to forever rid itself of the realist obsession and to find again its aesthetic autonomy" (18–19). The plastic arts may therefore follow the path of innovation, but they may do so only because photography took on the burden of the "mummy complex" that marked the beginning of plastic arts.

Cinema brings to completion this internal trend within art history, adding the ability to reproduce time to photographic objectivity: "For the first time the image of things is also an image of their duration, almost the mummy of change" (16). The existent no longer reappears only as it is and by means of an automatic process, but also as it is becoming, and the possibility of similarity becomes more or less complete. Hence, a close bond is established between cinema and reality: the former completely overlaps the latter and becomes its "fingerprint," more than its copy. Even better: by tracing reality in all its aspects, it continues it, "adding to nature rather than creating another" (18).

Of course, cinema's ability to heighten this latent feature of all figurative arts and of photography needs to be carefully cultivated. As we will see, it is necessary to avoid the shortcuts represented by "makeup"—even if effective—in favor of those moments in which the camera becomes a possibly involved witness. In short, some procedures need to be abandoned in favor of others. What really counts is not the isolated results or the different degrees of "verisimilitude" achieved by different films. Rather, what counts is the principle itself, for cinema boasts such closeness to the world that it can present itself as the replica and prolongation thereof. In this sense we are very far from the logic of illustration: more than a vignette, cinema evokes the Holy Shroud, that is, a figure emerging from the overlapping of a sheet and a body, in which the former keeps alive the presence of the latter. In other words, between cinema and reality there is an existential relationship, a deep continuity, and they belong to each other at an ontological level.

Beyond all metaphors (which, however, help to re-create the tone of Bazin's discourse, the core of which is often expressed through suggestions, hints, paradoxes), the underlying plot is clear: cinema adheres to reality and even participates in the latter's existence. It does so by virtue of that same psychological need that had led sculpture and painting to preserve the appearances of human beings against the flow of time and the threat of death. It does so thanks to the same technology that had already allowed photography to record events in an objective way. It does so also thanks to specific aesthetic choices, which enhance its ability to accompany the very flow of life. As a consequence, cinematic *realism* (which is at the same time psychological, technical, and aesthetic realism) [15] is not one among many measures, but the one that best describes the deepest nature of cinema.

We observe, therefore, a complete adherence to reality, even participating in its existence. This is a recurring element in all of Bazin's essays, even when it is confronted with other situations. At a historical level, for instance, the origin of this medium seems to be totally dominated by the myth of an absolute realism. The precursors of cinema, from Niépce to Muybridge to Lumière himself, pursued "a total and integral representation of reality." All the later achievements, from sound to color and Cinemascope, as well as the decreasing reliance on theatrical and literary models, simply reinforced this original vocation, so much so that, vis-à-vis some Neorealist films—such as *Ladri di biciclette*—it is possible to perceive that a perfect identity with life is achieved. "No more actors, story, or mise-en-scène; finally, in the perfect, aesthetic illusion of reality, no more cinema" (Bazin 1962:59). The aim of this medium, if any, is to fuse with the world.

The principle that cinema obeys becomes explicit in all those situations that we may call circular, in which the tight connection between reality and images allows them to trigger one another. The two poles interact freely, without having to move in a predefined direction. Bazin's very evocative analyses of war *réportages* find their place here. Bazin introduces the idea of battlefields as both the theaters where the destinies of whole nations are decided and the set of a show of great emotional power (people on the screen fight both to win and to be filmed). The final result is that "through its wars the world makes a cunning, economical move, for wars have a double aim, *history* and *Cinema* . . ." (Bazin 1958:31). Bazin deals in a similar way with Chaplin's mustache, "copied" by Hitler, who thus unknowingly got ready for the parody created by the actor in *The Great Dictator.* (Hitler, "by imitating Chaplin, had swindled him out of his persona, and Chaplin would not forget this. A few years later Hitler would pay dearly for this. By taking advantage, Chaplin took his persona back from Hitler in order to destroy it" [92]. In other words, a mask becomes reality, and reality becomes, again, a desecrating mask.) Bazin's analyses of the Russian films on Stalin can be grouped with these films. Such films are extreme examples of confusion of roles. (Stalin presents himself to the people mostly through cinema, which celebrates his myth. It is always through cinema, through documentary films, that he "visits" Russia. As his relationship with the world is developed almost exclusively through the images he envisions, "it would hardly be an exaggeration to say that Stalin came to believe in his own genius through the spectacle of the Stalinist films" [88].) Cinema allows this circularity as no other medium does and finds one of its roots in it.

Finally, the guiding principle of cinema—its underlying realism—determines both its taboos and its most intense moments. The taboos are connected with its fictional quality, which falsifies reality and creates situations and emotions that have no direct correspondence to it. Hence the prohibition, not only formal, against filming in two different shots what must happen in the same scene in order to be meaningful (this is the famous *forbidden montage:* separating with a cut the threatening beast and the threatened man means giving up the credibility of the situation). But taboos are also connected with the representation of something that involves a reality so exclusive as to prevent its reproduction. Hence the prohibition against representing love: "Love is experienced, not represented" (69). Above all, it is forbidden to represent death: "The representation of real death is also an obscenity, not a moral one anymore, as is the case with love, but a metaphysical one. One cannot die twice" (69).

On the opposite side of these taboos, we find the moments of greatest cinematic intensity. For instance, there are moments when reality appears on-screen in all its richness, so much so that the spectators themselves have the task of deciphering it, letting their gaze both wander freely and discover the world. This is the case of the sequence shot, where the event is presented in its integrity, "constantly demanding all of us: we must decide to choose this or that aspect of it." But among the moments of highest intensity are those

in which cinema so closely approaches a reality that is by itself "not captur-
able" that it clearly demonstrates an idea of the implicit risks and limits. This
is the case of documentary films about the war, in which the camera is in the
line of fire, or those about explorations, in which the cameraman faces death
while trying to steal one further image from reality (31ff). In all these situations, cinema reproduces the very breath of the world.[16]

This is the core of Bazin's thought, as it emerges mostly from the pages of
Qu'est-ce que le cinéma, the collection of his most significant essays. Of course,
it is necessary to clarify some of its elements. Even though he tries to view
realism as a need common to all arts, Bazin often defines cinema's position by
contrasting it to other fields of expression (see his comparative analyses of
cinema and theater or literature [Bazin 1959]). And even though he is interested, above all, in the aesthetic nature of the medium, he does not forget the
concrete work of the mise-en-scène or the economic and social factors on
which a film's realization depends. In this sense his theory is not as "idealistic"
as the critics of the 1970s reproachfully observed. It is also a "morphology"
and a "pragmatics" (to use a contemporary term) of cinema. Similarly, it is
necessary to specify both the origins and the consequences of Bazin's thought.
It is enough to mention a few elements: on the one hand, the influence on
Bazin of restless French Catholicism (from Legaut to *Esprit*); his distance
from Sartre's engagement (with his refusal of a "useful" art, and useful most
of all for its content: especially against Sadoul); and his closeness to phenomenology (as presented, for instance, by Maurice Merleau-Ponty).[17] On the
other hand, it is enough to mention Bazin's intense activity of promotion, as
a result of which he became involved in the creation of cineclubs and never
ceased to write for and promote *Cahiers du Cinéma,* with which he "brought
up" a new generation of critics and directors. Beyond these facts, however,
which are useful if we are to understand the environment in which Bazin
worked,[18] the basic, ever-recurring idea is still the same: that cinema, even
before representing reality, participates in it to the point of reproducing all its
depth and texture, freeing its hidden meaning, and showing its internal workings. In a word, cinema uncovers reality's essence.

Bazin's *ontological realism* consists in just this dream of "communion" together with "truth." This theory grasps extremely well some of the fundamental mechanisms of cinema or some of the reasons for its fascination: the
intimate persuasiveness of many of its images, the immediacy and significance
of what appears onscreen, the spontaneous attachment to what is in front of

our eyes. Finally, this theory starts from marginal or anomalous experiences to mark a recurrent need that will powerfully reemerge shortly afterward.

Let us conclude this analysis by trying to clarify this point. Bazin kept searching for examples of what he was saying in works that were marginal in terms of the dominant trend of cinema (not only Neorealism, but also ethnographic and scientific films, films for the young, etc., or Renoir's, De Sica's, Wyler's, or Welles' masterpieces, all of which were often intentionally viewed in a biased way). He spoke of something that in a way existed only as a necessary but underground trend or as a hypothesis still to be exploited. In short, his dream grasped the essence of cinema, but did not have much correspondence to the films actually produced at the time. This was a recurrent situation in postwar theory, as we have said. Yet what Bazin was watching for would shortly explode in the experience of *cinéma vérité,* in the use of 8 or 16 mm and videos, and, more generally, in all those moments, typical of the last decades, which tried to surprise reality at close quarters, which tried to catch it "red-handed." Bazin can therefore be called clairvoyant, or divining, for within the framework of classic cinema Bazin perceived its incandescent points and the symptoms of an imminent renewal. He prepared himself for the encounter, which his premature death would deny him, with one of the strongest traits of modern cinema: its need to melt into the flux of life.

2.4. Cinema as Documentation of the World: Sigfried Kracauer

If André Bazin's theoretical work seems prophetic and trend-setting, that of Sigfried Kracauer—a German scholar forced by Nazism to emigrate to the United States—is systematic and concrete. Bazin relies on extreme situations to grasp general underlying trends; Kracauer analyzes current behaviors to single out some basic capabilities. The former follows the radical hypothesis of a perfect identity between image and reality; the latter questions the assumption that people and things appear onscreen. The two scholars operated in different contexts, the former being a militant critic, the latter an academic. Their influence on the debate was also different. The former (who is still a reference point) has a central place in theory; the latter (who is being rediscovered), much less so. And yet their contributions may be viewed in parallel, as two different formulations of the same need: on the one hand, an *existential realism,* connected with cinema's possibility of participating in the life of the world, on the other, a *functional realism,* connected with the medium's ability to reproduce the outlines and document the existence of things. Let us now approach Kracauer's theory systematically by rereading one of his last books, symptomatically entitled *Theory of Film,* which in some ways is the summation of his research in the field.[19]

Kracauer, like Bazin, starts from an analysis of photography, considered the immediate forebear of cinema. If, in fact, cinema derives from the combination of various disparate elements—from the magic lantern to the phenakistoscope—still "photography, especially instantaneous photography, has a legitimate claim to top priority among these elements, for it undeniably is and remains the decisive factor in establishing film content. The nature of photography survives in that of film" (Kracauer 1960:27). The fundamental characteristic of photography is that it can reproduce the material reality around us, both recording the immediate aspects and revealing those aspects that are difficult to perceive at first sight. Photography, thus, has a realistic vocation, although it is often used for different aims. This fact has an aesthetic and a structural consequence.

First of all, even photography must obey a basic principle: "it may be assumed that the achievements within a particular medium are all the more satisfying aesthetically if they build from the specific properties of that medium" (12). Because in this case the specific qualities of the medium aim toward the reproduction of reality, the photographer, "in an aesthetic interest, must follow the realistic tendency under all circumstances" (13). In other words, photographers may try to express their own subjectivity, but if they want to achieve correct results, they must pursue a real "photographic approach"; "what counts is the 'right' mixture of their realist loyalties and formative endeavors—a mixture, that is, in which the latter, however strongly developed, surrender their independence to the former" (16).

Second, photography's realistic vocation underscores some of its "inherent affinities," four of which are especially worthy of attention.

First, photography has an outspoken affinity for unstaged reality. Pictures which strike us as intrinsically photographic seem intended to render nature in the raw, nature as it exists independently of us. (18)

Second, through this concern with unstaged reality, photography tends to stress the fortuitous. Random events are the very meat of snapshots. (19)

Third, photography tends to suggest endlessness. . . . In this respect, there is an analogy between the photographic approach and scientific investigation: both probe into an inexhaustible universe whose entirety forever eludes them. (20)

Fourth and finally, this medium has an affinity for the indeterminate. . . . To be sure, the traditional work of art carries many meanings also. But due to its rise from interpretable human intentions and circumstances, the meanings inherent in it can virtually be ascertained, whereas those of the photograph are necessarily indeterminate because the latter is bound to convey unshaped nature itself, nature in its inscrutability. (20)

So far we have spoken of photography, but a very similar discourse also applies to cinema. Kracauer admits that cinema implies elaborations and developments of its own and that it employs specific technical devices such as editing. He believes, however, that the basic properties of cinema "are identical with the properties of photography. Film, in other words, is uniquely equipped to record and reveal physical reality and, hence, gravitates toward it" (28). Cinema and photography both obey the same basic "aesthetic principle" and follow the same kind of "inherent affinities."

With regard to the first aspect, Kracauer recalls the rule that the more a work relies on the fundamental characteristics of the medium, the more aesthetically valid it is. Therefore, given cinema's characteristics, this may be achieved when, as with photography, films follow the path of realism. This seems somehow to imply a paradox, for all movies following this path, even those "almost devoid of creative aspirations, such as newsreels, scientific or educational films, artless documentaries, etc., are tenable propositions from an aesthetic point of view" (38). In fact, they embody the correct "cinematic approach," consisting of systematic attention to the outside world. On the contrary, those directors who simply try to express their own obsessions or dreams follow an aesthetically unmotivated path, betray the characteristics of the instruments they work with, and attempt mostly to observe concrete data. But, extreme cases aside, it is true that, "as in photography, everything depends on the 'right' balance between the realistic tendency and the formative tendency; and the two tendencies are well balanced if the latter does not try to overwhelm the former but eventually follows its lead" (39).

As far as the "inherent affinities" are concerned, they too are modeled for the most part on the ones described above. In fact, the interest in nature shown by photography corresponds to cinema's inclination toward the unstaged. It is true that most films rely on a mise-en-scène, but in the best ones it tends to disappear in favor of a complete illusion of reality. Also, photography's preference for casual facts finds its cinematic equivalent in the fascination with the fortuitous. From the very beginning this interest was shown in the American silent film comedies, full of incidents and disasters. Later, the same interest was evident in those movies filmed on the streets, mirroring a chaotic world. Another parallel is that, while photography tends to evoke the absence of limits, cinema shows "the chimerical desire to establish the continuum of physical existence" (63). We find examples of this in travelogues, which describe broad realities, or in documentary films, which linger on objects until they almost make their dimensions explode, or in some psychological films, which copy the technique of stream-of-consciousness by presenting a crowd of thoughts. Yet another similarity is the fondness photography displays for the indefinite, which finds its equivalent in the cinema's taste for the indeterminate and the formless. Although editing assigns facts a precise function within the plot, the best films manage to reconstruct the meaning of things as they appear before our eyes, in their indeterminacy and ambiguity. Cinema adds one more inclination to these four "inherent affinities" typical of photography, associated with cinema's ability to render the duration of reality. This is the inclination to follow the flow of life. Hence the valorization "of the stream of material situations and happenings with all they intimate in terms of emotions, values, thoughts" (71). Movies are interested in the succession of events, in the evolution of the world, of things and people alike.

Along this train of thought Kracauer adds that, although all that exists is theoretically filmable, there are "certain subjects within that world which may be termed 'cinematic' because they seem to exert a peculiar attraction on the medium. It is as if the medium were predestined (and eager) to exhibit them" (41). Among such subjects can be listed anything that creates an impression of concreteness (e.g., the close-ups of inanimate objects) or an impression of movement (chases, dances) or whatever part of reality cinema can underscore with its devices, although it is usually not the focus of our attention (that which is infinitely small, gigantic, transitory). The cinecamera, just like the camera, turns to the world in search of what is most congenial to it.

Kracauer's book touches on many other themes. Among them are the role played by the narrative component of a film, different acting techniques, the forms speech may assume, as well as the function of music in film, the audience's position, and the experience of the avant-garde. Yet the topic of our discussion—namely, the way in which cinema obeys the basic "aesthetic principle" and the different "inherent affinities" it follows, as well as the presence of privileged subjects—already suggests what is essential: by incorporating photography, this new medium inherits and develops the wish to reproduce physical reality. Its destiny, in short, is to become an even more faithful witness of the world.

Kracauer reaches conclusions that are very similar to Bazin's, yet (beyond the difference in the density of their discourses and in their influence on the debate) the two are separated by important nuances. For both, cinema is closely related to reality: but in Bazin this bond is the result of the overlapping of different parts, whereas in Kracauer it becomes the statement of what is. In fact, for Bazin cinema aims to interact with and act upon the world (so much so that its representation may disappear and become life itself); for Kracauer the medium must above all analyze people and things, with the attitude of an explorer or a scientist ("The supreme virtue of camera consists precisely in acting the voyeur"; or "Cinema is comparable to science" [44, 50]). As a consequence, for Bazin cinema brings out the intimate truth of reality; for Kracauer it simply presents the reality of facts. Of course, the German scholar suggests the existence of two levels of action. On the one hand, cinema "records" the already visible aspects; on the other, it "reveals" what is too small, too big, or too quick to be perceived at first sight. But this "revelation" does not go beyond appearances. It only focuses on them more clearly, without reaching the heart of a phenomenon. As stated above, for Bazin cinema's realistic basis derives from the possibility of *participation;* for Kracauer it emerges as the ability to *document.* The two trends are clearly defined: participation and documentation or truth of things and reality of facts. The theory of cinematic realism measures itself against them, and research gravitates around them.

2.5. Realism/Realisms

If Bazin's and Kracauer's contributions clarify the fundamental reasons for bringing cinema and reality together, the two scholars are not the only ones who deal with the notion of realism. It is therefore necessary to mention, although briefly, the contributions made by others. György Lukács devotes a whole chapter of his monumental *Aesthetics* (1963) to cinema, placing it between a section devoted to gardens and another devoted to what is pleasurable. Here Lukács relies on and applies the categories that are at the core of his previous work—and that have influenced other theorists of cinema, such as Aristarco. His starting point is that cinema is a *double mirror* of reality. First, it reproduces the world thanks to the photographic character of the film images for, due to cameras and technology, the outlines of things are presented on the screen in a very precise way and in all their immediacy. This first kind of mirroring reality implies a risk, for films are too close to everyday life and are therefore too tightly connected with the singularity (and visibility) of what they present. This mirroring does not seem to manage to convey the meaning of things through their whole—and thus more authentic—image. As compensation, this photographic mirroring gives films "a very significant authenticity" (Lukács 1963) that the other arts reach only "as the final result of the process of transformation that takes place in the reproduction of reality." The second kind of mirroring, which is more specifically aesthetic, is based on the ability to present not only the appearance of reality, but its universality and exemplary nature. This mirroring must therefore take into account the data at its disposal. A film will fail if it stops at the "immediate authenticity" of its images, as well as if it tries to contradict it. Instead, it should be able to express an "indeterminate objectivity." In order to do so, vis-à-vis the multiplicity and instability of reality, it should in particular represent a "unity of affective atmosphere." In other words, it should reconstruct a world complete and evident in itself.

As stated above, Lukács wrote his *Aesthetics* when his categories, originally applied to literature, had already had some results in the field of film theories. It should, however, be emphasized that his influence was visible in particular in the many defenses of socialist realism, both Soviet and foreign.[20]

On the other hand (this is really a different area and a different spirit: we will only try to define its broad outlines), the echoes of the study of cinematic realism reappeared in the debate on *cinéma vérité,* which flourished between the 1950s and 1960s and which made use of highly portable technology to document certain social or human situations from the inside.[21] This underscores the immediate truth of things, the absence of filters, cinema's ability to document reality.

But the idea that cinema is by nature a reflection and a continuation of reality is also behind research coming from other fields. Two names come to mind: for the 1960s, Pier Paolo Pasolini; for the 1980s, Gilles Deleuze (both will be dealt with in detail later).

Pasolini intervened in the debate initiated by semioticians. Starting from their line of research, he observed that cinema functions somewhat as writing does. It is a medium that "fixes" concrete behavior on film, just as lines on a sheet of paper "fix" words that are usually spoken. The real language is that of oral discourse, and the graphic signs are only a derivation. In the same way, the gestures through which we express ourselves are also a real language, which films merely collect, compress, and order. Thus, if cinema is a symbolic device, it is such only because it transcribes preexisting natural signs. In short, it is the "written language of actions," a language based on the world's, as the slogan created by Pasolini himself very effectively—and paradoxically—summarizes.

Deleuze, at least apparently, dealt with signs. For him cinema is a movement-image, which in turn consists of a perception-image, an affection-image, a drive-image, an action-image, etc., as well as a time-image, expressed above all by the crystal-image. These signs all reproduce a different state of reality, however. Among them are reality as perceived from a precise perspective, caught in one of its aspects (the movement-image), and reality that condenses a whole series of possibilities, open to totality (the time-image). This means that cinema is not a language, but the world itself, which presents itself at all its levels of existence, the world as it is and as it develops, as it appears and as it can be conceived.

Between Pasolini and Deleuze, at the beginning of the 1970s, there was a group of scholars who viewed the theories of realism as a target for polemics, so that the idea of the proximity of cinema and reality was examined in order to be dismantled and destroyed.

Let us now consider the position of journals such as *Cinéthique* and *Cahiers du Cinéma:* those who believe that onscreen images and sounds are a copy of what exists (as well as a means of expression) forget that they are first of all produced by work. Those who, instead, view films as a copy of the external world (as well as a reflection of the interior one) hide the only effective fact, namely, the process of production that lies behind a movie. Consequently, realism is a purely idealistic theory, hiding the materiality of the elements at stake, such as the technical, professional, economic, and ideological factors contributing to the creation of an illusion of reality.

Let us also consider, more generally, the debate on iconography, with the contributions of scholars such as Eco, Metz, etc.: the reproduction of the world is not a natural gesture, but derives from the application of current linguistic rules. Using a sequence of shadow and light in such a way as to make it recognizable as people or objects means organizing shadow and light according to highly codified principles.

Later we will return to all the positions mentioned above. For the moment, we will only underscore two aspects. First, it is necessary to insist that the bond between cinema and reality still continues to cause problems in some ways. For some it is a recurrent conviction, for others a presupposition to be destroyed, but for everyone it provides a background to be kept in mind. Second, it should be noted that the problematic becomes broader and broader, for the existence of new fields of study allows us to place cinema's realistic vocation along a wider horizon. Here we find the idea—initiated in the late 1960s—that the impression of reality coming from an image, the impression of truth emanating from it, needs to be connected with the notion of both *verisimilitude* (namely, the ability to reflect what exists) and *veracity* (namely, the ability to construct something that presents itself as what exists, with the help of signs). In short, it is a matter of both resembling reality and speaking as if it were true. Cinema manages to present reality through both a mirror game and a construction principle. This polarity, it should be noted, was already present in the confrontations between Zavattini and Aristarco and between Bazin and Kracauer. Here, however, it contributes to giving a new dimension to the problem. Realism no longer seems to depend on the medium as such, surrounded by factors that either reinforce or hinder this original vocation. Realism now also includes processes of perception (the ease or difficulty with which we relate what we see in an image to what we see in the world), mental habits (we rely on well-established schemes in order to recognize a certain figure), linguistic processes (the more or less effective ways of ordering the various elements), communication strategies (openly stating that we are telling the truth is sometimes more effective than simply telling it, without indulging in redundancy), etc. To sum up, it is clear that realism is a very complex matter, which needs a pluralistic (and multidisciplinary) approach. Before dealing with this complexity, which leads to a different area of the debate, it is necessary to deal a bit more with the postwar years and to examine a different train of thought, which relates cinema to the imaginary.

3 CINEMA AND THE IMAGINARY

3.1. Through the Looking Glass

Opposed to the more widely diffused idea of the cinema as a representation of the real, there was another idea that circulated during the same years: the idea that cinema is naturally able to embody the *imaginary*. What appears on screen is not the world, evident and concrete, but a new universe, where common objects and anomalous situations, precise data and impalpable feelings, recognizable presences and unreal entities, habitual behaviors and surprising logic are mixed. In other words, cinema defines a space that is other, where many more things than the ones around us may rightly belong. Therefore, we need to act like Alice when she returns to Wonderland. If we really want to make the journey we are invited to, we must not simply stand in front of a window to contemplate the landscape: we need to jump through the looking glass.

The expression "through the looking glass," which contradicts the most classic of the realistic metaphors, is a good starting point for the reconstruction of this section of the debate, but two preliminary observations are necessary. First, it should be noted that the hypothesis of cinema's ability to define a dimension that is "other" was already widespread before the war.[1] Indeed, it was even more widespread than the hypothesis of its merely realistic vocation, which was disliked by many because it seemed to impede the achievement of true aesthetic value. In the postwar years, on the contrary, it was the realistic hypothesis that enjoyed greater success, while the idea of the imaginary seemed too affected.

Second, the postwar years brought some changes to the hypothesis of the imaginary, if only to induce the explicit definition of the origin of the problem. What is central, in short, is the realization of something that the realist theories of the time seemed to hide: that is, the presence of a human being, directly involved in the process of filmmaking. Cinema is not an anonymous machine, which automatically records what exists and reproduces it. On the contrary, cinema stages very personal universes and asks each spectator to accept this. Cinema has much to do with *subjectivity,* and it is from this *subjectivity* that the imaginary derives.

As we have just suggested, the subjective dimension acts on at least two levels. First, it characterizes the world represented, which is always the product of a more or less personal elaboration, of a fantasy made perceptible. Hence, the first element of interest is the content of a movie, which is able to capture a dreamlike substrate or to arrive at the limits of phantasmagorias. But subjectivity also intervenes in our relationship with what appears on the screen. When we grasp the situation represented, we do not simply record it: we integrate it with what we know, suppose, and expect until we literally participate in it. Hence, the second element of interest is the very structure of the filmic image, its ability to trigger a personal reaction.

Our study will follow the development of both paths, which frequently cross (it could hardly be otherwise). It is possible, however, to distinguish between them. On the one hand, we find a discourse on the imaginary as the product of an *imagination* (and, thus, as a catalogue of out-of-the-ordinary themes). On the other hand, we find a discourse on the imaginary as the state we are in when we enjoy an image (and, thus, as a *dynamics,* activated by each representation).

3.2.   The Borders of Imagination: The Surrealist Tradition

Undoubtedly, the simplest way to speak of the imaginary is to recall that what appears on the screen is often extraordinary and inclines toward the marvelous. This is proven by the cinema's predilection for those paths that skirt enchanted landscapes and mental places, improbable objects and new life forms, dark visions and brilliant metaphors. The world of a film is not the empirical one we have before our eyes every day. It is a world made of the stuff of dreams, of obsessions, of mirages, of utopias. It is a world dominated by pure *possibility.*

This idea was at the core of the surrealists' interest in cinema during the

1930s. It is no coincidence that it reemerged during the postwar years thanks to one scholar, Ado Kirou, who explicitly continued the work of that movement. His most significant book (*Le surréalisme au cinéma*) is an authentic pyrotechnical display of paradoxes, provocations, cutting judgments, and mockeries of common sense. The book's point of departure is the idea that our society has reduced reality to its perceptible appearances in order to chain mankind to an everyday reality without wonders. Cinema overturns this situation. It recovers those usually hidden aspects; it presents things according to a logic that differs from the norm; it brings dreams to the surface and turns them into collective experiences. Not all films have the courage to pursue this objective to the end, and many simply mirror the world as it appears. But cinema by its nature lends itself to such an action, in that it manages to bind together places far from one another, to mix yesterday with tomorrow, to juxtapose the minuscule and the gigantic, to overlay the known and the unknown, to transform the foreseeable into the unusual, creating on top of all this a universe that we can believe in without effort. As a result, "For the first time in the history of mankind we possess a magical device endowed with an incredible power. More than in everyday life, we have been offered vaulting poles with which we can jump inside ourselves, break away from our everyday thought, and discover great poetry" (Kirou 1953:246).

In his book Kirou reviews many typical surrealist themes staged by cinema, including the journey to another place, the exposition of the impossible, love and Eros, the revolt, etc. At the same time, he offers an ideal counterhistory of the seventh art, made up of impertinent readings of the classics, of unknown works, of ghost-films (still alive in the author's memory, though they may never have existed). All this is accompanied by frequent references to Breton and a special interest in Buñuel. His conclusion can only be that "cinema will be surrealist" (263).[2]

We can find this kind of sensibility, with various accents, in other theorists, especially in French theorists, for whom the surrealist experience works as a kind of background. A journal like *Positif,* for instance, is full of such ideas.[3] But we should also think of those critics who defend the *fantastic*—understood not as a mere genre among many, but as an exemplary moment that helps us to understand the very nature of cinema. Almost at the end of the period under investigation we find a book by Lenne (1970), which gives a good idea of the limits (indulging mere cinephilia) and strengths (the ability to single out new centers of gravity) of this area of study.

Lenne puts his cards on the table from the very start. Beyond labels, "cinema should always be fantastic, even if this is not always the case" (Lenne 1970:17). The reason for this is that every image, even the most descriptive one, always contains something that exceeds factual reality. Imagination intervenes at all times, both by seeking to apportion and harmonize empirical data—as with classic cinema—and by playing with distortion and rupture—as with modern cinema. Similarly, cinema should be fantastic because it always makes the spectator "live" what it presents. Those who watch a movie, more than checking the verisimilitude or plausibility of the situations presented on the screen, allow themselves to "believe" in the image, giving complete mental availability to the film.

Thus, cinema is necessarily fantastic. It presents something other than reality that still provokes the spectator's assent (in a way that seems natural). It presents something that, although different from reality, makes us instinctively accept it. Later in his book Lenne analyzes the universes created by films, focusing in particular on some of the great polarities that periodically appear on the screen: monstrous and normal, order and disorder. Lenne also studies some key themes, like *Doppelgänger*, bestiality, physical alterations. He returns to some exemplary myths, like Dracula and Frankenstein; he touches upon some specific genres, like the marvelous or science fiction; finally, he synthesizes the "lesson" of the fantastic in an invitation to go beyond the accepted boundaries even at the cost of defeat. "Many characters lost themselves in their desperate search for the absolute; many vast projects, many great designs ended up in madness and death!" (Lenne 1970:193).

Lenne's method[4] is clearly not too different from Kirou's: both belong to a field of research that can rightly be labeled late-surrealist.[5] We could find other examples of this type, although their connections with this field are less clearly defined. We find authors who insist on the "unreal" nature of what appears on the screen or authors who defend a totally visionary kind of cinema.[6]

But it is now time to switch fronts. So far we have dealt with the contents represented on the screen. Now we will focus on an author whose attention goes more directly to the structure of the image, Edgar Morin, who brings us back to the heart of the 1950s. His scope is much wider than that of the two previous scholars, and his contribution to the field under investigation constitutes one of its central moments.

3.3. The Structures of the Imaginary: Edgar Morin

It may seem odd to place Morin in the field of ontological theories. This well-known sociologist worked within a discipline whose boundaries he systematically tried to surpass. Yet the work we will examine here (Morin 1956) appears to be different from the author's other works, which are in fact more methodological. Furthermore, he belonged to those who approach cinema from an anthropological point of view, so as to have great freedom of movement. Finally, he wished to create a dialogue with work such as Bazin's, which is representative of the first theoretical paradigms that appeared in the postwar years. All this requires that we analyze Morin's work in two separate sections. We will discuss him again in the chapter on sociology of cinema. For now, however, we will begin to discuss him within the framework of the ontological theories.

But let us enter into the substance of his contribution. From the first pages of the book it is clear that cinema is presented as something that (contemporarily with airplanes) "has hurled itself higher and higher, toward a dream cycle, toward the starry infinity—the infinity of the 'stars'—bathed in music, peopled by adorable and demoniacal creatures, far away from the everyday reality of which it apparently was supposed to be the handmaiden and the mirror" (Morin 1956 [1982]: 26). Thus, we are not dealing with a device devoted to the reproduction of the world and as such a captive of things; rather, we are dealing with a machine that takes us elsewhere, to another universe.

Morin's discourse becomes even clearer when, shortly afterward, he analyzes what lies behind this machine and, in particular, photography. It should be noted that Bazin and Kracauer also start their study with an analysis of photography. They too view it, in fact, as the most immediate predecessor of cinema, which gives the latter its own fundamental characteristics. But whereas Bazin and Kracauer admired photography's ability to seize reality directly, overcoming any human mediation, Morin admires its ability to involve the observers, to ask them to participate in the game, to turn them into its pawns. In this way, cinema does not appear as the offspring of an impassive recording device, but as the direct continuation of an involving experience.

Morin justifies his position by saying that considering photography a mechanical reproduction of reality does not allow us to understand why it manages to recall our experience so intensely, or why it can so easily familiarize us with what we have not yet encountered, or why it makes us feel so close to those who are no longer with us, all to such an extent that it becomes a talisman or a fetish. A picture is much more than a mere replica of what exists. It can be a persistent presence, a substitute, a source of emotions, an object of devotion. These properties of photography belong neither to the people or things represented in the picture through their outlines and forms nor to the technical device (the lenses, the developing tank, the cellulose acetate). These characteristics, instead, derive from what we ourselves put into the picture: our experience, our sensibility, our imagination. Hence the need to enact a real "Copernican revolution." "What seem to be the properties of photography are instead the properties of our spirit, which were fixed in the picture and then gaze back at us" (40). Also: "The richness of a picture is all that which is not there, but that which we project and fix in it" (41). Thus, photography is apparently an objective moment, but actually it owes its best qualities to the intervention of subjectivity.

Subjectivity is the point of this discourse. Morin connects the term not only to a psychological experience (the activation of mental facilities and the initiation of cognitive processes), but to a wider anthropological dimension (the "I" arises and affirms itself) and to a more properly linguistic dimension (the "I" posits itself as the source of either expressivity or communication). In any case, beyond these various determinations, what counts is the weight that subjectivity assumes. In photography what is represented acquires meaning because someone supplies it. The visible outlines are reassembled in someone's hands; the figures become animated because someone blows life into them. In short, the conspicuousness of an image depends on the gaze that passes over it. As Morin observes, the reproduction of things has, after all, always required a personal contribution. Such phenomena as the fascination exercised by shadows, the passion for reflections, and the seductiveness of the double rely on an internal impulse that gets in touch with external stimuli. Even photographs (shadow, reflection, double) appear to be a two-sided reality. They celebrate the encounter between something subtracted from the world and the perhaps tendentious reinterpretation of it; between elements copied by means of tracing paper and either a desire or a fantasy. In other words, the two sides of a picture's reality are objectivity and subjectivity; the second term follows the first, completing it and perhaps even overturning its importance.

Lumière's "cinématographe" is built on such terrain, and it goes even further. It is enough to think of the new elements at play: the image on the screen, free from its rigid support, accents its own immateriality and thus favors personal intervention. At the same time, thanks to the recovery of movement, it acquires thickness and body, so as to increase the tie to what is represented. The dark hall allows the spectator to concentrate on what is before his eyes, thus favoring the action of the film. The isolation and immobility of the spectator free his deepest self, the most secret impulses of the soul. In short, in Lumière's "cinématographe" subjectivity is superimposed on the objectivity of the reproduced events to an even greater degree. Thus, an apparatus born to give us back reality turns into a trap in which we are already imprisoned.

Following this logic, Méliès' contribution appears essential. He introduces a series of tricks, such as transformations before the audience's eyes, substitutions, apparitions and disappearances, double exposures, slow motion and speeded-up action. These innovations seem to contradict Lumière's documentary spirit in favor of a phantasmagoric, fairy-tale–like dimension; but in reality they further the development of cinema. On the one hand, these tricks uncover even more the magical background of both photography and "cinematography." In particular, they allow the recovery not only of the fascination with the reflection and with the double, but also of the meaning of metamorphoses, deriving from the changeability of characters and things. On the other hand, these tricks charge the world with new properties: because of these changing beings, the onscreen universe acquires fluidity, opens itself to the future, gets to know the intertwining and multiplication of time, observes the subdivision of spaces. Hence, "films cease to be *one* animated photograph and divide into endless, heterogeneous animated pictures or frames. At the same time, however, they become a *system* of animated photographs, with new spatial and temporal features" (70). In short, films develop a language, and what was once "cinematography," a mere recording device, becomes "cinema," a discursive mechanism that uses images and sounds, a tool for the fabulous.

Cinema is thus made of both a magical background and the acquisition of a language. The thread connecting the feeling of the double with, first, still photography and, then, the first experiments to record movements ends with Méliès, with the recovery of its starting point. It should be added that a similar maturation of the cinema is also revealed by the techniques now used to involve the spectator. It is the obvious feeling of magic and the unheard of linguistic ability of film that allow it to engross those watching it even more easily and to let the audience in a cinema bond even more with what is represented on the screen. Morin deals extensively with the spectator's affective participation. He analyzes its constitutive elements (the mechanism of projection-identification) and lists the techniques through which it can be enhanced (from the reproduction of objects and movement, already typical of "cinematography," to the absolute mobility of the camera, developed by "cinema" itself). He gives an overview of its effects (from the pleasure of recognition to empathy with "privileged individuals," such as the stars). As a result, this new medium completely reveals its nature: "Cinema is this very symbiosis; it is a system that tends to integrate the flux of films with the spectator's psychic flux" (111).

This unbreakable unity of observer and observed confirms, after all, the constant duplicity of cinema. No cinematic device is, so to speak, pure. To go back to the examples cited above, let us consider how the evidence of the image derives not only from the exactness of the reproduction, but also from a personal integration (it is "the coincidence of the *reality* of movement and of the *appearance* of shapes that determines the impression of concrete life" [124]). Similarly, let us think of how the rationality of an exposition derives both from the advanced use of the filmic language and from the reaching of deep expressive mechanisms ("cinema's reason derives from the same system of participation that gives its magic and soul" [173]; also: "Filmic language is not separate from its fluid and dynamic source, or participation in its nascent stage" [194]). Cinema is a mixed territory, a point of confluence, a point of fusion.

Of course, this shuffling of the cards is above all valid for two basic dimensions: the objectivity of the facts represented and the subjectivity of the observer, or the reality of what is reproduced and the unreality of the world on the screen. These two poles, in fact, rather than blending with each other, create a real circularity. The exactness of the reproduction starts the spectator's intervention and gives a new dimension to the world represented; and the spectator's intervention gives depth to the world represented while giving it firmness. "Subjectivity and objectivity not only overlap, but are constantly born again from each other, in a constant merry-go-round of objectifying subjectivity and subjectifying objectivity. Reality is bathed, skirted, crossed, and carried along by unreality. Unreality is modeled, determined, rationalized, internalized by reality" (159).

Where does all this lead? Morin makes it clear with the title of his work: this shuffling of the cards, this circularity, gives cinema the shape of the *imaginary*. In fact, the imaginary represents "the coincidence of image and imagination" (89). It is the place where the concreteness of fact lends itself to integration with the fantastic, where the experience of things is connected with a plan or an expectation, or even where the exactness of the images taken from the world confronts the motivations of the people who collected them. In short, it is the area *par excellence* where objectivity and subjectivity take turns. Thus, it is neither a space where things are what we want them to be or what we believe they are—independently of what they really are—nor the realm of an imagination free from all obligations or of an individual or collective illusion. On the contrary, it is a composite backdrop—consisting of opinions or wishes—against which our contacts with what surrounds us find their place. Or it is the set of attitudes, predispositions, and mental schemes rooted in individual and social life that both work as a filter and give a kind of cohesion to our way of apprehending things. If, therefore, the imaginary can be counterposed to reality, it is not because it represents falsity and lies, but because it adds to the objective facts the fluidity of participation. If it leads us to perceive another side of the actual world, it is not because it is the latter's simple opposite, but because it constitutes a moment of union between things seen and things experienced, between the certain and the possible, the here and the elsewhere. "The imaginary is the multiform, multidimensional 'beyond' of our life, in which we are all equally immersed. It is the infinite, virtual source of all that exists, or that is singular, limited and finished in time. It is the antagonistic and complementary structure of what is called reality, and without which, undoubtedly, there would be no reality for mankind, no human reality" (84).

We are thus in the field of the imaginary. If cinema is situated here, it is because of its genesis, its history, and its vocation. In fact, we should stress that it is thanks to this positioning that we can see to what extent it is both still deeply connected to magic and capable of becoming a linguistic tool. This positioning also justifies the duplicity of its nature, constantly suspended between dream and waking, between concreteness and personalization, between observation and fantasy. It is also this position that explains how the subjectivity of participation is always ready to erupt into the objectivity of the facts. Cinema is completely inscribed in the imaginary, through which it reveals its deepest nature.

What appears on the screen thus thoroughly reveals itself: "The secret messages, the deepest intimacy of the soul are there, alienated, carried through that imaginary which expresses so well both universal and twentieth-century needs" (214). There can be only one conclusion. Both a modern and ancestral machine, cinema allows us to photograph ourselves, our interior states, our drives, our attitudes, and our understanding of the world, to the point where it becomes either an "archive of souls"—as Morin notes in the conclusion of the work we have been examining (215)—or an "anthropological mirror"—as Morin notes elsewhere.[7] These are effective labels that overturn the metaphors dear to the theorists of realism and mark the need for another dimension, the imaginary.

3.4.   Trajectories and Pursuits

This, in extremely synthesized form, is Morin's discourse. It is very hard to express, because whereas his basic idea is well defined, it is presented in a way that privileges evocations, illuminations, suggestions, and urgings (the entire book is a constant "variation on a theme"). Yet his discourse is unavoidable, for it deals with the very core around which the theoretical hypothesis we are analyzing develops (his work, in fact, represents one of the highest points of the research of the 1950s).

Yet, if we consider the date of its publication, it will be noted that this work had a strange fate. Surrounded with an aura of great respect, it remained somewhat isolated, as if its contemporaries could not completely grasp the humors and intuitions that run through it. To discern clear, but perhaps indirect, echoes of Morin's work we will have to arrive at a more recent phase of the debate, which is marked by other concerns as well. When we do, we will rediscover the theme of the imaginary in discussions on the relationship between the cinema and the culture industry, conducted in a more properly sociological environment (see not only Morin's work, but also Abruzzese's). We will rediscover the problem of the audience's participation in what appears on the screen in the analyses of the psychological device at the basis of cinematic pleasure (see Metz, Baudry, Bellour). We will also rediscover the motif of subjectivity, as in the philosophical study of the symbolic functioning activated by cinema (see Silverman's work). We will rediscover an awareness of the intrinsic complexity of levels in studies that tend to see the new medium as a sign of different states of the world, ranging from the real to lived experience (see Deleuze, who is still very different from Morin, if only in the absence of any notion of subjectivity). In many historical works, which were not happy with elementary dualisms, we will also rediscover the renewed proposal of a thread that unites the magical experience of the double, photography, Lumière, and Méliès.

It should be repeated, however, that these are different fields of discussion, and we will deal with them later. For now, let us instead stay with the years from the second half of the 1940s to the first half of the 1960s and introduce a third major theoretical orientation, which revolves around the idea that cinema is, above all and intrinsically, a language.

4   CINEMA AND LANGUAGE

4.1.   Signs . . .

At first glance, it seems totally obvious that every film, by choosing certain segments of reality, certain kinds of shots, certain strategies, attributes a precise meaning to what it slowly unfolds before our eyes and openly transmits that meaning to us. Every film, in addition to representing either an interior or an exterior world, gives us information, impressions, ideas. It offers us meaning, and it makes that meaning's importance clear.

This much is obvious, but it is on these premises that the theoretical orientation we are reviewing considers cinema to be essentially a *language*. Cinema is seen here as a device that allows man to express himself and to interact (language as a faculty) and that provides him with a repertory of procedures or more or less recurrent signs that make expression and interaction effective (language as a system of signs). Thus, just like any natural language or such fields as painting—although in a different way—cinema appears to be a place for an elaboration of meanings that makes them perceptible, formulates them, and allows for their exchange with other people. In a word, cinema appears as the sphere of a *signification* and of a *communication*.

From a historical point of view, such a theoretical orientation has a double peculiarity. On one side, it is rooted in the prewar debate. The idea that cinema is a language had in fact already developed during those years. Also, many of the hypotheses proposed (not all of them, as we will see) are simply the reprise of well-established formulas. In short, there is a real scholarly tradition in fields such as that of film grammars that seems to have uninterrupted continuity. On the other side, however, this field of study underwent a radical shift toward the mid-1960s. The idea that cinema is a language was taken up by a new discipline, semiotics, which approaches the problem in a new way. In particular, semiotics no longer sees in language an intrinsic feature of cinema, capable of condensing the whole phenomenon within itself. It sees language as one of its many aspects, to be focused on from a specific point of view. As a result, the study of the *linguistic basis* of films—an element that permeates everything—is replaced by the study of the *linguistic features* of films, specific components of a broader phenomenon. Also, the essentialist, ontological approach ("by its very nature cinema is . . .") is replaced by a methodical, disciplinary approach ("from this angle, cinema emerges as . . .").

Thus, on the one hand, this theory has a more well-defined link with the past than in the previous cases. On the other hand, we have yet another point of rupture, marking the entry into the field of a new paradigm. If there is something at the historical level that characterizes the theoretical orientation we are about to analyze, it is that this is a moment of passage, a place of transit. But between these two extremes there is a large corpus of studies, often different in tone and value, but whose characteristics are generally homogeneous, distributed in most of the countries where cinema is the object of study. Many of these studies, as we have suggested, limit themselves to older themes. Others try instead to follow more personal paths. Finally, they all try to deepen our understanding of something that is self-evident, that is, the linguistic nature of films. Once the awareness that cinema means and communicates is reached, and that it does so openly, it is a matter of understanding how and why it does so.

Hence, there is a whole series of recurrent questions among the various contributions. We will try to organize them into a list, which may turn out to be somewhat boring but will, we hope, be informative. For instance, what exactly are the expressive means cinema relies on? In particular, what is the role of elements such as acting, set design, and music? How do they work individually and how do they blend with each other? Also, what kind of relationship exists between cinema and fields like the figurative arts or literature? What unites them and what divides them? And what are the traits that distinguish the filmic sign *par excellence,* the image? Moreover, what rules does the cinema follow in order to stage a specific reality and tell a story? Does a filmic grammar exist and, if so, what is it like? Finally, what is cinema's ability to signify and communicate based on? In particular, how does the shift between the showing of the world and the development of a meaning take place? What is the relationship between "showing" and "assigning a meaning"?

These are some of the questions around which the debate is centered. Starting from them we can map the development of this brand of film theory. In the following pages we will first examine three major areas of study, which in some ways also constitute the foundation of all the other critical contributions. The first area is concerned with the relationships between cinema and the other arts and looks for both analogies and interchanges among them. The second area deals with filmic grammars or the rules of the cinematic language. The third studies the image, its value as a sign, and its more aesthetic characteristics. For all three of these fields of study we will make references to the texts that are most significant for an understanding of the development of a debate that, as already stated, is quite homogeneous. Later we will focus on three contributions that, although different in dimension and influence, represent the attempt to get to the bottom of the question and to find out which conditions cinema must satisfy in order to be equated to a language, which paths it must follow in order to give a meaning to what it shows. We will start with Galvano Della Volpe's aesthetic project of a fundamentally anti-idealistic nature, which underscores the rational basis of cinema. Then we will study Albert Laffay, a rather isolated scholar who has only recently been rediscovered, who insists that narrative structures are elements that transform the flux of the images into a discourse. Finally, we will analyze Jean Mitry's theoretical work, which seems a bit like the end of this whole epoch and which is capable of underscoring the mechanisms behind all symbolic forms.

4.2.   The Components, Nature, and Rules of Film Language

We will start this analysis with an area more directly concerned with the relationship between cinema and other *fields of expression,* such as poetry, theater, dance, etc. Its aim is to measure similarities and differences between the so-called *seventh art* and the *arts* that came before it, as well as to underscore the areas where exchange takes place and those where each art retains its independence. Just as in the previous case, this field of study has its roots in the first years of the century. Before the war it aimed to show that even cinema, the newest among the expressive arts, enjoyed full aesthetic dignity (often achieved thanks to its differences from its predecessors). By the postwar years this phase of revindication had ceased, and the problem became that of identifying the range of action of the new medium, its possibilities and limits.

The bibliography is very large. There are analyses of the relationship between cinema and theater, which is considered its closest neighbor; studies of the relationship between cinema and painting; a very wide range of essays on the connections between cinema and literature; the initial work on the relationship between cinema and television, which already appeared to be a threatening competitor.[1] Within this panorama we also find very personal positions, such as Ragghianti's (1952). Ragghianti, continuing a trend that had started in the 1930s, seeks to earn cinema a place among the figurative arts, making it the continuation of painting.[2] Bazin's position (1959) is also very personal. In his work on the relationship between cinema and theater, he opposes the widespread belief that the former has to "breathe fresh air into" the latter. Instead, he defends the idea that film shots need to respect completely the mise-en-scène suggested by the theatrical text, while they must retain their voyeuristic quality so as to allow the spectator to enjoy this mise-en-scène better than in a theater. Beyond these more personal points of view, however, the debate appears to develop in a homogeneous—sometimes even boring—way, through references to the linguistic-aesthetic tradition, analyses of concrete cases, and attempts at generalizations.

We will now try to illustrate the modes of this debate. In order to shed some light on the situation in the United States, which has so far mostly been overlooked, we will briefly analyze a book by George Bluestone (1957), which deals with the relationship between filmic and literary narrative. It is an interesting work, which shows the incipient attention to cinema in American academia and which has been followed and quoted by many later studies. The opening idea of the book is that both films and novels "show," the former with the eyes, the latter with the mind. Thus, the ends of both are the same, but their means differ. The latter seems to be especially important. For instance, novels usually tend to try to overcome the mediation imposed by words between the perceiving subject and the perceived reality, which leads to their frequent recurrence to *tropes,* rhetorical figures adding vivacity and freshness to what is represented. Cinema, on the contrary, is in the opposite situation, for the image itself diminishes the distance between perceiver and perceived; if anything, it is the moment of symbolic mediation that is missing, and it only appears in the form of editing or of the combination of images and sounds. The presence of such differences does not imply, however, that novels and films should be alien to one another. On the contrary, we recognize many signs of reciprocal attraction, as in the case of filmed novels: here the two media try to join forces. Also in this case, however, we observe the alternation between moments of real convergence and latent divergence. The passage from the narrative text to the screenplay represents the point of greatest contact between the two media (a few years later Pasolini would speak of a somewhat literary reality). The possible divergence emerges with the finished film, which always tries to assert itself as separate from the literary work.

Bluestone analyzes some adaptations in detail, in order to see how this "hot" situation brings a variable relationship into play. He notes Ford's attempt in *The Informer* to make some internal states visible. He underscores how in *Wuthering Heights* Wyler attempts to make a story written for the nineteenth-century reader accessible to a twentieth-century audience. He suggests that in *Pride and Prejudice* Leonard proposes an analogy between the rhythms of the story and the dramatic relationships among the characters. Apropos *The Grapes of Wrath* he observes that Ford reverses the order of the key sequence, which brings the narration back to popular conventions. In Wellman's *The Ox-Bow Incident* Bluestone identifies the importance of the transformation of the ending, which adapts both the meaning and the structure of the original work to cinematic conventions. Finally, in his analysis of *Madame Bovary* he observes that Minnelli is unable to render Flaubert's means of constructing space, so that the film fails to achieve the novel's sculptural quality. All these examples not only show the kind of bond developed in the process of filmic adaptation between the source and the target work, a relationship that can range from re-creation to complete alteration. Above all, they underscore that films' attraction to literary models always requires— even apart from the case of adaptation—the will to find points of contact between the two media, together with the realization that they rely on different means of expression. Cinema and literature constantly tend both to converge and to diverge, and not only in the case of film adaptation.

The problems Bluestone focuses on have acquired importance and have remained at the center of scholarly investigation even in more recent years.[3] His insistence both on the common aims and different devices of cinema and literature and on the crucial role of adaptation in defining the relationship between the two gives a good idea of the topics of discussion among the theorists of the time.

Let us now move on to the second area of studies. The ones mentioned so far have approached cinema from the "outside." They focus on the expressive devices borrowed by cinema from the other arts and single out the arts that have some contacts with cinema. This second area of study, instead, approaches cinema from the "inside," with studies dealing directly with how a film works, trying to identify both the most common practices and the practices that appear to be most appropriate. This means that editing techniques, shots, camera movements, etc., are first systematically reviewed, then catalogued according to more or less rigid typologies and canons. In short, real *grammars of cinema* are compiled, repertories of filmic procedures with precise rules on how to apply them "correctly."

Such an enterprise blends the will to classify and the will to create rules. It has—yet again—a long tradition, with important antecedents in the 1920s and 1930s. In the best of cases, the focus here was on the directors' "practice," to identify the set of solutions that could be adopted in a film. In the worst of cases, a strict normative system, which functioned as a "cage," was constructed. This trend continued in the postwar years, with many examples of "grammars": by Bataille and Berthomieu in France, by Roger in Belgium, by May in Italy.[4] The last requires attention (first, because Italy, as stated above, is in some ways exemplary; second, because May was an interesting transitional figure, already active in the 1930s, who continued Spottiswoode's work). The first part of his work is devoted to the construction of a shot, with a typology of inclination, angle, and configuration, camera movements, blocking, light shifts. This part is followed by a broad section on editing, in which he analyzes the possible relationships among various shots, especially those that are direct or angled, inclined or inserted. At the end of the book we find a reflection on continuity and discontinuity in films, as well as a short analysis of the modes of nonnarrative editing, such as creative editing and rhythmic editing. But more important than the themes he treats is the assumption behind his work, expressed in the following statement: "Nature, objects, and peoples (plastic forms, in short) do not offer, in their generic aspect, any particular expressive characteristics. They acquire them only if seen from a certain angle and shown onscreen in a certain way" (May 1947:22). In a word, a film acquires its meaning not through the reality that is represented, but through the modes of this representation. Studying the "grammar" of cinema is thus fundamental in that it clarifies how a director treats reality and makes it significant.

This line of investigation includes not only "grammars" in the strict sense, but also all the contributions that, even without being inspired by the "grammars" of the natural languages and without claiming to arrive at a normative scheme, try to single out the expressive possibilities of cinematic language. Two examples of this are, among many others, the books by Marcel Martin (1955) and François Chevassu (1963), both of which were widely disseminated. The former, briefly, deals with the usual themes: shots, movement, lighting, set design, editing, etc. It also devotes special attention to such elements as ellipsis and punctuation, as well as unusually careful attention to the soundtrack and the story. Finally, it is very precise in dealing with the two fundamental boundaries of representation, space and time. The accent on these aspects reveals the position shared by Martin and other scholars close to him. What he is interested in, above all, is not the existence of fixed norms, but the variety of levels a film works on; not the recurrence of certain solutions, but the expressive richness of cinema; not the way each isolated element works in the abstract, but how certain suggestions are concretely realized. Thus, Martin's contribution emerges not as a grammar, but as a real *rhetoric* of cinema.

It should be added that this second field of study (which we have labeled "grammars and rhetoric" of cinema) continued beyond the period we are analyzing. In some cases it produced studies of a more "philosophical" kind (see Taddei's two volumes, which straddle two periods of research).[5] In other cases it was linked with the semiotic enterprise and was deeply transformed by this encounter (semiotics tried again, in a different conceptual frame, to discover the "rules" of cinematic language).[6] In yet other cases, this second area of study gave birth to a trend that could be called "neo-grammatical," developed through a series of books attempting to discover the organizational strategies of a film by stealing the "secrets" from both great directors and current films in order to identify the way films can and should be organized.[7]

Let us now move on to the third field of study, an area that largely overlaps the previous ones, in that it contains many of the themes and motifs we have already encountered. In addition, here we find special attention to what appears to be the cinematic sign *par excellence,* the *image.* Of what is it made? How does it manage to signify and to communicate? What impositions does it force on films? The answers to these questions usually come from the merging of many different elements: from the comparison between the image and other kinds of signs, such as speech; from the analysis of filmic narrative; from a series of affirmations inspired by psychology, aesthetics, or criticism; from surveys concerning cinematic technique; and from the discussion of concrete examples. The result is a very specific kind of study, often a manual, which is present in most countries everywhere and which could easily be subtitled "cinema as image language."

We will mention only two books of a clearly didactic nature as examples of this trend, just to give a feeling of the meaning and tone of these studies. The first is *Der Film: Wesen und Gestalt* by Walter Hagemann (1952). Starting in the late 1940s Hagemann directed the Journalistic Institute in Münster, and from his seminars emerged the generation that gave life to the journal *Film-kritik*. The theme of the image is analyzed in parallel with a wide range of questions: articulating space and time in cinema; rendering movement; complementing visual and auditory components; the dramaturgic structure of films; the many styles developed by the different national cinemas; the aims the new art seems to pursue; etc. All this is nothing new (Hagemann's inspiration dates back to prewar authors, some of whom, like Béla Balász, are still active). Hagemann, however, tries to offer a complete overview that will allow the reader to understand the linguistic (as well as aesthetic and broadly social) basis on which cinema operates.

Our second example is similar to the first: it is Luigi Chiarini's *Arte e tecnica del film* (1962). Chiarini directed the Centro Sperimentale di Cinematografia, in Rome, and became the first cinema professor at the university level in Italy. His book was published almost at the end of the period under study. But because it was the product of the reexamination of older texts, it reveals a lot about the main debates of the two previous decades. The question of the image is presented first through the illustration of the fundamental cinematic techniques (subject, treatment, screenplay, acting, shooting, editing) then through the discussion of the relationship between cinema and the other arts (the spectacle in general, theater, figurative arts, narrative). Within this framework, Chiarini devotes some pages to a specific comparison between images and words. With the latter, he argues, it is possible to represent precisely the meaning of a situation while leaving its outlines somewhat blurred. With the former the situation is reversed. Although very specific objects are represented (a chair, for instance, is *a* chair and not another one), their meaning often varies (a chair may mean different things in different films). In other words, in the first case, the reality evoked by words is variable, while signification is stable; in the second case, reality is stable, while signification remains variable. Hence an important corollary: "When they express concepts, words in this respect have a higher synthetic capacity than images; when, instead, they attempt to give us an objective (and as analytical as possible) representation of reality, they can neither achieve the completeness of images nor compete with the latter's synthetic power. Similarly, images cannot express concepts" (Chiarini 1962:233). Thus, words and images have opposite qualities: the former aim toward the concept, the latter toward the referent; the former are highly synthetic, the latter analytic. Films must take these differences into account and act accordingly.

Many other examples could be given, but the two mentioned above give us an idea of what is at stake. We have now presented the three great areas of study of this debate. They often blended with each other, and in these years they gave birth to a kind of study that is somewhat obsolete today and yet has not completely disappeared. It is not by chance, in fact, that at the beginning of the 1970s Perkins resurrected this tradition. (His book discusses the characteristics of reality on the screen, "both reproduced and imagined, a creation and a copy" [Perkins 1972:70]. The criterion behind the representation of this reality is, first of all, coherence, through which "the film-maker creates significance" and the spectators "recognize meanings at all levels" [116].) Nor is it a coincidence that Carroll, a historian of theory, tries to reevaluate this period through Perkins' book.[8]

We now intend to remain within this time frame, but to approach three works of a more markedly seminal nature, devoted to the definition of not only *how,* but also *why* cinema is a language. The authors we will include in this analysis are Galvano Della Volpe, Albert Laffay, and Jean Mitry. They are prompted by different interests (Della Volpe was a philosopher looking to cinema for confirmation of more general hypotheses; Laffay was a man of letters, for whom cinema was an elective subject; Mitry was a historian and a theorist who devoted his entire life to cinema). They also moved in different dimensions (Della Volpe worked to upset the still dominating Crocean aesthetics in Italy; Laffay's starting point was narratology; Mitry embodied the "classic" tradition of cinematic studies). They are even different in terms of the dimension of their contributions (from Della Volpe's rather few pages to the huge "opus" written by Mitry). Grouping these three authors together, however, effectively presents the courses taken to explain the linguistic nature of cinema.

4.3.   The Foundations of Language: Della Volpe and the Rationality of Images

In the most famous of his essays on cinema, "Il verosimile filmico," Della Volpe questions Eisenstein's well-known sequence about the stone lion rising.

He observes how, undoubtedly, it is impossible to translate such a sequence into words, since expressions like "revolutionary lion" or "even stones revolt and shout" would appear to be artistic banalities compared to the sequence itself. Yet it is also true that this sequence "contains transfers, symbols, abstract ideas, just like a verbal or literary image" (Della Volpe 1954:62). It is even possible to observe, more generally, that every filmic image, in its completeness as an *edited, dynamic-visual image,* consists of "specific, defined, and defining forms and ideas." Also, its ability to communicate or to express consists of "such ideas, or else universal definitions and, in short, of the *discursus* of intelligence" (Della Volpe 1954:66). Hence the first point: filmic images do not simply construct concrete references, but also rely on a rational basis. Similarly, they do not simply evoke generic sentiments, but also introduce precise concepts. In this sense they are thus related to any other sign, which in order to be such must have a well-defined meaning.

Thus, filmic images have an intellectual component, which perfectly overlaps with their representational capacity and which assimilates them to a sign. The consequences of this structure of the image need to be mentioned briefly at this point, if for no other reason than that they complete the picture. First, it is necessary to reformulate the traditional opposition between form and content. It is not the case that on the one hand we have a visible organization and on the other hand an idea to communicate. The situation is more complicated than this. First, in fact, we need to take into account that it is "thanks to their symbolic or ideal nature that artistic (filmic, etc.) images become specifically a *form,* and thus communicative or *expressive*" (Della Volpe 1954: 67). To this *form,* understood as the possibility of signifying, concretely correspond "very defined and discriminate *forms* (in the plural), that is, *ideas* or *empirical* or 'full' concepts" that allow an "effective communicativity of the image" (67). Finally, "the 'fullness' of the concepts obviously takes us back from form (idea) to *content.* The latter, in turn, in general can only be called the *sensible* or the *experienced,* or in other words *matter,* the *particular* where the idea (the universal) can be defined so as to become the 'idea of something,' for otherwise it is nothing" (67). In other words, the fact that images possess a discursive dimension, or simply the fact that signs mean something, does not belong to the realm of mere hearsay. Instead, it is granted by the simultaneous presence of a symbolic structure, of clear and separate concepts, and of concrete thought, by the presence of a form (in the singular) understood as the expressive principle, or basis, of forms (in the plural) understood as specific or defined expressions, and of content, understood as the concrete action of referring to something. It is evident that, beyond the extreme architectural complexity, a rich dialectic among the terms at stake is established. We have a real "reciprocal *functionality* of form and content" that tightly connects the two realities.

Second, the conjunction of representational power and rationality in the image also leads to the reevaluation of the *artistic techniques* characterizing cinema. As we have seen, in fact, the ability to signify connects the latter to the other arts, while some of the solutions it offers cannot easily be translated into other aesthetic realms. Thus, having to identify some specific traits on a common basis, we realize that "it is possible to distinguish between them thanks to the different expressive *devices* and *semantic* techniques already separating, within the realm of art, film (edited, dynamic-visual images and symbols) from literature (with its verbal symbols and images) and painting (with its 'abstract' static-visual symbols and images)" (Della Volpe 1954:70). In other words, filmic signs are not characterized by their expressive amplitude (which, on the contrary, they share with the whole realm of art), and even less by a specific representative power (which they achieve like any other). Instead, they are characterized by the materials and procedures with which and through which they are constructed. Within this picture, what acquires importance is, of course, the almost "physical" nature of the references and the editing process, understood as the possibility of comparisons, successions, metaphors, etc. In other words, cinema is marked by the presence of *edited, dynamic-visual* symbols.

Third, this conjunction in the image of rationality and representational power generates the notion of *filmic verisimilitude*. This is a very important notion, designating "the foundation of the *artistic* constitution of the filmic image" (Della Volpe 154:74). Sometimes, when we watch a film, we wonder why it contains a detail we find disturbing. We then realize that this does not happen because this detail is "fake" or a "bad copy of reality," but because it goes against "the *deep coherence,* the *reasonableness* of the director's own *premises,* against the final effect, the director's goal: to achieve credibility, to arouse interest, emotion" (72). Thus, we compare the out-of-tune visual detail not with the exactitude of the representation, but with an internal rhythm of the director's discourse; not with the assumed "truth of the facts," but with the way in which they are presented. In short, we do not react "only with our eyes, but also with our experience and with our unitary, rational (ideal) feeling for things, with our (experienced) *reason*. This confirms what we have discussed above, i.e., that art is—in its modes—a relationship between ideas (reason) and matter, an empirical concept" (72). Filmic verisimilitude is the very measure of this complex order, which allows us to accept even the most impossible details as long as they are coherent and to reject even the most exact ones if they appear to deviate from the film's internal logic. Above all, verisimilitude allows Della Volpe to reiterate once again that images speak to us, fully, using the language of ideas and concepts.

So far, we have discussed Della Volpe's main contribution on cinema.[9] The major points of his discourse are clear. He claims that there exists in the image, no less than in words, a rational component; he postulates the existence of a dynamic between form (understood as general symbolic structure), forms (understood as the structures of each single expression), and content (understood as concretely expressed thoughts). He also insists on the role of technique in defining the outline of a sign. Finally, he contends that the coherence and reasonableness of a work are the only standards capable of defining the "verisimilitude" of what is said. Let us add that Della Volpe's position must be viewed within the framework of his battle against Croce's thought, still dominant in Italy in the 1950s. Above all, Della Volpe attacked Croce's reduction of language to a purely aesthetic fact, as well as his definition of art as a "pure, lyrical intuition," close to feeling and imagination and far from any need (and ability) to communicate. Images—in particular cinematic images, which apparently are detached from any rational dimension—become the basis for a dramatic shift, with effects that are felt beyond the realm of film, making it possible for us to find the very roots of filmic language.

4.4.   The Foundations of Cinematic Language: Laffay and the Narrative of Films

Albert Laffay, the scholar we will now focus on, was an author whose collected writings provoked no obvious reaction at the time of their publication in 1964. He was, however, rediscovered in the 1980s as one of the fathers of cinematic narratology. We will present his work in the light of this. Laffay connects the definition of cinema as language to the presence of a story that orients images and sounds. In so doing, he underscores a second kind of possible "foundation." After the idea of an intrinsic rationality (which, we repeat, Della Volpe defended against Croce's sentimentalism) we have now the idea of a pervasive narrativity (which Laffay prefers to Bazin's realism). The work of this French scholar deserves a careful, step-by-step analysis.

At first glance, cinema undoubtedly appears to be a replica of the world. It "aims to give us the impression of the solidity and solidarity of things" (Laffay 1964:18). Hence the impression that films always represent objects and bodies in their concreteness and rootedness. A closer analysis, however, shows that the world on the screen has only an *appearance* of reality, but is not truly real. The effectiveness it seems to possess turns out to be totally ineffective (the things we deal with are separate from us, and we cannot intervene in them). Likewise, the consistency it seems to have is the product of a mere illusion (we are not dealing with things, but with representations of things). In short, we are faced with "a world simply covered with a thin film of life, which is only almost real and, indeed, beyond our reach" (28).

This illusory quality and ineffectiveness depends on many factors, such as the transfiguration of reality that takes place in all the arts. "By itself, reality never has an aesthetic quality. If cinema is an art, it needs to be something other than a double of the world" (23). Another factor is the presence of explicitly unrealistic elements in films. It is enough to consider the music that invades the represented universe, detaching it from the world that surrounds us and setting it afloat. "The musical accompaniment does not simply build a sonic prison that leaves the spectator face to face with the film; but thanks to its symbolic value it establishes a relationship with the events on the screen, sustaining and transforming them" (34). But beyond any individual factor, there is only one key element: the necessary and constant presence of a *narrative* dimension.

In fact, cinema is based on narrative, always and in any case relying on it. This happens because narration satisfies some of its fundamental needs. The first is the need to make reality legible on the screen. By itself, reality reveals its vague outlines, confused distances. In order to represent it, it is necessary to highlight isolated components, the mutual relationships among them, and their specific functions. In short, one must bring to light a key for deciphering it. Second, cinema also needs to reorganize the universe to be represented. By itself, this universe is open and dispersed. In order to represent it, it is necessary to frame it with a beginning and an end, structure it, put it into perspective. In other words, it must be assembled according to lines of force. Third, cinema needs to succeed in composing the materials it uses. By themselves, these materials may be put to any use, but if one wants to use them on the screen, it is necessary to give them a precise role and to define them as a whole. In other words, we need to give them form. To summarize, we observe the need to make reality legible, to reorganize the universe that is our starting point, and to compose the various materials. A story is capable of satisfying these needs, because of its ability to underscore facts and characters, to delineate a plot, and to guide exposition. It is indeed so capable of doing all this that stories become integrally connected with cinema. If we look closely at these needs, however, we realize that they are the same as those behind the translation of existence into representation. A story satisfies them so well that it becomes the decisive factor in the construction of a simulacrum of reality. In this sense, as stated above, a story has the greatest responsibility in defining the dimension of *appearance* that dominates the screen.

Yet by espousing narration cinema also finds something else in it. In fact, a story not only makes the real world become a filmic, ineffective reality; it also makes it possible to give meaning to what is represented. In other words, narrative is not only a filter for representation, a mechanism that does not realize anything. It is also the realm where a real discourse is carried out. The proof of this lies in the very operations around which it gravitates: promoting legibility, ordering, and shaping. "A cinematic story is sustained by an *underlying logical plot,* by a series that is related to *discourse*" (68). Thus, the cinema's assumption of narrative as its own measure in order to allow the representation of reality means entering the realm of discourse, making cinema into a language.

This is the core of Laffay's thought. To further synthesize it, we can say that if cinema is not reality itself, but its representation, it owes this to narrative's ability to make things legible, to reorganize them, and to insert them into a composition. Since the frame of a story is of a discursive nature, however, by espousing narrative cinema becomes a linguistic device. This central idea leads the French theorist to many other points, of which we will consider only the one that is most current. By permeating the images and sounds, narrative weaves a thread that holds both together. Thus, in a film we find a comprehensive design, a pervasive immanent logic. Neither can be confused with what directors explicitly want to say or with the producers' decisions. Rather, they emerge as a virtual linguistic *focus* placed beyond the screen, but one that, nonetheless, literally guides the game. Hence the need to acknowledge the existence of an abstract figure, like a master of ceremonies, the *grand imagier* whom we confront before all else. This is what recent narratology calls the *implied author,* or the *enunciator,* namely, the general instance that incarnates the very act by means of which film allows itself to be seen and understood. In other words, this is the principle according to which film functions, what moves it as a discourse. Laffay intuits the presence of this abstract figure that delineates films, and he exalts its linguistic quality. This is the main reason for his rediscovery in the 1980s. But beyond his beautiful pages on the *grand imagier,* what really counts is the core of his thought, which we have tried to isolate: cinema finds in narrative both a necessary accomplice and another reason to call itself a language.

4.5. The Foundations of Cinematic Language: Mitry and the Structure of the Symbolic

The last author we intend to deal with in this section is Jean Mitry. His monumental theoretical work, *Esthétique et psychologie du cinéma,* along with his equally monumental *Histoire du cinéma,* emerges as the crowning achievement of the whole line of thought that we are surveying.[10] Therefore, if we devote more attention to him it is not only because he shows us a third way to establish cinema's linguistic nature, through reference to the very structure of the symbolic order, but also because his contribution is exemplary.

The exemplary quality of his work is apparent in its title, where the main terms, *aesthetics* and *psychology,* recall two traditional realms of discussion. Mitry turns them into the designated territory where cinema needs to be situated. In fact, every film appears, on the one hand, as the product of an expressive intention that is more or less realized and, on the other hand, as the moment in which thoughts are organized, constructed, communicated. That is, a film is both a *work of art*—at least potentially—and a *linguistic object* in which ideas are manifested. Thus, the aesthetic and psychological dimensions are not random standards to be adopted, and they do not act upon film from the outside. If they are inherent to it, this is because of a real *internal* necessity.[11]

Such a belief is reflected by the way in which Mitry organizes his work. The beginning of the first volume presents the aesthetic framing. He questions how art was born ("as with science and philosophy, the origin of art is rooted in religion," then detaches from it, separating itself from the other areas, although never completely disrupting this bond [Mitry 1963 : 15–16]); he distinguishes the various arts (and "cinema is the only one among the arts to be an art of both time and space" [27]); he compares cinema and creation (a film is a collective *job,* the *work* of an author, understood not as such, but as the author *of* a work [30−44]).

This first frame is followed by a psychological-linguistic one. Expressive devices and language are opposed (with the former "we access a vague, imprecise idea through an emotion"; with the latter "we access emotion from the idea" [47−48]). Mitry already hints at this point at the linguistic nature of cinema (in fact, cinema is "an aesthetic form, just like literature. However, although it uses images as a means of expression, it is a language because of its logical and dialectical organization" [47−48]). Mitry reiterates the connection between thought and language (the latter being a way to both translate and shape the former, so that the latter relies on the former's operations, namely, "conceiving, judging, reasoning, ordering according to relationships of analogy, consequence, or causality" [59]). Finally, Mitry compares the filmic and verbal language (they use different symbols, but have the same basic mental structures, namely, the operations of thought [see Mitry 1963 : 59]).

Starting from this point, Mitry's work is explicitly devoted to images. He intends to refute (and dismantle) the idea that a film can provide "absolute immediacy." In fact, reality seems directly present on the screen, presenting itself as it is, without the mediation of any symbolic structure. In this sense, films seem to *show* more than to *mean.* After a deeper analysis, however, we understand that even filmic images fully deserve to be called *signs.*

First, they are such because of the functions they are able to fulfill. On film the images are never isolated, but are connected to one another by similarity, by contrast, or simply by succession. Thus, every image acquires value not by itself, but thanks to its connection to other images. The mere fact that one image follows another means that an image acquires precise *implications.* For instance, presenting in sequence a gunshot and a man falling down makes the shot a cause and the fall an effect. Such implications characterize the first way in which an image signifies, making of the image what Mitry calls a true *symbol.*

An image can also be a sign, however, because of the *processes* engendering it. In fact, "although it is similar to what it represents, it *always* adds something to it" (126). Let us consider a table, any table, in a western movie: "*This* table is there because a table needs to have this specific function and be a part of the action. Thus, we are not only seeing *this* table, but—with it and through it—also the *idea* of every possible table and of the *necessity* of a table. Through this object, it is the concept itself that finds itself at play in the drama" (128). Such a generalization of what is in itself particular, such an abstraction of what is in itself concrete, defines the second way in which an image signifies. Mitry calls it an *analogon*.

Thus, the filmic image not only *shows:* it *signifies* both because it acquires new value through its combination with other images (symbol) and because it initiates a process of generalization and abstraction with its own presence on the screen (analogon). This already proves that, behind the impression of immediacy that filmic images give us, there is a precise capacity for significa-tion. In any case, with Mitry we find confirmation of this at another level:

At the level of the perception of reality, there is no difference between a chair and its image, so much so that at the cinema I see the real chair through the image of it that is shown on the screen. However, I also perceive an image. *Inasmuch as they are represented,* filmic images appear to be similar to the im-mediate images of our conscious mind. However, *inasmuch as they are represen-tations,* filmic images are aesthetically structured forms. It follows that, if the limits of the screen are not only a *mask* (cache) for the reality represented, they become a *frame* (cadre) for representation. Therefore, when we take into consideration a filmic image projected on the screen, we find ourselves: a) in front of an image perceived as a real space, seen through a small window; b) in front of an image projected on a flat surface, organized in a frame or in relation to it. (170)

Thus, we observe some sort of intrinsic duplicity in the image. On the one hand, it tends to annul itself in what is *represented* in it (a portion of the world, seen through a small window). On the other hand, it appears as a *representation* (a space that is other, enclosed by a frame separating it from the world repre-sented). The former aspect seems to emerge at once, but in the long run it is the latter that defines the true nature of the filmic image.

In short, we observe a shift from the represented to representation, just as before from showing to signifying. These two elements need to be viewed in parallel, as both tell us that the filmic image not only consists of reality as shown on the screen, but works in a realm of its own, that of signs, of figures. Above all, these two elements need to be emphasized, because it is thanks to them that we can reach the goals our work has set for itself.

The first of these goals, although it is constantly reiterated, is after all con-tingent, for it is Mitry's battle against the theories of realism. For him this is merely a naive trust in the content that is represented on the screen, which fails to grasp the process that makes content representable, the process that makes what appears on the screen manage to pass for real. Believing in the theories of realism means accepting appearances without understanding the modalities of their appearance, mistaking what a film shows for something concrete. Taking an image for reality means succumbing to a *trompe-l'oeil*. Bazin and his followers are victims of this illusion.[12]

The second goal is, instead, crucial, for it implies understanding in what sense cinema is a language. Mitry has already suggested this connection at the beginning of the volume, and in the light of what he has been saying this idea becomes even clearer. The fact that filmic images signify *more than* show, that they are representations *more than* the represented, detaches them from the initial reality and generates a new reality. Through its relationship to the images nearby, through its ability to offer concepts, through the fact that the frame of the screen restructures space and time, each image annuls[13] the thing that it is the image of, makes reality not real. The world on the screen may be more or less similar to the world that surrounds us, but it is a world apart, with its own measures and patterns. As a consequence, filmic images are part of language above all because, as in every language, they create a parallel and autonomous universe, which cannot be confused with the one we live in. Still, the fact that an image signifies because it starts by showing, and that it is a representation because it starts with the represented, allows it both to detach itself from and to keep in touch with reality. What appears on the screen is different from reality (for instance, it is such "inasmuch as it is representation, because of the values structuring the information an image contains and placing them within a noncontiguous space which is dimensionally different from the real one" [178]). At the same time, however, the onscreen reality is in some ways reality itself ("inasmuch as it is represented, because the information appearing in an image is an image of reality" [178]). Thus, it is possible for the filmic image to be an entity in and of itself and to establish a connection with its ideal starting point. More generally, it is also possible for the filmic image to play the game that is the basis of every symbolic structure, consisting of closures and openings, differences and identities. Thus, filmic images may be said to be similar to a language because of what they are based on, that is, their ability both to be different from the world and to become its substitute, its emblem, its representative.[14]

The core of Mitry's thought is here: he reiterates the intrinsic "linguistic nature" of films, not only at the level of their logic organization, as previously suggested, but also at the level of their basic components, images. The latter's nature, as sign and representation, gives cinema its linguistic base. We should also add that in his monumental work Mitry not only states and reiterates this,[15] but also tries concretely to articulate it. This is his third goal: after establishing that cinema is a language, he intends to discern the forms that organize it.

It is impossible to summarize the numerous observations the French scholar makes in this regard, but they are all closely related to the points just mentioned. Let us give an example. The borders of the image, as we have said, allow a figure both to become autonomous from reality and to evoke the "essence" or the "idea" of what is represented. Starting from them, Mitry introduces a discourse on filmic space and time, on the composition of the frame, and on the kinds of shots. There are four kinds of shots. We have a *descriptive image,* in which the camera merely records any portion of reality. We have the *personal image,* in which the camera makes some choices, emphasizes certain objects more than others, establishes symbolic relationships among different objects. In a word, it manifests the author's "view of the world." We also have the *semisubjective image,* which "adopts the point of view of one of the characters, who in turn is placed in an objective—and yet privileged—way within the frame" (Mitry 1965:77). Finally, we have the *subjective image,* in which the camera takes the place of one of the characters, who stands outside the frame, with whom it identifies and through whom it sees. On the other hand, investigating the ways in which images are connected among themselves makes Mitry explore different kinds of editing and cinematic rhythm. As far as editing is concerned, we have the *narrative montage,* which simply aims to ensure continuity of action. Then we have the *lyric montage,* which relies on continuity in order to express ideas or feelings that transcend the drama; the *montage of ideas,* which allows the total elaboration of the film *a posteriori;* and the *intellectual montage,* which dialectically determines ideas rather than expressing them (see Mitry 1963:358). As far as rhythm is concerned, we have the rhythm of the various shots, the rhythm within the shot, etc. Mitry also analyzes broader phenomena, from the study of subjectivity to the structures characterizing the cinematic tale through time.

But the central point of Mitry's work is still what we have already hinted at. The image is both sign and representation; cinema is therefore language. On the one hand, we have his idea based on the will to show that whatever appears on the screen is not really itself, but its reformulation ("what is represented is perceived through a representation, which of necessity transforms it" [Mitry 1965:11]); on the other hand, the idea that the "framing" of the image, together with its juxtaposition with the other images of the film, creates a separate world, which nevertheless reminds us of the world around us in its essential characteristics.

This basic belief guides Mitry even in the final section of his work, where he discusses the newly born semiology of the cinema. He apparently shares the goals of the new science, and yet he rejects it, for reasons that are easy to explain. First, Mitry tries to highlight the mechanisms that are *specific* to cinema and mistrusts generalizations. It is true that film images support the structure of the symbolic (and we have insisted on this point more than Mitry himself). It is also true, however, that they do so through their procedures (consider the role of the frame or of montage), which are peculiar to them and cannot be found elsewhere. In other words, a semiological approach that programmatically intends to take into account the whole field of signs can only seem mistaken to Mitry, who, in the second place, tries to underscore those mechanisms that are *intrinsic* to cinema and reveal its true nature. If cinema is a language, it is such in itself, because it is the way it is. Thus, a semiological approach can only seem questionable to Mitry, for it connects the various properties of an object to the point of view from which it is observed, and in this sense it does not study its intimate characteristics, but only those aspects pertaining to the chosen perspective. Mitry and the emergent semiotics, thus, study the same things. For both an image is a sign structure, the place of a representation. What changes is the epistemology, which, in the first case, studies the essence, and, in the second, the method.

Laffay and, above all, Della Volpe are not that radical (in particular, the latter is far from any explicit ontologism).[16] Yet even for them the linguistic quality of cinema is an intrinsic characteristic more than a pertinent aspect. With Mitry this becomes totally clear, in part because his polemic with the innovations of semiotics is explicit;[17] and in part because he likes to base his work on an established tradition of thought, and he wishes to remain faithful to a previously established way to approach the field.

This very bond with the past, which he masterfully represents, together with his incomprehension of the new times—whose needs he does not understand—makes Mitry the ideal figure with which to conclude our survey of "ontological theories." His contribution emerges today as the perfect mirror and the final act of a whole epoch of research. In the following pages, after a short "interlude," we will encounter a different way to conduct such research.

5 AN INTERLUDE:
THE FEELING OF THE NEW

5.1. Movements

Before confronting the second great theoretical paradigm of the postwar years, it is necessary to examine the wide range of contributions that accompanied the birth of a *new cinema* between the beginning of the 1950s and the end of the 1960s. Among them are the essays that first led the way to and then supported the Nouvelle Vague in France; those that supported the experience of the Free Cinema in England; those that defended and explained the motivations behind such movements as the Cinema Novo and the Tercer Cine in Latin America; those that accompanied the development of the New American Cinema (NAC) in the United States; those that gave their support to the Neues Deutsches Kino in Germany; and those that elsewhere, from Italy to Eastern Europe and Japan, were interested in the "young cinema" or the "independent cinema."[1] These are very dissimilar writings, hard to group under a single label. But there is also a common thread that runs through them, which we will follow.[2]

As far as the differences are concerned, it is important first to note that these movements developed neither contemporaneously nor in parallel. They both crossed paths and kept a distance. The incubation period of the Nouvelle Vague was quite long, before it exploded at the end of the 1950s. The Free Cinema was the product of more homogeneous trends, but lasted for a shorter time, in the second half of the 1950s. The new Latin American cinemas started to operate at the end of the 1950s (the Argentinean Escuela de Santa Fe) and continued throughout the following decade (the Brazilian Cin-

ema Novo at the beginning of the decade, the Argentinean Tercer Cine toward the end), until the beginning of the 1970s (Espinosa's Cine Imperfecto,
Sanjinés' didactic cinema), in a succession characterized by discontinuity. The
New American Cinema attracted the most attention at the end of the 1960s,
although by then it had been active for quite some time, and eventually it
divided itself into a whole range of experiments that were tendentially separate from one another. Other movements emerged in the 1970s, directly connected to the "political cinema" of the post-1968 years.[3]

The differences increase if we look at the cultural contexts. In France the
spark of the renewal came from the wish to evade social commitment and to
make room for subjectivity. On the contrary, in England we find the wish to
reiterate and radicalize the commitment to oppose "conformist" politics, a
position appropriated by the political left. This is a reference to the "angry
young men," with their novels and dramas built around ordinary events and
told in an ordinary language. In Latin America the call for something new
emerged within the framework of the struggles for national liberation from
colonialism and capitalism and was paralleled by the rediscovery of popular
and autochthonous traditions. Meanwhile, in the United States New American Cinema followed in the footsteps of the historical avant-garde (thanks to
the mediation of people like Maya Daren) and in connection with the figurative arts (on the one hand, Pollock's *action painting,* to which Brakhage refers; and on the other hand, pop art, which finds in Warhol its "prophet"
both in painting and in cinema).

More differences emerged from the discourses that each movement used
to promote its poetics and from the speeches that supported its filmic practice.
What pushed the Nouvelle Vague forward was above all critical contributions
and *querelles.* The Free Cinema was sustained by explicitly political interventions. The new Latin American cinema was accompanied both by analyses of
the social and cultural reality of each country and by directors' reflections on
their own activity. The New American Cinema relied on "manifestos" similar to those that had initiated the historical avant-gardes, as well as testimonials
from the inside, catalogues of works, presentations of collections, etc.

Despite such diversity, we can still identify a commonality, the shared *feeling of the new.* There was an initial need to break with traditional ways of
making and conceiving of film. After all, the long-established global order of
cinema (the cinema System and cinema as System, as they would say at the
end of the 1960s) already showed signs of decay. Within this picture, films

needed above all to appear as an individual filmmaker's work, whether he spoke for himself or in the name of a collectivity. It was necessary to be responsible for the means of expression. One's own work had to be the first witness to this principle.[4] This had many consequences: a greater awareness that the form assumed by a film was a crucial factor; the refusal to reduce the cinema to the status of a mere tool, without considering the reasons behind it; the search for new and truer narrative and expressive solutions; and a parallel experimentation with new and freer production formulas. We will focus above all on three points: the need to establish a more direct and deeper relationship with reality; the demand not to limit the discourse on reality to a simple mirror of empirical data; and a special attention to the language through which it expresses itself.

The presence of a common ground allows us to explore the field transversally. Rather than attempting a portrayal of each movement and of the debate it generated, we will try to emphasize the main recurrent ideas, on the basis of which we will discuss similarities and diversities. We will focus on the works of the main movements (Nouvelle Vague, Free Cinema, the New Latin American cinemas, New American Cinema), and we will analyze the most "programmatic" works, those that do not account for individual poetics (this book refuses to take this approach) but that define "lines" that are in some ways exemplary.

5.2.   Marking a Break

Breaking with the past was the first imperative. All movements intended to react against a past that, because of its constituted schemes, had become too narrow and rigid. The break was to take place on all fronts, both in the practice of filmmaking and in the formulation of new critical categories.

The Nouvelle Vague expressed this desire above all through the pages of the *Cahiers du Cinéma,* the monthly journal founded in 1951 by Bazin and Doniol-Valcroze. François Truffaut's "Une certaine tendance du cinéma français" (1954)—generally acknowledged as both the manifesto of the new movement and the most lucid attack against the "tradition of quality"—appeared in this very journal. Truffaut's attack on what current criticism called "good" cinema was three-pronged. First, "good" cinema was dominated by "scriptwriters' films," or works where the visual and more clearly cinematic part was a mere translation of or complement to the literary part. This implied not only privileging the story as opposed to the mise-en-scène, but also considering the director's work irrelevant, since the director found a "prepackaged" film in the screenplay. Second, this "good" cinema perpetuated a trick through the "literary cover." The audience was provided with works whose level was apparently high, works that seemed different from each other, whereas they were merely the product of the same recipe, a recipe that did not even take into account the peculiarities of the original novels. Finally, the "psychological realism" that "good" French cinema boasted about as one of its prerogatives was only a pretext to make entirely commercial films seem *engagé.* This was "an antibourgeois cinema, made by the bourgeoisie for the bourgeoisie," which "pretended" to be up-to-date while it was actually escapist. Hence the need to react against the "tradition of quality," against the cinema that was ironically called "de papa." It became necessary to insist on filmmakers, rather than scriptwriters, on art rather than empty technicalism, on the truth of things rather than masked ideologies.

Across the Channel, the Free Cinema also preached and practiced a break with the past. Its main target was the conformism that had long dominated England and that had reduced culture to regret for a glorious past, rather than a mirror of the present; to a glossy illustration of the good old motherland, rather than an analysis of the troubles experienced by the nation. On top of this, there was an aggravating factor: cinema had become the expression of only one class, the bourgeoisie, and of that class's "hysterical refusal" to face social and political problems. Thus, a radical critique of English society was needed, one that would uncover England's false faith in a nonexistent "humanism" and "liberalism," its lack of engagement vis-à-vis its most painful problems, its affected taste for tradition. At the same time, it was necessary to reject a purely illustrative cinema, dominated by the escape toward the *divertissement,* ready to be snobbish in order not to deal with the existence of such classes as the proletariat. What was needed, on the contrary, was for films to follow the path of freedom (from the rules of film industry, from the obligation to be successful, from professionalism at all costs, from stylistic conventions, etc.). Thanks to this freedom, films could aim toward the goal of talking about contemporary reality (Anderson 1957b).

The wish to break with the past was also shared by the Latin American "new cinemas." Their targets were, however, different from those mentioned so far. In an ideal synthesis of the trends of the Brazilian Cinema Novo, Glauber Rocha observed that the Cinema Novo should have nothing in common with the artistic-bourgeois aesthetics typical of a certain European cinema, the popular-commercial Hollywood aesthetics, or the populist-demagogic Moscow aesthetics (Rocha 1981). Thus, it was necessary to start on a path of *decolonization,* leading far from both the cinema of the dominators and that of the supposed liberators, for both oozed ideological conformism. In order to achieve this, Brazilian cinema had to recover autochthonous expressive forms, the primitivism that characterized the culture of the country, and thus it would acquire a popular and national connotation.

Even in Argentina, Solanas and Getino fought for a decolonized cinema, both in terms of taste and in terms of thought. However, their goal was to develop *counterinformation.* In fact, underdeveloped countries show more than anywhere else that knowledge is a monopoly of the dominant classes. These classes, which share interests with international capital, privilege the development of models of thought similar to the ones of the more advanced countries. Hence the necessity to break with imported schemes and find other points of reference. Cinema could and should appropriate this aim (Getino and Solanas 1973).

The New American Cinema's rupture with the past, instead, was played out at home, with Hollywood as the opposing team. The proof of this came from the designated role played by New York, in opposition to the West Coast, in both geographical and ideological terms. Here Jonas Mekas, Shirley Clarke, Gregory Markopoulos, and Robert Breer started their battle against the prevalence of industrial logic even in the field of cinema and against the pervasiveness of the American Dream. An article published in *Film Culture* toward the end of the summer of 1961 summarizes their intentions and goals: "We do not want false, polished, slick films. We prefer them rough, unpolished, but alive. We do not want rosy films, we want them the color of blood" (Film Culture 1961). Under the rather generic label *underground,* these directors' experiments taught the whole world a new approach to cinema.

The wish to break with the past that, in slightly different ways, was shared by all these movements reveals a different way to conceive of the cinema. We find direct proof of this in the journals that supported and encouraged these new film practices. They are the *Cahiers du Cinéma* for the Nouvelle Vague, first *Sequence* and later *Sight and Sound* for the Free Cinema, *Film Culture* for the New American Cinema, etc. Similarly, further proof of this comes from the work of cultural promotion and organization done by many of the future protagonists of this phenomenon (as, for instance, in the film circles in Rio or

Bahia, where the nucleus of the Cinema Novo developed). As a result, new critical categories were disseminated that will be of use in examining both "national" and "foreign" works.

We will now delve into these categories.

5.3. The Name of the Author

The aspect on which these movements seem to insist the most is the centrality of the figure of the *auteur*. It is not the first time that cinema has spoken of this "authorial quality." [5] It is only from the 1950s onward, however, that the interest shifts dramatically from the star, the producer, and the scriptwriter to the director and that a film is considered a direct expression of the director's personality. Within this picture, the *auteur* becomes more important than the film itself. The signature guarantees the value, the quality of the work.

The idea of the *auteur* developed mostly within the framework of the Nouvelle Vague.[6] The first suggestion came from a fortunate contribution by Astruc (1948), who suggested considering the camera analogous to the pen. One should express oneself with images and sounds just as freely as with words. The famous formula of the *caméra-stylo* had more than one positive implication. Films were equated to all other forms of expression. The shooting (when the camera is working) acquired more value than the preparatory phases (such as writing the screenplay). Finally, what appeared on the screen was "personalized" to the highest degree, for it was the result of an individual "meaning." As a result, the director's role as a mere "metteur en scène" gave way to that of an artist, a peer among peers. Thus, the director was promoted to the role of the creator of the work, the only person responsible for it.

The effects of this on the field of criticism could be seen at once. Film was seen as a testimony to a personality that manifests itself despite and through any form of conditioning (even the industrial one). It became a deposit of the feelings, obsessions, and thoughts of an individual expressing himself through images and sounds. It became the fingerprint of a single person, not the work of a group of "camera managers," as Truffaut said, adding: "I believe tomorrow's films will be even more personal than a novel, as individual and auto-biographical as a confession or a journal. . . . Tomorrow's films will be made by artists for whom shooting is a terrific, exciting adventure. Tomorrow's films will look like those who filmed them" (Truffaut 1957:18).

The "politique des auteurs," which from the mid-1950s onward defined the cultural path of *Cahiers,* perfectly exemplified this principle.[7] Its core was the rejection of the critical tradition of "content." The attention shifted from what a work said (or tried to say) to how it actually said it. It was not the theme, but the style of a movie that revealed its *auteur*'s attitude and orientation. Hence the interest in the ways the medium was used, in how directors "interpreted" cinema and "bent" it to their expressive requirements. The true task of the critics, then, became identifying within a film the "traces" of the person who conceived it and at the same time pointing out the films containing such "traces," as opposed to the films conceived by directors without a real personality.

This led to the development of very refined observational techniques (the spiral construction and the obsession with numbers that are recurrent in Hitchcock's films were thus emphasized). It also led to the idea, however, that *auteurs* "sign" their work, no matter what, whereas non-*auteurs* may make good films, but will never make a masterpiece. As a result, a small pantheon was created, containing the names deserving attention and respect: only Bresson, Renoir, Rossellini, Hitchcock, Hawks, Ford, and few others should be studied (and admired). Thus, this new critical trend revealed its provocative quality. Bazin himself underlined its excesses in a couple of essays, where he distanced himself from the reduction of a work's dimensions to those of its author and from the tendency to develop an actual cult of personality.[8]

This did not prevent the underlying hypotheses behind the "politique" from spreading and acquiring definition.[9] Andrew Sarris, a critic of the *Village Voice* and contributor to *Film Culture* (see in particular Sarris 1962 and 1970), most successfully relaunched these ideas. He opposed to some degree the position of the critics of *Cahiers.* First, he insisted that films should not be studied in isolation, but within the context of the history of cinema. A masterpiece can be judged such only when it stands out against a background. Second, he demanded that the economic and industrial system should not be forgotten, but kept in mind in terms of both the limits it imposes and the possibilities it offers. An author's vision of the world can only be translated into a full image when it relies on the means at cinema's disposal and avoids the limits implicit in the production machine. Finally, Sarris asked that the pantheon of directors worthy of attention become not an elite club, but an open list, to avoid falling back on the romantic view of the artist as an extraordinary "genius." With these exceptions, he believed that the notion of authorship needed to be defended and reinforced, for it permits emphasis on the ability of some directors to "sign" their work through constant, recurrent stylistic traits. Similarly, it allows the isolation of a deep meaning in some films, emanating from the tension between the director's personality and the material he works with.[10] The critics' task, then, is to underscore the personal and coherent use of cinema's expressive devices, as opposed to a purely rhetorical use (using black and white to "suggest realism" at all costs) or an innovative use (relying on incongruous solutions in the rest of the film). Similarly, the critics' task is to reconstruct the existence of an underlying impulse, which manifests itself even through small elements—such as breaking a certain rhythm—and yet testifies to the intensity of the person expressing himself through the film, to his ability to give shape to a work. In other words, the critic should recognize the *style* and the *élan vital* that turn a director into a true *auteur.*

These are the fundamental elements of the *auteur theory,* the American version of the French *politique des auteurs.* If we step back and examine the debate that developed around the Free Cinema, we find a similar interest in the *auteur,* but also some diffidence toward him. In fact, the English movement refused to conceive of art as the manifestation of an individual universe, as a pure manifestation of the self. Instead, it is necessary to keep an eye on the world, to take into account the information offered by reality. This does not mean, however, that the director should disappear behind the objectivity of the camera. The way cinema looks at reality is in any case the product of a stance taken toward things, and in this sense it should be "oriented." Hence the idea of a *witness-auteur.* The latter collects the stimuli coming not just from the soul, but from the events happening around him, while at the same time he does not renounce confrontations or judgments and does not evade responsibilities.[11]

Even the debate in Latin America had to reckon with the figure of the *auteur,* but changed its connotations even further. As an example, let us look at the "manifesto" introduced in Cuba by Julio García Espinosa (1973). His "imperfect cinema," which was immediate, everyday, devoid of the embellishments of commercial products, and interested in ongoing struggles, was not created by a demiurge-director, but by a *collective auteur.* It was promoted by the people themselves, who turned from spectators into actors. Thus, the alienation typical of bourgeois art was overcome. There was no longer any separation between producers and consumers. Being able both to promote and to enjoy a film made people "their own masters" as never before.[12]

Along this line, other theorists of the new Latin American cinema also emerged. Bolivian director Jorge Sanjinés repeated the refusal of the notion of the bourgeois, isolated artist and supported the "popular, revolutionary, and collective art where we always find the style of a people, of a culture that includes a group of individuals, with their general and specific way to conceive reality and with their personal way of expressing it" (Sanjinés 1979).

Variations of this idea can be found, still in Latin America, in the notion that the director should stay in touch with the national culture and should work toward the creation of a critical, more prepared, and more revolutionary audience (Santiago Alvarez). It is also seen in the notion that a man of cinema should become instead a man of the people, until he finds a personal dimension within the dialectic of people/antipeople and fatherland/anti-fatherland (Octavio Getino).[13]

To summarize what we have discussed, among the various movements subscribing to the "feeling of the new" we find three great authorial figures: the author as the only source of expression, the only one responsible for his film (Nouvelle Vague, but also NAC); the author as witness of his time and society (Free Cinema); and the author as spokesman for the popular experience (the new Latin American cinema).

Now we will move on to other problems, in particular the relationship between cinema and reality.

5.4. The Horizon of Reality

At first glance it would seem that the importance given to the author's figure diminishes the interest in the reproductive quality of cinema. Insisting on subjective mediation reduces the objectivity of the images. All the movements under investigation here, however, affirm that cinema is also a mirror of the world and that this is its most natural vocation, its true revolutionary force.

We have already mentioned that Bazin's lesson influenced the Nouvelle Vague. The idea that, in copying reality, cinema somehow continues it, reveals reality's hidden meaning and discloses its intrinsic truth, becomes a fundamental lesson for the new French filmmakers. It is not by chance, then, that Rohmer's essay "Le celluloïd et le marbre" (1955, later in Rohmer 1984) finds "cinema's most immediate privilege in the possibility of exactly reproducing reality." It is in fact from this starting point that the new "language of things" may express "something different" as compared to all the other languages, namely, the interiority, spirituality, and universality of all that surrounds us. Cinema "carries with it something that before it had been unsuspected," the "secret song of the world that can awaken us through its magic." It is, however, necessary to distance oneself from a naive realism that takes advantage of the reproductive potential of the medium in order to make the filmic tale more believable. Realism should not reduce itself to mere verisimilitude. "If, by virtue of the very fact of being shown, what appears on the screen acquires a more intense feeling of truth, I do not see why the flat law of verisimilitude should reign there sovereign." Rohmer reinforced his point (1954) by accusing his colleagues of being the slaves to a realistic "pseudo-aesthetics."

Even with the Free Cinema the concept of realism assumed a fundamental importance. However, this term was understood not in the generic meaning of adherence to reality, but in the much more precise notion of "documentary." Indeed, realism as pursued by the British movement was more "direct" and "immediate" than the one theorized by the French directors. It was the realism of those movies that show life with no need of comment or explanation, without cuts or additions. It was, in short, a witness to reality in its forgotten aspects. In an article in defense of the Free Cinema (1957a), Lindsay Anderson stated that documentaries should be one of most exciting and stimulating contemporary forms of expression and that there is nothing richer, more fantastic, surprising, and full of meaning than real life. But this strong passion for reality does not diminish the *auteur*'s importance. In fact, as Anderson himself added, the new British cinema presented *tranches de vie* (slices of life), carved with the knife of a specific point of view. In particular, what counts is the effort to tell a story taking place among the people, with proletarian characters. The *auteur* has the task of showing reality in its everyday dimension, in its least spectacular aspects.

This declared rejection both of the extraordinary dimension of reality and of its rendering in spectacular terms was echoed by Glauber Rocha: "Young directors despise huge spotlights, cranes, imposing machines. They prefer a hand-held camera, a portable tape recorder, small spotlights, and actors without makeup in natural environments" (Rocha 1963). Thus, there was a desire to avoid any manipulation and to reach instead the heart of things. Along this path one should not be stopped by squalor and poverty: "Latin American hunger is not only an alarming synonym for social poverty. It is the essence of its own society. Here lies the tragic originality of the Cinema Novo, as compared to world cinema. Our originality is our hunger, and our greatest misery is that our hunger, being truly felt, is not understood" (Rocha 1981). Rocha's *aesthetics of hunger* was rooted in the need for realism, even if it left room for flaming, baroque solutions.

Realism was also advocated by other new protagonists of the new Latin American cinemas. For instance, Espinosa strongly defended those films that are born from an original impulse to denounce the most hidden, and for this reason often forgotten, realities. In this case, cinema's adherence to reality produces—more than the didactic effect wished for by Rocha—a directly revolutionary effect. In fact denunciations "serve as information, as evidence, as a further weapon for those who fight." Even better, they can "show the processes generating the problems," thus leaving a "cinema that illustrates aesthetically the ideas and concepts we already possess" (Espinosa 1973). Thus, "imperfect cinema" is also built on such elements as pursuing reality, showing its mechanisms, changing our way of thinking.

Sanjinés also advocated realism without limiting it to an objective reproduction of reality. The lever to be pulled is both the people and their thirst for knowledge. "As we need to talk to the people, what do the people want to know? People are more interested in finding out how and why poverty comes about, who is responsible for its existence, how to fight it. They want to learn the various systems of exploitation and their backgrounds, as well as the historical truth which they have always been denied. They want to know the faces and the names of murdering, exploiting cops. They want to know causes and effects" (Sanjinés 1979). Again, realism is a means of instruction, of sensitization, of uprising: a fighting realism.

Finally, with Gutiérrez Alea we have realism as the negation of appearances and the return to the real social reality experienced by the spectator.

A socially productive spectacle should deny everyday reality (the false values that have been frozen by the ordinary consciousness) and establish the premises of its own negation, namely, its negation as a substitute for reality and as an object of contemplation. It does not emerge as mere escape or consolation for the anguished spectators, but favors their return to the other reality—the one that momentarily led them to enter into a relationship with spectacle, that allowed them to evade, enjoy, play . . .—and does not leave the audience pleased, tranquil, relaxed, pacified, and defenseless, but stimulates it and arms it for practical action. (Gutiérrez Alea 1981)

To sum up, realism emerged as a revelation of essence for the Nouvelle Vague, as a means of witnessing for the Free Cinema, and as denunciation for the Latin American cinema. It is never "reproductive fidelity," however. It is more interested in grasping the hidden side of the world (its secret heart, the marginal situations, the logic of events) than in tracing the outlines of things. Hence a systematic opening in the opposite direction: if realism exists, it often emerges only by passing through the realms of the imaginary.

5.5.   The Role of the Imaginary

As a matter of fact, for the new cinema reality is never a material to be transposed on the screen in a mechanical, cold, and sterile way. Instead, it needs to be "reinterpreted" by the *auteur,* on the basis of a personal engagement that makes him search for what is hidden behind and inside appearances and that is directly evidenced by the way in which the film is constructed.[14] Consequently, the truth of things does not necessarily coincide with their appearance. Instead, it often manages to emerge only if these appearances are pumped up and even allowed to explode.

Yet again following Bazin (according to whom "there is not just one, but many realisms; every epoch looks for its own"), the Nouvelle Vague stubbornly defended a "personal image" of reality. It is true that cinema should respect the intrinsic truth of things; however, it is also true that every director's duty is to seek this truth along a personal path. It is significant, in this sense, that Rohmer compared the director to an architect: both express themselves through their work, no matter how "industrial" this work may be. Both make use of reality, not abstractions, in doing so. Above all, both are a very special kind of creator, for they do not "invent" from scratch, but "rewrite" in a personal way the material at their disposal, which they cannot disregard (see Rohmer 1984). In short, directors are artists who start from a given reality and readjust it according to their vision, harmonizing concrete "facts" with a personal and fictional universe. We are facing the "aesthetic paradox" that Bazin had already attributed to cinema: unifying the realistic and the artistic aspect, giving up the objectivity of matter for the personal imaginary.

The opening of the imaginary was also invoked by the new Latin American cinemas. An example of this is Glauber Rocha's "concrete surrealism," which he theorized about during the second part of his activity as a director. The exasperated use of metaphors and the fantastic delirium not only testify to his interest in both the baroque and the surreal, but are above all justified as an attempt to recover the fantasy (and daydreams) typical of popular culture. Restructuring reality in a new system is a way to talk to the people from their own point of view.

The New American Cinema also often stepped beyond appearances, in the name of a new freedom of vision. By then many, whether in their everyday life or in their artistic activities, used "an eye unruled by man-made laws of perspective, an eye unprejudiced by compositional logic, an eye which does not respond to the name of everything but which must know each object encountered in life through an adventure of perception" (Brakhage 1963 : 120). If up to that point cinema had not managed to achieve this, it was not automatic that the new cinema should do so.

By deliberately spitting on the lens or wrecking its focal intention, one can achieve the early stages of impressionism. One can make this prima donna heavy in performance of image movement by speeding up the motor, or one can break up movement, in a way that approaches a more direct inspiration of contemporary human eye perceptibility of movement, by slowing the motion while recording the image. One may hand hold the camera and inherit worlds of space. One may over- or under-expose the film. One may use the filters of the world, fog, downpours, unbalanced lights, neons with neurotic color temperatures, glass which was never designed for a camera, or even glass which was but which can be used against specifications, or one may photograph an hour after sunrise or an hour before sunset, those marvelous taboo hours when the film labs will guarantee nothing, or one may go into the night with a specified daylight film or vice versa. One may become the supreme trickster, with hatfuls of all the rabbits listed above breeding madly. (123)

The personal image, the imaginative nature of the people, and the imagination of the magician: the movements dominated by the "feeling of the new" also presented these solutions. After all, it was but another way to reinforce their vocation. Along such a path, in fact, the Nouvelle Vague once again reclaimed the author's crucial role; Latin American cinema inaugurated a more powerful and persuasive reading of reality; the New American Cinema explicitly declared its distance from traditional cinema.

5. 6.   Which Language?

The last aspect on which these movements insisted is the linguistic quality of cinema. A film "tells," "expresses," "communicates": it possesses and uses a language of its own.

Astruc's idea of a *caméra-stylo* underscores this very dimension.

Cinema is simply becoming a means of expression, just like all the other arts before it, especially painting and novels. After successively becoming a fair-like attraction, and then an amusement like the boulevard theater, and then a means of preserving the images of an epoch, it slowly becomes a language. In other words, it becomes a form through which artists can express their own thoughts, even if they are abstract, or translate their own obsessions, just as with essays and novels. For this very reason, I call this new age of cinema the age of the caméra-stylo. (Astruc 1948)

For Astruc, thus, the linguistic quality of cinema is connected to the latter's ability to *express* a personal world and to give shape to *thoughts*. And it is the very expressivity and conceptuality of cinema that the theorist-critics close to the Nouvelle Vague would take into account and emphasize.

For Free Cinema, instead, what counted above all was the ability of a film to *communicate* information. Cinema must adhere to reality, showing its true face rather than the comfortable versions that are usually provided. At the same time, it must publicly display this reality, making it known and understood. In this sense, a language is more than a means to manifest personal feelings and thoughts. It is a tool with which to record the states of things, presenting them to people and investigating their life and dynamics. Cinema has social utility and a vocation of service that must be respected. "One of the most powerful ways of helping people to feel this [the English reality] is by making films" (Anderson 1957b:161).

The need to communicate also strongly emerged in many statements about the new Latin American cinema. For instance, Sanjinés (1979) believed that "cinema's goal must be to insist on the possibility of communicating with the people." The people must in fact be led to understand the situation in which they live. "Communication, in revolutionary art, must aim to build the capacity for reflection." On the other hand, the people are not only the recipients, but also the authors of a film, although through the figure of a spokesman-director. From this point of view, it is also necessary to "consider that a new, liberated, and liberating language cannot be achieved without penetrating, investigating, and integrating popular culture, which is alive and dynamic." Thus, it is necessary to communicate both in order to make things understood and through the means elaborated by the people. Along this path, cinema will range from documentary coldness to fablelike creativity.

In the New American Cinema attention to language was central. The radical difference between the filmmakers' works and those of the directors of the industrial system, in fact, emerged here. The two pursue very different paths, ranging from a language that is as realistic as possible to one that is conceptual, abstract. In all cases, however, linguistic choice is synonymous with aesthetic choice, and the search for a certain form is justified by the fact that cinema is an art. Thus, Jonas Mekas can write that the new American filmmakers "seek to free themselves from the overprofessionalism and over-technicality that usually handicap the inspiration and spontaneity of the official cinema, guiding themselves more by intuition and improvisation than by discipline" (1959). This means that cinematic language is not a cage where we are held prisoners, but a continuous exercise in creative freedom. At the same time, this language is not given once and for all, but must be close to the mobility of things. For this reason it has been compared both to artistry and to experimentalism.

Thus, language is an instrument that gives shape to expression and thought. In the last analysis, it is a form of writing, as it appears from the theories allied with the Nouvelle Vague. For the Free Cinema language meant exploration and denunciation and was therefore emphatically communicative. For the Latin American cinema it was a language to be used for communicating with the people through the expressive forms of the people itself. For the New American Cinema it was a language that is "other," claiming the right to art and experimentation. Again, we notice the existence of a common element, which varies in each movement. Like the elements treated above (the need for reality, the opening toward the imaginary), this element brings us back to one of the great points of the theoretical debate of the immediate postwar years.

To conclude, therefore, we can say that the most interesting feature of the studies about and in support of the "new cinemas" is their very ability to reconsider the nuclei of investigation circulating in those years, to project them on the need to break with the past, and to correlate them with the authorial presence. As a result, we have an original theoretical synthesis, open to many variations. In addition, we also observe that a contact is established perhaps for the last time between theory and filming practice. Later the two will become more and more separated.

6 METHODOLOGICAL THEORIES

6.1. 1964: The Metzian "Breach"

In 1964 an essay that would have a very loud echo appeared in the fourth issue of the French journal *Communications:* Christian Metz's "Cinéma: Langue ou langage?" Metz focuses his attention on an idea that was developing in those years, the idea of a general science of signs or semiology (it is not by chance that the same issue includes Roland Barthes' "Eléments de sémiologie," which is almost the "manifesto" of this idea), and wonders what chance cinema may have to become the object of this new science.

Now, this is certainly not the first time that a parallel has been seen between cinema and the universe of signs. As we have already said, the 1950s saw the writing of "grammars of cinema": films were compared to other forms of expression, and the "foundations" of film language were investigated. Metz's gesture, however, is totally new. By asking under which conditions cinema might become the *object* of semiology, he first refers to a research field, then verifies the possibility of placing in that field the phenomenon under investigation. In fact, his position requires, first, that a point of view from which to look at cinema should be defined (in our case, semiology, the science that studies signs); then, that cinema should be approached from that point of view (underscoring only what the latter is interested in— in our case, the dimension of signs). As a consequence, this phenomenon is not investigated in itself, for its intrinsic characteristics. Rather, it is examined from a certain perspective, which brings up certain features, emphasizes certain compatibilities, and sheds light on certain elements rather than on others.

In this sense, Metz stops thinking that cinema, if it is a language, is such on its own. If it is a language, this is only because it can be taken in a certain way. The study of cinema as an intrinsically linguistic reality is thus replaced by the study of the linguistic aspects of cinema or, even better, by a linguistic study of cinema.

Thus, we are dealing with a kind of research that is profoundly different from the research we have studied thus far. Rather than attempting to define the nature of cinema, to focus on the essence, here the inquiry is predisposed to analyze the things that fit into its specific frame of mind and thus to focus on what pertains to the slant of this investigation. Also, a more natural way of looking, directly perceiving what lies before our eyes, is replaced by a more educated way of looking, the product of a specific competence, which depends on the methods of the investigation. Furthermore, the way of looking that attempts to exhaust the global nature of the object in question, to grasp the core from which everything else derives, is replaced by a way of looking that instead focuses on the selection and the systematic quality of the object. Finally, he proposes to replace the way of looking that pursues the truth of things, as revealed in themselves, by a way of looking whose main focus is to assure the correctness of its inquiry.

Of course, this passage is not totally explicit in Metz's essay. There are pages, such as the initial ones, that seem to deal with cinema "as such" (yet his ambiguity is positive, for it refers to measures that are still widely used). Let us look clearly at the dilemma present in the title, however. It does not indicate a will to define cinema (what is cinema in itself: *langue* or *langage?*). Rather, it indicates the essay's enrollment in a field of research (the question has meaning *only within semiology,* for it is within the scope of this science that the "rigid" systems of signs—*langues*—were juxtaposed to "flexible" systems—*langages*—during those years). Thus, the question concerns more the *discipline* we start from than the phenomenon we are dealing with.

Let us add that the success and relevance of the essay depend not only on the dawning of a new way to conceive theory, based on a pertinent, systematic, solid analysis. With Metz there also emerges a new kind of scholar, whose formation is more scientific than cinematic, who works for research laboratories or in academia, more than as a critic; who publishes in journals that specialize in some discipline, more than in journals dealing generically with the "seventh art." Above all, such a scholar is connected with specific disciplines from which he borrows the tools for his investigations. Thus, this scholar also prefers to have other objects of study (literature, television, etc.), rather than to deal merely with cinema, and to study them using the same methods, instead of continuing to occupy himself with cinema from new perspectives.

In other words, "Cinéma: Langue ou langage?" introduces a shift in the approach to the filmic phenomenon and in the kind of topics leading to this approach. A new research *paradigm* is born, as well as a new *generation* of scholars. The *ontological theories* are followed by the *methodological theories:* besides semiology (or semiotics, as it is more currently called), psychology, sociology, and in many ways also psychoanalysis. We will approach these fields one by one. Also, we will return to Metz's essay to examine its content. Before doing so, however, it is necessary to clarify a point. Is "Cinéma: Langue ou langage?" totally new? Are there no antecedents to it? Indeed, if Metz's essay is to be identified with the birth of a new paradigm, it should be noted that another research experience, somewhat isolated compared to the main currents of the debate, had already brought up these same problems.

6.2. 1946: Filmology, a Foreshadowing

In the immediate postwar years a French scholar, Gilbert Cohen-Séat, observed that it is impossible to find a common denominator for the very different factors that cinema involves. Therefore, it is advisable to make a few distinctions, first of all between *filmic facts* and *cinematic facts.* "The filmic fact consists of the expression of life (the life of the world, the spirit, the imagination, of beings and things), through a system of combined images (visual—natural or conventional—and auditory—sounds and words). The cinematic fact, instead, consists of social circulation of sensations, ideas, feelings, and materials that come from life itself and that cinema shapes according to its desires" (1946:57). These two orders of facts work in close connection. Cinema represents universes and at the same time connects them to social life. Inasmuch as it is a specific *institution,* it functions through the very complementarity of the two dimensions. Therefore, it is necessary to conceive an approach that preserves in the background a feeling of the unity of this phenomenon, while it uses the appropriate tools to approach all the elements at play. In short, it is necessary to prepare an investigation that both pursues a "totalization of experience" and relies on an "ordered vision" (60).

Cohen-Séat calls this area of research *filmology.* He views it as teamwork with multiple points of view, where all the disciplines play a role, from sociology to aesthetics, from psychology to linguistics, from psychophysiology to psychoanalysis, each ready to confront the aspects pertaining to its field of competence. Similarly, he views it as an attempt that, on the basis of these same disciplines, should be "deeply unbiased and scientifically objective, and, difficult as it may be, totally disinterested" (64). Tendentiousness, the lack of factual data, and recurrent prescriptiveness should not be considered virtues. Thus, we are far from the generic and generalistic approaches typical of "ontological" theories. Instead, we find a different spirit, which valorizes pertinence, systematicity, rigorous control of observations, and the possibility of interconnecting them. In short, as Cohen-Séat suggests, we find ourselves in the field of a "methodical enterprise" (63). And even if many of his pages may puzzle us in that they tend more toward the imaginative rather than toward the methodical, what is really important is the appearance of a precise requirement.

Cohen-Séat's suggestion was immediately well received. The year after his book was published the *Revue Internationale de Filmologie* was founded, and it hosted contributions on cinema from scholars belonging to different disciplines. In 1947, in September, the first International Convention of Filmology was held in Paris, with many participants. Various organizations were founded, such as the Institut de Filmologie de l'Université de Paris and the Bureau International de Filmologie. The second International Convention of Filmology was held in Paris in February 1955. Finally, at the beginning of the 1960s, during an international conference on the modalities of visual information, the *Revue* moved on to Italy, where it continued to be published with the new title *Ikon*. Over two decades many extremely enlightening essays were published both in *Revue* and in *Ikon*. Besides those published in this journal, to which we will refer in the following chapters, it is enough to mention the beautiful collection of essays edited by Etienne Souriau, representing the work of the Parisian Institut (Souriau 1953). These essays treat all aspects of cinema, ranging from the impression of reality afforded by the images on the screen to the spectator's attitudes, which oscillate between activity and passivity; from such structures as filmic time and space to the function of elements like scenography and music; from film's problems with art to the role of the fantastic dimension in films. Let us add that this collection (in which Souriau himself tries to delineate in an extremely modern way the main features of the filmic universe, as opposed to those of the real world) opens with an attempt to create an adequate "vocabulary" for filmology. Here we find terms that will later enter our current lexicon, such as "diegetic" and "profilmic." Above all, however, we observe the will, on the one hand, to avoid the imprecision and terminological casualness of the "ontological" approaches; on the other hand, to draw a systematic map of the key concepts so that, while each of them explores a specific area, all of them work as common background to the research.

After all, this wish to turn over a new leaf, to start over, is one of the most remarkable features of filmology. It is true that it is not the first time that cinema has been approached with a scientific spirit. But here a comprehensive project is taking shape. It is also true that for each discipline cinema is more a way to broaden its horizon than a really different object of study. Still, their seriousness in dealing with it is the same. In short, with all its limits, filmology constitutes an essential experience. The demand for a method, which semiotics brings back to the foreground and manages to turn into a deeply shared need, finds full expression in filmology. In the 1950s this experience remained comparatively isolated with respect to the rest of the debate, and it was lost during the 1960s (because some of its promises were not kept, such as the integration of the disciplines, which would remain a dream). Its presence was important, however, for a whole line of research, which it directed and motivated.[1]

7 PSYCHOLOGY OF CINEMA

7.1. The Cinematic Situation

Among the disciplines called upon by filmology, psychology was the fastest to answer the call. This is partly because it was already used to studying cinema. Besides Münsterberg's extraordinary *Photoplay,* which dates back to the 1910s, it is worth mentioning the many contributions of the 1930s, which sought to emphasize the effects of images and used film as a testing ground.[1] However, it is also partly because psychology is especially interested in the first great concept elaborated by filmology, that of *cinematic situation.* This term refers to the cluster formed by screen, cinema, and spectator, where processes such as recognizing and deciphering what is shown, giving in to the pleasure of the stories, identifying with the characters, and fantasizing and personal reelaboration take place.

It should be clear that the *cinematic situation* is interesting not only for psychologists. On the contrary, one of the most original contributions made by filmology suggests developing an integrated study of this reality, so as to grasp all its aspects, from our attitudes before entering a cinema to behaviors during the projection, from the rituals preceding the show to the effects of personal tastes. The result would be a "phenomenology of film," which would account for our actual way of being spectators (Feldmann 1956). Yet this same contribution is aware of the centrality of psychological studies; and psychology views the *cinematic situation* as a unique object. Thus, here we will offer an overview of the contribution of this discipline. We will follow the ideal order of the psychological dynamics that develop in the *cinematic situation* and will discuss studies of perception, comprehension, memorization, and participation.[2] After analyzing the research connected with filmology, we will complete the picture with some more recent investigations, inspired by the "ecological" and above all the cognitive approaches. In fact, if it is true that the "circle" promoted by Cohen-Séat reinforces to the highest degree the relationship between psychology and cinema, it is also true that the former continued to be interested in the latter even after the end of the experience of filmology, toward the mid-1970s.

7.2. Perception

The *Revue Internationale de Filmologie* has published many essays on how a film is perceived when it is projected on the screen. Some scholars, like Wallon (1953), emphasize the elements of the perceptive acts; others, like Rey (1954), analyze the perception of movement. Still others, like Michotte (1948 and 1961), explore the quality of "reality" we assign to the objects on the screen. In a volume on the "cinematic experience," Dario Romano (1965) summarizes and consolidates these studies. First, he examines the luminous stimulus coming from the screen. It is well known that the succession and alternation of frames and instants of darkness make the illumination of the screen discontinuous. The spectator does not record the "gaps," but instead perceives a continuous illumination. This can be explained thanks to the "critical frequency of fusion" or the "frequency of the stimulus, where the physical intermittence is no longer phenomenally present, even as the variation of the intensity of the source of light" (Romano 1965:10). The cadence of twenty-four frames per second guarantees the end of the "flickering" (still present with the first projectors, with only eighteen frames per second) and completely eliminates the gap between light and darkness.

Later, Romano approaches the problem of movement. The spectator deals with two different orders of phenomena: "a rather extreme range of movements, relatively slow, in which the conditions of the psychological stimulus correspond to those of real movement" and "a wider range, where the stimulus-conditions are those of the stroboscopic movement" (35). In this second case the impression of movement derives from the pairing of two still images, separated by a small temporal interval. A film exploits this possibility and relies on the close succession of the otherwise still photographs to render the sequence of the action.

In addition to these two orders of phenomena (the former, we repeat, is rarer and based on a "real" stimulus; the latter, common to all cinema, is based on an illusory effect), we also have the so-called induced movement, according to which "an object is experienced as moving when its spatial relationships vary with respect to other objects in the field of vision that serve as a frame of reference" (38). The simplest example is that of a car at the center of the screen, with the landscape around it moving sideways. We assume that it is the car and not the landscape that is moving, because the latter is our frame of reference and the former is our variable. At the cinema, however, the audience also has another possibility, that is, to use its own position within the cinema—rather than an element of the represented world, such as the above-mentioned landscape—as an anchor point. In this case the frame of reference is represented by the environment where the projection takes place, and the things moving on the screen become the variables. It should be added that these two systems are both parallel and alternative, which explains why at times we perceive something that is still on the screen as moving (and we move with it), while at times we perceive the movement of what is actually moving (and we remain still).

After the question of movement, Romano examines that of space. It is currently believed that one of cinema's great limits is its inability to reproduce the three-dimensional nature of real environments. The flatness of the screen and the camera's monocular lens (the depth of an image is perceived thanks to "retinal disparity," the difference in the image as perceived by each eye) hamper the rendering of the third dimension in a film. Some stylistic efforts (such as placing people or objects on different planes) or some technological attempts (such as 3-D cinema) only make this inability more evident. Romano starts by dividing the problem in two. "On the one hand, we need to consider how the perception of the distance separating a given object from the observer takes place (the impression of something being close and far); on the other hand, we need to examine the mechanisms that mediate the impression of an object's corporality and plasticity" (53). It will then be possible to realize that all the clues to three-dimensionality are present in cinema. Among the factors contributing to the perception of the depth of an environment, we have the gradient of depth (the farthest things appear placed on the surface in a more regular fashion), the longitudinal movement (the dimension of an object varies, the closer or farther away it is), the parallax of movement (an object acquires a different angular speed, according to the observer's distance and its own and the observer's movement), the aerial perspective (distance diminishes clarity, and the farthest part acquires a purple nuance). Among the elements contributing to the perception of plasticity and corporality of an object, instead, we find chiaroscuro and stereokinesis (the impression of depth deriving from the movement of a figure on a plane).

After the problems connected with the perception of space, Romano moves on to examine how the audience reacts (or fails to react) to the images, taken as a whole. He analyzes such phenomena as the constancy of an object's dimension. (We do not perceive people as giants if they are in the foreground or as dwarfs if they are in the background, but we assign them a specific dimension, which remains stable through time. We may, however, perceive that they change location.) He investigates the perceptive mechanisms that allow us to experience an image in perspective (where it is important to notice that "experiencing a photographic representation in perspective means above all interpreting specific two-dimensional configurations according to three-dimensional schemes and structures, which only partially derive from the stimulus itself and are mostly postulates, perceived as such by the subject" [110]).

Finally, in the last part of the volume, Romano approaches the problem of the "impression of reality" of cinematic images. They are faithful copies of the world, of which they seem to present many aspects. Apropos this point, however, it is necessary to make a distinction. First, if it is true that the objects appearing on screen, having a volume and being able to move, have an intuitive quality of reality, it is also true that the audience is aware of their illusory nature. Thus, it observes this world as if it were real, but knows that it should not believe in it completely. Second, if it is true that at the level of perception an image possesses many of the phenomenal characteristics of the real world, it is also true that they involve artificial, fictional features. Thus, while watching a movie we see a blend of stimuli that are like those offered by reality and others that belong only to the filmic universe. Hence, "there is not only a contradiction between what we *perceive as reality* and what we *know is reality,* but also between the perceptive data themselves" (163). As a result, we have the impression of experiencing some real events, but we realize that this reality does not completely belong to our world. We should add that the evocation of the actual world has a great structuring power for film (being a copy helps it to acquire its meaning) and helps us to assume various degrees of "psychological distance" from what we see, so that we can enter or exit the universe presented by the film.

We have given a very brief overview of Romano's book, without mentioning the studies that form its background and that it continues. Because it characterizes very well the "state of the art," however, we can form a fairly clear idea of the interest in cinema shown by psychology of perception, and particularly by the branch that is most involved in the project of filmology. We should also note that the research continues outside this project. An example of this comes from J. J. Gibson's studies, based on an "ecological" model, or from Hochberg and Brooks', based on cognitive psychology (a branch of great interest among cinema scholars—especially American—in the 1980s). Or, moving further away from the initial project, we also find the resurgence of the theme of the "impression of reality," used by semiology and psychoanalysis. We will mention all of this later in this book.

7.3.   Comprehension and Memorization

We will now move on to another series of questions, related to the audience-film relationship at the level of the *comprehension* and *memorization* of what appears on the screen. We will begin with two quick observations. First, the frame of reference becomes less static, for there are different interests at stake, such as those of the cognitive models and those of the progressive age. Second, cinema loses its specificity: films are used as one test of comprehension and memorization among many others, without too much consideration of their own peculiarities. But let us closely examine some of the studies published in the *Revue Internationale de Filmologie*.

Among the contributions worth mentioning are those by René and Bianka Zazzo. Their goal is to find a correlation among the various degrees of mental development and the various difficulties of cinematic language, "in order to find out which needs films must respond to and to what extent they actually do so" (Zazzo and Zazzo 1949: 30). In order to achieve this goal, first a scale of mental values is developed, organized around factors such as relational thought (the ability to unify dispersed data), decentralization (the ability to assume alternate points of view), and mobility (the ability to invert past and future, virtual and actual, etc.). Then the various difficulties of the filmic discourse are placed along a scale, in order to understand at which mental age and to what extent procedures such as the shot/reaction shot and the fadeout are grasped or more generally the spatiotemporal structure of a movie, the role of the various characters, etc. In their first experiments, the Zazzos obtained results that confirm that "the significance of a relatively long sequence (5 minutes) is perceived globally much earlier than imagined. A film's dynamism induces the dynamism of narrative at the age in which a child is still at the stage of enumeration or of static description," while "the comprehension of the temporal ellipsis is probably much later" (Zazzo and Zazzo 1949:130).

An interesting experiment conducted by Mialaret and Méliès can be connected to the Zazzos' research. Their investigation is organized as follows. First, three short films are prepared, equivalent in terms of content but very different in terms of style and language. The first is constructed only on the basis of full views. The second alternates full views, close-ups, and extreme close-ups, uses parallel editing, and has a faster rhythm. The third also uses the subjective shot and the fadeout. Second, the three films are shown to a sample of four-year-olds, eight-year-olds, and twelve-year-olds in order to cover the main stages of child development. Finally, the children are asked to repeat what they have seen or to identify the images of a film from a pile of pictures. The results of this experiment can be summarized as follows. First, language difficulties do not seem to be a discriminating factor in and of themselves (on the contrary, "a very articulate film, with many different levels, is more accessible for a young spectator's mind" [Mialaret and Méliès 1954: 227]). Second, if anything it is the reconstruction of the action recounted by the film that presents a problem (the younger children do not always retroactively connect one plane to the others, while the older ones do it automatically). Finally, the greatest difficulty seems to be connected to the reconstruction of the environment.

Obviously, the studies conducted by the Zazzos and Mialaret-Méliès are not the only ones on audience comprehension. On the contrary, this is a field rich in contributions. These two cases exemplify both the techniques and the goals of the research, however. In practice, it all boils down to grasping the relationship between the film's linguistic "mechanism" and the spectator's cognitive "mechanism," in order to see to what extent they trigger each other and where, on the contrary, they may act independently. A consequence of this (and this is the most relevant theoretical implication) is that cinema does not operate just on the basis of naturalness and spontaneity. On the contrary, it requires both automatic processes of recognition of reality and symbolic and discursive conventions, both the immediacy of what is represented and the specificity of the representation. In short, if, as is often said, cinema is some sort of "universal language," interpreting its signs is not something to be dismissed lightly.

Such a dialectic is confirmed at another level of the film-audience relationship, that of *memorization*. This is another theme dear to filmology, and to illustrate this we will refer to two experiments coming from this very discipline. The first one, conducted by Fraisse and De Montmollin, analyzes both what remains at the end of the projection ("immediate memory") and what remains after a longer time ("deferred memory"). In the first case, "what remains is a function of the relationship between the images and the story told; a logical or affective restructuring takes place in overall impression" (Fraisse and De Montmollin 1952:55). We therefore remember those details that represent the climaxes of the action, and we impose an order on them that may be subjective. Moreover, we need to keep in mind the enormous condensation of the perceived data, which concerns the reconstruction of space, the recomposition of time, and the distribution of the various points of view that take place. In the second case we have, instead, a large amount of data loss and a readjustment of the global picture. With the passing of time "forgetfulness flattens the acoustic and visual images; it totally eliminates both their accessory and characteristic details, or those defining the meaning, the originality, and the coordinates of the story told by the film. The memory we retain of the action is in the last analysis a passe-partout, a stereotyped tale" (68).

Much of this information was detailed in experimental research conducted by D. J. Bruce. Two different preoccupations lie behind it: reconstructing "the general form that memory takes" and understanding "the influence on memory of a break deliberately introduced in the continuity of the perceived action" (Bruce 1953:21). In order to achieve these goals, three variations of a short movie are prepared: the first is totally coherent, the second contains a congruent interpolation in the story that is told, and the last inserts an incongruent interpolation. Bruce observes, for instance, that in all three cases we remember those details about the action and the progression of the story that enable us to construct a comprehensive picture of it; that the interpolation may be totally forgotten, or perceived as an independent element, or more often integrated in the content of the film; that the process of restructuring the various perceived fragments requires the presence of many subjective elements; finally, that what a film implies but does not show is generally remembered as something that has really been seen. "The result is the shaping of a partially autonomous structure, which defines the way in which the other perceptive elements will be recovered, and which implies a smaller or bigger shift from the literal interpretation. This process must be understood as characteristic of memory" (37).

The two contributions we have mentioned briefly give a good impression of the research on this theme. The problem is studying how the audience, reconstructing a film after a longer or shorter time, restructures the various data and creates something that may be independent of what it has really seen, but that helps in filing the experience. Thus, we are dealing with an increasingly ambivalent process. If perceiving a film means balancing real and artificial characteristics, and understanding it means allowing a greater intervention of the mediations of language, remembering it means making a powerful reelaboration of what we have acquired. Even better, it means allowing the intervention of a mental *rewriting,* which seizes the initial elements and appropriates them.

7.4.   Participation

The last of the psychological dimensions emerging in the *cinematic situation* is that of participation. What is at stake here is the special "empathetic" relationship connecting the audience seated in the cinema and what passes on the screen, the "involvement" in the spectacle that leads to the point of "experiencing" it directly. Within the field of filmology, this theme is approached by Michotte (1953) in an essay that is in some ways ground-breaking. First, it should be noted that participation manifests itself in various degrees: vis-à-vis a spectacle, the audience may remain indifferent, but it may also synchronize its own movements with the actors' or mimic them or even fully identify with them. In this last case we pass from mere "motor reactions" to real "empathetic relationships." Thus, participation is the most interesting, but also the most problematic topic. In fact, how can the spectator literally forget himself to identify with someone else? A first suggestion comes from the analysis of our perceptive mechanisms. On the screen we see the movements of various objects and people "fuse" into a whole, and in some ways we "fuse" with them too. A second suggestion comes from the kind of people we identify with. They are usually the hero or the heroine of the story, with whom it is somewhat common to establish a close bond. The third suggestion comes from the analysis of our general conditions when we watch a movie. Our relative immobility and relaxation in the seat help us lose contact with our body; darkness and isolation make us forget we are in a theater; the intensity of the visual stimulus increases our attention to what happens onscreen; etc. The effect is that the spectator suspends the recognition of himself to identify with someone else.

This is the general picture delineated by Michotte. Many others have worked on this theme, however. Still within the field of filmology, it is worth mentioning Ancona's works, which investigate the correlation between participation and aggressivity. Ancona observes that the former deeply influences the latter, but also that films, by making participation easier, may "regulate" aggressivity, to the point where they have a real "cathartic effect" (Ancona 1963). Also, we should mention the works on participation with respect to different film genres. Here we find another contribution by Ancona (1967), who analyzes the interplay of involvement and detachment taking place with comic films. Finally, still remaining in the field of filmology, we find works that investigate the relationship between participation and understanding, such as Lucia Lumbelli's interesting contribution, on which it is necessary to say a few words. She explores the *passivity* induced in the cinematic audience. She wonders if it is true that the audience tends "to accept all that is presented on the screen, to question it less than would happen in other situations" (1974:53). The answer comes from a series of experiments. In a short fragment of a film, an incongruity is introduced to see to what extent the audience realizes its presence. The same incongruity is introduced in a passage from a book, to see if the reader is more or less aware of it. The same phenomenon is verified with a passage taken from a documentary film. The three kinds of incongruity are then compared: logico-verbal (at the acoustic level), iconic (at the visual level), and tonal (at the level of the tone of voice). Finally, the perception of a live situation is compared to that of a filmed situation. In this way, Lumbelli anchors the audience's passivity to observable indicators, in order to check their impact empirically. Her conclusion is that "filmic communication seems to stimulate less of a critical attitude than a verbal one, both when the content of a movie is dramatic and narrative and in the case of merely informative and documentary films" (178). Furthermore, "the direct observation of an event seems to help the audience's perception to focus more easily than does audiovisual reproduction" (178). Finally, the influence of a logical incongruity is less strong than that of certain perceptive impressions, such as a change of tone. At the same time, however, it is necessary to drop certain frequent schemata and certain divisions that have no foundation. "It now seems more reasonable to say that both words and images can be used in a rational or an irrational way. What counts is a deep knowledge of the tendencies and possibilities of the medium, so as to utilize it in the way that is most suited to reaching specific ideological and educational goals" (185).

7.5.   Beyond Filmology: The Ecological Approach and Cognitive Psychology

The panorama of filmology consists of many more studies than those analyzed in this book (which were chosen because they are both exemplary and intrinsically interesting). A look at the issues of *Revue Internationale de Filmologie* and then *Ikon* will convince us of this. It should be noted that filmology is not the only branch of the ongoing research, however; but we have had strong reasons for privileging it so far. It cannot be said too often that filmology introduced a scientific approach to cinema for the first time and that, during the 1950s and 1960s, it hosted the most important psychological contributions on the topic. But when the references to this experience started disappearing, especially in the second half of the 1970s, other lines of enquiry emerged, close to filmology in spirit. We should mention the many works of Baroni, Cornoldi, and others on how a film is experienced and remembered. They connect memory with emotional processes, which are analyzed on the basis of the physiological modifications taking place inside the spectator (Baroni 1989). Thanks to a series of experiments conducted with the help of some sequences from *Eye of the Needle,* their work familiarizes us with the cognitive processes, pulse rates, rate of breathing, muscular tension, etc., that accompany our experience as spectators. Thus, we discover that scary scenes raise our "emotional temperature" and stimulate memory, while sad scenes lower the "temperature" and can be forgotten more easily.[3]

The postfilmology age, however, is also—and above all—characterized by a change of framework in the study of cinema. The research of filmology, especially on perception, was for the most part inspired by the Gestalt school,[4] and when the 1970s witnessed an increasing interest in the field, other frameworks became the source of inspiration. We should mention J. J. Gibson's contribution, which is based on his "ecological" approach (Gibson 1979, 1986). This approach relies on specific ideas. First, perception means retrieving some invariable structures that are present in the constant flux of shifting stimulations called reality. Second, the information necessary for a correct perception is present in the world and only needs to be "collected" by each individual through the senses, without relying on previous knowledge, mental models, or interpretive schemes. Third, the analysis of how a person moves through the world is crucial to this "collection." Perception relies on individuals' ability to connect the movements perceived by their eyes and the voluntary movements of their body.

Starting from these principles, Gibson confronts cinematic vision. His idea is that the camera, projector, film, and screen form a device capable of generating the same perceptive situation as the audience would experience if faced with real events. In fact, the scene of the screen, limited by a frame and viewed by a spectator placed in the middle of the theater, corresponds to the temporary optic field of a human observer placed in a natural environment, perhaps behind a moving window. Furthermore, the richness and continuity of the events staged on the screen generate a flux of stimulations equivalent to the mutable one that reality affords us. Above all, the camera's ability to shift the angle of vision stimulates the change of position the observer in question would make within that environment. The spectator, even if confined to his seat, has some optical indications that generate kinesthetic effects, together with impressions of moving through the represented scene. Finally, we should add that the image's two-dimensionality creates no problems whatsoever. The information relative to the three-dimensional structure essentially emerges through the changes of light perceived by the human eye, regardless of the fact that such light may be natural or coming from a screen offering merely its representation. The conclusion is that cinema allows the audience to experience a totally real situation at the level of perception.

Among the various factors at play, Gibson insists above all on the camera and its movements, for they allow us to orient ourselves within the world appearing on the screen. "The modes of camera movement that are analogous to the natural movements of the head-body system are, in this theory, a first-order guide to the composing of a film" (1986:298). In short, we can assure a film's perfect intelligibility only if we conceive a spectator who is identical with a "natural" observer and if we take into consideration the latter's way of perceiving "naturally."

This is the core of Gibson's work. But a more sensitive reprise of the research took place toward the end of the 1970s, thanks to the school of cognitive psychology. In particular, we are referring to the work of Hochberg and Brooks. In the following decade they would influence a wide number of film theorists. Unlike Gibson, their basic idea is that perception is an activity based on reconstruction and hypothesis. Observers do not simply record information present in the flux of reality, isolating some invariables and exploiting their own movement. Instead, they "process" the data, thanks to some mental framework that allows them to interpret what lies before them and to develop expectations as to what will happen.

Hochberg and Brooks approach cinematic perception on these premises.

First, the two scholars agree that films tend to appear as faithful *surrogates* of reality. On the screen we have "an optic array, a field of patterned light, that is in its essential features similar to that produced by the scene or event itself" (Hochberg and Brooks 1978:261). The reproduction of movement in its various forms (stroboscopic movement, induced movement) seems to confirm this. But when we move from the dimension of movement to the spatiotemporal dimension, we realize that films are something other than surrogates. Films are a real *construction*. Let us now think of how a camera selects fragments of reality and rearranges them in a new universe, different from the original one. Here we are no longer dealing with a "facsimile" of reality, but with something "existing only in [the director's] imagination and in the perceptions of his audience" (272). Hence, there are two specific points of interest: the camera's "work" in representing onscreen reality; and the spectators' mental activity of "reconstruction" of what lies before their eyes.

The camera works at various levels. The creation of depth of field is of special interest. The image on the screen is of course two-dimensional. Yet it is enough that the camera moves through the scenic space for the various elements to be placed into perspective. Hochberg and Brooks examine the four basic camera movements: boom shots, dollying, panoramic shots, and zooming. They argue that only the first two provide all the information allowing the spectator to correctly perceive spatial tridimensionality. In any case this impression of depth does not come "naturally" from the image (as Gibson thought), but is "inferred" by the spectator starting from the information at his disposal. Thus, boom and dolly shots are more effective than zooming and panoramic shots, because the observer's cognitive activity finds in them a better point of engagement.

But how does the spectator operate? How does he "process" the information at his disposal? How does he perceive as three-dimensional a two-dimensional scene? How does he manage to see, or to construct "a mind's-eye space that is many times bigger than the screen on which the momentary image is projected" (273)? The crucial element is the presence of a series of "cognitive maps." The spectator has certain "mental schemes" that allow him to invest actions, figures, and canonical events with meaning, that allow him to make hypotheses and to verify what he is seeing. The stimuli coming from the screen are interpreted according to a certain hypothesis, which will or will not be confirmed by the rest of the film, viewed through a well-structured process of adjustment and comparison of the elements at play.

Thus, it is thanks to these "mental schemes" that the spectator decodes the situation before him, expectations, etc. Also, thanks to these schemes, he "reconstructs" in his own mind what the film tells him, albeit little by little or only in part.

Of course, all this implies that the director should provide information so as to allow the spectator to make adequate inferences. Hochberg and Brooks analyze, for instance, the editing separations where each frame recaps and enlarges on the previous one, or the "establishing" and "reestablishing shots," which offer a general view before the details show specific aspects or portions of it. Similarly, they try to draw a diagram of the optimal rhythm a story may have.

Their study of cinema was continued in later works, which were devoted to more specific problems, such as filmed dance (Brooks 1989; also Brooks 1985 and Hochberg 1989). But what we should like to emphasize here is the reason behind the interest shown by film theorists in the 1980s in cognitive psychology. Cognitive psychology is able both to uncover the mechanisms of recognition and reelaboration of images and sounds and to provide a foundation for the spectator's "linguistic" action. Let us think in particular of an author like Bordwell and of his book on narration (Bordwell 1985). He relies on the results of cognitive psychology to explain how images and sounds literally make "meaning" without the intervention of semiotics (on the contrary, they emerge as an alternative to the explanations offered by this discipline).

Conversely, in the 1980s there was also a resurgence of psychological studies, including the Gestalt school, which looked for a somewhat "global" theory of representation. The theory plays with a plurality of approaches rather than adopting a single point of view. Jacques Aumont comes to mind, with his book devoted to the image (Aumont 1990). He carefully and competently reviews the results obtained by psychology. He emphasizes the connections—rather than the conflicts—between them and other results. His final goal is to examine all the levels at which visual representation works.

In both cases, however, we are far from a rigidly disciplinary interest, from its limits and specific objectives. Instead, we are in a different area, which could well be called post- or interdisciplinary,[5] and which we will explore later. In so doing, we will identify some references to the field of study we have just analyzed.

8   SOCIOLOGY OF CINEMA

8.1.   Meetings

The meeting between cinema and sociology, behind its apparent inevitability, hides a dark side. Cinema has long risked becoming just another object of research for sociologists, a phenomenon to be added to others already under examination, and merely a means to emphasize the common nature of social reality rather than its peculiarities. Viewed in this way, cinema belongs to a wider panorama, where, however, it is inevitably lost. Cinema becomes one of the many mass media, one of the many industrial organizations, one of the many places where culture reveals itself. For film scholars, in contrast, sociology has long risked becoming a useful but truncated tool for their investigations. It is true that it is important to understand how film affects certain social trends and behaviors, or to what extent it reflects the aspirations and fears of a community, or to which productive structures it refers. It is also true, however, that it is not possible to avoid wondering what makes a film a presence that is often more meaningful than others, where its depth comes from, in which direction it is going, what ensures its identity.

Let us say at once that this double sense of uneasiness clearly expresses the difficulties that underlie all disciplinary approaches. On the one hand, we have a method (in this case, sociology, but also psychology and semiotics), which has been developed in fields often far from that of films and which finds a new application only by analogy with previous experiences. On the other hand, we have a field of study (cinema) that already has its own tradition of studies and that tends to insist on certain research topics and points for reflection. Nothing prevents the meeting of these two sides, but it is evident that mutual dissatisfaction may arise, especially at the beginning.

In our case some basic misunderstandings—inherited from the previous debate, but still active in the immediate postwar years—play a role. Let us consider film scholars' habit of working on specific and symptomatic cases. Conversely, sociologists work with statistical relevance and vast amounts of data. It is indeed very difficult to combine qualitative and quantitative approaches. Let us also think of film scholars' profound attention to works and authors and the sociologists' interest in collective phenomena and the industrial machine. These approaches evoke two different dimensions that do not seem compatible: art and social processes or the world of commodities.[1]

After the end of World War II, sociology of the cinema made an attempt to overcome divisions and separations, in the name of a view that is both more precise and more accurate. In the 1950s psychology preferred to take more secondary roads (the new approach, while developing, did not seek to interfere directly with the "main body" of film research, which still had the flavor of essentialism). Similarly, semiotics managed to break off from the extant formations and redefine the situation of the debate (but this happened in the 1970s, when the time had come for a change); sociology, instead, chose to act from the inside. It slowly annulled the oppositions among different fields; it introduced broader concepts; it widened the field of the phenomena that need to be investigated and prepared the way for the various fields to converge. As a result, it affirmed the validity of a methodological approach, which it tried at the same time to broaden as much as possible.

It should be noted that filmology once again became from the very beginning the perfect interpreter of such an exigency. We refer to two works by G. Friedmann and E. Morin, published in the *Revue Internationale de Filmologie*. In the first (Friedmann and Morin 1952) the two scholars defend the centrality of sociology. Cinema is "a human fact, the unity and deep reality of which cannot be understood and explained without the converging attention of all the disciplines that study man." In the second essay (Friedmann and Morin 1955) the contents and methods of the sociological approach are delineated. The idea is that "every film, whether an art film or an escapist one, whether it deals with dreams or magic, should be examined as an entity." The subjectivity it is charged with can and must be studied objectively. Consequently its features, being empirically controllable, "can enlighten us about the dark areas of our societies, those very areas that correspond to what, in other words, we call collective representations, the collective imaginary, collective oneiricism, or collective affectivity." Friedmann and Morin's ideas have no major resonance, but the type and the tone of the discourse are very indicative of the lines along which the discipline moves.

If we take the whole area studied by sociology, we realize that it can be divided into four parts.

The first includes the contributions that confront the *socioeconomic aspects* of cinema. They are among the first to examine—without inferiority complexes and with an explicit disciplinary slant—a reality that risked remaining in the background, secondary to the film's artistic dimension. Such studies, which at first were viewed as "parallel" to the aesthetic approach, uncover a truly common basis for both the socioeconomic and the aesthetic aspects.

The second area is dominated by the interest in the cinematic *institution*. It focuses on elements such as professional profiles and production routines, the mechanisms of taste and evaluation criteria, the kinds of offerings and the consumption processes, etc. Furthermore, cinema's structures are compared to those of other social organizations. The idea is to uncover a real system, capable of integrating different aspects, dictating behavioral rules, and providing precise statutes for its components.

The third area is characterized by the desire to bring cinema back to the broader picture of the *culture industry*. Scholars' attitudes may differ (from the apocalyptic to the integrated, to use a famous formula); but they all share the idea that the game should be played on a comprehensive terrain, and with rules different from those of the past.

The fourth area includes those contributions that explore the *representations of the social* used by the cinema. The idea is that every film, even those telling the most improbable stories, somehow reenacts the society around it. Using this portrayal as a starting point, some scholars reconstruct the spirit of an age. Others try to understand what a culture keeps visible and what, instead, it prefers to hide. In any case, what is investigated is the film's ability to be a "sign" (which should be questioned as such) of the reality where it develops.

We will now focus on each of these four areas of research.

8.2 Cinema as Industry

Peter Bächlin's work *Der Film als Ware* testifies to the interest shown in the immediate postwar years in the socioeconomic aspects of cinema. Its opening is significant. "In a capitalist economy a film, as an intellectual production, has all the prerequisites to be a *work of art,* but it is also, of necessity, a commodity, because of the various industrial and commercial operations required by its production and consumption" (Bächlin 1945). Thus, as in the best tradition, we have art versus the commodity. The latter component cannot be underestimated without damage, however: it coexists with the former and often even dominates it. This depends on the fact that economic factors are especially linked in the field of cinema. "In our age there are some products of the intellect (literary works, paintings, musical compositions) whose commercialization emerges only from their dissemination; with cinema every creative work is commercialized, from the screenplay to the distribution of the film to the theaters." But this also depends on evolution of the medium. "While technical progress has been continuous, the artistic and intellectual problems presented by the production of a film have become more and more secondary under the pressure of commercial considerations." Thus, from both a structural and a historical point of view, it is clear that in our case the merchandising dimension coexists with the artistic one, and even overrides it. Thus, we have the need to study thoroughly and specifically the economic-industrial components of cinema.

In order to obey this imperative, Bächlin studies some of the crucial stages of cinematic history. He examines the period of its origins and the advent of sound, the preeminence of the Hollywood model and the attempts to create national cinemas, the emergence of monopolies and the periodic crises that characterize the field. This analysis is followed by some theoretical reflections, which require attention.

First, Bächlin addresses the most prominent characteristic of films, the fact that they are a mass product. This is a direct consequence of cinema's industrial organization, of its distribution and consumption on a large scale. This very mass dimension is what unifies the various parts of the cinematic "machine": the number of films is a function of the number of spectators, and vice versa, distribution being the mediating factor between these two poles.

Second, Bächlin examines the organization of the cinematic enterprise. He focuses on the various phases of the industrial process, the tasks involved, the corresponding financial assets. These themes are paralleled by a broad analysis of the "risks" run by cinema: production risks (the possibility of interrupting work on a film, the difficulty of changing the final result, the irregular output of the artistic and technical collaborators, etc.) and consumption risks (related to the market). The presence of such risks, Bächlin says, turns the cinematic product into a commodity. The more necessary it is to be careful, because of the amount of money invested in a movie, the more the intellectual and aesthetic needs "give in to financial considerations." In short, risks are the main enemies of art.

Third, Bächlin analyses the relationships among production, distribution, and consumption. One of the elements holding together the various moments of the life of a film (its opening, distribution to the various theaters, and screening by the audience) is, as we have said, a function of film's being a mass product. Many elements reinforce this mass dimension of cinema: when we pay for a film, we pay for a commodity that we do not possess, but only enjoy (Bächlin was writing when videotapes did not yet exist); there are different kinds of theaters (first-, second-, third-run and rerun houses); the ticket is fairly cheap (cinemas cost less than theaters). A second element common to production, distribution, and consumption is standardization. Its application implies both the use of the "most rational form of labor" and the search for the "highest use value." Hence, on the side of production we observe such phenomena as the division of roles and the specialization and coordination of the various tasks (the studio as an assembly-line producing film); on the side of consumption, we have the search for the maximum enjoyability or "universal appeal" (film as a product that knows no boundaries). We should add that standardization "implies mediocrity, formulas, and constantly provokes artistic compromises." Some signs of this are the creation of the "star system, the limitation of the subject matter to certain determined categories, and propaganda." At the same time, however, it should be noted that the fact that spectators *choose* to go to the cinema, for their own satisfaction, limits the tendency toward stereotype and repetition. "The use value of a film prevents standardization from developing beyond a certain limit. Thus, the difficulty encountered by producers is finding a balance between an individual and a standard film form."

This short overview has not considered all the topics approached by Bächlin. The three points we have lingered upon (films as mass products, cinema as an industrial organization, and the convergence of production, distribution, and consumption), however, are enough to suggest the scholar's territory. This picture reinforces the traditional distinction between art and commodities while at the same time it inverts the order of the elements at play. The market dimension of cinema is not counterbalanced by expressivity;

it is the latter that is influenced by the former. Thus, Bächlin removes art from its niche and submits it to a different kind of reasoning. What he may lack is a theory of the mutual interactions of the two poles. He does not grasp the complexity and multiplicity of the bonds between the terms at play, which grant their unity. His understanding of the phenomenon is limited to the parallelism of the various components.

Such a theory, characterized by the will to valorize an essential side of the film phenomenon, but not by the need for synthesis, is the basis for many later contributions. Among them, Mercillon's work (1953) on the American cinema deserves attention. It presents both the preoccupations typical of a socioeconomic approach to cinema and a more acute sense of history, which manifests itself through an in some ways canonical periodization. This can be seen in the first pages of the volume:

I. From 1896 to 1908 cinema is born and takes shape. It is first controlled by its inventors and then by businessmen. At this stage cinema is a "competitive small business"; competition is tough, but the investments are minimal. But in 1909 there is a first attempt at consolidation and the great battle for control of the market begins. II. From 1909 to 1929 is the age of conflict among various trusts, characterized by three dominant facts: the creation of the cinema's first monopoly; Adolph Zukor's predominant influence on the new industry; the role of the "small" banks. Every enterprise tries to obtain an absolute monopoly, and although none manages, a certain concentration of business takes place. III. From 1929 to today, thanks to patents such as those for sound in films, which they control with the help of talkies, big banks start to play an important role within the film industry. The depression allows the tightening of the banks' actual control. Five corporations will finally dominate the industry, which will create an original oligopolistic structure and interact with some degree of fair play. A goal is thus achieved with their domination. (Mercillon 1953)

Mercillon's analysis stops at the beginning of the 1950s. Today cinema's situation has changed. But the phenomena he focuses on offer a good example of what this kind of research is interested in—the mechanisms that control the film industry, the importance of technology and finance, the shaping of dominant positions, and the transformations taking place in each sector.

There are a great many other works that should be mentioned. Among those devoted to specific fields, reference should be made to Durand's work on consumption (1958). The author first defines the idea of film audience; next he analyzes how the market for films has evolved and changed, both in the short and in the long run; then he concentrates on how demographic factors, such as gender, age, class, etc., influence film consumption. Finally, he approaches the problem of preferences and how to measure them. Among the always numerous and valuable theoretical studies, the works by Bizzarri and Solaroli (1958) and Quaglietti (1980) on Italian cinema are worth mentioning. They underscore some of the particular traits of our cinema, such as its fragile independence and its financing from the state. The works by Prokop (1970) likewise deserve attention. In covering the development of American cinema from its embryonic phase to that of becoming an international monopoly, they greatly broaden the field. Janet Wasko (1982) focuses instead on the relationship between industry and finance, as seen through a series of case studies. The works by Degand and Bonnel are among the studies that are most topical. They analyze primarily the birth of new production systems (Degand 1972) or the boom of cultural consumption and of leisure time (Bonnel 1978).

It is important to note that such contributions tend to follow Bächlin's theory more or less explicitly, both valorizing and ghettoizing the economic and industrial aspects. From the 1960s on, this theoretical framework progressively deteriorated. The scholars of the field were the first to promote its renewal. They began by systematically connecting industrial and economic factors with aesthetic and linguistic ones. Along this line, Thomas Guback's work is extremely interesting. He analyzes the penetration of Europe by American cinema (Guback 1969). In so doing, on the one hand, he compares the European and American ways of filmmaking, and he reconstructs the pattern through which they both clash and converge, by emphasizing the attack and defense strategies of each. On the other hand, he tries to see the effects of such an expansionist policy on the films themselves, which he examines. Above all, the French group gravitating around Patrice Flichy and Bernard Miège has done some very interesting work. First, they connect cinema with the media system. Second, all industrial or technical choices are viewed together with their ideological or political implications. Finally, films are seen both as economic goods and as signifying structures (*La production du cinéma* 1980).

This renewal is also promoted by language scholars, who, in turn, attempt to broaden the field. Significantly, such notions as "production mode" or "apparatus," introduced by Heath, Elsaesser, and others, have been rethought.[2]

Finally, the renewal is connected with new methods for dealing with the history of cinema: instead of monothematic analyses (the history of cinema through films and authors, the history of its industrial structures, etc.) a multi-dimensional approach emerges, which juxtaposes, compares, and mixes the various factors. The work of Bordwell, Brunetta, and Sklar moves in this direction. Because their work involves approaches different from the ones so far examined, we will deal with their results later.

8.3. Cinema as Institution

Another parallel field of study had already pointed out the necessity of merging the various factors at play. These were the surveys that intended to uncover cinema's influence on society, analyze the films' ability both to trigger attitudes and behaviors, trends and values, fashions and expectations, and to introduce new professions, new styles and languages, new criteria for evaluation of aesthetic products. The range of the phenomena under investigation is clearly broader than it previously was. Industrial and financial elements are combined with decidedly social aspects. We also observe a partial change in the criteria of the approach: socioeconomic analyses are replaced by more strictly sociological (or socio-anthropological) analyses. The obviously complex object of such surveys, together with their method, seeking to establish broader connections among the factors at play, allows this second field of study to emphasize the existence of a plurality of levels and of coherence in their functioning.

Many of these studies are of a purely empirical nature, belonging to a tradition already established before the war, especially in the United States.[3] Others attempt a more theoretical approach. The latter tend to insist not on the art-commodity dichotomy but, rather, on the correspondence and convergence among the various components. The idea that best represents these efforts is that of the *cinematographic institution.*

This concept appears in Friedmann and Morin (1952) and refers first of all to cinema's industrial structure. The latter incorporates different realities, such as production and consumption, routines and creativity, economic goods and social values, concrete behaviors and mental attitudes. This structure makes its components function in syntony according to more or less canonized rules. Thus, speaking of cinema as an institution means viewing it not merely as an enterprise, but as a *social organization,* as a device that, on the one hand, incorporates and gives a feeling of belonging and, on the other hand, dictates the rules of behavior.

The idea of the cinematographic institution probably derives from Friedmann's more general interest in "social machines." This idea plays an apparently minor role in Morin, who, of the two, would continue to study cinema. However, the impression is that it influences Morin's work on at least two levels: method and content. At the first level, it is important to notice that Morin's approach is always somewhat syncretic. Even when he follows a clearly disciplinary framework, a method, Morin prefers intersections and syntheses (his most famous book, *Le cinéma ou l'homme imaginaire,* presents a partially different approach: here he tries to grasp the "nature" of the phenomenon under investigation, rather than analytically decomposing[4] it). His preference confirms that he attempts to grasp cinema both in its multifarious nature and in the totality of its being an entirely human fact. Morin's horizon fuses anthropology and sociology (Morin 1954). Therefore, the idea of the institution is behind his work, even when it is not stated explicitly.

The idea of the cinematographic institution also influences Morin at the level of content. The themes he deals with are always somewhat transversal, relating to many interconnected areas rather than isolated ones. His analysis of the *need for cinema* is typical in this sense. Morin considers the necessity that leads large portions of the population to devote part of their time to film consumption. They enter a theater, watch a show, recognize and identify with a story, develop some opinions on it, and follow specific behavioral rules. According to Morin, this phenomenon has three major characteristics. In the first place, film consumption tends to be universal. Consequently, the audience emerges not only as a conglomeration of specialized segments, each with its own taste and expectations, but also as a unity that recognizes its own shared desires. Second, film consumption tends toward stagnation, that is, toward the exhaustion of the need to go to the cinema: it "induces us to posit the theoretical and practical problem of the limits of universality, of cinematic saturation, and of reluctance toward the cinema" (Morin 1953b:10). In the third place, film consumption is characterized by differences, discontinuities, and disturbances. For this reason, we study "the way in which the need for cinema is autonomous from and dependent on the social environment that surrounds, breeds, or alters it" (10). These three characteristics allow Morin to write a history of the cinema's audience. Regardless of the greater or lesser completeness of the picture, his work is striking in that it introduces the idea of cinema as a machine that both incorporates different components and somehow gives them a regular rhythm. In other words, it introduces the idea of the institution.

This is also valid for Morin's other works, from his more traditional text on the relationship between cinema and violence (Morin 1953a) to the more innovative study of the star system (Morin 1957).[5] This could also be said for many studies in the same field, ranging from analyses of professional groups to studies of collective behaviors.[6] What matters, in such cases, is that the materials and levels in question should reveal not only diversity, but also complicity and synchronization.

The term *institution* explicitly reappears in Ian Jarvie (1970). He uses it first to distance himself from those scholars who only deal with films that are considered "beautiful," rather than with the cinematic machine itself. Instead, Jarvie is concerned

with the whole galaxy of production, marketing, portraying and being-reflected-in-the-audience, and to a certain extent with appraisal and the sociological factors which may help explain why a film is good or bad. In the end, of course, the artist's technical mastery, imagination, creative discipline and control over his material, must make at least some of the difference between good and bad films. Yet these qualities are not totally individual: possibly certain social structures and organizations are more conducive than others to giving the artist the opportunity and incentive to do well. (Jarvie 1970:xvi)

Therefore, any aesthetic criteria should also be viewed in light of their social basis: the idea of the institution helps to understand the meaning of the judgments we express every day.

Jarvie also uses the term *institution* with polemical tones against a restricted notion of the sociology of cinema. The latter, he believes, cannot be reduced to some sort of "psychology of the social conscience," entirely focused on questions related to the effectiveness of cinema as a means of propaganda or to its influence on the audience. On the contrary, it is necessary to refer to a framework that considers the ways in which cinema and society influence one another, the audience's ability to manipulate and use the cinematic situation, and the "structural impact of films as an institution among existing institutions, not as content among possible contents" (7). Only a global and globalizing view can provide valid answers.

Starting from these two points, Jarvie introduces a "critical sociological method" that tends to explain phenomena and not just describe them. In the case of cinema, this method develops through four questions: "Who makes films and why?" "Who sees a film, how and why?" "What is seen, how and why?" "How do films get evaluated, by whom and why?" We do not intend to offer a survey of Jarvie's answers, nor do we want to summarize his analyses (some are good, such as his study of the various professional roles and of the artistic responsibilities they imply; others are not as good). His basic approach, connecting four different areas, and his initial requirements that aim for a vision of the whole show rather clearly the meaning and the importance that the idea of the cinematographic institution has for him.

During the 1960s this term enjoyed a certain popularity. It reappeared in such works as Simon's (in Collet et al. 1975). Toward the end of the decade it was further enriched by Metz and Odin. The former (Metz 1977b) recognizes the existence of a threefold machine: the industrial one, which works toward the output of products that are as effective as possible; the mental one, which seeks to perpetuate the spectators' capacity to enjoy film; and the one that finds expression in critical, historical, or theoretical arguments, which attempt to valorize each work. In Metz, therefore, the institution is something that guarantees what psychoanalysis calls a "good object relationship" with a film. Odin operates more on the side of semiotics than of psychoanalysis. For him, there is a mechanism regulating both the modes of film construction and those of its reading. The institution is the social device, very much like any language, that allows the interaction of a *sender* and a *receiver* (Odin 1983). We will not dwell at this point on the work of these two scholars. It will be dealt with later, because it belongs to a different disciplinary field.

8.4. Cinema and the Culture Industry

The third area of study is also characterized by the desire for a synoptic view, but it relates cinema to a sphere that both includes and determines it: the *culture industry*. In this way, rather than grasping the structure of a machine, this approach situates cinema in a common landscape. Rather than identifying isolated functions, it seeks a global horizon.

This line of thought's point of departure dates from the postwar years[7] and can be found in a famous chapter of Horkheimer and Adorno's *Dialectic of the Enlightenment* (1947). The first striking feature of the culture industry is its uniformity. On the one hand, it distributes highly homogeneous products:

"For culture now impresses the same stamp on everything." On the other hand, it links all its compartments. "Films, radio, and magazines make up a system which is uniform as a whole and in every part" (Horkheimer and Adorno 1947 [1972]: 120). Some would explain this situation in purely practical terms. Mass diffusion requires uniform products and homogeneity. But this explanation mistakes effect for cause: mass consumption is a consequence, rather than the origin, of the new industrial system and of the new kinds of products; "the attitude of the public . . . is a part of the system and not an excuse for it" (122). Therefore, the reasons for the uniformity of the culture industry are to be found elsewhere: in the inertia of the technical and personal apparatus or in the "determination of all executive authorities not to produce or sanction anything that in any way differs from their own rules, their own ideas about consumers, or above all themselves" (122), and particularly in the economic dimension that permeates the cultural industry. In fact, economic motives integrate the sectors of the culture industry at ever higher levels because of "the dependence of the most powerful broadcasting company on the electrical industry, or of the motion picture industry on the banks." The same is true for new product distributions, which are created for economic reasons. "Marked differentiations such as those of A and B films, or of stories in magazines in different price ranges, depend not so much on subject matter as on classifying, organizing, and labeling consumers. Something is provided for all so that none may escape" (123).

Let us dwell on this last point, the rigid homogeneity of the various products, which is disguised by their apparent diversity. "That the difference between the Chrysler range and General Motors products is basically illusory strikes every child with a keen interest in varieties. . . . The same applies to the Warner Brothers and Metro Goldwyn Mayer productions" (123). This homogeneity is the result of overwhelming *standardization:* production models dictate fixed formulas. Among other consequences, this tends to eliminate any content. "The ostensible content is merely a faded foreground; what sinks in is the automatic succession of standardized operations" (137). Hence, *works* as the site of authenticity and truth are liquidated, and *schematism* triumphs as a perfected and functional piece of machinery: "As soon as the film begins, it is quite clear how it will end, and who will be rewarded, punished, or forgotten. In light music, once the trained ear has heard the first notes of the hit song, it can guess what is coming and feel flattered when it does come. . . . The development of the culture industry has led to the predominance of the effect, the obvious touch, and the technical detail over the work itself—which once expressed an idea, but was liquidated together with the idea" (125). The creative work loses, and clichés win. In other words, art dies, together with all that used to be connected with it.

The point is that the culture industry indicates *the death of art,* an idea that finds many confirmations. For instance, today's cultural consumers are deprived of any possibility of participation and intervention. They are victims of the "stunting of the mass-media consumer's powers of imagination and spontaneity" because of the product that "prescribes every reaction" (126, 137). But the death of art also manifests itself as the transformation of creativity into mere technical mastery or into linguistic virtuosity: producers introduce and impose jargon with "such fine nuances that they almost attain the subtlety of the devices of an avant-garde work" (129), and yet they do not engage in a corresponding search for truth. Just as art's death manifests itself through a totally degraded notion of individuality ("pseudoindividuality is rife: from the standardized jazz improvisation to the exceptional film star whose hair curls over her eye to demonstrate her originality" [154]), it manifests itself even more in the new role ascribed to the artists, who have become mere aesthetic experts ("Formerly, like Kant and Hume, they signed their letters 'Your most humble and obedient servant,' and undermined the foundations of throne and altar. Today they address heads of government by their first names, yet in every artistic activity they have are subject to their illiterate masters" [133]). Then the possibility of deviation, of difference, of alterity, falls by the wayside: if art used to mean violating norms and opening toward the possible, all we have here are confirmations of what already exists. In turn, the character of aesthetic objects as mere commodities emerges. "Putting on a show means showing everybody what there is and what can be achieved" (156).

With its death, art is therefore *equated with the commodity.* This feature is nothing new in itself. "That art renounces its own autonomy and proudly takes its place among consumption goods constitutes the charm of novelty" (157). On the other hand, it is vain to try to resist the convergence of art and goods. "Those who succumb to the ideology are precisely those who cover up the contradiction instead of taking it into the consciousness of their own production" (157). Instead, the problem lies in the fact that a complete identification of the two deprives them of any freedom of movement. Even as a commodity, art should guarantee the useless within the kingdom of utility.

"The use which men . . . promise themselves from the work of art is itself, to a great extent, that very existence of the useless" (158). But, inasmuch as it is a commodity, art also displays its utility: on the one hand, it is a "commodity" that helps to deal with our need for distraction and relaxation; on the other hand, it is a "commodity" that helps us to earn prestige or to feel "with it." Art's functionality not only represents a new form of slavery ("The work of art, by completely assimilating itself to need, deceitfully, deprives men of precisely that liberation from the principle of utility which it should inaugurate"); the more it is pronounced, the more such functionality deprives art of its residual identity ("No object has an inherent value; it is valuable only to the extent that it can be exchanged") (158). Once it is mistaken for an instrument of entertainment or production, art disappears even as a specific kind of commodity. Its aim (which is not even defined) devours its objective texture; its finality (ready to become a social obligation) destroys its body.

It is only by taking into account these points that it is possible realistically to represent the present.

Even today the culture industry dresses works of art like political slogans and forces them upon a resistant public at reduced prices; they are as accessible for public enjoyment as a park. But the disappearance of their genuine commodity character does not mean that they have been abolished in the life of a free society, but that the last defense against their reduction to culture goods has fallen. The abolition of educational privilege by the device of clearance sales does not open for the masses the spheres from which they were formerly excluded, but, given existing social conditions, contributes directly to the decay of education and the progress of barbaric meaninglessness. (160)

Thus, several consequences emerge: mystification (damaged goods are provided, lacking the substance they promise); impotence (the greater circulation of art does not uplift the masses, but spreads barbarism); the complete flattening of all values (an art object is as valuable as a public park: cultural goods reduce everything to a common denominator). Moreover, the *totalitarianism* of the cultural industry emerges: a reality devoted to control, to the elimination of difference, to profit, to domination. To speak of art, then, of its survival, and of the possibility of its fruition is a fundamentally pathetic gesture. For any art that is proffered the compensation is contempt ("When thrown in free, the now debased works of art, together with the rubbish to which the medium assimilates them, are secretly rejected by the fortunate recipients" [161]); advertising is the dominant model, from which there is no escape ("today every monster close-up of a star is an advertisement for her name, and every hit song a plug for its tune. Advertising and culture industry merge technically as well as economically" [163]). The aesthetic object is like a slogan, communicating the lack of a real perspective.

We are aware that a few quotes and some symptomatic references are not enough to reconstruct one of the densest and most complex discourses developed in our age. Still, some points of the Frankfurt School should be clear: the decision to relate cinema to the whole machine of the culture industry, rather than to a specific industry (therefore, notions such as "cinematographic institution," even if useful, appear to be biased with respect to the field under investigation); the attempt to shed light on some general trends, of which cinema is the greatest witness (homogeneity, standardization, commodification); above all, the impression that it is false to distinguish between art and industry, social and aesthetic components, because the two terms have now merged, and the first has given up its autonomy, because their encounter has transformed its own nature.

This last point is essential. After Horkheimer and Adorno, scholars began to perceive as useless the attempt to preserve these presumably independent territories and to distinguish that which is intimately connected. It seemed better to erase the old categories and to look behind the façade of the new reality. From a historical point of view, perhaps Horkheimer and Adorno's greatest achievement was elimination of the prior conceptual framework. The purely *negative* dimension of their discourse was later criticized, however. As is well known, their analysis sought to reveal the predisposition to domination of the culture industry, familiar from other moments of modernity. The rationality of the Enlightenment, on which our age depends, has produced new forms of totalitarianism because it reduces thought to an instrument for the government of nature and society. Only another kind of rationality, more self-reflexive and critical, may assume a liberating value. Many later scholars believed that such a radical condemnation of the present, such a clear-cut denunciation of the aporias of the Enlightenment, and such an alternative dimension of liberation are not totally justified. Therefore, although they preserved the ideal tension that sustains Horkheimer and Adorno's discourse, they tried to articulate its analysis and conclusions more clearly.

We do not intend to give the details of the revisions to the approach developed by the Frankfurt School. We would, however, like to mention Edgar Morin's work on *L'esprit du temps* (Morin 1962). This book does not dismiss the tension between production and consumption, nor does it present as finished the dialectic of repetition and invention. Similarly, it suggests that we cannot speak of one mass culture, because the latter is part of a multicultural complex; it also suggests that the role of the imaginary has not been suffocated, but on the contrary is as active as it can be. We intend, rather, to analyze the conclusions reached by the revisions made to the Frankfurt School. To this aim, we will present as representative the work of Alberto Abruzzese (1973, 1974, 1979).

Instead of a view "from the outside" that operates in the name of a past that risks becoming mythical or in the name of a future that risks being utopian, Abruzzese prefers to view things "from the inside," confronting existence and accepting it as given. Only in this way is it possible to understand the real mechanisms at work in the field and to figure out what position to assume regarding it.

Looking "from the inside," for instance, leads us to perceive the culture industry as uniform, but not as monolithic. Its history, of which Abruzzese (1973) gives an overview, punctuates and articulates its surface. Two points emerge from this history. On the one hand, the negative moments of critique and rejection always end up appearing as productive moments. Thus, denunciation suggests possibilities of development (Schopenhauer's opposition of genius and the masses put the intrinsic potentialities of the author-audience relationship in focus). Similarly, rejection suggests new modes of involvement (avant-gardes unconsciously provide advertising with new ideas). On the other hand, no path is ever linear or goes only in one direction. There are phases during which we recover older values, others when we plan new social relationships; structured and uncertain phases; humanistic and technological phases. Therefore, one should not think of the culture industry as something uniform and static. On the contrary, it is continuously subject to reversals and phase discrepancies. Its history appears, thus, to be extremely varied, despite its tendency toward the transformation of the individual into a consumer and the work of art into a commodity. Indeed, it is so varied that it even contains antibodies, generated by the system itself and ready to upset the most stable balances.

The second point is that within the progressive success of the culture industry accelerations do not necessarily represent defeats. For instance, with the development of the mass media and, above all, of cinema, intellectual work quickly ceases to be an enterprise entailing craftsmanship and likewise loses the ability to control the entire production process. Instead, it becomes an industrial task, parceled out, mechanical, salaried, often anonymous, and fundamentally marginal. In other words, it becomes "abstract work." Yet to think that this should mark the loss of a "truer," "richer," or "more human" dimension is totally misleading. "All abstract work represents the most advanced terrain for the political organization of work; in other words, for the awareness of one's own alterity with respect to capital and one's centrality within the productive process as such. . . . The more the industrialization process forces intellectual work to become anonymous, collective, mechanized, and salaried, the closer it gets to the concrete possibility of organizing one's *identity* in political terms (that is, once again, inside production)" (Abruzzese 1977:11). Therefore, an apparent regression masks an opening to new and more concrete maneuvering room. The cultural operators (or the "aesthetic experts," as Horkheimer and Adorno used to call them) can still effectively manage themselves, even if they have lost their autonomy. They only have to do it at the level of organization and politics.

The third point is that, when we move from the area of production to the area of consumption, the dynamics and potentialities of the culture industry become increasingly evident. First, all the themes, motifs, and figures that man has developed over time come into play. For instance, cinema once again takes up traditional myths and tales, while at the same time it amplifies facts taken from the news or more recent topics of discussion. Such constant recycling of the collective imagination is important in that it allows us to revert to formulas that have already been tested and to invest them with new meanings. In this way, apparently schematic solutions reveal unsuspected valences. If we think of the obstinacy with which cinema explores the traditionally delicate borders between culture and nature, the individual and society, we understand that filmic stereotypes are the direct heirs of deeper archetypes. Similarly, if we think of how obsessed cinema is with two of the typical characters of mechanical civilization, the beast and the robot, we understand that such stereotypes emerge as true symptoms of the shadowy zones of our age (Abruzzese 1979). We should not, therefore, speak of the poverty and simple-mindedness, but of the *richness* of the cultural industry. While apparently providing escapism from reality, it may unconsciously make us think about the world we live in. Second, the spectator's participation comes into play. Mass media texts tend toward self-referentiality. With their symbols and stories, they show us the means through which the latter are produced; by traversing wide sections of the imaginary, they also display the mechanisms regulating our imagination. This makes readers or spectators aware of their role and allows them to associate the text's work with their own work. In other words, being exposed to objects that reveal their own origins and function makes us familiar with the machine, internalizes it, and continues the production process. The production of the text elicits more production. We should not, therefore, speak of the consumers' slavery and servitude, but of their *complicity*. The extra work necessary for the cultural commodity to achieve its ends, to fulfill its destiny, comes from the consumers; the same holds true for the extra work that, mostly in the form of memory and desire, is the secret engine of the culture industry (177ff.).

The idea of the *richness* of the supply and of the *complicity* of the consumer may be disconcerting. Yet, besides shedding light on real circumstances, it also suggests the outcome of the processes at work. On the one hand, the culture industry has the ability to exploit its own capital and to broaden its range of action. Consequently, art does not become consumer goods, but consumer goods become art. We observe, therefore, an *aesthetization of the commodity* and not a commodification of aesthetics, as Horkheimer and Adorno believed. On the other hand, the readers' and spectators' involvement in actually "productive consumption" does not lead to their subjection to the machine. It makes them assume its rhythms and potentials. A *technologization of the body* occurs, not a loss of personal abilities, as Adorno and Horkheimer thought. The picture presented by the Frankfurt School is thus totally reversed. The response to the impression of totalitarianism is the effective possibility of a *reappropriation*. The culture industry is neither vacuous nor tyrannical: it is a factory that runs through us and that needs to be dealt with, used, and conquered once again.

8.5.   Cinema and the Representation of the Social

The previous pages have presented cinema within the framework of a wider horizon, where it did not play a primary, but only a secondary role. It now comes back as a protagonist with those scholars who believe that films, even fictional ones, always portray the society around them.

One of the most representative contributions in this field is Kracauer's *From Caligari to Hitler* (1947), a study of the cultural atmosphere that preceded the advent of Nazism. His basic theory is that "through an analysis of the

German films deep psychological dispositions predominant in Germany between 1918 and 1933 can be exposed" (Kracauer 1947:v). This idea is paralleled by more general observations. "The films of a nation reflect its mentality in a more direct way than other artistic media for two reasons. First, films are never the product of an individual"; therefore, individual and idiosyncratic choices are less determinant than elsewhere for the final product. "Second, films address themselves, and appeal, to the anonymous multitude. Popular films—or, to be more precise, popular screen motifs—can therefore be supposed to satisfy existing mass desires" (5). In other words, we have a working *group* and *broad* consumption. This *collective* dimension at both levels makes films the perfect *social testimony*.

A second important point is that "what films reflect are not so much explicit credos as psychological dispositions—those deep layers of collective mentality which extend more or less below the dimension of consciousness" (6). In short, cinema sheds light on what is not said, what is hidden, what is underground. Let us look at the negligible gestures that accompany an actor's aging: inasmuch as they are marginal, they bring to the surface things that are hardly ever admitted, namely, one's own way of relating to others and to the world. Such unperceived behaviors, being automatically recorded by the camera, emerge as the "visible hieroglyphs" of the invisible dynamics of human relationships, in turn "characteristic of the inner life of the nation from which the film emerges" (7). Similarly, "What counts is not so much the statistically measurable popularity of films as the popularity of their pictorial and narrative motifs. Persistent reiteration of these motifs marks them as outward projections of inner urges. And they obviously carry most symptomatic weight when they occur in both popular and unpopular films, in grade B pictures as well as in superproductions" (8). In short, insistence winds up as the stronger force. Therefore, these subliminal and reiterated elements define cinema as a *social testimony* in that cinema grasps both the *unobserved* and the *recurrent*. Its horizon is a culture's *unconscious*.

A third important point is that "to speak of the peculiar mentality of a nation by no means implies the concept of a fixed national character" (8) because all collective trends and emotional states are part of a historical moment. Yet historical evolution does not depend only on political, economic, or social reasons. All cultural components, even the most minute and hidden, play a relevant role. Let us look at pre–Nazi Germany. "Behind the overt history of economic shifts, social exigencies, and political machinations runs a secret history involving the inner dispositions of the German people. The disclosure of these dispositions through the medium of the German screen may help in the understanding of Hitler's ascent and ascendancy" (11). Cinema is therefore a *testimonial* tightly connected with *history:* it allows the integration of more traditional approaches with the data coming from *social psychology.*

These initial clarifications of Kracauer's are followed by a wide-ranging analysis of German cinema between 1918 and 1933, which we will not present in detail. Such premises make clear in fact that the scholar's interest lies mainly in the possibility of grasping German cinema's ability to represent the emotional states present in the society of the time and to foreshadow the following events. Kracauer's observations conform to his research program. In the 1910s and 1920s films with a sexual background, and costumed epics that fuse history and individual psychology, were very successful. Kracauer explains this by observing that the former "testified to primitive needs arising in all belligerent countries after the war" (45); the latter, instead, soothed "the wounds of innumerable Germans who, because of the humiliating defeat of the fatherland, refused any longer to acknowledge history as an instrument of justice or providence" (53). Similarly, Kracauer perceives in *Caligari* the dominant dilemma of the early 1920s: "the soul wavering between tyranny and chaos, and facing a desperate situation: any escape from tyranny seems to throw it into a state of utter confusion" (74). Again, he divides the films of the very early 1930s into two groups: those that manifest antiauthoritarian tendencies, and yet contain no positive indications, and those that celebrate the war hero, the leader, or the active rebel, and in so doing help to give vent to extant authoritarian tendencies. Paradoxically, his conclusion is that German cinema offers such a precise portrayal of the contemporary mentality that later events can only confirm it. With Nazism "Homunculus walked about in the flesh. Self-appointed Caligaris hypnotized innumerable Cesares into murder. Raving Mabuses committed fantastic crimes with impunity, and mad Ivans devised unheard-of tortures. Along with this unholy procession, many motifs known from the screen turned into actual events" (272).

Beyond these isolated observations, let us reinforce the idea that the theoretical core of Kracauer's work lies in his premises. Films reflect the society around them. Their very nature—works collectively produced for mass consumption—allows them to reflect the motifs at work in a given society better than any other kind of text. They underscore the subterranean, hidden aspects of society, to the point of illustrating its unconscious. They mark its historical evolution, uncovering its dynamics. In short, cinema is a perfect *witness,* and as such it is a precious *source* for the work done not just by the historian, but by the sociologist.

Such premises clearly recall Kracauer's previously mentioned idea of cinema as a realistic device. Our choice to separate his twofold contribution depends on the fact that his *Theory of Film* presents an essentialist dimension that is diminished by a deep methodological awareness in the previous *From Caligari to Hitler.* Clearly, today Kracauer's position lends itself to criticisms. The author correlates filmic representation and social motifs in a simplistic manner (a consequence of the notion of reflection). The determinism with which he explains the dynamics of facts (probably intrinsic to his notion of history as a mere causal succession) is also striking. The importance of Kracauer's work is, however, undeniable: he demonstrated that cinema may be of interest not only for scholars of aesthetics, but also for historians, and, above all, for sociologists. He reminded them that what is at play is more than a machine, bound to new production models, markets, professions, and values. It is a mirror of society, ready to reflect its most secret components and its subtlest tensions. He defined films' role as both testimony and source. In other words, Kracauer presented movies as an essential *document* for understanding how each culture represents itself, its alternatives and its options.[8]

Kracauer's ideas have had many followers, both direct and indirect. Among the former are Giorgio Galli and Franco Rositi, whose work (1967) compares pre-Nazi cinema to the contemporary American industry. The social and political situation of the two countries is similar: if, in one case, we have Hitler and, in the other, Roosevelt, this is in part because of the fact that American movies privilege optimism and effectuality, thus suggesting to American society the "antibodies" with which the crisis can be fought.[9] Among the latter are Martha Wolfenstein and Nathan Leites, whose work (1950) examines the way in which three cinematic traditions (American, English, and French) represent affective relationships: between men and women, parents and children, subjects and objects of desire, even "butchers" and victims. Their starting point is in some ways the opposite of Kracauer's. Films belong to those "daydreams" that embody our wishes, aspirations, and feelings. And yet cinema does reflect reality, although not like a mirror; cinema "reflects" as a dream does, altering the external contours of things, but retaining their meaning. Hence, we have the opportunity to see what three different cultures think and say about a broad area of human life, even through the filter of such genres as melodrama or comedy. Wolfenstein and Leites, it should be noted, have a different and also less-articulated view of cinema than Kracauer. Still, they make better use of the tools of quantitative survey, thanks to their reliance on the methods of "content analysis." Together with *From Caligari to Hitler,* their work is among the first of many studies on "the cinemato-graphic image (of youngsters, family, deviance, etc.)" published in the following decades.

Mark Ferro also reelaborates Kracauer's problematic by studying the relationships between cinema and history. Films testify to social reality in four principal ways. First, through content: the situations shown on the screen suggest what a society thinks of itself, its past, others, etc. The suggestion may be positive: the representation concretizes the way a society views itself. It can also be negative: since the representation contains frequent incongruities and lapses, it also shows what a society knows without wishing to acknowledge, what we may call its latent side. In this sense, cinema may well emerge as a "counteranalysis" of some sort (Ferro 1977 [1988]: 29 ff).

Second, films testify to social reality thanks to their style. Let us consider editing decisions as an example. In *Jud Süss* Veit Harlan uses crossed fadeouts to move from the castle to the ghetto, from the protagonist's traditional attire to his more modern costume, from gold to the dancers. Such shifts perfectly reveal some Nazi obsessions: for instance, the idea that the Jews' appearance may change, but their nature never will; that their money may foster vices. Even the way a subject changes may be revealing: in *The Third Man,* Carol Reed disregards Graham Greene's directions and in so doing "he substitutes a morality of Good and Evil for a morality of ambiguity" (129).

The third way in which film connects with society is by acting upon it. It has numerous, and often contradictory, possibilities of intervention: mobilization of the masses, indoctrination, counterdocumentation, glorification, etc. Images are not simply a mirror, but also a weapon. The appearance of one form of action as opposed to another is a precious detail, testifying to the dynamics running through a society. It reveals which projects inspire it, which forces stir it, and which problems threaten it.

The fourth way a film reveals a more general situation is connected with the way in which it is read. Every society interprets texts in its own way: it takes note of certain aspects and suggestions and overlooks others. Cinema, too, is subject to this rule. Renoir's *La grande illusion* is an exemplary case.

When it was first released, before the war, it was hailed as a pacifist work that aimed to bring different peoples closer; after the war, it was accused of being too kind to Germans and slightly collaborationist. A film's reception, therefore, provides useful information about the ideological substrate that dominates any society.

Ferro's contribution both broadens and displaces Kracauer's themes. Cinema is a *testimonial* not so much because it fully reflects a society, but because it is an *indicator* of its blind spots, mental processes, possible dynamics, and accepted answers. Along this line we also find the work of Pierre Sorlin, whose research is valuable for its deepening of these insights. If it is true that cinema portrays society, it is also necessary to wonder what kind of portrayal it offers. Films never duplicate reality. On the contrary, they select only fragments of it, charge them with meaning, make them functional for a story or a thesis, and recompose them into a new unity. In short, movies transcribe reality and do so with their own devices, cuts and exemplification, emphasis and editing. Hence the view that, in order to understand what kind of portrayal is at stake, it is necessary to take into account the *construction of films,* that is, the "process through which the cinema of an age captures a fragment of the outside world, reorganizes it, makes it coherent, and produces, starting from the continuity of the sensible universe, a finished, circumscribed, discontinuous, and transmissible object" (Sorlin 1977:270). No society ever appears on the screen as it is, but according to the requirements of the expressive devices of its time, the director's choices, the audience's expectations, and the very idea of cinema.

As a consequence, the filmic image shows not just a situation, but the *visible* side of a society. "The visible side of an epoch is what image makers try to grasp in order to transmit it, and what audiences accept without surprise"; it is also "what seems to be capable of being photographed and presented on the screens of a given age" (68, 69). Thus, the visible side defines what we are aware of, the way in which we notice it, the shape we give it in order to communicate it to others, and the importance we ascribe to it in context. Two social groups are directly responsible for it: filmmakers and spectators. Through them, however, the whole society reveals its perceptive habits, mental schemes, canonical configurations, and focuses. More specifically, through its visible side a society reveals its interests and the way it frames them; it reveals the horizon of what it believes to be worthy of discussion, "the perimeter within which it is able to pose its problems" (69). Moreover, through its visible side it displays its recurrent obsessions and representations, the "fixations" (230) that occupy its imaginary. Finally, this visible side allows society to show its orientations and how it applies them, that is, how it solves its problems and how it interprets reality. Something radical, then, comes into play. It is not merely an attitude, but a way of seeing and consequently of learning and knowing the world; it is a mentality or an ideology. This visible side reveals the mentality and the ideology of a society: it tells us through which representations the latter reelaborates reality and takes hold of it,[10] so much so that its fluctuations or multiplications indicate a very deep tension, which is connected with the introduction of new world views.

With Sorlin, we are clearly very far from Kracauer's mimetic model. Cinema does not represent a society, but what a society considers representable. In the first place, cinema

underscores a way of looking; it allows the distinguishing of the visible from the invisible and thus the recognition of the ideological limits of perception in a certain age. Second, it reveals sensitive areas, what we called fixations, that is, questions, expectations, uneasinesses, all of which are apparently secondary, but the importance of which emerges from their systematic reappearance in films. Finally, it presents different interpretations of society and of the relationships developing inside of it. Under the cover of an analogy with the sensible world, which often allows it to pass as a faithful witness, cinema creates a fictional universe by reverting to comparison, matching, development, repetition, ellipsis. (242)

We repeat: cinema tells us what a society literally sees, to which key images it entrusts its thoughts, which elaborations it carries out. Similarly, it informs us about the oversights, censorships, and prohibitions that run through it. In other words, cinema does not provide us with an image of society, but with what society considers an image, including a possible image of itself. It does not reproduce society's reality, but the manner in which it deals with reality.

Sorlin's view preserves (yet shifts and in a sense radicalizes) films' value as testimonials. His position is understandable if we take two elements into account. The first is that Sorlin, despite his privileging of sociology's interests (it is not by chance that the title of the work under discussion is *Sociologie du cinéma*), appreciates the lesson of semiotics, for which all representations are first of all conventional linguistic constructs.[11] The second is that he, even though following Kracauer, does not forget that cinema is also a machine that functions according to precise rules (production routines, aesthetic criteria, communicative codes) and toward specific ends (economic, expressive, and ideological). This last point is fundamental. Kracauer separates the theme of cinema as social portrait from the other sections of sociology. Instead, Sorlin brings them back together. We must consider cinema as a productive organism, a complex institution, and a field of values belonging to mass communications, in order to be able to appreciate its ability to be a testimonial. In other words, cinema can mirror reality only inasmuch as it is a social reality itself. The idea that the visible side of an epoch should be grasped through its definitions and functioning, and that we can spy on reality only through these, confirms the need for synthesis that Sorlin uncovers.

We can conclude our remarks here. We started with the subordination of social and economic aspects to the aesthetic ones; we have observed that a first research trend aimed to rehabilitate the former, while keeping them separate from the latter. We have also presented a second research trend, which instead tried to bring the two together inside the same machine, and a third one, which tried to further broaden the field of investigation, reconnecting cinema with the culture industry. Finally, the last trend posed the problem of the image of society in film. To conclude, we must admit that inasmuch as cinema belongs to society, it may be the latter's image, and the back-and-forth movement between cinema and the world may be the most radical sign of its destiny.

9 SEMIOTICS OF CINEMA

9.1. The Foundation of the Discipline

Besides psychology and sociology, the third discipline that systematically studied cinema after the war was semiotics. The unusual fate of the discipline makes it a somewhat special case. It emerged in the mid-1960s, immediately outmoding many of the current discourses. In turn, the early 1970s found many scholars from various disciplines still feeling challenged by its theories. Then, in the years that followed, a good number of contributions boasted of being "beyond" or "against" semiotics. The semiotic approach created fractures, aggregations, resistances; its presence both accented and realigned other theoretical formations. This occurred because semiotics, more than other disciplines, tended to highlight certain fundamental points: on the one hand, the dissatisfaction with discourses that are too general, with impressionistic observations, with the search for essences; on the other hand, the need to define its own interests, to deploy rigorous analytical procedures, to make use of well-defined categories. These features characterize the *methodological approach* that semiotics of cinema seemed to want to embody. This identification with methodology exposed semiotics to controversy. Its will to being scientific was perceived by some as a turning point, by others as a sign of its aridity and asceticism. Its attention to the instruments more than to the objects of analysis was for some a sign of its rigor, while for others it was an excuse for abandoning the concrete reality of cinema. Its indifference toward the previous debate was for some the proof of its achieved autonomy, and for others a sign of mere presumption. But this identification with methodology also placed the semiotics of cinema in a privileged position. It marked the beginning of a comprehensive attitude toward research and served as an "example" of a whole style of investigation.

After all, such a style—based on the rejection of essentialism and on the adherence to method—was already apparent in the essay that started the whole field of studies: "Le cinéma: Langue ou langage?" by Christian Metz, published in 1964 by *Communications* (later in Metz 1968). At its core, as we have already mentioned, we find two fundamental problems. On the one hand, the question of range is raised, whether cinema does or does not belong to the phenomena that semiotics deals with,[1] and thus whether it can be studied with the instruments elaborated by the discipline. On the other hand, there is the question of merit, of whether cinema has a *language system [langue]*, a coded repertoire of symbols, figures, or formulas to which it constantly refers, or whether it is instead a matter of *language [langage]*, a mostly spontaneous, self-regulating discourse.

These two questions are closely connected. In fact, only if cinema has a language system may it fully become an object for semiotics, because the latter deals with complex, meaningful structures, more than with autonomous or scattered facts (or so it seemed, when Metz's essay was published). But these two questions, above all, depend on each other. When wondering whether cinema has a language system, or is a nonsystematic language, we already view it from the standpoint of semiotics, if only because we apply some of the discipline's categories to it. In itself, cinema may be many things; it is only semiotics that posits such an alternative. For this reason, we may say that the question of range logically precedes the question of merit. Given the situation, what matters is defining a point of view and checking to see how it holds up, more than defining the phenomenon.

These ideas run through Metz's essay, although not in such a schematic form. It is well known that the answer to the dilemma epitomized by Metz's title is in favor of *langage*. If we look at it carefully, cinema is not a language system *[langue]*, even if a scholarly trend, personified by Eisenstein, has tried to prove that it is capable of abstract meanings and to present cinema as a "new Esperanto." It is not a language system for at least two reasons. On the one hand, cinema lacks double articulation, which is the fundamental feature of all natural languages. A verbal discourse may be subdivided first of all into separate, meaningful units (monemes or words) and second into meaningless units, which are, however, able to construct arbitrary signifiers (phonemes or isolated sounds). Instead, cinema has neither fixed meaningful units (each shot is unique) nor meaningless units (each section of a shot is already meaningful). On the other hand, and more generally, "cinema is not a language system because it contradicts three important characteristics of the linguistic fact." If "a language is a *system* of *signs* used for *intercommunication*" (Metz 1968 [1974]: 75), cinema does not have a system or consist of signs or have intercommunication as a goal. First, a film does not rely on a system such as a dictionary, in which each term acquires its identity through its orderly opposition to others. On the contrary, it is the result of an alignment of different shots, relying more on the combination of scattered elements than on a selection of the elements of a paradigm. Besides, a film's images cannot be equated to signs in any strict sense (as can words). Each shot is already an enunciated phrase, a sentence, because what appears on the screen (e.g., a dog) means at least "here this is" (in our case, "here is a dog"). Finally, a film does not work at the level of communication, but of expression, or at a level where "meaning is somehow immanent to a thing, is directly released from it, and merges with its very form" (78). In other words, a film shows; it does not signify.

For Metz, cinema is therefore not a language system, a *langue*. It has no double articulation and it does not fully satisfy any of the "three elements of definition." Yet this should not discourage us. Even though the main object of semiotics is such a "strong" system as language systems, we need to acknowledge that there is another legitimate attitude: "to look at the semiological endeavor as open research, permitting the study of new forms; 'language' (in the broad sense) is no simple thing—whole flexible systems may be studied as flexible systems, and with the appropriate methods" (89). In short, with felicitous intuition, Metz contradicts his initial conclusion, that cinema lacks the features of a language system and therefore that semiotics must leave it aside. On the contrary, he suggests that the chosen point of view should be maintained (this is, after all, what matters), adding to its rigorous formulation a more open attitude so that even simple linguistic facts may be recovered. The essay ends with a sentence that clearly suggests hope: "The time has come for a semiotics of the cinema" (91).

9.2.   First Explorations and Contributions

"Le cinéma: Langue ou langage?" immediately provoked, as stated above, a far-reaching debate about both the question of range and the question of merit. Of the many scholars who participated in it, above all Umberto Eco, Gianfranco Bettetini, Emilio Garroni, and Pier Paolo Pasolini should be mentioned. It is not by chance that these authors are Italian, because these studies started mainly (but not only) in Italy, thanks to two international conferences on the language of film, held in Pesaro during the Mostra del Nuovo Cinema [the exhibit of new cinema] in 1966 and 1967.[2]

Bettetini (1968) is in agreement with both of Metz's "proofs" of the fact that cinema does not correspond to a language system. In general, it is correct to separate these two terms, above all if we think that filmic signs, unlike linguistic signs, do not always mean the same thing for everyone. They lack both a stable reference in varying situations and sociality. Cinema is, however, endowed with double articulation, only it is different from that of natural languages. Films can in fact be divided into nuclei representing a given situation, then into isolated technical elements, such as lighting. The first kind of unity ("iconemes") corresponds to the way speech is articulated into sentences, more than into words. The second corresponds to the articulation of words, more than of isolated sounds (lighting is already meaningful in and of itself).

Eco (1968) intervenes on the subject of double articulation, but tries to dismantle its "myth." It is true that natural languages are endowed with it; however, there are systems characterized by single articulation (i.e., bus numbers, as a whole, denote a certain route, but the numbers are not indicative of anything in and of themselves) and by multiple articulations.[3] Cinema belongs to this last group. On the screen, we can identify "iconic semes" (i.e., a tall, blond man) that may be subdivided and analyzed as smaller "iconic signs" (nose, eyes, etc.), composed of meaningless "visual features" (angles, curves, etc.). A frame is articulated into meaningful units (semes and signs) and into unities that function as pure signifiers (figures). If we move from the frame to the shot, a third articulation is added to these first two. The portions of a gesture (the blond man frozen at various stages of his movement) construct a whole gesture (the blond man's complete movement). The separate "cinemes" make up "cinemorphs." Thus, we have three articulations: from the figures we move to the "semes"; from these (which are already meaningful within the frame, but which are only suspended moments within the shot), we move to "cinemorphs." This shows that cinema is a "strong" semiological system, which simply happens to be different from those usually given as examples. For this reason it requires special attention.

Garroni's contribution (1968, expanded in 1972) is in some ways more general. He acknowledges the legitimacy of Metz's question of range, but not the question of merit. The opposition of *langue* and *langage* may be misleading: a *langue* is the only way a *langage* may be "coded," that is, it may be limited through fixed possibilities, recurrent behaviors, and structural regularities. In short, a *langue* is *langage* as seen in its schematic, normative dimension. Thus, the problem is the degree to which the scholar may "formalize" the phenomenon under investigation: high in the case of natural languages, still low in the case of cinema. But nothing whatsoever hampers the semiotic approach. We need not wonder what cinema resembles but which codes it deals with.

Eco shares this view of Garroni's (he compiled a list of the codes at work in visual messages), which sets the debate on a very productive path. Metz himself tries to systematize the way in which cinema organizes shot sequences, reaching what he calls the "large syntagmatic category of the image track," that is, a typology of sequences (Metz 1968). Naturally, many more scholars have contributed to this project.[4]

Pasolini's position is unusual. On the one hand, he is one of the first to participate in the debate with a series of contributions, later collected in *Empirismo eretico*. On the other hand, at times he relies on semiotics in a deliberately undisciplined way. Pasolini, too, starts with the realization that "cinematographic languages do not seem to be based on anything: no communicative language is their real basis" (1972: 171). This is confirmed by the fact that images are not comparable to stable, general, and abstract terms such as those presented in a dictionary. "No dictionary of images exists. There are no predefined images, ready for use" (173). Consequently, filmmakers have to invent their own signs for every film, even before charging them with an expressive value. And yet, despite the lack of a language as their basis, films communicate. They transmit meanings that the audience grasps. This occurs because cinema relies on that "common patrimony" represented by the objects that surround us, the gestures we all use, and the attitudes impressed on our faces. Cinema exploits the signs of reality, appropriates them, and reuses them. In this sense, "reading" a film equals "reading" the world. "The receiver of the cinematographic product is also used to visually 'reading' reality . . . [,] which also expresses itself through the simple visual presence of its acts and habits" (172).

The first step is the "visual presence" in cinema of signs of the world. If we move a step further, however, we can maintain that such signs constitute a real language, the basic human language. "Actions can be seen as the first and principal form of human language, inasmuch as they establish a relationship of reciprocal representation with others and with physical reality" (203). All the rest, including verbal language, comes later: "The languages that are written and spoken are but the integration of this first language: the first information about a man comes from the language of his physiognomy, behavior, clothing, rituality, corporeal techniques, actions, and, finally, his spoken and written language. After all, it is thus that reality is reproduced by cinema" (204).

In other words, cinema traces the language of actions. It assimilates its signs and reproduces them. Now, such a procedure is somewhat similar to that of writing as compared to oral speech. Just as writing takes live speech and preserves it without betrayal, similarly cinema traces natural behavior and fixes it without alteration. Pasolini insists on this equivalence (which, he notes, may seem crazy). In both cases, we are dealing with an instrument that preserves prior experience by recording it. Hence the possibility of clearly defining the terms at play. "Our whole life, with its actions, is a natural, living cinema: in this sense, it is linguistically equivalent to oral language in its natural or biological moment" (210). Conversely, cinema "is but the 'written' moment of a natural and total language, namely, our acting within reality. In short, the . . . 'language of actions' has found a means of mechanical reproduction, similar to the convention of written language as compared to oral speech" (210).

The core of Pasolini's thought is his idea of cinema as "written language of reality." The author is certainly aware of the risks inherent in his discourse. The most immediate risk involves overlaying cinema and real life to the extent that their differences become imperceptible. But Pasolini is not afraid of this danger. "To put it as simply as possible, in all films we recognize reality, which speaks to us just as it does in everyday life" (246). So much so that general semiology, which has the primal languages of acting and of physical presence as its objects, can be "both the Semiology of the language of reality and the Semiology of the language of cinema" (247). The identification is therefore possible, but we should keep in mind that there is an audiovisual reproduction, bound to special modalities that can be described in a specially designed grammar. Pasolini defines this grammar (which includes "orthographic modes," "substantive modes," "qualification modes," and "verbalization or syntactic modes"). He also observes, however, that such a grammar has a limited autonomy, because in the end reproduction "re-creates in cinema the same linguistic characteristics of life when it is understood as language" (247).

The second risk run by Pasolini is that of betraying the semiologic enterprise by "naturalizing" language instead of seeing how it is "encoded" culturally. He is not afraid of this risk either, because, on the one hand, we should remember that gestures and objects never appear as "brute facts," but bear the traces of the way we have experienced and lived them: they have, in short, a dimension that is connected with their story. On the other hand, however, we should not forget that their meaning is inscribed within reality, regardless of the way we observe the latter; that this meaning is connected with such natural archetypes as "peacocks spreading their tails, cocks singing after intercourse, flowers displaying their colors during a given season" (247). Reality communicates this meaning to itself, to those inside of it, to those belonging to it. Thus, semiotics should not hesitate to approach the spontaneity of life, instead of cultural constructs: it will find grist for its mill.

At this point it is clear that Pasolini establishes a parallel between a disciplinary discourse and some kind of utopia: reality speaking by itself and cinema as its faithful mirror. Many later scholars (for instance, Deleuze) would enhance these very extra- or antidisciplinary aspects, insisting on the idea of intimacy between cinema and life and on the idea of the naturalness of signification. Yet, at the time, this contribution helped above all to generate new questions and to indicate the complexity of the mechanisms of representation. Therefore, despite its deliberate eccentricity, it fit perfectly within the debate.[5]

9.3. Broadening the Field

By the end of the 1960s and the beginning of the 1970s the semiotics of cinema had emerged as a reality fully involved in the process of expansion. By then a great many scholars had taken part in the debate. In Italy, besides the scholars mentioned above, we find Brunetta, Grande, Tomasino, Tinazzi. It is also necessary to mention that journals such as *Filmcritica* and *Cinema e Film* showed interest in this new approach. In France we find Odin, Chateau, Marie, Jost, Ropars, Simon, and the journal *Ça Cinéma*. In England there was a more political slant in the work of Wollen, Heath, and the group gravitating around *Screen*. In Belgium Gheude and Peraya founded the collective Quazar.

In Germany Knilli edited an important issue of *Sprache in technischen Zeitalter,* while Koch worked more at an epistemological level. In the Soviet Union Ivanov and Lotman were among the protagonists of the Baku semiologic circle. In Poland Alicia Helman founded a real school of research in Cracow. In the Netherlands we find Peters. In Spain, Urrutia and, later, Talens. In Japan, Asanuma. And many more.

Research took place at all levels, too. Scholars focused on the "codifiability" of cinematographic language (Lotman 1973; Ivanov 1975) and on the latter's relationships with other languages; on "filmic materials" (Helman 1970) and on each of the two "sides" of such materials (for the sound track, see Brunetta 1970; for the image track, see, for instance, Peters 1981); on the status of the frame (Gheude 1970) and on the "rhetoric" of the image (Knilli and Reiss 1971); on filmic language as a "system" (Grande 1974) and on the interrelations among the various codes of a single film (Bailblé, Marie, and Ropars 1975); on the relations between language and reality (Urrutia 1972; Tomasino 1978); on the relationship between linguistic and biological factors (Koch 1971); on strategies of analysis (Talens et al. 1978) and on the usefulness of semiotics for criticism (Tinazzi 1972), etc.

This list is, intentionally, somewhat chaotic, in order to convey the impression of the excitement within the field. We can identify a common feature, however: the will to make the models relied on more "flexible," the desire to experiment with new analytical categories, and the decision to focus on aspects thus far left out of the cinematographic phenomenon.

The three contributions we are about to examine, by Peter Wollen, Sol Worth, and Christian Metz, respond to these very needs. We will start with Wollen's book (1969). In the chapters on "The Semiology of the Cinema"[6] the author laments the inflexibility of the notion of sign that was elaborated in the wake of Saussure. Fortunately, one can also turn to the teaching of Charles S. Peirce, in which the sign appears as a multiple entity. Referring to one of Peirce's tripartite divisions, Wollen reminds us that the term *icon* identifies a sign representing its object mainly by similarity (e.g., an illustration or a diagram), while the term *index* identifies a sign establishing an existential relationship with its object (e.g., the symptoms of an illness naturally refer to reality), and the term *symbol* defines an arbitrary sign, the product of an explicit convention (a word or an emblem). Such tripartite division may be useful for critically rethinking the history of cinema, insofar as it sheds light on recurrent trends. Under the heading of the *index* we can in fact place all realistic research, with its firm belief in an immediate and spontaneous relationship with the world: from Feuillade to Flaherty, from Stroheim to Murnau, from Renoir to Rossellini. Under the heading of the *symbol* we can place Eisenstein's films, seen as the extreme point where images intend to play on conceptual and therefore conventional mechanisms, rather than on a direct representation of things (the stone lion, which metaphorically suggests the insurrection). Under the heading of the *icon* we find Sternberg's work. Thanks to his systematic reinvention of reality and to its transformation into some sort of ghost of life, he departs from reproductive realism and from conceptual games, to enter a dimension characterized only "by virtue of similarities."

Even before defining the field from a historical point of view, however, such a tripartite division helps us to make some of cinema's fundamental traits clear. First, it allows us to grasp its complexity. Unlike other languages that work with only one of the three types of signs, cinema has an "aesthetic richness" that "springs from the fact that it comprises all three dimensions of signs: indexical, iconic, symbolic" (Wollen 1969:141). There are never pure solutions on the screen, but always a combination of elements that is always subject to change.

Second, because of this very peculiarity, it seems inappropriate to compare cinema only to verbal languages: it is better to connect it with fields that have the same semiotic richness. Hence the need for a study that investigates "the whole range of communication within the visual sensory band, from writing, numbers, and algebra through the images of photography and cinema" (Wollen 1969:139−140). We can determine which connections count only when we look at the whole field.

Third, this tripartite division allows us to appreciate the choices made both in the name of uniformity and in the name of dispersion. Along with scholars who assign a dominant role to indexes, symbols, or icons, we also find those opting for somewhat unstable juxtapositions of these elements. Both trends are revealing: the former (with the above-mentioned names) reminds us of possible directions; the latter (personified by Godard) reminds us that a film is always a puzzle of signs, rather than a (false) monolith.[7]

These are the essential traits of Wollen's thought. He presents exigencies that were widely confirmed at the beginning of the 1970s. Bettetini (1971) also attempts to reuse Peirce. He distinguishes between a realism that is dominantly iconic, which focuses only on the reproduction of physical outlines, and a realism that is dominantly indexical, which tries to "get in tune" with the world. Thus, Hoensch (1976), an exponent of the Stuttgart School, attempts to analyze the possibility of applying to film a more wide-ranging typology than that of index/symbol/icon. But the search for new frameworks goes in even more directions. Brunetta (1974), for instance, explores the birth of narrative in Griffith through the concepts provided by Chomsky's generative linguistics. Lotman (1973), on the other hand, studies the ways a film organizes its signification against the background of a more comprehensive semiotics of culture. But for now we will move on to Worth's contribution.

In "The Development of a Semiotic of Film," published in 1969,[8] Worth approaches some of the problems typical of those years. For instance, he discusses the appropriateness of applying linguistic categories to cinema. He lists the advantages and then exposes the limits of such an operation. He also attempts the definition of the "cinematographic sign" *par excellence,* namely, the frame, which he calls a videme and which he subdivides into units of shooting (cademes) and units of editing (edemes). Yet this and other observations are located in an unusual context. Worth believes that it is necessary to study both the semiotic basis of a film and the way in which it concretely "acquires" meaning and "passes" it from a sender to a receiver. Indeed, this very operative dimension of the phenomenon is, so to speak, its fundamental element. Hence the necessity of this double objective before all else: "to describe a film as a process involving the filmmaker, the film itself, and the film viewer; . . . to define film communication accordingly, so that it relates this process to some of the current research in psychology, anthropology, aesthetics, and linguistics" (284).

In the first part of this essay, Worth actually focuses his attention on the transmission and reception of a film. According to him, the director starts from a conglomerate of interests, preoccupations, beliefs, and feelings that sustain his expressive will (Feeling-Concern). When such a conglomerate decides to communicate, it is embodied in a narrative organism, a structured story (Story Organism). The story, in turn, is made concrete in a series of represented events, constituting the body of the film (Image-Event). The spectator follows the same path, backward. He recognizes the events represented, collects them into a unitary narrative organism, and, on the basis of his experiences and expectations, infers their expressive, initial motivations. Let us add that this second itinerary may trace the first one exactly. When this happens, the reverse path takes place, as in a mirror. But this second path may also take parallel or alternative roads. In this case we will have, rather than specularity, the complementarity of transmission and reception.

According to Worth, focusing on the communicative process described above has some important advantages. On the one hand, the same basic problems of cinematographic semiotics, such as its basic unit or the relationship between filmic and verbal language, find a more adequate solution and are bound to a concrete dynamics without remaining questions of principle. On the other hand, the aim of connecting different kinds of approaches can finally be realized. The communicative process involves many factors and dimensions, thus lending itself to a multiple analysis. We should add that Worth, in the last part of his essay, tries to apply Chomsky's models to cinema. He perceives them as the most appropriate models to use in order to account for the way that communication occurs and for the possible interchange of observations, with interesting results.

Worth's ideas are important because they bring to our attention the communicative dimension, which the first semiotics largely neglected, and because they discover pertinent new aspects. Worth worked hand in hand[9] with a group of psycholinguists who during the same years tried to focus on the kind of information provided by films, the functions of each channel (visual or auditory), the spectator's engagement with images and sounds, the syntactic or semantic models underlying what a film shows, the presence of such phenomena as ambiguity, recursivity, incongruity, redundance, etc. Among them, the name of Calvin Pryluck (Pryluck and Snow 1967, Pryluck 1968) comes to mind. These scholars, too, start from filmic communication, which they make into a multidisciplinary field of study and a specific object of research, capable of generating very productive models.

Let us now move on to Metz. *Langage et cinéma* represents for him a twofold and contradictory stage in his development. It pursues to the end the structuralist theory behind his first studies and it outlines the possibility of going beyond this theoretical stance.

Metz highlights the first aspect through a series of distinctions. He underlines the difference between "concrete objects" and "ideal objects" or between reality taken in its immediate and empirical aspects and reality reconstructed on the basis of systematic surveys from a precise point of view. Similarly, he notices the difference between "unique objects" and "nonsingular objects," that is, between a reality that manifests itself in a single example and a reality that manifests itself in various instances. We have the opposition of the world as it is and the image of the world as drawn by scientists. In the same manner, we have specific events as opposed to moments that are common to many events. These two alternatives help us to understand fully both the realities dealt with by semiologists and the paths they follow.

Realities, first. If we combine the alternatives, we have four cells, respectively: the *text* (something concrete and singular: this given film); the *message* (something concrete but not singular: a certain way to play with lights in a film, which belongs to a specific text, but not only to it); the *code* (something constructed by the scholar, which is nonsingular: the "grammar" of illumination); and the *singular system* (constructed and singular: the way a text is organized, a film is built, all of which is the core of the study). It is important not to confuse these four entities and constantly to keep in mind which one we are talking about.

These alternatives also help to clarify the paths followed by semiotics. As a rule it starts from the text and message and moves toward the code and singular system. In other words, it starts from what "precedes the analyst's intervention" and arrives at something that is "only a form of logic, a principle of coherence" (Metz 1971:79). This path is typical of the disciplines with a structuralist imprint, which try to account for each phenomenon by uncovering its underlying structure and finding in the latter a principle of intelligibility. It should be noted, however, that if one aims to isolate the singular system one is dealing mainly with a film, for the singular system is the structure underlying a single event, a text. If, instead, one aims for the codes, one deals mainly with cinema, which consists of all the elements that any film uses or may use. These two paths are different and should never overlap.

Metz tries to cover both of them. He starts with the codes, which he divides according to their applicability. (Some cinematographic codes are general, common to all films; others are specific, and typical only of certain film groups; some are nonspecific, shared by cinema with other "arts," etc.) Then he lists them (the iconic-visual codes that give meaning to images and that cinema shares with painting and photography; the codes of mechanical duplication that regulate the mechanisms of reproduction of the world, which cinema shares only with photography; the codes of audiovisual composition, concerning the relationship between images and sounds, which cinema has developed on its own, etc.). Metz derives an important idea from this study: *cinematic language* is a two-sided reality. On one side, it is the whole of the specific codes (only that which makes cinema what it is); on the other side, it is the set of all the codes that are used to construct a film (a set that is part of cinema, even if a code may come from elsewhere). In short, it is a hard and pure core and at the same time the aggregation of different elements. Thus, all previous anxieties about defining cinema once and for all, separating it from the other media and arts, cease to exist. Cinema is not characterized by one feature instead of another, but by an ordered set of codes, the central core of which belongs only to cinema, unlike its peripheral areas, which connect it with other media and arts.

After examining codes, Metz moves on to the singular system or the structure that underlies a film. Here his point of view is slightly different. By uncovering the design behind each work, in fact, he realizes that what is at play is not only an ordered system of codes, but also an operation that is performed on them. A singular system derives from the overlapping of elements (space and time organization, acting techniques, lighting procedures) that are ready to clash with one another, to redefine one another, to establish new connections. It is true that they later integrate and give birth to a new unity, but while doing so they also leave behind some areas of friction and disequilibrium. Most importantly, they cannot conceal the tensions and reformulations they went through. In other words, even before being an organic distribution of components, the singular system is above all a product of their intense interaction. Behind its design we perceive the presence of maneuvers that consist of constant moves and countermoves. In order to account for this aspect, it is necessary to place the idea of *writing* next to that of *structure*. In this way, we go back to a "work on the codes, which starts from them, goes against them, and the result of which—temporarily 'frozen'—is the text" (291). Thus, the structuralist theoretical stance gives way to a much more turbulent horizon: the underlying structure counts no more than the dynamics that brought its development and that keep moving it. Concepts such as force, becoming, and energy enter the field and dominate, as we will see, discussions during the years that follow.[10]

9.4.   The Textual Turn

We have presented the work of Wollen, Worth, and Metz as emblematic of the desire felt by semiotics in the 1960s and 1970s to broaden its framework. Wollen referred to Peirce and in so doing widened the notion of sign that was current until then. Worth insisted on the communicative dimension of cinema and thus suggested new elements worthy of attention. Metz thoroughly explored structuralist theory and at the same time introduced elements with which to overcome its limits.

The years we have covered marked the broadening of the discipline; the years that followed marked instead its dispersion. The increasing number of studies led scholars to lose sight of their connections and almost to forget their common roots. The branches of the semiologic tree both spread out and distanced themselves from one another. Furthermore, many of these branches underwent grafts: semiotics developed some of the typical preoccupations of the period, such as the need to "dismantle" the dominant ideology, and came closer to other fields of study, like psychoanalysis and Marxism. From these new contacts emerged new branches of research, each with a direction of its own. Finally, there was a shift in the research field itself. The focus was not only cinema as a whole, but also more restricted areas, such as genres (the western, for instance), or production areas (for example, experimental cinema), or even a particular film. Although the final aim was still to provide general observations, the specificity of the objects under investigation eventually increased the distance between the various analyses.

Thus, the field of study fragmented. Old borders were extended, external areas were added, and new provinces were created. All this led to dispersion.[11] This does not prevent us from recognizing some fundamental trends. In particular, a new form of sensitivity was developing about both procedures and objectives. Such sensitivity, which could already be glimpsed in the works discussed above, characterized what some have called the "second semiotics."[12]

First, we observe a progressive departure from the taxonomic and static stance of structuralism, which was more and more openly and radically criticized. As a result, instead of defining "classes" of signs or codes to which to assign each occurrence, there was a tendency to emphasize trends and orientations, both local and global. Typologies were replaced by lines of force. And, instead of reconstructing the whole design behind a sequence or a film, the point-counterpoint of the various elements was delineated. The idea of *process* replaced that of system.

There was also a progressive redefinition of the object of research. The focus shifted from cinema as a set of possibilities to cinema as a field of realizations. One looked at the modes and conditions of a concrete work rather than at a repertoire of shapes and codified procedures behind every individual choice. Films (or a set of films or parts of a film) became the true center of interest. Indeed, one spoke of the *filmic text,* an idea that we saw emerge already in Metz's work and that was used frequently in these years. Some scholars, still tied to tradition, used it to define an ordered set of auditory and visual signs. Most of them, however, perceiving the increasingly dominant shift of point of view, used it instead to describe the interaction of elements, an open game among components, in short, a *process.* How can we define this process? This question generated many answers.

In the 1970s one usually referred to the process that gives body and shape to a film. The focus was on the "linguistic work" done with its basic materials: the "writing" (another term already used by Metz) dictating its composition; the "production" that originates the film. In a word, the focus was on the *signifying practices* that traverse and drive film. Hence, the idea of text tended to be indifferent to contents: the signifieds did not count, but only the signifiers with which a film was constructed. As a consequence, the idea of text was tendentially indifferent to the fact that this content "changed hands." What mattered was not the transmission of something, but the linguistic operations displayed by a film.

Toward the end of the decade a new trend emerged. One began to refer to the process of *communication* (already anticipated by other scholars, such as Worth). The focus shifted to the conditions that a film should respect in order to be recognized as such, to be interpreted correctly, to find its place in the correct situation, to obtain the required effects, etc. It was important to see how a text can be used in a social context, rather than reconstructing the work that gave form to it; to uncover the basis of its practical operation, rather than giving an overview of the tensions and conflicts running through it; to list its recurrent characteristics, rather than pursuing its latent potential; to define its optimal balances, rather than judging its ability to upset the rules. In short, rather than being "tendentially infinite productivity," as the scholars of the first school called it, the filmic text becomes "the theater of a series of communication strategies," as a slogan of scholars of the second school suggested.

These two schools have, of course, various founders and interpreters. Behind the first we find, clearly, Barthes, Derrida, Kristeva, with their intention of overcoming a merely functional view of language and their interest in the way some works (mainly, but not only, avant-garde) constantly play with their own constitutive elements. Journals such as *Cinéthique* and *Cahiers du Cinéma* played a major role in this, with their decision to "dismantle" the filmic machine and to see what ideological effects it has, and in particular with their will to denounce as merely illusory cinema's pretense to reconstitute reality for us. This background is easily discerned, for instance, in Marie-Claire Ropars' studies and in her notion of "writing." Briefly, Ropars postulates the adoption of a point of view that reverses the traditional perspective. Instead of reconstructing the meaning of a film, it is necessary to break its mechanism, to create friction, to change the order of its pieces. In so doing, we will see that its various components only apparently converge and overlap. Indeed, every structure hides a constant movement, which brings into play elements that have neither a definitive role nor a predetermined place; every structure is a kind of pure field of tensions, where everything is defined by its possibility of clashing with the others. Hence the idea of text as mere difference: it consists of "structural conflicts, which cannot be reduced to a synthesis, which by definition remain active and open" (Ropars 1981:122; see also Ropars 1976). Therefore, films are not tools with which one represents a world or constructs a discourse. Rather, they resemble a kaleidoscope, with its aimless and endless combination and recombination of colors.

The references to the avant-garde and political engagement are, however, not limiting. Even scholars working more inside the semiotic debate refer to a signifying practice as the moment that founds the filmic text. One of them is Bettetini (1975), with his notion of "production of meaning" and "mise-en-scène." His work analyzes a double hypothesis. On the one hand, we find a close connection between the material "fabrication" of a film (the production itself) and the "fabrication" of a film as a signifying object (the "production of meaning"). Both aim to build a world through "mise-en-scène." On the other hand, this two-sided operation is typical of any discourse, either visual or verbal, pictorial or literary. The "mise-en-scène" also takes place on a written page, in a picture, or in a conversation. In other words, Bettetini sees an analogy between the concrete organization of a film and the operations that make it a symbolic object; and this merging of levels is typical of every text. Hence, it is possible to find some common traits and to conduct a widely integrated analysis.

As far as the second research school is concerned, it was initiated by those scholars who, during the decade, attempted the construction of a "Textgrammar" or a "Texttheorie": Petöfi, Van Dijk, Schmidt. Going back to this field of studies, Casetti (1980) suggests defining the filmic text as a coherent, complete, and communicative entity. As in the other discourses that populate our social space, what appears on the screen tends to gravitate around a central theme, to develop between a beginning and an end, and to shed light on a recognizable meaning. This happens thanks both to internal maneuvers, allowing the connection of elements otherwise different from one another (editing comes to mind), and to the contribution provided by the spectators, who give shape and meaning to what they see. Other scholars work in the same direction. Möller (1978), for instance, concentrates on the filmic sequence. He emphasizes both its basic syntactic structures, or how the various elements are connected with one another, and its interpretability, or how the spectators can go over it and grasp it. Starting from Peirce, he believes that the compactness and meaningfulness of a filmic sequence lie in the fact that it stimulates the configurations and procedures of human actions.

This brief overview has sought to summarize the two definitions of filmic text that were developed in the 1970s and referred to by later scholars: the idea of a field of constantly open tensions as opposed to the idea of a compact and functional organism.[13] It is, however, impossible to end this discussion without mentioning a fundamental point: the definition of the notion of text was very much indebted to the circulation of film analyses in the same decade, in particular of the so-called textual analyses. They consist of a minute description of a work (or of a segment thereof, or of many works) and of the discovery of the principle at work behind it. In many cases, the interest in the object itself is paralleled by the desire to challenge the categories in use or even to create new ones. These are not, therefore, mere practical exercises, but also often theoretical explorations. Roger Odin has covered on more than one occasion the trends, methods, and aims of these studies (Odin 1977, 1988). Aumont and Marie mapped them out, too, with special reference to their descriptive procedures and broad themes (Aumont and Marie 1988). Finally, Bellour, one of the pioneers and initiators of these studies, recounted their development in the form of a passionate autobiography ("D'une histoire" in Bellour 1979).[14]

We will return later to textual analyses and their role. For the moment, we will try to improve our description of the general situation. The notion of filmic text (emphasizing the moment of its realization, rather than the set of its virtualities) and the antistructuralist attitude (focusing on the processes, more than on the system) define the fundamental direction of semiotics from the 1970s onward. These ideas strengthen smaller fields of research, four of which we will introduce in the following paragraphs. These include the investigation of the narrative act; exploration of gaze and point of view; study of filmic enunciation; and the attempt to apply to cinema the model of generative grammars.

9.5. New Research Trends: The Act of Narration

The narrative dimension of cinema attracted semiotics from the start. It is not by chance that Metz, in seeking the stable structures that films rely on, started from sequential organization in the cinematographic narrative. A typology derived from his inquiry, the "large syntagmatic category" (Metz 1968), which tried to prove that cinema, too, had a "language" (or at least the outlines of a "language") of its own; this "large syntagmatic category" is destined to be reexamined and modified many times.[15]

Among the modifications, the suggestions made by Gardies, Chateau, and Jost stand out. In a series of contributions devoted to the modern cinema, the authors suggest renewing the "large syntagmatic category" in two ways. To the eight types of sequences isolated by Metz in classical cinema should be added new types, used by experimental cinema. Also, the description of cinema's basic structures should be paired with a study of the way in which each film uses them, even if it does so paradoxically (Chateau and Jost 1979; Gardies 1980; Chateau, Gardies, and Jost 1981). New syntagma are therefore introduced: the thematic sequence (in which a theme, and no action, is illustrated), the parametric series (in which no sequence of events, but a game of variations takes place), and the free series (in which the pure accumulation of events dominates) (Chateau and Jost 1979:105ff.). Above all, the tensions developing among the various elements of the story come into focus (e.g., the visual and auditive clash in Robbe-Grillet's films [Gardies 1980:45ff.]); the study of the dissonances emerging from the alignment of the sequences (with the accompanying crisis of linearity, still in Robbe-Grillet [Chateau and Jost 1979:193ff.]), leading to the discovery of an antinarrative dimension inside the story. As a result, cinematographic narratology comes closer to films and their internal dynamics, thus giving body to the textualist and antistructuralist trends mentioned above.

The birth of a new sensitivity is also evident elsewhere. Let us consider in particular a work by Seymour Chatman (1978) about cinema and literature. The book, clearly influenced by Gérard Genette's contemporary studies, consists of two parts. The first one deals with what is narrated, with the *story*. The story includes events (something happens) and existents (something exists). Events are divided into actions and happenings. Actions involve specific individuals (they are "changes of state brought about by an agent or one that affects a patient": running, speaking, thinking, etc. [Chatman 1978:44]). Happenings have no personalized cause (they are not provoked, but endured: rain, being overwhelmed, shipwreck, etc.). Instead, existents are divided into characters, individualized entities, and settings, simply containers for events. A story arises from the combination of these four kinds of elements: a combination that is both organic—where all the components are required to cooperate—and hierarchical—where some elements prevail over others (the character "makes the story" more than the setting) but within the same class (some events constitute fundamental moments, the so-called nuclei, and some peripheral moments, the satellites). What matters, in any case, is that there should be a basic structure on which the tale relies.

In the second part of the book, Chatman changes both his topic and his stance. The object of his study becomes *discourse* or the way in which the story is concretely narrated. At this level the essential feature is the more or less explicit presence inside the narrative of the addresser and the addressee of the narration. Therefore, we have totally impersonal discourses, which merely describe some facts; discourses that bring subjectivity into play, which either reproduce a stream-of-consciousness or reveal the author's voice; and explicitly self-reflexive discourses, which comment on what is narrated, parody it, etc. What matters, then, is no longer the existence of a supporting structure, but the initiation of a dynamic between the addresser and the addressee of the narrative. We are dealing with a set of moves, rather than with a coordinated series of components, with an orientation, more than with a comprehensive design.

Therefore Chatman, too, in moving from the first to the second part of his book, begins to follow the new research trends. He leaves room for the texts and their internal dynamics. Of course, his field of research is different from Chateau, Gardies, and Jost's: he focuses on classic cinema (and literature) as opposed to avant-garde cinema. Similarly, he also focuses on different processes: the "exchange" between the addresser and addressee of the film (or the book), as opposed to the reformulation and subversion of the preexisting codes. In both cases, however, the accent moves from the existence of general characteristics transcending isolated realizations (*narrativity*) to the object in which these characteristics are embodied (the *narrative*) and, above all, to the act giving shape to this object (*narration*).

Narration is the great research theme from the end of the 1970s onward.

Let us examine a far-reaching contribution by Nick Browne, who follows the path indicated by Chatman.[16] Browne, too, believes that the study of the story, that is, "the actions, speech, and perceptions of the character," must function as part of the study of "the set of rhetorical mechanisms through which the narrator presents the story to the spectator" (Browne 1982:58). In order to understand how the sender addresses a receiver it is not necessary to refer to either a director's psychology or the audience's sociology. It is enough to look at the way in which the protagonists of the communication are inscribed in the object communicated through the presence of suggestions, stances taken, comments, perhaps through a character whose role is that of the sender's alter ego. Hence the dominant idea of Browne's book: it is possible to "read a story" as though it represented in symbolic form the exchange that takes place between directors and their audiences.

Through an analysis of a sequence from *Stagecoach,* Chapter 1 considers the role of the spectator. Browne observes that the scene of the meal at Dry Fork Station is constructed around a double series of images: on the one hand, we have objective shots of a group of characters, including Lucy; on the other hand, we have shots that are almost subjective, showing Lucy's gaze directed at Dallas and Ringo. As a result, the two female characters receive two very different treatments. Lucy is both a character in action (objective shots) and the source of a gaze (her subjective shots); Dallas, instead, is only the object of other people's gazes (Lucy's subjective shots). The audience should immediately identify with Lucy, who lends the audience her eyes; instead, the film generates a clear sympathy for Dallas. This happens because the "spectator's position" is determined by at least two elements: the presence of someone or something "guiding" his perception of the events represented and what appears on the screen, the presence of which evokes certain values and elicits a greater or lesser adherence to them. Hence the spectator's capacity for double identification, with a gaze (identifying with the camera or an observing character) and with the object of a gaze (accepting or rejecting what appears on the screen). In *Stagecoach* it is clear that there is a conflict between these two forms of identification. The audience does not know whether it should take sides with Lucy or with Dallas, each the center of one form of identification. A reading of the film slowly solves the problem by restructuring one and gradually confirming the other.

It is clear that the spectator's options are determined by the strategies adopted by the narrator. "The spectator's place . . . is a construction of the text which is ultimately the product of the narrator's disposition towards the tale" (11). Appropriately, the second chapter is devoted to the narrator. How does his role unfold in a film? A narrator must first of all exhibit a character's experience and comment on it. Exhibiting experience means illustrating both concrete behaviors (acting) and cognitive behaviors (seeing, imagining, etc.). The character must be seen moving in the world and perceiving the world.[17] Commenting on experience means instead constructing a standpoint from which to judge it. The characters are always presented from a certain point of view, now favorable, now unfavorable. Similarly, the narrator establishes a relationship with the audience. While following and judging the characters, the narrator provides the spectator with ideas both on the structure of the narrated events and on how to interpret them. The narrator places all elements on the screen and tells us how to handle them. This process leads the narrator to a position of simultaneous solidarity with and distance from the story he is telling. We understand his position from what he shows us and from what he thinks, even "against" what he shows. In short, "the narrator is associated with the exhibition of images but is, ambiguously, both *in* and *behind* them. He takes a position in and on the story" (42). Browne confirms this with his study of *The Thirty-nine Steps*.

Chapter 3 deals with the characters. Besides acting on their own, they also function as mediators between narrator and spectator. They both reveal the narrator's attitude toward the narrated material and guide the spectator's perception of the story. Often this mediation is obvious (think of the characters functioning as "critical conscience" or "onstage interpreters" of what happens, obvious alter egos of the author or the spectator). In other cases, especially in modern stories, this same mediation is hidden (for instance, in *Au hasard, Balthazar,* the protagonist is nonhuman). The fact remains that characters "bridge" the exchange between the sender and the receiver of the tale.

Here we will interrupt this overview of narratological studies.[18] We will return to this theme later on, in particular when dealing with the work by Jost and Gaudreault. The two scholars both develop and broaden the horizons of the ideas we have just illustrated. Now we will move on to another field of study, dealing with the way in which the filmic narrative influences the gaze.

9.6.   New Research Trends: The Construction of Point of View

Although still interested in the filmic text and its dynamics, this area of study does not focus on the act of narration itself. With the appearance onscreen of the addressee and addresser of the story, it focuses instead on the construction of a point of view capable of both "anchoring" and giving a certain "slant" to the story. A dynamics is established between seer and seen, bodies and eyes, screen and theater, and so on.

This is neither an innovative theme (cinema has always presented itself as the field of the gaze) nor exclusively the object of semiotics (in these same years other disciplines, such as psychoanalysis of cinema and feminist film theory, were deeply interested in this topic). We will limit ourselves to mentioning two works that give an idea of this field of study. *Mindscreen* (Kawin 1978) is explicitly connected with narratological studies. The opening question is "Who narrates a film?" The response sheds light on at least four ways in which images and sounds suggest an explicit "source." The narrator may manifest himself first of all through the use of subjective shots. While watching film we literally "share" eyes with someone who "shoots" reality. But the narrator also affirms his presence by introducing a particular point of view that runs through the scene. While watching film we "share" the emphasis on a specific detail. Above all, the narrator can signal his presence by constructing a "consciousness" that filters all events. While watching film, we "share" the author's sensitivity or imagination, aligning ourselves with his "mental eye." Finally, the narrator may emerge through the process of self-reference: while watching film we "share" the author's sense of self. Additional cases could be defined, connected with the auditory component. An example of this is the voice-over, which leads us to follow film while "sharing" the words of the person who, beyond the scene, introduces or comments on the facts.

What all these ways of suggesting the presence of the narrator have in common is that they "conjugate" the film in the *first person*. There is an "I" that guides images and sounds. There are also ways to conjugate a film in the *second person,* as in the films slanted toward the spectator's point of view (e.g., propaganda films), and ways to conjugate a film in the *third person,* by presenting the events in a neutral and anonymous way. Films in the first person, however, have the advantage of making clear the presence of a *point of view* that guides the narration. Even better, they manage to embody a *subjectivity* that permeates both images and sounds. The storyteller leaves his mark on his tale. He offers both a story and himself as its sender.

The problem of the point of view and of subjectivity reappears in a profound study by Branigan (1984). The book is about subjective shots, that is, those shots in which onscreen reality is seen through a character's eyes. Branigan develops his analysis in various directions. First, he tries to define the notion of subject more adequately, whether that subject is a film's author, a spectator, an internal narrator, or an acting character. He perceives subjectivity as a type of position that derives from the fact of presenting or following a story. Hence the reference to the presence of a point of view: what is narrated is always seen from a certain perspective. It is perceived by someone (point of view as perception), felt (point of view as attitude), filtered (point of view as identification with an observer), said (point of view as language used), or created as an effect of following the story (point of view as a logic of reading). In this picture, the subjective shot is but one of many ways of constructing the point of view. Its protagonist is the character on the scene, ready to lend his eyes to the camera and the spectator.

In order to be subjective a shot must follow some rules. Its canonical structure requires two frames, one that represents someone who is looking (*point/glance*), the other representing the object of this gaze (*point/object*), and a relationship of temporal simultaneity or continuity between them. Starting from this basic structure, it is possible to define different kinds of subjective shots or point of view shots. The simplest is the one that mobilizes the axis of perception (*perceptual point of view shot*): the object is presented exactly as it appears to the character's *eye*. The second frame will then have to be taken from the exact point where the observer is placed on the scene in the first frame and provide a normal representation of the object. This simply simulates the action of "seeing" on the part of an onscreen witness. Its possible developments are the "closed" point of view shot (if A is the seer and B is the seen, the sequence is A-B-A); the delayed or suspended point of view shot (B arrives after the insertion of other frames); the "open" subjective shot (B never comes); the multiple point of view shot (A-B-C-B-D-B . . .).

In addition to the subjective shots through which an onscreen observer confirms the presence of an object, there are others that broaden the relationship between the two. Some shots present what an observer sees, but not from the exact place where he stands: for instance, they may appear in a mirror at which we know the character is looking or be an object that we know belongs in his field of vision (*character reflection*). Here we no longer have a point of view shot in the literal sense (Branigan speaks of *metaphorical point of view*). Yet the awareness that the object is seen by a character "subjectifies" the shot. In the opposite case, a shot shows something the observers see only in their minds. These are either altered perceptions or imagination. Hallucinations or dreams illustrate this case (*character projection*).

After this extremely accurate study of the structure, typology, and variations of the point of view shot, Branigan inserts a historical section, in which he studies various films of the modern age, in particular, Fellini's *8½* and Oshima's *Tokyo Senso Sengo Hiwa*. The book concludes with a long metatheoretical section, in which the author presents his approach and compares it with other views of narration and representation and clarifies the rationalist orientation of his work. A film takes shape when the spectator "reconstructs" it on the basis of both the directions coming from the screen and his own mental schemes. In other words, the film is not a *given,* but the result of a real *process.*

Branigan's work has many merits. He deals with a theme of increasing importance, the forms of the gaze in cinema,[19] giving it both a general frame and a strict formalization. Further, in his final pages, he combines semiotics and cognitive psychology, indicating a path that would be increasingly followed. We should also add that studies on the point of view would continue, often with references to Branigan, although with different slants. Among these works are those by Dagrada (who is close to Eco's semiotics) or Fontanille (who follows Greimas) and, above all, Jost (who follows Genette).[20] And we find the point of view once again in another field characterizing the "second semiotics," in considerations of cinematographic enunciation.

9.7. New Research Trends: The Role of Enunciation

This research area emerged at the end of the 1970s and profoundly marked the entire following decade. Here we will merely touch upon it, because we will talk about it in more detail when we reconstruct the major tendencies of the second half of the 1980s. Yet we should also keep in mind that the interest still lies in the text and its dynamics. In fact, the term *enunciation* defines the set of operations that give body, so to speak, to the linguistic object. Scholars focus on the "act" through which someone uses language's possibilities to create discourse or the "shift" from virtuality to manifestation. In our case, enunciation is what, starting from cinema's intrinsic potentialities, allows a film to take form and manifest itself: to present itself as *text,* as *this* specific text, and as this specific text in this specific *situation.*

The echo of ideas that we have already encountered is obvious, ideas like "signifying practice" and "writing." The focus shifts, however. The theory of enunciation sheds light on the formation of the text, rather than on the perennial instability to which it is doomed because of the combination and recombination of its elements. Moreover, the theory of enunciation shows that texts are never the anonymous product of language functioning by itself, but are always "from someone," "toward someone," "of a certain time," and "in a certain place." Finally, the theory of enunciation shows that texts are never guiltily neutral or transparent, but always retain a trace of the gesture that gave them birth. Therefore, attention shifts to the way in which the filmic text is delineated, rooted, and self-referential. Instead of describing the work as something that "gets lost" in the play of its signifiers (as the theorists of "writing" had done), the theory of enunciation highlights a positive and complex movement.

The three main centers of interest we have just outlined (the filmic text's *construction, placement,* and possible *self-referentiality*) are the guidelines for the contributions of the theory of enunciation. This explains the research on point of view, understood as the mechanism that connects films to the moment when "someone" looked at the world and filmed it, and when "someone else" watched it again, on the screen (Aumont 1983; Casetti 1986). This explains the studies concerning the way in which filmic gazes and voices connect a "source" and a "destination" (Collins 1979; Jost 1983; Simon 1983; Bettetini 1984). This also explains the studies of the ways in which verbal and visual enunciations are related (Marie and Vanoye 1983); of the ways of constructing the diegetic world (Chateau 1983); of the presence of shifters even in films, that is, of signs that refer to the communicative situation itself (Simon 1978 and 1981; Bettetini 1979; Casetti 1986; Metz 1991 also devotes a long discussion to this point). The list could go on. We will come back to this trend later, when we compare the results of the "second semiotics" with other research trends, in order to present a set that profoundly marked the 1980s.

9.8. New Research Trends: Generative Models

This group of inquiries starts from the underlying syntactic or semantic structures and focuses on how a film takes shape. The problem here is similar to that of the theory of enunciation, but the approach is different. The scholars of that theory attempted to see how a text develops from a group of virtualities; here, instead, they emphasized that a text realizes a sort of latent communicative project. The theory of enunciation focused on how, in taking shape, a text is rooted in a given situation and reflects the mechanisms that gave birth to it; here, instead, scholars focus on how a text, in realizing this project, organizes the flux of information. Within this area we find attempts to apply to cinema the models of generative-transformational grammar. What appears on the screen is seen as deriving from the progressive rewriting of elementary structures, which are slowly clothed with images and sounds. A sequence like "shooting man/falling man" is "generated" by later transformations of an "agent/action/patient" structure, which elsewhere could also have a linguistic manifestation ("John opened fire on Jim") or a different cinematographic manifestation ("MS man/BCU gun/MS second man/LS environment . . .").

Among the studies moving in this direction, we should mention Carroll 1980, Möller 1986, Chateau 1986, and, above all, Colin 1985. Colin gives strong reasons for applying generative-transformational linguistics to cinema. There is no substantial difference between the mechanisms of a film and those of a natural language; an audiovisual representation is constructed and interpreted much as is a verbal sentence. In both cases, "ideational content" is clothed either with images and sounds (in a film) or with words (in a novel). When the form of the manifestation changes, neither the basic meaning nor the logic that brings it to the surface changes. Colin supports his hypothesis with many examples, comparing written and visual texts, fictional and documentary films, etc. Moreover, he studies the communicative dynamics that develop on the surface of a text: the way in which the underlying structure manifests itself, emphasizes some aspects and obscures others, takes some facts for granted and insists on others, anticipates some elements and delays others. A text literally modulates the information. In particular, the tension between what is said or shown and what is about to be said or shown is essential. In a film, we need to examine the sequence of the frames or the direction given to the camera movements. Expectations, surprises, and reinterpretations are strictly dependent on this tension.

9.9.   Semiotics and Postsemiotics

In the preceding pages we have given an overview of four main areas of study: the first deals with the act of storytelling as it emerges in narrative; the second underscores the role of the point of view in "slanting" a film toward either pole of communication; the third focuses on the formation and situation of a film; the last reconstructs the shift from underlying schemes to discursive manifestation. These four ways account for the *dynamics* present in a *filmic text*. Yet this brief overview has forced us to use ellipses and cross-references. In that it focuses on the text and its dynamics, the "second semiotics" is an open field, characterized by centrifugal movement. Interests broaden, and the search for new sources of inspiration emerges, as does the wish to compare itself with other disciplines. Consequently, we have a kind of genetic mutation. Style becomes less rigid, but also less rigorous; more agile, but also more eclectic. Disciplinary limits decrease; methods fade into a more carefree and less controlled attitude. Semiotics itself changes, if not into antisemiotics, into postsemiotics. Here ideas, themes, even the obsessions of the previous discipline are studied and delineated; and scholars whose formation is rooted in the ideas discussed above work side by side with scholars attempting new combinations. It is thus inevitable that we will return later to this field of study, which is rich because of its tradition and because of the deviations that make it new.

10 PSYCHOANALYSIS OF CINEMA

10.1. Cinema on the [Analyst's] Couch

The fourth major field of inquiry that can be related to methodological theories is psychoanalysis. Some might find this statement incorrect, because psychoanalysis is not characterized by a "method" in the same way as the other disciplines. At times it even refuses to be defined as a "discipline." Without delving into this, it is important to note that the psychoanalysis of cinema has generally behaved like any other scientific approach, establishing criteria of pertinence, interpreting data, elaborating models, and seeking verifications of its postulates. Of course, some works exhibit a vaguer theoretical stance, especially when references to Freud, Jung, or Lacan are a mere borrowing of keywords. And other works reveal the desire for a comprehensive explanation over the need for systematic assessments. This was in accordance with the tendency in the 1970s to turn to psychoanalysis in order to respond to fundamental questions, rather than using it to explain how cinema functions. This very fact defines this approach not as antimethodological, but as a moment of confrontation between the methodological and the postmethodological. In the 1970s, in fact, psychoanalysis was one of the pivotal points that led from one kind of sensibility to another. For this reason, we have chosen to discuss it here, at the end of our overview of the theories of the second generation, as both the ideal closure of an experience and the ideal start of a new paradigm.

Keeping these facts in mind, we can draw a map of the various contributions of the psychoanalysis of cinema.[1] If we look at the entirety of postwar contributions, three recurrent paths emerge. We will not analyze in detail the first and most frequented of them, which views psychoanalysis as a critical method. It either prepares an inventory of the signs present in a given film or systematically reviews its discursive procedures, in order to grasp something hidden or just below the evident surface, something that defines a deeper, more complete, and authentic "truth." In short, it reconstructs what a film says without explicitly meaning to, the revealing symptoms, what is repressed that has an effect. This takes place in a spontaneous extension of the analyst's couch: the director becomes the patient, the film the discussion, and the critic (but also the astute spectator) the analyst.

Two examples of this procedure (very different in terms of quality) are the books by Fernandez (1975) on Eisenstein and Spoto (1979) on Hitchcock. In both cases the authors look for "traumas" that mark the childhoods of the respective directors, generating certain "complexes" that are reflected in their works by recurrent themes or figures. We do not intend to comment on this use of psychoanalysis (at times very approximate, even if it was originally authorized by Freud himself). After all, as already suggested, it relates more to the theory of criticism than to the theory of cinema.

The second path belongs more to our field of investigation. Instead of using films as "clinical material," it examines them in themselves, in order to emphasize features of film that are pertinent to psychoanalysis. In particular, it focuses on the analogies between films and products of our unconscious (such as dreams), in order to find out if the mechanisms of the unconscious can explain how movies work. In this case, it is not filmmakers who are analyzed through their work, but cinema itself, through its manifestations, that, so to speak, lies on the analyst's sofa. But we are about to cover this terrain more carefully.

10.2. Films and Dreams: Recollections and Overlappings

Scholars had noticed from the very start the similarity between films and dreams. After the war this theme reemerged with filmology, following the latter's systematic analysis of the *cinematographic situation*. Lebovici presents it organically in "Psychanalyse et cinéma." The first aim of this essay is to present film as a means of expression that is very close to oneiric thought. Many features seem to prove this, especially their common visual character. Just like cinematographic language, "a dream as a whole is almost exclusively visual"

(Lebovici 1949:50). They also share the possibility of great freedom of movement. "As in dreams, filmic images are united neither by temporal bonds nor by strong spatial connections" (50). Both lack a rigid principle of causality. Just like oneiric images, filmic sequences proceed on the basis of "relationships of contiguity and imagination" more than on the basis of logical relationships. There is even the presence of a general coincidence of "grammar." "Are such technical procedures as fade or tracking shots not the same as those a dreamer uses?" (50). Finally, they both recur to suggestiveness. As with dream images, with film images "nothing is explicit; they only suggest." His conclusion is that "all classical kinds of films offer the spectator very oneiric material" (50).

Starting from this point, Lebovici pursues a second aim: showing that the film spectator, given the situation he is in, can be compared to the dreamer. Again, there seems to be evidence of this. First, the conditions of the projection—the dark theater, the isolation of the bodies, the psychological abandon, the unreality of the images—are similar to those characterizing sleep. Besides, films induce an empathy, far from mere passivity, and closer to "a certain state of relaxed communion" (53) similar to the dreamer's relationship with his dreams. Finally, the slight dizziness with which the spectator leaves the cinema is "analogous to the semi-sleep of the dreamer who refuses to leave his dreams and wishes to prolong the various episodes in a rêverie" (54). We should also add to this list the identification processes (which lead the spectator to identify with a character) and the projection processes (which lead the spectator to lend his problems to those living on the screen). In short, real transfers take place with the filmic spectacle. This confirms not only the close relationship between films and dreams ("a film is a dream and material for dreams"), but also the idea that there is some continuity between the two that makes film directly involve our psychic life: because of the way in which film is usually presented to us, the experience to which it invites us, the dynamics it originates (in particular, the way in which it "flatters narcissism, in the mythological sense of the word" [54]).

We have used Lebovici as an example, but there are many scholars who adhere to this line of research. Cesare Musatti, in an essay published at the same time as the one mentioned above and in the same journal, takes up the comparison between films and dreams and notes how the representations elaborated by each have a peculiar "appearance of reality," which makes them both a copy of and something different from life. This characteristic of both cinematographic and oneiric images at least partially explains why it is so easy to transfer material back and forth between films and dreams. Often, in fact, passages from a film end up in our nocturnal reelaborations. If we add that many clinical cases present "cinema phobias" due to excessive identification it is understandable that psychoanalysis should find it legitimate to work on cinema, which is based on mechanisms fully involving the psychic universe.[2]

These problems also recur outside the field of filmology. At times they develop out of a more general study of the relationship between oneiric and artistic productions. In this case, the aim is to shed light on the psychic processes behind both.[3] At other times it is connected to studies on the representation of dreams and dreamers in films: here the aim is to discover, through such presences, the roots of the fascination exercised by the cinema.[4] Finally, these problems often—at least recently—merge with a third path along which psychoanalysis's interest in cinema developed.

10.3. Cinema and the Psychic Apparatus: An Identity of Function?

This path seems to be a radicalization of the preceding itineraries. Cinema is seen as directly modeled on our psychic apparatus. Rather than being a means to reach certain secret nodes or the equivalent of certain unconscious manifestations, cinema emerges as a phenomenon that extends and encompasses the structures and dynamics that are the object of psychoanalysis. Therefore, the cinematographic situation reintroduces key moments that either are fundamental for the development of the self or give rise to neuroses and psychoses. Thus, the procedures behind films reproduce the mechanisms that construct dreams, mental lapses, and hallucinations. Similarly, through some of cinema's recurrent images, such as the double, the mirror, the mask, or, at a stylistic level, shot/reverse shot, where seer and seen stand in opposition, the unconscious of cinema itself can be discerned. As a result, psychoanalysis is no longer the study of some aspects of the cinematic phenomenon, but the key to an understanding of its basis and its functioning.

In order to better frame this kind of study, it is necessary to recall its context. First, it developed in the early 1970s, when psychoanalysis was extremely successful. There was great interest in the mechanisms behind ideologies, particularly in the way in which subjects represent themselves and their social experience. In this context, psychoanalysis appeared to be the most appropriate instrument for analyzing the dynamics underlying such representations and for uncovering their background and roots. Hence a double effect: on the one hand, the wide "diffusion" of psychoanalysis, which broadened the range both of its interests and of its concepts (often by scholars who did not belong "professionally" to the field); on the other hand, an "integral" use of psychoanalysis, increasingly guiding the study of all forms of representation and providing models that somehow revealed its foundations (in order to denounce its ideological implications).

Second, this path developed under the banner of Lacan's rereading of Freud: this explains both the wish to connect psychic and linguistic phenomena and the explicitly antipositivistic style of the inquiry. Without wishing to make illicit and questionable syntheses, we should recall both Lacan's suggestion that the unconscious is structured just like a language and the idea that this structure is predicated upon differences and subtractions. Like any structure, it consists of a set of relationships that define its elements through opposition. Like any signifying structure, it needs a nonpresence, because each sign may acquire value only insofar as it "stands for" or "is a substitute for" something that is actually absent. In short, like linguistic structure, psychic structure is defined through opposition and lack (represented by the phallus and fear of castration). Such differentiality and subtraction may either be accepted and made to act or hidden and compensated for. It is typical of the *imaginary register* to create an impression of illusory fullness. One can think of those (mental, iconic, etc.) representations that seem to offer us a world, while in reality they deprive us of it, that give the subject the impression of controlling the game, while actually determining his position and actions. Meanwhile, it is typical of the *symbolic order* to leave things wide open. The content of representations appears as the effect of a constant recombining of the signifiers (like a pure *trompe-l'oeil*). The subject emerges as an entity that is neither outside, nor above, but inside the chain of discourse (like a signifier among signifiers).

This is the background of this research. It can easily be grasped in the studies by Jean-Pierre Oudart and Jean-Louis Baudry, who analyze the role that cinema assigns to the spectator.

Oudart published an essay of great consequence in *Cahiers du Cinéma*. He introduces Lacan's notion of *suture,* which defines "the subject's relationship with the chain of his discourse." For an understanding of how it works at the movies, it is necessary to start from the fact that every scene presented on the screen extends itself beyond the ideal "fourth wall" that should enclose it, into a hypothetical space that we never perceive but from which the scene is perceived: an invisible field, a field of Absence, corresponds to every visible field. The spectator or, rather, his imaginary image is situated in this field. Oudart refers to the spectator who occupies the missing field as the "Absent One." What appears on the screen can therefore be considered the signifier of this Absence and of this Absent, and its presence reminds us of what is not there. What is lacking gives it its essence. In other words, "the image has access to the order of the signifier" (Oudart 1969a: 37) in relationship to the Absence. The signifiers a film provides can gradually connect and unite, giving rise to a "signifying whole" that continues to be pervaded by a feeling of subtraction, to be affected by the Absence. Let us look at the shot/reverse shot, that very peculiar procedure, so typical of cinema. What happens when two shots "face each other"? On the one hand, as usual, an invisible area, a lack, emerges; on the other hand, however, at least in the second shot, a visible someone or something also intervenes, situated in this same zone and thus eliminating the invisibility, the lack. In short, the shot/reverse shot creates an empty space and fills it at once. In the space of the Absent, then, a nonpresence blends and overlaps with a presence. It becomes an imaginary filmic space, allowing the shots to echo, to expand toward someone or something that somehow "is there"; thus, rather than the signifier of a lack, it becomes a segment of an accessible world, a momentary glimpse of the signified.

The *suture* is the very "abolition of the Absent and its resurrection as something else" (38). It is the transformation of an empty cell into a populated, imaginary space that connects the shots both backward (finding a new position for the fragment just seen) and forward (creating expectation for the new fragment). In other words, it is a game through which the signifying chain posits an Absence, converts and exploits it in order to fuse itself and close in on itself. It is a game that rotates around the space of a subject–spectator that is posited by the movie as an Absent, but also reintroduced as an element that guarantees the movie's fluidity and fullness. Let us add that such a game is not only connected to the shot/reverse shot, but starts every time the film works on its shots as if they were portions of an actual, coherent world (thus overcoming the logic of the meaningful whole). Let us also add that not all films work this way. Such authors as Bresson or Lang seem to "dismantle" this mechanism, as though to show its operations bared.

Oudart returns twice to the suture theme: first, in a work published soon after the previous one (1969b), where he insists on the terms of the problem and exemplifies the two possible cinematographic practices it can initiate; then in a later work (1971) where he analyzes the "reality effect" ("effet du réalité") deriving from a "sutured" representation (the scene seems to "hold" just like the work) and its opposition to an "effect of the real" ("effet du réel"; things acquire a "texture" of their own that makes them "be there" regardless of the rest). Let us now move on to another author, whose work still revolves around the role of the spectator as subject and the dynamics at work around him.

We are referring to two essays by Jean-Louis Baudry respectively in *Cinéthique* (7–8, 1970) and in *Communications* (23, 1975) and published in a later work (Baudry 1978).[5] The earlier essay has a very broad scope (therefore we will need to come back to it later); it tries to identify the ideological effect of the cinematographic "machine" as such, regardless of the content presented by a film. Such effects gravitate around two phenomena: the hiding of the work that makes reality a cinematographic representation and the construction of a transcendental subject upon which the spectator can rely. As far as the first phenomenon is concerned, let us consider how the camera transcribes reality into a series of frames lacking both light and movement in themselves and how the projector, by reintroducing light and movement, transforms these frames into an image that, on the screen, has the same appearance as reality. When such passages are made clear, they produce an effect of knowledge; when they are hidden, they produce an ideological surplus value, just as hiding the productive process of some good leads to an economic surplus value. Needless to say, the cinematographic "machine" seems to have been created in order to follow the latter path. As far as the second phenomenon is concerned, it is also rooted in the way in which the apparatus works. The camera is a direct heir of the "camera obscura" of the 1400s, and it reintroduces the idea of a space that is organized according to a central perspective. The origin of the lines of perspective coincides with the observer's eye, which thus both dominates reality (with a gaze that literally models the world) and departs from it (with the vanishing point on the same axis). Hence, the observer can constitute a transcendental subject. Yet again, this is reinforced through the way in which the projection is organized. The screen, the theater, and the seats seem to reintroduce the mechanism behind Lacan's mirror phase, during which a child, between eight and eighteen months of age, creates a first version of his "ego" as an imaginary construct. The dark theater encourages extreme visual concentration; the seats we sink into put us in a state of reduced motor activity; above all, the screen takes us to the mirror of our childhood, where we saw the reflection of a body (ours) and recognized ourselves in the features of an "other."

This is the core of the matter: the spectator constructs himself as a subject because cinema reproduces an essential phase of the formation of the "ego"; watching pictures slowly compose themselves until they emerge as a whole, we follow the same path through which we saw ourselves whole and outside ourselves. It is clear, therefore, that the spectator should identify both with the actor on the screen (a projection of the spectator's ego) and with those people who give them life, that is, with the ego of which they are a projection. The identification always takes place with a *subject,* whether diegetic or extradiegetic, with an entity that roots its own identity in the ego (with the ideological consequences that this entails). In any case, cinema may well emerge as some sort of substitute psychic apparatus. To make the connection even more explicit, the set of the elements at stake in the "cinematographic situation" may be simply called an *apparatus* or *device.*[6] Baudry returns to the theme of the cinematographic apparatus in his essay published in *Communications.* Here he expands his comparison to the situation described by Plato in the famous myth of the cave. The analogies between the elements evoked by Plato and those at play during the projection are evident (the prisoners, chained to their seat; the fire behind them; the shadows, reproducing the outlines of things; the back of the cave, where the shadows are projected, etc.). Similarly, there are analogies with the elements at work in our dreams (for instance, the peculiar impression of the reality of the oneiric images). The problem is then what kind of *desire* emerges from these situations. Fundamentally, it is a desire for perception and representation; even better, it is a desire to experience a hallucinatory reality or a more-than-real reality (the product of the overlapping of perception and representation). Cinema acquires in a very concrete way what a dream provides us with in a physiological manner, so to speak, and what Plato tells us in the form of a myth. It provides us with "a perception with the features of a representation, but which appears as a perception." Along this path, it allows us to face something that has both a hallucinatory nature and an extraordinary impression of reality. In this sense, cinema is really an auxiliary psychic device: it is a "simulation machine" that constitutes us as subjects and satisfies our most deeply rooted desires.

Oudart's and Baudry's work was continued, redefined, and integrated by many other scholars. We are not going to analyze in detail the intense debate that ensued. We will, however, return, in other contexts, to some of these essays. Now, instead, we will move on to another branch of these studies, which is contemporary with and connected to the one presented above.

10.4. Filmic Processes and Images

The close relationship between cinema and our psychic life emerges not only from the way in which a subject is modeled, but also from the trends and themes that films repeatedly introduce. Within what we identified as the third area of research, another line of inquiry is intertwined with the previous one and yet partially differs from it. Its focus is on the filmic text, more than on the screen/theater/spectator complex. Its objects are the *signification* processes that films activate and the images they elaborate, more than the cinematographic device.

An example of this trend comes from Thierry Kuntzel. In a series of innovative works, he repeatedly introduces a basic idea: that the making of a film relies on the same mechanisms that allow the making of a dream. Hence the notion of *film work,* modeled exactly on the notion of *dream work.* In both cases we are dealing with a game of reprises, transformations, new beginnings, and camouflage that takes place either between a latent content and the manifest dream or between two states, two levels, or two parts of a film.

Kuntzel increasingly clarifies his hypothesis. For instance, in a work on a short, experimental cartoon (Kuntzel 1973), he observes that a film is two different things at the same time: a celluloid strip running through a projector and a work coming to life on the screen. In the shift from one stage to the other the acquisition of movement takes place, together with the erasure of the isolated frames. The latter, however, continue to act, but tacitly. The situation can be summarized as follows: when the film runs through the projector, it both "unwinds" and "moves out of range" (the French *défilement* has both meanings). In short, the *film work* is first of all this shift from one stage to the other, with its gains and losses, or, in the language of psychoanalysis, with its repressions and its residues. We need to add, however, that the film work also affects the development, the increasing unfolding of the text. Two great processes emerge at this level, bringing us back to the dream work: condensation and displacement. The former takes place, for instance, in Lang's *M,* when the various threatening signs presented at the beginning of the film clot together, so to speak, in the killer's shadow (Kuntzel 1972 : 36). The latter can be seen, for example, in Schoedsack's and Pichel's *The Most Dangerous Game,* when the various themes systematically presented at the beginning (such as the sickness or the sharks) are scattered and disguised throughout the narrative (Kuntzel 1975a [1980]: 55).

These last remarks allow us both to better understand how the *film work* develops and to see to what it is connected. Its counterparts are the *images,* such as the shadow, the sick man, the shark, which emerge from the text's surface and tie it to recurrent reference points. We are not dealing with fixed symbols defining a psychic condition, but with elements that structure the signifying chain and indicate the dynamics that move it. It cannot be said too often that images have to do with the signification process of a text; even before its signifieds, they have to do with its significance. Some of these images, such as the sick man or the shark, are typical of the film in which they appear. Others, such as the door or the book—still in *The Most Dangerous Game*—seem to have a wider value. Others still, such as the double or the mirror, seem to take us back to the *film work* as such, to its constitution as an audiovisual text.

Hence, we can return to the *cinematographic apparatus.* By letting us perceive the work behind a film, the last two images also define the components of the "machine." Indeed, as we are still dealing with something close to the psychic apparatus, they also uncover more general facts. Let us once again take an example from *The Most Dangerous Game,* the sequence where Eva and Rainsford try to escape Zaroff by entering a dark cave and observe with apprehension, from inside, the illuminated entrance. Zaroff appears in the light, calls the two fugitives, and shoots an arrow, without hurting them. This situation reminds us both of the film's projection and of the "primitive scene" that in some ways cinema reactivates. Eva and Rainsford stand in the position of the spectators, who watch the screen, the only point of light in a dark theater. Their different attitudes also (the woman fears the imminent danger, the man does not) replicate the indecisiveness of the spectator, who remains suspended between having empathy with and keeping himself detached from the spectacle. Finally, the use of subjective shots, by making the spectator see exactly what the characters see, further confirms this analogy. As a consequence, however, the flesh-and-blood spectator can, in turn, see the characters through whose eyes he observes the onscreen events. Therefore, he remains "one step behind" the characters representing him in the film. He finds himself in the position of Melanie Klein's Grete, who can spy on her parents better than her little brother can, because she stands behind him and a little farther back. Zaroff, too, confirms these analogies. He is the image of what appears on the screen, which presents itself without being able to see. And he is the image of the pair of parents, who act without even suspecting that they are being spied on. The sequence we just analyzed, in other words, has a double and combined value. It presents a

global device: in an enclosed scene (the space between the trees and the entrance to the cave, the bed), some actors are seen who do not see (Zaroff, the pair of parents); in another scene, separated from the former by a stage (the entrance to the cave, the posts of the bed), there is a spectator, who watches—or tries to watch—the "primitive" scene (Rainsford and Eva, the little brother) and who, in turn, is watched by another spectator (Grete, the spectator of *The Most Dangerous Game*). This latter spectator gains a divine knowledge by watching the two scenes at the same time, and often seeing *better* than the former spectator, who belongs to the scene, and is hiding. (Kuntzel 1975b:96–97) [7]

Of course, Kuntzel's works touch upon other problems as well. In particular, he focuses on the process of analysis itself, which he views as participating in, rather than remaining outside, the work of signification. Hence, his writing often either mimes the film's dynamics or willingly resorts to such devices as puns, through which one meaning emerges from (and is hidden behind) another. Such attention to the modes and reasons behind an analysis, together with a study of the processes and images at work in cinema, also characterizes the work of the scholar who perhaps best represents the research trend under investigation in this chapter: Raymond Bellour.

Between the late 1960s and the late 1970s Bellour wrote a series of precise analyses mainly of American movies, especially by Hitchcock, Lang, and Minnelli, which he later collected in one volume (1979). Here he focuses on many fundamental points, especially on how classic cinema activates a structure that relies on the constant interplay of symmetries and asymmetries, internal references and interruptions, repetitions and variations. This is made possible by three factors. First, by the presence of real "rhymes": classic movies constantly revert to shots, or groups of shots, that present identical characteristics, at the level both of form (the same kinds of shot, or movement, keep reappearing) and of content (the repetition of the same actions, such as seeing). Let us think of *The Birds,* for instance, and of Melanie constantly traveling back and forth through Bodega Bay, or of *North by Northwest,* and of the airplane attack on Thornhill: Bellour studies these two sequences, which are both constructed around the systematic repetition of a group of elements. Another factor is the use of condensation and displacement. The constant reappearance of the same content leads both to shots that integrate characteristics previously belonging to separate shots and to shots that "rewrite" previous shots. An example of this comes from *The Birds.* On the one hand, the four shots where a seagull strikes Melanie present a condensed version of what is at play in the second part of the sequence. On the other hand, they reintroduce in a different way the idea of the aggression, already suggested by Mitch's glances at her (to strike and to strike with a glance). Another example comes from *North by Northwest.* The shots that end the airplane attack, on the one hand, reintroduce previous situations, in reverse order (arrival and departure). On the other hand, they redefine Thornhill's relationship with all means of transportation (means of aggression and means of escape). A third factor contributing to this same structure is the introduction of many breaking points, where all the balances and correspondences are broken by the presence of shots that change the established order and insert new data. Sometimes such breaks rhyme, but they always mark anomaly and irreducibility. A case of anomaly is found in *The Birds,* namely, the detail on the cage of the lovebirds that Melanie gives Mitch's sister. Here we observe the loss of the gaze on the part of both Melanie and Mitch (in the passage, dominated by the construction looker/looked at, this detail is not seen by anyone, not even by the person who offers the present). An example of the lack of irreducibility can be seen in *North by Northwest* (a film that also introduces rupture as the loss of the look). The airplane does not perfectly integrate with Thornhill's system of transportation and requires other possible associations.

Around rhyme, substitution, and rupture classic cinema constructs a structure based on both equilibrium and disequilibrium, which gives films a peculiar pace, made up of redundancies, belated echoes, sudden irruptions, later integrations. This structure can lead to a kind of "systematic perversion" where everything fits together. It may, however, also remind us of the existence of an asymmetry that is always latent. Above all, this structure seems to be the basis of the essence of the story itself, both in cinema and elsewhere. A narrative always starts with something that is not clear and usually ends because all the pieces fall (or at least seem to fall) into place. In between we find a thick net of repetitions that, on the one hand, try to fix the imbalance that originated the story and, on the other hand, try to find a new balance around which to end it. In short, we have repetitions of difference (that both hide it and remind us of it) and repetitions oriented toward a solution (that resolve the story and themselves). This is the keystone of classic narrative cinema (we could also say of narrative cinema *tout court*).

This structure, which aligns and combines symmetry and asymmetry, is typical of all stories; a narrative (either managed optimally as in classic cinema or based on new balances as in modern cinema) exists because of a laceration, a repetition, and an agreement. Besides being the foundation of narration, this structure also introduces desire and its submission to the law, which fully charges our psychic universe. Let us consider the repetitions of difference and the repetition oriented toward a resolution. They seem to follow perfectly the dynamics of our drives, with their often lacerating outbreaks, their repeated appearance, their continually changing disguises, their (apparent) regulation. Indeed, it is just this dynamics of the drives that seems to provide the model for the game cinema plays with great ability and recursivity. In this sense, we need to broaden the equivalence between the processes at work in a film and the psychic processes. It concerns not merely such devices as condensation and displacement, but the very foundations of this edifice. After all, the configuration of the shot/reverse shot already shows that cinema follows the paths of our psychic processes. Both diversity and mirroring intervene in this cinematographic procedure, which expresses almost at its purest the relationship that a subject entertains at the imaginary level with an object. This relationship, in turn, consists of the desire for the incorporation of the object and the discovery of its otherness. The Bodega Bay sequence from *The Birds,* yet again, exemplifies this: a man and a woman; a look that increasingly binds them; the logic of desire, marking the alternation of the shots.[8]

We can even go one step further. The underlying structure of classic narrative cinema brings us back, even before the dynamics of drives in general, to an element that concerns me more than any other, the emergence of desire and its submission to the law: Oedipus. "We need to perceive the fate of Oedipus and of castration even in the smallest textual device, as if through a constant vibration" (Bellour 1979:245). Oedipus knows well the repetition of difference and the repetition oriented toward a resolution. He uses them to exorcise his infraction (his attraction to his mother), to effect a substitution (the "other" instead of "her"), to hide his fear (of castration), and to impose his return on the establishment (family, society). Difference and similarity, rupture and recomposition, are at the core of the Oedipus story. It is in this light, then, that we need to view the existence of rhymes within film, which end up taking care of the insertions, and the existence of that overriding rhyme that marks the *récit* and transforms mere splinters of reality into a coherent, continuous, and accessible world. Oedipus marks both film as a signifying object and the filmic narration. Indeed, these two levels establish a correspondence in reference to Oedipus. "The film is subdued, it submits to the narrative as the subject submits to Oedipus. In this way, it narrates what the body of the film never stops miming, namely, the shift from one equilibrium to another, from a first term to a second that repeats and resolves the previous one" (244). Bellour confirms and reinforces his point. There is a connection between the structuring of a film and the structuring of its narration. The latter amplifies the movements that shape the former, regulating its rhythms and cadences so as to become the source of its rules; from the amplified and regulated movements of both emerges a constant reference, Oedipus.

Classic cinema refers to Oedipus also in terms of the stories it tells. Let us consider the constant family setting, the presence of maternal and paternal figures, the explosion of desire and, together with it, of violence, the fear (of castration), the inauguration of a relationship with the other sex, the substitution of the parental figures, the submission to the institution of marriage, etc. The myth of Oedipus keeps being told. An excellent example comes from *North by Northwest*. Bellour underscores Thornhill's relationship with his mother; the symbolic killing of his father (Townsend, the paternal figure); Eva's appearance on the scene (she is the mother's exact opposite); the sudden development of a drive connecting sex and death (the conversation in the sleeping car); the threat of castration (the tiny straight razor and shaving brush); the "evil father's" aggression (Vandamm); Thornhill, who needs to grow up (the conversation at the hotel after the airplane sequence); the ambiguity of Eva's role (object of desire or *femme fatale*); the discovery of a "good father" (the professor); a conflict that cannot be put off anymore (to whom does Eva belong?); Thornhill, who both dies and is born again because of Eva; the final submission to the law's dictates (the stone faces of the presidents, the "fathers of our fatherland"); Eva, who becomes "Mrs. Thornhill" (like his mother, in his mother's place); and finally pleasure ("Come on . . ."). We could give many more examples, besides *North by Northwest,* where no immediately recognizable symbols appear, but where the position of the elements introduced charges them with values aiming in this direction (the "net" of meanings is what counts: see the transportation system in *North by Northwest*).

Beyond the stories that are being told, we find support in the very structure of films, of their narration. After all, there is complicity between the stories that are told and the structure behind them. "The systematic accumulation of symmetries and asymmetries along the whole film chain . . . never stops miming, reproducing (for a mutual production) the scheme of the family relationships establishing the space of the narrative" (261). In short, a correspondence is established between the parental system presented by the film, consisting of difference and mirrorings, and the game on which the film relies, in turn consisting of mirrorings and difference. Yet again, we observe a close solidarity among the various levels at which cinema operates. Just as before we spoke of a solidarity between the body of the film and the narrative practice, now we observe a similar relationship between the body of the film and the narrated events: an intimate solidarity under the sign of Oedipus.

One should also examine in the light of Oedipus many elements that classic cinema presents systematically: the theater scene, in addition to the family one; the image of the artist, besides that of the father. These elements take us back to the cinematographic apparatus: the theater as the place of the mise-en-scène; the artist as the concretization of the director-enunciator. Similarly, we should analyze many stylistic features, including the shot/reverse shot. The latter, as we already said, expresses an "object relation" in which, we now realize, the man is always (or almost always) the scopic subject, and the woman the object of desire. Through the alternation of shots, this relation enacts the obsession with lack and the multiplication of differences. In order to conclude, let us go back to that very delicate and decisive part of a film, the end. Bellour suggests that the end represents the phase where the pieces of the mosaic fit together, so that desire submits to order. At this point, the movement that originates the film comes to a sudden stop. Yet the same power that opened the narrative allows it to be concluded. This power works at various levels, from stylistic matters to the events in which a couple is involved. It finds its rhythms and obligations in the echoes among the various levels, as well as in the whole construction of the system. In that this power never stops, it gives the filmic text an infinite productivity. Bellour calls this game of constant openings and closures "blocage symbolique," to imply that it represents confrontation with the law and consequently the point of access to the realm of the symbolic.

As Bellour himself insists, his analyses are impossible to summarize (190);

similarly, his ideas as we have presented them lack the power they derive from his personal style. Still, through him we have focused on one of the contributions that most characterized the debate on cinema and psychoanalysis. We will encounter other essential voices, such as Heath. In an attempt to bring together the many threads woven in the previous pages, we will now consider Christian Metz's *Le significant imaginaire,* a wide-ranging text that attempted to both close and relaunch this debate.

10.5. The Imaginary Signifier

In his book Metz both touches upon and reformulates the many points of which we have given an overview. Part three (which he wrote first), for instance, both continues the analogy between the oneiric and the cinematographic experiences and introduces some important corrections to it. First, "the dreamer does not know that he is dreaming; the filmic spectator knows that he is at the cinema" (Metz 1977b [1982]: 101). A different knowledge, therefore, characterizes the protagonists of the two situations. Second, "filmic perception is a real perception (is really a perception); it is not reducible to an internal psychic process" (109). We have, therefore, a different relationship with the outside. "A dream responds to the wish with more exactitude and regularity: devoid of exterior material, it is assured of never colliding with reality," while "as hallucinatory fulfillment, the fiction film is less certain than a dream" (112, 113). Finally, "a narrative film is usually much more logical and constructed than a dream": therefore, the former entails a secondary process, which is less marked in the latter. Hence a displacement of the analogy: the spectator's experience is closer to *daydream* than to *dreaming,* to *rêverie* than to *rêve.* Hence, too, a new division of the field: "the dream belongs to childhood and the night; the film and daydream are more adult and belong to the day, but not midday—to the evening, rather" (137).

Part one of Metz's book posits his fundamental question. The author aims to uncover the ways in which the *cinematographic signifier* is constructed, the signifier with which the spectator measures himself and in which he searches for a "good object." The question is, which of its features "call most directly on the type of knowledge that psychoanalysis alone can provide?" (42). He identifies three main areas: specular identification, voyeurism, and fetishism.

We can perceive the borders of the first area if we consider that "film is like a mirror. But it differs from the primordial mirror in one essential point:

although, as in the latter, everything may come to be projected, there is one thing and one thing only that is never reflected in it: the spectator's own body" (45). According to Lacan, in the mirror children find their image and the matrix of their subjectivity. By seeing themselves, they learn to recognize themselves. At the cinema this identification game is impossible. "But *with what,* then, does the spectator identify during the projection of the film? For he certainly has to identify: identification in its primal form has ceased to be a current necessity for him, but he continues, in the cinema—if he did not the film would become incomprehensible, considerably more incomprehensible than the most incomprehensible films—to depend on that permanent play of identification without which there would be no social life" (46). In short, although our subjectivity has already gone through the fundamental steps (primordial mirror, primary identification), it still needs to find constant confirmations, supports, applications. At the movies the spectators may well identify with a character of the fiction, or with the actor playing the role, but they can also identify with themselves. This is an apparently impossible step (as we have seen, "contrary to the child in a mirror, [the spectator] cannot identify with himself as an object, but only with objects which are there without him" [48]). Still, it is fully understandable if we consider that cinema implies a double, although unitary, "knowledge." When I watch a film, "I know I am perceiving something imaginary . . . and I know that it is I who am perceiving it. This second knowledge divides in turn: I know that I am really perceiving . . . and I also know that it is I who am perceiving all this" (48). This is how spectators identify with themselves or, even better, with themselves "as a pure act of perception (as wakefulness, alertness): as the condition of possibility of the perceived and hence as a kind of transcendental subject, which comes before every *there is*" (49). The spectator is a transcendental subject, rather than an object, as well as identifying in turn with the camera eye or with the director's point of view.

As far as the area of voyeurism is concerned, we observe that "the practice of the cinema is only possible through the perceptual passions: the desire to see, . . . which was alone engaged in the art of the silent film, and the desire to hear, which has been added to it in the sound cinema" (58). Unlike other sexual drives, the peculiarity of this perceptive desire is that it never wishes to incorporate the object of its desire. Instead, it keeps it separate, at a distance. This is what happens with voyeurism, which indeed "always keeps apart the *object* (here the object looked at) and the *source* of the drive, i.e., the generating organ (the eye)" (59). Hence, an interesting connection emerges. "The voyeur is very careful to maintain a gulf, an empty space, between the object and the eye, the object and his own body: his look fastens the object at the right distance, as with those cinema spectators who take care to avoid being too close to or too far from the screen" (60).

This analogy does not really clarify the manner, for we might apply it also to other arts (such as the theater) and spectators. Cinema does more than this. It widens the gap between desire and object. On the one hand, "the spectacles and sounds the cinema 'offers' us (offers us at a distance, hence as much *steals* from us) are especially rich and varied: a mere difference of degree but already one that counts" (61). On the other hand, "cinema only gives [its data] in effigy," thus placing them in the realm of the "inaccessible from the outset, in a primordial *elsewhere,* infinitely desirable (never possessible), on another scene which is that of absence" (61). By showing the world in the form of images, cinema both makes it appear and deprives us of it. What is represented seems both to be there (or we would not recognize it) and not to be there (or we would not need its images). Indeed, it is exactly because we are deprived of the world that the latter's image may establish itself. This is what originates the desire that binds us to a film, our perceptive desire. "What defines the specifically cinematic *scopic regime* is not so much the distance kept, the 'keeping' itself (first figure of the lack, common to all voyeurism), as the absence of the object seen" (61). Consequently, cinema relies on some sort of voyeurism in its pure state, on the creation of an unbridgeable gap, on the impossibility of access. Of course, other conditions are of help to this phenomenon: "the obscurity surrounding the onlooker," "the aperture of the screen with its inevitable keyhole effect," "the spectator's solitude," "the segregation of spaces which characterizes a cinema performance, but not a theatrical one" (64). In the last analysis, what matters is that "For its spectator the film unfolds in that simultaneously very close and definitively inaccessible 'elsewhere' in which the child *sees* the amorous play of the parental couple, who are similarly ignorant of it and leave it alone, a pure onlooker whose participation is inconceivable" (64). After the mirror, the primal scene: the fundamental elements of an individual's psychic life penetrate deeply into the cinematographic machine.

A few words are enough to give us an idea of the area of fetishism. Its object is mainly the cinematographic technique or cinema as technique. "The fetish is the cinema in its *physical* state" (75). How cinema comes into being is, therefore, the core of its interest: "A fetish, the cinema as technical performance, as prowess, as an *exploit,* an exploit that underlines and denounces the lack on which the whole arrangement is based (the absence of the object, replaced by its reflection), an exploit which consists at the same time of making this absence forgotten" (74). Sublime dolly shots, wonderful "plan sequences," extraordinary takes, all tell us about the reality we lost, while at the same time they present themselves as adequate substitutes for this loss. They both hide a lack and admit to it between the lines. According to Metz, this process blends a total love with the effects of knowledge.

Specular identification, voyeurism, and fetishism are therefore the elements through which a film on the screen actually acquires substance. Thanks to the dynamics underlying these phenomena, the *cinematographic signifier* comes into being. With this signifier Metz also sheds light on the way in which the cinematographic "machine" works, at least at the stage of the film projection. Besides the signifier, the *apparatus* is also at the core of these pages. As far as the *processes* and *figures* go, they reappear in the last part of his book, which is devoted to a careful overview of condensation and displacement and of the relationship that these two psychic dynamics entertain with both two linguistic axes (the paradigmatic and the syntagmatic) and two rhetorical devices (metaphor and metonymy). In this section there emerge, on the one hand, the steps that every film takes in order to acquire the final shape with which it presents itself to us; on the other hand, the elements with which its work is intertwined. Metz's book ends with an analysis of the crossed fadeout, which is exemplary in this sense: he calls it a "stylistic figure" that brings to the surface the very processes that most subtly manipulate the filmic text, the film as text.

Metz's book certainly deserves a more detailed analysis because of its great resonance. Instead, we will end our overview of the psychoanalytical studies of cinema here (later we will return to some others). The reason behind this is that Metz still works on problems of method. His work aims at a systematic clarification of concepts and an evaluation of their appropriateness. In other words, while confirming the existence of a close interpenetration of some sort between cinema and psychic life, Metz carefully retains the idea that psychoanalysis is a *tool* for the study of reality, rather than a totalizing and exhaustive view of phenomena. After Metz, or despite him, the debate would often slide toward another kind of sensitivity, less concerned with the "disciplinary" dimension and less strict with all-encompassing models. After all, this chapter started by mentioning that psychoanalysis represented, historically, the essential point of passage between a methodological and a post-methodological approach. It worked like a very fragile bridge, which can be crossed, though perhaps only once, but which still guarantees the connection between the two banks of the river.

Similar episodes of escape from the "cages" of the methodological approaches took place especially at the end of the 1970s within the other disciplines that developed an interest in cinema, such as psychology, sociology, and semiotics. A new procedure emerged, a new paradigm came forward, as we will see shortly.

11 FIELD THEORIES

11.1. From Methodological to Field Theories

During the 1970s a radical change in the approach to film theory took place, often imperceptibly and sometimes along indirect routes. The methodological approach, which applied to cinema the point of view and the tools of a specific discipline, gave way to a freer, more direct, and perhaps even more intense approach. We have already mentioned some of its features and will now focus on its most significant aspects.

This new paradigm has three main characteristics. First, the scholars' attention focuses on the relationship between the observer and the object observed. Theorists no longer take refuge in the anonymity of scientific discourse and the objectivity of their propositions. On the contrary, they come out in the open, declaring their presence, justifying their perception of cinema, often relativizing it but always making it personal. Similarly, the object of the theory no longer appears as an inert reality, passively submitting to analysis. On the contrary, it interferes with the gaze that traverses it, often openly resisting it, and always contributing to its orientation. As a result, the boundaries between the roles of the observer and the observed, of the theorist and cinema, start to blur, and an open dialogue is instituted, in which the two partners exchange positions.

Second, within this new paradigm it becomes very important to posit "good questions." Theory no longer derives from a cold analysis of the facts, but from the emergence of problems that reveal the scholars' preoccupations with the systematic nature of the object that is being studied. Therefore, it is essential to understand both what we need to ask of cinema, in order really to grasp its meaning, and what cinema wants us to ask it, for it to show us its depth. The selection of a strategic question, around which to develop the discourse, constitutes a decisive moment.

The third characteristic of this new paradigm is its attention to concrete texts, to films. Films are no longer invoked only to illustrate what happens within the whole body of cinema. Instead, they are analyzed in their particularity, in their individuality. This does not imply the renunciation of a general understanding of phenomena (this is still film theory, rather than the theory of films). It implies, instead, that generality is seen as a goal that can be reached only by starting from the singular, from the unique, even from the idiosyncratic. All that this requires is that our starting point should lead us on an interesting path. Hence a feeling of exaltation and an increase in the connections with the field of films: the points of interest are chosen not as mere exemplifications of current trends, but rather because of their exemplarity. Their comparison, furthermore, does not provide us with unifying rules, but with a network of occurrences that can testify to behaviors, processes, and trends.

These three characteristics (focusing on the interaction between observer and observed; identifying important questions; paying attention to works, to films) not only describe a new way of making theory, but also allow us to understand how we arrived at this point. The increasing success of hermeneutics in the 1970s was the first element that led to this shift. This phenomenon goes well beyond our field of study. It involves philosophy, literary criticism, scientific and historical research. Among other factors, the end of structuralism, the spread of deconstruction, and the increasing use of "micro-histories" contributed to it.[1] To remain in our field, let us merely observe that the emergence of this new sensibility led to a change in the theoretical framework in at least two ways: on the one hand, it forced scholars to reveal themselves, to come to terms with themselves, to question themselves on their way of questioning their objects. On the other hand, it led scholars to doubt the functionality of the research techniques, which had dominated in the methodological field, and to make room for the practice of interpretation.

Another factor that led to this new paradigm came from the reemergence of "global questions" that go beyond each isolated discipline to bring into play something common to all. A great interest in the subject, for instance, emerges in psychoanalysis (the formation of the ego), semiotics (the presence of an implied author and spectator), aesthetics (the role of the director-creator), society (individual/mass dialectics), with constant cross-references between sectors. Once again, this trend did not only affect film studies. In other fields, too, such as literature, science, and history, there was a tendency to posit questions that are common to many approaches and fields (such as the question of the subject, which emerges in all the above-mentioned fields). If we limit our analysis to our field, we realize that the tendency to focus on one fundamental question helped in many ways to reorient film theory. It broke the rigid articulation of the disciplines and showed how precarious their independence from one another was. It also uncovered connections among the various research fields, points of suture, transversal trajectories, and in so doing it helped to redefine the field of the debate.

A third factor that led to this new paradigm came from the practice of textual analysis, whose name underscores that researchers approach a film as a real text, where they find all the data they need. From the early 1970s onward, and following the example of scholars such as Bellour, Kuntzel, and Ropars, the habit of describing in detail a film, a sequence, or a group of films, in the attempt to reconstruct their internal logic, their signification processes, themes, etc., became widely diffused. Again, this passion for analysis went beyond the field of films. Literary theory and general semiotics, for instance, turned more and more to detailed, precise comparisons with certain texts (i.e., Barthes' *S/Z* or Greimas' *Maupassant*). Within our field, textual analysis (we call it analysis, but it is mostly an interpretation) affected the transformation of the theoretical framework in at least two ways. First, by emphasizing the elaboration of categories, rather than their application, it interrupted the priority of the deductive model that was typical of the methodological approach. Second, by focusing on objects as seen in their concrete aspects, it discovered the existence of differences behind an apparent homogeneity or of connections between things that had previously been considered separate.[2]

The new paradigm came into being through the success achieved by hermeneutics, the interest felt in "global questions," the diffusion of textual analyses. It did not develop progressively or linearly, however. For instance, the need to introduce a new form of investigation did not lead to the complete rejection of the disciplines. Often the latter were merely required to become more flexible, open, and understanding. This happened with cognitive psychology, textual semiotics, and sociology of culture, which kept alive—but also integrated and corrected—the methodological tradition in the 1980s. Another example: sometimes the need to identify interests that were common to many fields made scholars look backward in order to recover themes that had emerged previously during the debate, perhaps even in ontological theories. Deleuze is one of them. His studies on cinema as a form of reality and of thought derived from his rereading of Bazin (and Pasolini). Finally, the necessity of starting from specific films did not always lead to a disenchanted, mobile gaze. At times the scholars ended up building cages around themselves that were as rigid as, if not more rigid than, those that preceded them. The debate on cinema and ideology, which developed during the 1970s, with its tendency toward the schematic and the repetitive, was an example of this.

11.2. A Complex Geography

The preceding statements help us to understand that the newly developed theory was neither uniform nor compact, unless perhaps in its essential traits. We are dealing with a varied landscape, maybe an archipelago, rather than a continent.

The characteristics of this paradigm are responsible for its many outcomes. The more we insist on the relationship between observer and observed, proceed through problems, and rely on the texts, the more we create differentiated areas and trajectories. We have a plurality at both the stylistic and thematic levels. As far as style is concerned, some scholars still stick to the factual; others pursue interpretation to its extreme limits; some give in to the pleasure of drift, and others return to normative principles; some compare objects, others upset their placement, etc.[3] As far as themes are concerned, scholars focus on the dynamics that control films, seen in their presuppositions and aesthetic, ideological, and social effects; they wonder what a representation is and how it may "account for" reality, or what narration is and how it may "imply" a spectator; they study the relationship between text and context and project them onto the becoming of history.

Yet the variability of the frame of reference does not imply a lack of identity. We are dealing here with a series of research areas whose borders do not necessarily fit together but which stay in contact with each other thanks to underground connections that are maintained by the reintroduction of similar obsessions or sensibilities. Or we have research areas where at times the same language is not spoken, but where there is the will to "translate" the discoveries made by some in the directions provided by others. Above all, we are facing research areas that have in common the traits we already know, namely, the ability to reflect on their own procedures, the presence of a central preoccupation, and the systematic study of specific films. Finally, these research areas are strengthened by the progressive institutionalization of the research itself. During these very years film theory appeared on the scene as a well-defined field, with journals, books, and courses devoted to it.

This peculiar arrangement of the field is the reason behind the choice of the name of this paradigm. *Field theories* means that we are dealing with research fields that are both autonomous and interconnected, delimited and yet open to new connections. Each is characterized by a central problem and by a series of branches that connect it to other sectors. We could call them "discussion fields": they have an identity of their own, and often (but not always) they are open to the new; they are rich in experiences and passwords, yet have long, stable roots.

We will now devote our attention to these research *fields*.

12 POLITICS, IDEOLOGY, AND ALTERNATIVES

12.1. 1968 and Beyond

The year 1968 is for some a turning point, for others an accident along the way; for some it represents the opening up of new horizons, for others the last utopia; for some it is a page that needs to be erased from our history, for others it is a moment to be remembered with neither repentance nor regret.[1] In the (small but not meaningless) field that is the focus of this study, 1968 marked the beginning of a debate that dominated the entire following decade and that served as a background for later studies. In its more general and simpler form, this debate developed around cinema's political value.

The dual concept of cinema-politics had forcefully demanded attention before, for instance, with Neorealism. Behind the emphasis on the intrinsic documentary value of films lay the hope that cinema could help to develop an awareness of the negative aspects of reality and to mobilize all the forces that intended to correct them. Each work could and had to participate in a larger battle than the merely aesthetic one. To different degrees and with different orientations, other research trends had seen cinema as a weapon, as a terrain of confrontation, as an aid to various sides. After all, certain widespread attitudes, such as denouncing escapist cinema, expecting directors to discuss collective events, the possibility of uniting the people and the intellectuals thanks to this new medium (such attitudes were typical of Neorealism, and of the latter's anticonsumerist and antibourgeois attitudes, but also existed inside other movements), all remorselessly betrayed a political implication.

Yet after 1968 something changed. Previously, the most common approach to the problem was to refer to a political position, to define the nature of cinema, and to show a connection between the two. From 1968 onward, this order was reversed. One tried, first, to identify cinema's behaviors; then, to grasp their political implications; finally, to project the implications onto the map of the whole of society. The movement was not from politics to the movies, but from movies to politics. We will see shortly that this did not always hold true and that, in any case, different interpretations emerged. It is, however, a fact that a new path was inaugurated. Many factors typical of these years contributed to this: for instance, the perception of art as a particular battlefield, rather than as a mere extension of the battles fought inside society; or the perception of the intellectual as a specific political subject, rather than as a mere "fellow traveler"; this led to the impossibility of speaking of the "subordination" of either art or the intellectual to rules developed elsewhere. The result was that cinema's "taking sides" with politics was replaced by a more articulated and complex dialectic, by an overlapping, a tension, a give and take. Cinema voiced political issues by itself and invited everyone to reflect on them.

If this new path represents the first background element, the second and more traditional one concerns the activity of the scholars engaged in the debate. The starting point is the study of the paths that cinema usually follows and of those that it could be useful for it to start following. This is the descriptive stage, often leading to a "chart" of the various kinds of film, where each appears in a different position. The next step is judging the work that has been done and that can be done, uncovering the options the theorist considers best. At this stage even theory is charged with political value by taking part in alliances and alignments. Finally, and very frequently, the films that seem to embody the desired tendencies are forthrightly valorized, both defended in journals, books, and reviews and shown at festivals, protests, and meetings. At this stage the theorist becomes militant.

Thus, there is a movement from cinema toward politics (more frequent than the reverse), which is combined with analysis, judgment, and promotion. These two elements are the starting point for our reconstruction of a debate that was of great consequence both in 1968 and afterward.[2]

12.2. The Problem of Ideology (I)

During the first months of 1969 *Cinéthique,* a young and combative French journal, published an interview with Jean Thibaudeau and Marcellin Pleynet. Both were editors of *Tel Quel,* a literary journal that was famous for voicing the newest cultural trends. In this interview, Pleynet made a surprising re-mark. Before asking what art shows or how, he said, one should ask through what medium. Before judging the degree of someone's militancy, on the basis of either content or language, one should define the camera's role. The cam-era is not a neutral tool, which "can be used for this or that, to the left or to the right, indifferently." On the contrary, it is "a tool that spreads the bour-geois ideology before anything else" (Cinéthique 1969). The camera presents an image of the world that is constructed directly on the model of the "sci-entific perspective" of the fifteenth century. This means that it never records reality as it is, but as it is restructured on the basis of a figurative code. Fur-thermore, it excludes everything that does not fit into a system consisting of a vanishing point and orthogonal lines. Finally, it pretends to behave similarly to the human eye, according to the laws of perception. The image on the screen, therefore, depends both on strong norms and on equally strong cen-sorship; and yet the "scientific" patina of the procedures behind it turns it into a "natural" image of the world. Consequently, although it does not mir-ror reality, this image may pretend, and even persuade us, that it does. Instead, it is necessary to emphasize that a camera elaborates a representation of reality that is *its own,* although derived from the world. It depends on a code that both rules and shapes and that is only apparently "immediate" and "faithful." If, therefore—as Althusser suggested[3]—ideology has to do first of all with representations, cinema inevitably sides with ideology. It continues and re-launches the "specular vision" that Humanism, in the 1400s, had developed to support the emergent bourgeoisie.

Pleynet's invitation to take into consideration the basis of cinema and to connect it with a precise ideology is what triggered the debate. Two issues later, in number 5, *Cinéthique* published an essay written by its director, Gér-ard Leblanc, and a long essay by Jean-Paul Fargier. Both essays attempt to redefine the forms and tasks of political cinema. Leblanc studies in a very critical way a group of films that, by focusing on either the working class or the young, pretend to represent a turning point. Instead, he argues, they keep doing what bourgeois cinema has always done, that is, presenting on the screen a world on which we can project our desires and through which we can compensate for what we lack. In other words, these films give us the illusion of participating in experiences that may not be ours, instead of mak-ing us aware that we are watching a spectacle. They aim to show us a more or less truthful slice of life, instead of telling us what lies behind their images and sounds. In this way films do not break with the bourgeoisie, whose interest, at the movies and elsewhere, lies in "hiding the productive work that is the origin of surplus value" (Leblanc 1969:4). The bourgeoisie, instead, wants "to show the world (it does not matter which world) on the screen without showing (without letting us see) cinema's work on elements that are not natural" (5). Leblanc mentions other films that, unlike those described above, in his opinion actually break with the bourgeoisie. Among them are Pollet-Sollers' *Mediterranée* and Hanoun's *Octobre à Madrid*. They "do not present compensations to the spectator, but invite him to consciously participate— author and spectator are here finally on the same level—in the production of images and sounds that no longer hide the material nature of their inscription on film" (4). In short, these films break away from the impression of reality that was so dear to bourgeois cinema. They display the material conditions of their existence and free the spectator from the position to which he is usually confined. What these films do should be supported and continued, because this is the only way for cinema to connect with ongoing battles. "Bourgeois cinema will never really be threatened (and cinema will never really be articulated as a practice of transforming the world) until filmmakers produce films that tell everything about themselves: their economy and their means of production, starting with the prohibitions proposed by idealist cinema" (6).

Thus, on the one hand, we have films that perpetuate the realist illusion, as if they were an extension of life; and, on the other hand, films that present themselves for what they are, clusters of images and sounds. At the same time, we have the apparently natural functioning of the "cinematographic machine," as if it were a neutral presence; we also have the laying bare of the materials and processes on which this "machine" relies, and in particular of the labor invested in it. This is the difference between these two kinds of cinema. One, while stating that it is *engagé,* is actually still tied to the bourgeois modes. The other, instead, looks for new ways to connect itself with the ongoing class struggle.

Fargier, too, returns to this difference. A film influences the way in which individuals portray things in their minds. It influences their images of themselves and of the world around them, images that constitute ideology. Cinema's political action consists, then, above all, in providing or removing the awareness of what is really happening. In particular, it addresses the "subjective factor" that accompanies every struggle, "namely, the proletariat's class conscience" (Fargier 1969:18). But how does cinema affect this subjective factor? How does it exercise its ideologic function? First and foremost, it "*reproduces* the existing ideologies, and is therefore used (it does not matter whether consciously or not) as a vehicle of the circulation process of ideology" (18). In this sense, cinema needs to be evaluated above all for the view of the world that it supports. Second, cinema "*produces* an ideology of its own, the impression of reality. On the screen there is nothing but reflection and shadow, and yet the spectator develops at once the idea that there is reality as it really is" (18). In this sense, cinema needs to be evaluated above all for the view of the world that it provides as cinema. This view relies on naturalness and transparence and depends more on the medium used than on what it says or how. This second ideological function of cinema is very important, but it is the hardest to attack. Some films, however, have tried to break the illusion of reality and to uncover the material conditions of the existence of images and sounds. Although it is difficult to give the latter a determining role in political struggle, they no doubt help to redefine our idea of cinema. They uncover its weaknesses and suggest new possibilities for cinema. In other words, images and sounds belong to a *theoretical practice* and are political inasmuch as they develop our knowledge (at the level of theory) of what cinema is, is not, and can be. Such theoretical work is invaluable: "at the movies, the circulation of knowledge takes place concomitantly with the production of the knowledge of cinema" (20). The knowledge a film transmits is connected with the knowledge that concerns it. By taking all this into account, one can hope that a *materialistic and dialectical cinema* may emerge: materialistic in the sense that it shows the material conditions of its existence; dialectical in the sense that its will to talk about itself affects the processes of its fabrication and its reception.

Fargier continued his analysis in two further essays, published in the immediately following issues of *Cinéthique* (Fargier 1970a and 1970b). In the first he states that if cinema intends to remain the reflection of something, it must not be the reflection of a preexisting reality (the world around us or the author's interior world). Rather, it must be the reflection of the work that shapes it, thus becoming "the reflection of a process." Similarly, the work that shapes a film should not be considered a linear route from an initial project to a finished product, but a complex and articulated activity, in which at least three spheres of activity overlap: economic practice (concerning the financial operations connected with production and distribution); technical practice (all the optical, mechanical, physical, chemical operations that are present at the stage of the shooting and the editing); aesthetic practice (which covers the modes of representation and which plays the most important role).[4] In the second essay, Fargier focuses on one of the films that *Cinéthique* considers exemplary, *Mediterranée*. The film breaks with the traditional forms of representation in various ways. First and foremost, it does not re-present a world, but questions the way in which it is portrayed. Second, it does not refer to a predetermined meaning, but lets meaning emerge from the relationship among the shots. Third, it does not rely on a space-time connection that gives unity to the world on the screen, but on editing that limits itself to juxtaposing its constituents by connecting colors, movements, and so on. Finally, it gives the voice-over the task not to illustrate, but to provide a counterpoint to what we see.

Moreover, *Cinéthique* presents a clear picture: cinema concerns first of all ideology, that is, the way in which individuals represent themselves, the reality around them, and their mutual relationships.[5] Therefore, cinema's political nature can be measured in two ways: on the basis of its ability to break the monopoly of the bourgeois ideology (tied to the idea of naturalness and ready to hide the labor behind each kind of commodity) and on the basis of its ability to increase the knowledge that allows us to evaluate the processes that are really at work. At this level, it is necessary to distinguish between idealist cinema (which presents itself as a mirror of reality and erases the labor that produced it) and materialistic and dialectical cinema (which tells everything about itself, shows its own materials, and inscribes on itself its own contradictions). This latter kind of cinema, by promoting a "scientific" knowledge of cinema or, if you will, by placing itself at the level of theory, has progressive political value.

12.3. The Problem of Ideology (II)

A reaction to Pleynet's suggestions and to *Cinéthique's* proposals also came from *Cahiers du Cinéma,* starting with two essays by Jean-Luis Comolli and Jean Narboni, entitled "Cinéma/Idéologie/Critique." The first, which was published at the same time as the fifth issue of *Cinéthique,* attempts to define the "position" of the journal. Its starting point is the acknowledgment that a film is, on the one hand, "the product of a specific economic system" and, on the other hand, "the product of the ideology of the economic system that produces and sells it," namely, capitalist ideology (Comolli and Narboni

1969a : 12). Capitalist ideology permeates the world around us, of which it provides a specific representation, instead of allowing us to perceive it as it is. A film, while believing it traces the world, traces a predefined image of it. "Cinema is doomed from the very first meter of film shot to reproduce things not in their concrete reality, but as they are refracted by ideology" (12). This makes ideology the absolute master of the field. Its representations form a wide and cohesive picture, and all the elements that are included in a film, "subjects, styles, forms, meanings," duplicate "the general ideological discourse." But such a situation makes ideology give itself away. As soon as it represents itself in a film, it places itself, so to speak, in a display window, thus risking the exposure of what it is really like through "its own self-representation" (13). Therefore, cinema's critical function can also emerge from the study of the conditions of its own existence. As the representation of a representation, it can uncover what it portrays by showing its imagistic nature. Or it can question what it refracts by asking how it refracts it. Any film that duplicates ideological discourse can become evidence against that discourse. What matters is that the film display self-awareness and not accept working in silence.

These observations allow Comolli and Narboni to escape the strict dichotomy suggested by *Cinéthique,* according to which it is possible only to be either inside or outside the system of representation that bourgeois ideology imposes. *Cahiers,* instead, believes that while some films do not hesitate to follow this ideology, others reject it completely and work on different terrain. Yet there are also films that fight it in an indirect way, without losing their effectiveness. This is the case with cinema that denounces the system of representation imposed by ideology by reconsidering its own role as a tool of representation. Its focus on the basic principles and internal mechanisms of representation (perhaps even accompanied by a partial attempt to change the situation) "causes a swerve or rupture, with respect to its ideological function" (13).

In any case, Comolli and Narboni's new film typology is essentially structured as follows. On the one hand, we have films that are "blindly faithful" to the dominant ideology and above all "totally unaware of their fidelity" (13). On the other hand, we have films that openly denounce the dominant ideology by opposing the traditional forms of representation. In between, with different degrees of radicalism, we have films that criticize the dominant ideology both by working on representation and by introducing explicitly political themes, films whose critique focuses only on one component of the system of representation, such as the form of the story, and films that rely on procedures that mark some critical points (such as the technique of "direct cinema"). Finally, we have films that seem to be entirely within the bourgeois system of representation, and yet end up dismantling it, not because they shatter the ideology that presides over them, but because they lay bare the image that ideology gives of itself. This last group, which includes for instance Ford's, Dreyer's, and Rossellini's films, deserves serious consideration.

After defining its position, *Cahiers* returned to the relationship between cinema and politics in the following issues. Besides Comolli and Narboni's second essay, which refuted the position of its *Cinéthique* rivals, we should mention the essays by Bonitzer (on the *habitus* of the film watched in a theater); by Daney and Oudart (on the equivalence posited by bourgeois ideology between vision and knowledge and the status of the "visible" in reality and in its filmic representation); again by Comolli (who criticized a film by Costa-Gavras as unable to question itself on its own working procedures) and Narboni (who praised a film by Straub because it does the very opposite); and so on.[6] Similarly, while there were reviews that were more and more "partisan," there was also the continuation of the publication of Eisenstein's writings and an extended discussion of the political value of the Russian cinema in the 1920s and 1930s. Possibly, however, the most effective contribution to the debate made by *Cahiers* came from a series of "exemplary readings" of films, made by the journal's collective (the journal had now changed and tried to organize itself as a militant group).[7] In particular, the analyses of Ford's *Young Mr. Lincoln* and Sternberg's *Morocco* constituted a kind of challenge, because they studied two films belonging to the group that is both the hardest to defend and the closest to *Cahiers'* heart: films that remain within bourgeois ideology, but clearly show all its sides. The "reading" attempted by the journal uncovers the principles that rule the film, which should work silently, and yet are revealed through their effects. By "foregrounding" this work aims to "let the film say what it says through what it does not say," "to let what was already silently there emerge" (Cahiers du Cinéma 1970).[8]

In order to understand how these analyses are structured, let us quickly look at the analysis of *Young Mr. Lincoln*. On the one hand, the film emphasizes a precise ideological plan. It affirms values like private property and respect for the law. It connects history with myth and sees the realization of destiny in Lincoln's life. In it the political and the moral dimensions overlap, thus suggesting that any political position depends on an ethical choice. It exalts the role of the family and the positive side of rural culture. On the other hand, however, *Young Mr. Lincoln* transgresses its own purposes. The very wish to translate its ideological project into images and sounds, together with the obligation to compare this project with the ways in which images and sounds concretely intertwine, leads Ford's film to make moves that seem excessive and distorting. The plot is sometimes forced. There are gaps in the development of the story, unexpected accentuations, sometimes obvious and sometimes unforeseeable solutions, all of which fully show at what cost and with how much work this translation takes place. This brings about a real *deconstruction* of the original project. By trying to embody a certain view of the world, the mise-en-scène gives it away. By entering the film, the ideological project shows its true nature. Because of its own wish to translate the ideological project into images and sounds, translation leads to betrayal.

Cinéthique believed that cinema could break its ties with the dominant ideology only by situating itself elsewhere in a completely new field. *Cahiers* believed instead that the rupture could also take place along internal lines, through the reformulation of the initial design. Allow us to repeat that for the former the ideological slant of a film depends on the way in which the reproduction of the world is approached (what matters is escaping the traps of specular vision: it is necessary, therefore, to break the illusion of reality and to display what is really at stake, in terms of work and materials). For the latter, the ideological slant given to films also depends on the way in which they take charge of the representations that circulate in a given society (what matters is not being foolish servants: hence the usefulness of transmigrations, which create obstacles and initiate contradictions). The difference in accent allows for more maneuvering room. It is no longer necessary to dream of extreme (and even slightly utopian) solutions. It is also possible to recover the past, in order to see how many classics, even without knowing it, are resistant. The clash with the dominant ideology consists of both major frontline battles and apparently minor—and yet often decisive—skirmishes. A good example of this kind of struggle comes from the way in which many films *deconstruct* their initial project.

12.4. The Problem of Ideology (III)

At the time when these two positions were being defined, a third one emerged too, which opposed both the previous ones and approached the problem differently. In a series of articles published in *La Nouvelle Critique* (and later collected in a volume),[9] Jean Patrik Lebel insists that the ideological value of a film depends neither on the functioning of its technical apparatus nor on the directions taken by the mise-en-scène, but on the way directors use their materials, on their ability to exploit the medium, and on the reactions that they generate in the public.

In short, Lebel accuses *Cinéthique* and *Cahiers* of essentialism and mechanical thinking. Both journals believe that the ideology of film lies in something "intrinsic," that is, in the way the camera works or in the reproductive nature of the medium; they also believe that it is enough to break the impression of reality or the tendency to mirroring in order to free oneself from servitude. In reality, cinema is a tool, and nothing more. It is tied to a function (freeing and reproducing reality), which it passively performs; and it has scientific bases, such as the laws of the propagation of light, allowing the construction of an image that is "faithful" to reality. "The camera is not, in itself, an ideological apparatus. It does not produce any specific ideology, nor does its structure condemn it to reflecting the dominant ideology. It is an ideologically neuter instrument, inasmuch as it is an instrument, an apparatus, a machine" (Lebel 1971:26). Neither do the procedures of the mise-en-scène themselves have ideological connotations. They are a linguistic means (once again, mere instruments) of expression for some meaning. In order to judge a film's ideological position, therefore, it is necessary to take into account other variables: first and foremost, how the "filmic signs" are used (their use may ratify their traditional connotations, contradict their superficial meanings, or reveal some ephemeral aspects). Second, one must consider the director's ability to make the best of his material working conditions (which may involve limited means, some unforeseen events, the resistance of reality itself, and so on). Third, the effects on the audience must be taken into account (along with the possibility, therefore, of affecting the orientation and attitudes of public opinion, as well as the possibility of changing the social meaning of cinema itself). A film, in short, is a tool, and it should be judged on the basis of the way in which it is used, the objectives one wishes to pursue, and the effects one achieves.

The scholars' reaction to Lebel was immediate. Among other things, *Cinéthique* published an essay by Baudry that goes back to the theme of specular vision, and *Cahiers* published a series of articles by Comolli on the role of cinematographic technique in the construction of an ideology. We will start with Baudry's essay, published in issue 7–8 of *Cinéthique* and republished a few years later in a separate volume (Baudry 1978). Its goal is to provide further proofs of the idea that cinema, in the guise of a "machine" that merely obeys scientific laws, actually has ideological effects because of the very way in which it is conceived. These effects gravitate around two phenomena: the concealment of the labor that turns reality into a cinematic representation and the construction of a transcendental subject that serves as a support for the audience. The first phenomenon already concerns the "instrumental basis" of cinema. The camera transcribes reality into a series of frames, which, in themselves, lack both light and movement; the projector, by reintroducing light and movement, translates these same frames into an image that, on the screen, looks like reality. In this shift the difference between the starting point (the world) and the finishing point (an image of the world) is reduced to zero. The transformations that took place are hidden from our sight. And the final result is charged with ideological surplus value, just like all commodities, which are charged with an economic surplus value because they conceal the production process.

The second phenomenon is also rooted in the way in which the apparatus functions. As the direct heir to the "camera obscura" of the fifteenth century, the camera presents a space organized on the basis of central perspective. This places the spectators in a privileged position. Because their eyes coincide with the point from which the lines of perspective diverge, they have the illusion of dominating the world (reality unfolds for them), while at the same time giving it life (the filmic reality is their own projection). Thus, the spectators become transcendental subjects: they are the beneficiary and the motor of the game, not *de facto*, but at the level of the imaginary. This move is further reinforced by the ways in which the projection is organized. The screen, theater, and seats all seem to reintroduce the device behind Lacan's mirror phase, in which a child between eight and eighteen months of age produces a first sketch of the "ego" as imaginary formation. The dark theater restores extreme visual concentration; the soft seats place us in a state of reduced motor activity; above all, the screen takes us back to the mirror of our childhood, where we saw the reflection of a body (ours) and we recognized ourselves in the features of an other. Therefore, cinema reproduces an essential phase of the formation of the "ego." By constantly reexperiencing it, the spectators are confirmed in their role as subjects, and thus in the image of someone who, starting from the "self," can order the world and his own experiences. The ideological effect is clear. The idea of subject, of this subject, hides the reality of social relationships, our true role as pawns in a game that escapes our control. It gives us the illusion that we are dominators, even while we are being dominated.

As well as confirming and intensifying the theme at play, Baudry introduces into the debate a reference not only to Marxism, but also to psychoanalysis: Althusser meets Lacan. The importance of Comolli's series of articles (published in 1971 and 1972 in *Cahiers*) lies instead in giving (or at least trying to give) the debate a historical dimension. Comolli asks us to consider the cinematographic "machine" as a whole. Focusing only on the camera risks being partial and distracting, because this restricted focus analyzes only the most visual component of this machine, thus serving as an accomplice to the ideology of "visibility," which is supposedly being contested. The focus here is instead on the whole machine, including its hidden parts. From this starting point, Comolli approaches two historical elements of great importance: the birth of cinema and the death and resurrection of depth of field. In short, the birth of cinema should be viewed neither as the mere perfecting of the "camera obscura" nor as a series of personal inventions. The forces behind its growth are, on the one hand, economic demand (the will to profit from a growing commodity sector, namely, the "spectacle"); and, on the other hand, social demand (the ever-stronger need to "see the world as it is," to develop our eyes in order to make them the instrument of our knowledge). The explosion of these two demands in the second half of the nineteenth century gave birth to a series of experiments both in the field of reproduction of reality and in the field of its "mise-en-scène," culminating in the birth of the cinema. In short, the invention of cinema is determined by ideology (the dream of "true vision"), as well as by economy (expanding capitalism). The second element approached by Comolli concerns, instead, the disappearance and reappearance of depth of field, between the mid-1920s and the early 1940s. Depth of field employs the kind of shot that seems closest to the fifteenth-century model of representation. Usually, the disappearance of depth of field is connected with a technical exigency, namely, the shift from orthochromatic to panchromatic film, with the use of incandescent lights instead of arc-lamps, which produce weaker light and force filmmakers to open the lens, thus reducing the focus. Once again, things are more complicated than this. It is true that, previously, the need for "true vision" required the presence of a space that was usable in its totality (a "landscape-space," open to nature). From the mid-1920s onward, however, this need was expressed in a different form. What gives the image credibility is the possibility of re-producing the world even in its nuances (which panchromatic film does), together with the linearity and cogency of the plot (hence the creation of genres), and, above all, the possibility of reproducing on the screen the sound dimension.[10] The ideological question, however, always rules the game, and not vice versa. Technique never comes first, but always follows.

We will end our overview of a debate that continued to develop in dif-ferent directions here (one thinks of the choice made by *Cinéthique*—and presented in a very long collective text in issues 9–10, 1971—to abandon the field of cinema and to focus on the organization of the political-cultural avant-garde). The picture was clear anyway, and it served as a reference point for a long time still. In order to question cinema at a political level, it is nec-essary to approach the problem of its ideological role. In order to do this, it is necessary to analyze the functioning of the basic machinery and the modes of representation of cinema. Such modes of representation, in turn, rely on a "transparent" image (reality itself seems to appear on the screen), on a "full" subject (the spectators have the illusion of dominating what is offered to their sight), and on a "linear" plot (narrated stories that develop without obstacles and without gaps, as if there were no contradictions in life). The real political action of the cinema is denouncing this choice, which is tied to cinema's own origins, either by reversing it or by revealing it.

12.5. Semiotics/Materialism/Psychoanalysis

The first two 1971 issues of the British journal *Screen* published a translation of the previously analyzed essays by Comolli and Narboni, Leblanc, and Fargier. Their impact was immediate. They at once initiated an open battle, which led *Screen* to play a major role for several years both as a participant in the debate and as a battlefield. This was no simple replication of the French debate. The institutional and cultural context in which the journal worked together with the themes it emphasized and the results it achieved all made its experience something special.[11] First and foremost, *Screen* was not born as a "partisan" journal, but as the organ of an association working in the educa-tional field. This justified its constant attention to the institutional compo-nents of political discourse, as well as the fact that many internal and external ruptures were motivated by disagreements that extended beyond pure "the-ory."[12] Second, *Screen* was close to a (literary and filmic) critical tradition that was both empirical and allergic to abstract categories. This explains its effort to introduce more modern reading "methods," inspired by semiotics, psychoanalysis, and sociology. Third, *Screen* thought that for the previous generation of filmmakers and critics the idea of "engagement" implied the desire to voice one's rage. It therefore tried to broaden the concept and to view this engagement as a connection between personal testimony and formal research, between artistic and political practice. Finally, *Screen* operated in a context where the (filmic or literary) work was viewed as the expression of an "author" and as the display of a "world." This brought about the need to emphasize that the representation of things and of the self is no passive gesture and that one needs to take into consideration other elements. In short, *Screen* was very attentive to the institutional dimension (it often interrogated its own situation vis-à-vis the state apparatus, while the French remained tied to the logic of the "little group"). *Screen* was still very interested in the human sciences (it translated Metz and Todorov, using them to produce some "exemplary analyses"; [13] the French, however, quickly dismissed such approaches as structuralist semiotics). *Screen* tried to reconsider the relation between politics and aesthetics, starting from different historical experiences (it reexamined Brecht, as well as Eisenstein and the Russians, and it accepted contributions by Fortini and Fofi, as well as Kristeva; the French, instead, remained more united). *Screen* questioned tradition and its investigative tools (it approached themes such as the author and realism, in order to dismantle the presuppositions of current criticism; instead, the French did so for reasons that were more internal to theory). This outlook is perhaps too cut and dried (although preferable to portraits of *Screen* as nothing but an epigone of *Cahiers* or *Cinéthique*). If both France and England believed representation (both conveyor and field of ideology) to be at the center of the problem, this belief met with a slightly different sensibility after crossing the Channel.

These facts, although presented briefly, show how *Screen* articulated the framework of its interests. It worked between 1971 and 1980 (when the journal's change of format signaled the end of an epoch). It was animated by both the contribution of such scholars as Colin MacCabe, Steven Heath, Ben Brewster, Paul Willemen, Peter Wollen, and Geoffrey Nowell-Smith and the spirit of a collective.

Let us start with the problem of the "method," in particular with the taking up of semiotics. Why choose this discipline? The answer is that semiotics decisively helps to destroy the idea of the work's immediacy and organic nature, the assumptions of traditional approaches such as author theory. The filmic text, on the contrary, appears as what it is: a totally constructed object; better still, a place where the various materials, levels, and codes enter into contact and conflict. In short, the filmic text is a zone of contradiction and conflict. Heath's extraordinary analysis of *Touch of Evil* deals with this very issue: the filmic text as the field of impossible balances.[14]

Yet one should neither close film in on itself nor view it as the mere interplay of codes: it is instead necessary to connect it to the broader field of social processes. Historical materialism allows such a connection. Its ideas (see Brewster and MacCabe's editorial in vol. 15, no. 1, 1974) help us place films in history, which is viewed as the set of the "essential struggles and conjunctions which have produced the present." One should not risk paying too much attention to the formal dimension, to the author's role, to the world that is reproduced on the screen. Instead, one should reexamine the lessons of those who have shown us how to deal with the relationship between a work and its time, between artistic and social practice: people like Eisenstein and Brecht, who "have both been actively involved in the revolutionary politics of this century, but have also been fascinated by the problem of the sign— of the processes of signification." Finally, it is necessary to pursue certain goals: reconstructing the scenarios in which a film evolves; understanding its actual role, especially if the film is called revolutionary; studying the effects of technical progress; all of this, while at the same time continuing to destroy the idea of textual unity and trying to connect its ideological effect with the dynamics of signification.[15]

When we reconnect films with social space, we cannot help asking who acts, for whom, in what guise. This is the problem of the subject, or rather of its constitution inside and above the text. Psychoanalysis teaches us how the subject develops from the confrontation between the imaginary and the symbolic dimension, from the tension between the fullness that the "ego" believes it possesses and a lack that constantly threatens it, from the conflict between a continuous onslaught of identifications and a sense of dispossession. Starting with vol. 16, no. 1, in 1975 (with Brewster's lucid opening editorial), *Screen* devoted increasing attention to psychoanalysis.[16] It perceived this discipline as a way to complete the study of both the internal and external functioning of texts and also as a unique instrument for forcefully positing the problem of the linguistic and social *identity* of those who are involved in the life of a film. We should mention that the perception of an "excessive" use

of psychoanalysis (what is more, in Lacan's esoteric version) led some contributors to leave *Screen* around mid-1976. It was also this interest in subject
and identity, however, that allowed the journal to initiate a series of questions
that became fundamental to the Anglo-American feminism engaged in film
theory.[17]

Screen examined the intersection of semiotics, materialism, and psychoanalysis, convinced that only these disciplines can ask cinema the "right"
questions: questions about the profile of the filmic text, the role of social
space, the construction of subjects and identities. It also believed that only
through these questions as a group was it possible to grasp the ideological
value of the medium and its political substance. It should be clear that this
is a postdisciplinary (rather than transdisciplinary) use of a group of "methods," resulting in what has been called (sometimes affectionately, at other
times polemically) the "Metz-Althusser-Lacan paradigm." This paradigm
played a major role in the debates of the 1970s and provided a basis for later
approaches.

Besides this, the core of the journal's activity, other elements that are
connected to it deserve attention. In particular, two questions were both important for the debate and the cause of conflict. How "important" is the ideological with respect to the political, and which "examples" should be valorized and supported? The first develops from Althusser's acknowledgment of
the "relative autonomy" of ideology with respect to politics (and economics).
Now, "how much" autonomy does ideology have? If it has a lot, the ideological struggle (and, in particular, the denunciation of bourgeois modes of
representation and the discovery of alternatives) is very useful; if it has only
a little, the only thing to do is to enter directly into the field of political
struggle. A whole issue (4, 1978) is devoted to this question. The journal's
position (see the opening editorial) is that the space of representation initiates
"negotiations" of some sort among ideology, politics, and economics. It is
therefore necessary to avoid both determinism (one of the three dominating
the other two) and partiality (each has a life of its own). MacCabe (in his essay
"The Discursive and the Ideological in Film: Notes on the Condition of Political Intervention") believes that the central problem is the subjects' position, which is defined through discourse. If, however, one intends to reveal
the mechanisms behind this position, "one needs an analysis which can identify the other ideological practices with which the discourse is imbricated,
but also the specific effectivity of the discourse itself" (MacCabe 1978:32),

that is, the real problems it touches upon. Beyond these positions, it remains a fact that the problem of the degree of ideology's autonomy uncovers a latent opposition between those who believe that representation is *the* field to be examined and those who believe that it is only *one* of many such fields, and not even the most important. To put it more simply, the disagreement is between those who want to continue to work with theory (MacCabe, Heath, and Brewster) and those who want a stronger connection with politics (Willemen).

The second question asks which films should be analyzed and valorized. Which should be studied as "symptomatic"? Which should we defend because of its "exemplarity"? Again in this case two tendencies emerged inside *Screen*. On the one hand, there were those who paid attention both to popular culture as expressed by current (cinema or TV) products and to those authors who made popularity a condition of their work, even when it meant going against the current. On the other hand, there were those who were interested in both the avant-garde and experimentalism, that is, in those experiments that did not worry about the public (or at least did not seek the mediation of the public) and that wanted to break with tradition, suggesting radically new things. To put it bluntly: soap-opera deceptions (to be dismantled) or Brecht's cunning (to be understood), against the personal reasons of the underground (to be turned toward new goals) or the rigor of the London Film Coop (to be appreciated as radical practice). *Screen* was open to both sides; some editors were more engaged in the former (Nowell-Smith, MacCabe), others in the latter (Wollen). In both cases, some key factors were at stake, but the alternative reveals two different strategies. One considered the complexity of the dominant system, without ever overlooking its relapses and weaknesses; the other chose to openly oppose the existent and broke habitual attitudes (and pleasures) in the name of the possible. We have, if you will, critical attention and militancy rooted in the social, against research characterized by slightly prophetic outlines, choosing few interlocutors and placing itself at the level of aesthetics.[18]

These are the two main alternatives offered by *Screen*. The impossibility of untangling them (together with some events both internal and external to the editorial staff) caused a shift in tone and content toward the end of the decade. Still, the journal's activity during the key period of its life remained as a point of reference for a whole generation of scholars, while the issues it raised initiated further research itineraries (especially across the ocean, where *Screen* exercised great influence).

12.6. The Role of the Avant-Garde

In these years we frequently observe the temptation (emerging in *Screen*) to call exemplary those avant-garde films that radically break with tradition in the name of purity. Some journals, indeed, turned this option into their banner. They believed that it is impossible to separate political engagement from aesthetic research. For them, breaking with the dominant discourse, so charged with ideology, implied rejecting the current procedures and solutions. Only constant linguistic experimentation would allow cinema to free itself from its traditional bonds and to move toward new, richer horizons.

Among these journals, *Afterimage* deserves special attention. It displayed no "strict" editorial position, as was the case with *Screen* or *Cahiers;* yet its interest in the avant-garde as the testing ground of cinema's "political nature" remained constant for over a decade.[19] The issues of the journal that received the most attention are 4 (1972) and 5 (1974): they contain, in particular, two "programmatic" texts, one by Peter Wollen ("Godard and Counter-Cinema: *Vent d'Est*"),[20] the other by Noël Burch and Jorge Dana ("Propositions").

Wollen views Godard's *Vent d'Est* as the manifesto of a *countercinema* that is radically opposed to the current, orthodox one. The film introduces at least seven turning points. First and foremost, the narrative shifts from "transitive" to "intransitive": the story no longer develops *linearly,* from one episode to another, but presents gaps, jumps, digressions, moments that are closed in on themselves, and so on. Second, identification is replaced by estrangement: rather than relating to the characters' experiences, we are kept at a distance and aware of the scenic fiction. Third, there is a shift from transparency to foregrounding: language is no longer the imperceptible vehicle of the narrated events, but places its mechanisms before the spectator's eyes. A fourth change is that the single diegesis is replaced by a multiple one: the film does not present a unitary, homogeneous world, but a world that is dispersed and heterogeneous. A fifth difference is marked by the shift from closure to aperture: rather than internal, mutually reinforcing references, there intervene references to other films, other narratives, and other media. Next, pleasure gives way to unpleasure: spectators do not experience satisfaction in following the story, but rather are hurt or challenged by what they see. Finally, reality takes the place of fiction: the actors no longer play roles, but interpret themselves while being at work in a film, in this film, which thus shows what it really is. As a result, all the characteristics of cinema as we usually understand it are dismissed, and a new path is inaugurated, where nothing is taken for granted.

Wollen defended the avant-garde elsewhere. We should at least mention his essay "The Two Avant-Gardes," published in *Studio International* in 1975. It compares the experience of the filmmakers belonging to the London Film Coop with those of such directors as Godard, Straub and Huillet, Hanoun, and Jancso. In the first case, we are dealing with a form of inquiry that is very close to that taking place in the field of painting. In the second case, the cinematographic tradition is the starting point for experimentation. Despite the divergence of references and actions, it is important to keep these two trends together, in order to understand where we are going.[21]

Burch and Dana start instead from the revisitation of the history of cinema. Many attempts have been made, in the past, to dismantle and subvert the dominant codes. Not by chance, they often occurred in contexts that were connected with the historical avant-gardes. One thinks of *Das Kabinett des Dr. Caligari,* where the normal way to construct a space is shattered, or of *Čelovek s Kinoapparatom,* which reveals the fabrication processes of film; or of *Vampyr,* where the border between objective and subjective vision disappears. The goal that underlies these attempts is to make the construction principle of the work evident, instead of letting it act silently; to let the structural and serial bonds come to blows (embodied, respectively, by the organization of the plot and the juxtaposition of recurrent themes), instead of allowing their cooperation; and to find substitutes for the systems of representation in use, instead of reusing them without discussing them.

On this basis, Burch and Dana introduce a new taxonomy of filmic forms, the criterion of which is the degree of adhesion to dominant cinematographic codes. The more distant these codes, and the more systematically distanced, the more the ties with the current ideology are broken and real issues emerge. In particular, Burch and Dana's map includes films inspired and explained at all levels by the dominant codes; films explained by the codes, but where the presence of a style hides this; films that only partially defy the codes' ideological determinations; and, finally, films that, although ideologically determined, question their determination through the place they give the codes and the way they play with them (Burch and Dana 1974:46, 48). They exemplify each category with a film, which is carefully studied. For the first category, they choose Lang's *The Secret behind the Door,* where—despite everything—the traditional devices are applied; for the second, Welles' *Citizen Kane,* where the reliance on the codes in use is paired with some departures, shaping a personal style. Dreyer's *Gertrud* explains the third category. It questions such important issues as the construction of space. The plot of this last film is systematic enough to give us an idea of what the fourth category is like. Here all of the illusory dimensions are dismissed; the rules through which a text is constructed are easily seen, and the spectator may become aware both of the object in front of him and of his own place.

Afterimage is, of course, not the only journal engaged in defending the avant-garde. We should also mention *Artforum,* which published two important essays by Annette Michelson, one on Dziga Vertov (1972a), the other on contemporary experimentalism (1972b). Breaking with the traditional modes of representation introduces a new aesthetic dimension, where the material nature of the work and the objectivity of its procedures are heightened.

12.7. Echoes of the Debate

Following the affairs of several journals[22] has allowed us to reconstruct the outline of the debate. This choice was not fortuitous. In these years journals played a major role in the development of the debate: they introduced passwords, they promoted mutual comparisons that were often ferocious, they searched for internal clarity, and they published manifesto-like essays. These procedures corresponded very well to the spirit of the time. In these same years, those who were occupied with politics typically worried about the "correct line" (paying attention also to nuances), belonged to a (small but pure) group, and tended to privilege open conflict (without mediations).

Yet the emerging preoccupations and orientation were a widespread patrimony. Many scholars argued the necessity of questioning the political and ideological value of cinema without even considering the lines of work that we have outlined. Let us, then, look at a broader horizon and analyze other contributions (some of which were published by these same journals), regardless of the different positions of each journal.

13 REPRESENTATION, UNREPRESENTED, UNREPRESENTABLE

13.1. The Critique of Pure Representation

The debate on the ideological and political value of cinema triggered more wide-ranging reflections, from which the debate drew many suggestions. At stake was a strong critique of the way in which *representation* had been viewed and practiced. Many scholars participated in the debate. Some focused on the perverse effects a certain kind of representation has on individuals and on social groups. Others were more interested in denouncing the falsehood of many current solutions and envisioning new ones. Others intended to dismantle the assumptions behind the idea of representation.

The starting point was the need for new measures. Representation had long been perceived as an imperceptible filter of reality, as a mediation that readily dissolves. To the idea of transparency we should oppose the concept of *opacity*. Representation had also been seen as a means of both fixing appearances and giving form to an interior universe. To the idea of functionality we should oppose the concept of *resistance*. Finally, representation had been viewed as a device that allows the organic illustration of a world, as well as its ordered perception. To the idea of fullness we should oppose the concept of *dispersion*.

Why does such a substitution take place? The idea of representation as mirror, instrument, and synthesis derives from our conception of it as a *re-presentation*: something that at the moment is not here (reality) returns in a different form (images). Without a doubt, absence and presence overlap in any representation, yet the relationship between these two terms is not so linear. One wonders what the substitution act relies on: what forces it mobilizes, how much work it takes. Furthermore, one wonders what legitimacy allows a substitute to replace an absent. It does so in the name of what principle, in view of what advantages? Finally, one wonders to what extent the substitution takes place: what it deprives us of, what effects it has. We then realize that the mimetic, functional, and symbolic dimension of representation is a mere illusion: we encounter its consoling and abusive double, both a beneficent and a poisonous remedy, an extension that fills the eyes while hiding things. Hence the importance of such concepts as opacity, resistance, dispersion, which tell us that representation is no convergence of present and absent, but an open tension between a replacement and that which has been replaced, a result and the work behind it. In order to understand what is at stake, we need to accept this conflict, change point of view, and maybe even give up the word *representation* itself, which is now too compromised.

In a word, the debate is characterized by a feeling of opposition, against representation as re-presentation, and against the capabilities that are usually attributed to it. The goal of this is to uncover the elements of tension and to find new capabilities, even if they lead us to excess and emptiness; to say good-bye to the key word of the debate, which is itself distracting.

Despite this common background, the scholars' contributions display a great variety of themes and tones. Generally speaking (though simplifying somewhat), we can identify three major kinds of contributions: *philosophical, aesthetic,* and *militant.* In works of the first kind, representation is opposed as an idea. The conception of re-presentation perpetuates a logic that focuses on the being-there of things, rather than celebrating their loss. Hence the need for a new conceptual horizon, a transformation of the unrepresented and the unrepresentable into strengths. Its outcome is a truly negative thought, with contributions from thinkers outside the discourse on cinema, such as Derrida and Lacan.[1] Works of the second (aesthetic) kind attack representation as a model of the current artistic practices, which aim only to stage something, whether external reality or an experience. Instead, we need to give a work back its materiality and make it first and foremost an object rather than a mirror. Incidentally, many of these works are modeled on the "manifestos" that are so typical of the historical avant-gardes of the twentieth century. Works of the third (militant) kind condemn the effects of representation: portraying the world ("that" world, and in that specific "manner") means imposing a deviating view of things. People do not become aware of the real conditions of their existence, of the actual situation they live in, and of the actual relationships regulating society. Only a discourse that tells everything about itself or that demonstrates its tools and procedures will manage to break the illusion that is the foundation of ideology.

We will now focus on some of the works that punctuated the debate, starting with a famous essay by Roland Barthes that interrogates the constitutive mechanisms of filmic representation.

13.2. Barthes and Obtuse Meaning

By the mid-1960s Barthes had greatly contributed to the establishment of semiotics, with both his *Eléments de sémiologie* and his works on narrative and the "system" of fashion.[2] Between the 1960s and 1970s Barthes called his project into question. It is impossible either to reduce every work (a novel, a report, a film, etc.) to an ordered system of signs or to reduce the sign to the juxtaposition of a signifier and a signified. Indeed, in a text different constitutive elements enter into a kind of struggle, which involves them first of all in their materiality. Therefore, such notions as writing, sign-function, etc., are unable to account for the situation. A text is not just the means of a signification, or a communication, but an open laboratory, the space of a "writing."

This was the context when, in 1970, Barthes published in issue 222 of *Cahiers du Cinéma* an essay called "Le troisième sens" (later translated into English in 1977). His point of departure is a frame from *Ivan Groznij* where two courtiers pour some gold on the czar's head during his coronation. This frame displays three levels of meaning. The first is "the informational level, which gathers together everything I can learn from the setting, the costumes, the characters, their relations, their insertion in an anecdote with which I am (even if vaguely) familiar" (Barthes 1970 [1977]: 52). At this level communication takes place or a series of immediately graspable data is transferred. The sciences of the "message," such as old semiotics, deal with it. The second is the symbolic level, signaled by the presence of the gold. It is more complex than the previous level, if only because it can, in turn, be decomposed. Various symbolisms are in fact at play: referential (present in ceremony that is filmed); diegetic (tied to the theme of wealth in the film); authorial (connected with the value that this theme has in Eisenstein's whole work); and historical (tied to the meaning gold has always had for man). The sciences of the symbolic, the second semiotics, psychoanalysis, dramaturgy, etc., deal with this level. But there is also a third level, harder to identify and define, and yet "evident, erratic, obstinate." It can be perceived in a few details and in the way they are presented, such as "a certain compactness of the courtiers' makeup, thick and insistent for the one, smooth and distinguished for the other; the former's 'stupid' nose, the latter's finely traced eyebrows, his lank blondness, his faded, pale complexion, the affected flatness of his hairstyle" (53). At this level, meaning neither depends on the presence of something on the scene nor merges with the dramatic elements of the episode that is being narrated. It is more than the indication of a presence, and at the same time beyond the narrative. Thus, it stands in opposition to the symbolic meaning, which could be defined as *obvious* (etymologically: what comes ahead); this third meaning can be called *obtuse,* both because it is broader than the others (like the obtuse angle, as compared to the right angle) and because it stands outside the sensible and the measurable (like an obtuse individual as compared to one who behaves appropriately). In short, this meaning is beyond measure, it is something *excessive* or *exceeding*.

Let us try to clarify its outlines. Other images, not only Eisenstein's, suggest that often the *obtuse meaning* derives from the disguising of some character, in particular of those disguises that, although obvious, never stop attracting our attention. It has to do with an artifice that is both pastiche and fetish. The same thing happens when we touch upon the erotic sphere. The obtuse meaning derives from radiant beauty and from its opposite, ugliness and the ridiculous, and from something else, namely, uneasiness and, perhaps, sadism. Yet again it has to do with both explicit elements and intriguing facts, with moments of clarity and question marks. What characterizes the obtuse meaning, then, is its ability to define something that draws us in, something touching and sensitive: *emotion* is its first realm. We are not talking of a sappy emotion, but of "an emotion which simply designates what one loves, what one wants to defend; an emotion-value, an evaluation" (59).

In this respect, we may well say that the obtuse meaning does not belong to the order of articulated language, but rather to that of *interlocution*. It involves the relationship between image and observer "over the shoulder or on the back of articulated language" (61). Obtuse meaning emerges without being foreseen by a language, unlike the meaning of words. It has no pre-established position in a text, unlike the elements of syntax. It even baffles linguistic descriptions: it can only be pointed out, underscored, reconsidered.

Consequently, the obtuse meaning is a striking presence that imposes itself outside what an image means or wants to relate. It operates beyond the functionality of signs. It is a *supplement* to a game that is self-sufficient in itself, but the observer depends on it, in order to establish a relationship with what he is observing.

Emotions, interlocution, supplement: the excessive nature of the third meaning begins to acquire definition. Let us add that its excessive nature emerges above all with respect to the narrative. The obtuse meaning is indifferent to the story that is being narrated and to the latter's meanings; besides, it is in a constant state of depletion. It lacks information of its own. It may be compared to an accent that punctuates and underlines certain details of the scene. Because of these very characteristics, the obtuse meaning never represents an intensification or an enrichment of the narration but, rather, its counterpoint: by remaining outside the succession of the events, by creating a pause, and by establishing a new rhythm, it emerges as antinarration par excellence. "The obtuse meaning is the epitome of a counter-narrative; disseminated, reversible, set to its own temporality, it inevitably determines (if one follows it) a quite different analytical segmentation to that in shots, sequences, and syntagms (technical or narrative)—an extraordinary segmentation, counter-logical and yet 'true'" (63).

Subverting narration is only the tip of the iceberg, for the very idea of representation is under discussion. The obtuse meaning does not, in fact, belong to the logic that makes of the image an instrument with which to accomplish "restitution" or "expression." On the contrary, it operates outside of every finality, every economy. It doesn't compensate for or capitalize anything. This happens because in the last analysis the obtuse meaning invests *signifiers without signifieds,* material presences that lack explicit counterparts, which, if anything, function like a kind of rebus. Obtuse meaning is connected with details that do not "say" anything other than that images are constructed with withdrawals, juxtapositions, and deviations and at the same time with chiaroscuros, lines, and contours. What emerges is the body of a figure, and not what the figure illustrates. Obtuse meaning is also connected with details that attract the observer's eyes because of their capacity for resistance, because of their intransitivity: a question, not an answer, emerges here. Therefore, representation is doubly in crisis. On the one hand, it has to acknowledge the concrete game that underlies it; on the other hand, it has to go beyond itself, in order to find elsewhere, in a gaze running through it, its real reason for existence.

It is easy to recognize here the themes so dear to the later Barthes. Let us think of the suggestive pages of *Camera Lucida,* where photography is seen as a mere composition of lines and is at the same time connected to its ability to "puncture" the observers, to call them directly into play.[3] Let us return to "Le troisième sens." The dimension investigated by Barthes takes us to the heart of the *filmic,* the quality that makes a film a singular object (in the sense of both unique and unusual), instead of the usual, canonical working out of the possibilities afforded by cinema. The third meaning, therefore, explains the filmic. It testifies to a dimension that cannot be reduced to any instrumentality and predefined order. It marks the emergence of significance, rather than of communication and signification. It is the opening to an alterity or maybe to a utopia such as "a representation which cannot be represented" (64).

This is Barthes' position. He dismantles representation in the name of its concentratedness and emotional involvement with the spectator. The final praise of the still, an element that serves as a mere interval but that is also, once frozen, an element of unforeseeable availability, fully confirms the author's framework.

A different and complementary move (although perhaps less rich than Barthes') comes from Lyotard in an essay called "L'a-cinéma," which was published in 1973 in a special issue of *La Revue d'Esthétique:* the "movement" of representation marks its point of rupture.

13.3. Lyotard and the *A-cinéma*

In these years Lyotard actively participated in the broad philosophical movement denouncing the "violent" character of Western thought, guilty of a systematic suppression of difference and alterity, and devoted, instead, to systematicity and identity. The pair *discours* and *figure,* which provided the title for a book that Lyotard had published two years before "L'a-cinéma," makes this polarity explicit. On the one hand, we have the *discursive* or that which presents itself as logical, ordered, meaningful; on the other hand, we have the *figural* or something that is felt before being understood, which expresses a force, rather than meaning, which has an existence before having a function. Even better, on the one hand, we have representation, understood as the organic construction of a world; on the other hand, we have the auroral and undetermined source of representation, the amorphous, from which representation can take shape.

Lyotard shows that Western culture literally abolishes the figural in favor of the discursive. Galileo with his idea of science, Renaissance painting with the primacy of perspective, Hegel and his philosophy—all reduce and expunge the metaphorical, the multivalent, the contradictory. Nonetheless, the figural continues to press forward. With Mallarmé or Cézanne representation moves toward the other and incorporates it, transforms itself, and dissolves.

The contrast and coexistence of the figural and discursive become clearer if we reconsider the Freudian primary and secondary processes. The former is characterized by the uncontrolled flux of psychic energy and is ruled by the pleasure principle, aiming exclusively to free itself from unwanted tensions. The latter is guided by the reality principle, leading the energetic dimension of the unconscious to a normalization, in view of the requirements of the external environment. Similarly, the figural is dominated by power and energy; instead, the discursive gathers the stimuli that underlie it, recognizes them, and disciplines them. Thus, the drives that move language become a meaningful, coherent, functional saying; the desire to speak becomes a discourse.

This, in very broad strokes, is the framework for "L'a-cinéma."[4] This essay returns to the points we have just seen. First of all, Lyotard observes that cinema is the inscription of movement, that is, of something that has to do with energy and drives. But not all movements are actually accepted; on the contrary, many are either excluded or erased. Let us think of the way in which movies usually reject what is fortuitous, badly framed, badly printed, badly regulated, untidy, dirty, or misshapen. Professional norms require that all that is either exceedingly intense or not part of an overall order should be left out. All that remains is what refers us back to something else and reveals a system of connections, or, in short, what can be compared and unified.

After all, the function of the mise-en-scène shows this. First and foremost, it helps replace reality with its representation. "To arrange a mise-en-scène means to mark a limit . . . and to establish a relationship of representation or duplication between one region and another" (Lyotard 1973 : 363). It also helps unify all the data into a single design. To arrange a mise-en-scène means to make an ordered and uniform whole. We have, thus, the separation between reality and its double, with the former's repression in favor of the latter, and the elimination of what does not lend itself to being recognized, coordinated, and restrained. Hence, "if we view it in light of this primordial function of exclusion, which is operative both inside and outside of the area of film, the mise-en-scène always acts as a factor of libidinal *normalization*" (364).

It is precisely this necessity of normalization that is a key factor. All that is inside or around a film is brought back to the acceptable, the commensurate, the organic, and the well-formed. We repeat: libidinal normalization "implies the exclusion of everything on the set that cannot be reduced to the body of the film and, off the set, to the body of society" (364). Hence a reformulation of the question we usually ask ourselves. The question is not how or what to represent, but how and why "the exclusion or the foreclosure of all that is judged to be unrepresentable, because it is not recurrent" (364) takes place.

As the transcription of movement, cinema is not always subject to this rule, however. The unrepresentable belongs within its horizon. The *a-cinéma* (the negative of current cinema, or current cinema from a negative perspective) obeys different laws and standards. Its logic is the same as that of pyrotechnics, namely, the exaltation and the waste of forces. Thanks to this, films stops being "an object of value that stands for another object, with which it composes, compensates, and reinserts itself into a whole that is regulated by some constitutive law" (359). Rather, it becomes a place where erotic energy that is invested in it is "promoted, displayed, and burned in vain" (359). In short, a pyrotechnic film does not "economize" movements, but accepts them all in their integrality, not so as to make them productive, but to turn them into an opportunity for *jouissance,* for enjoyment.

At this point, "two directions open up for the conception (and production) of a cinematographic object that conforms to the requirements of pyrotechnics. These two poles are immobility and the excess of movement. When we let ourselves be pulled toward these two antipodes, cinema stops being an orderly force: it produces real (that is, vain) simulacra, intensities of enjoyment, instead of consumable and productive objects" (360). An extreme exemplification of the path of immobility comes from the *tableau vivant:* the fixed nature of the image, the suspension of becoming, the characters' construction through their poses all underscore the relationship between who sees and who is seen and at the same time make the latter a "victim" of the former. The path of excessive movement is instead best exemplified by *lyric exaltation.* Rather than interrupting its flux, a film amplifies it to an extreme degree; it is characterized by accelerations, abrupt turns, shifts of scene, alternating shots, etc. As a result, the focus is on what supports the image, more than on the latter's content; the signifier acquires more intensity than the signified, and the spectator himself becomes a "victim," more than is warranted.

Beyond these two extremes, however, pyrotechnics emerge every time the drives intervene as what they are, as forces in action, without rigid regulation. *A-cinéma* needs to step beyond the threshold of the economic, the mimetic, the representative, and to open up to those movements that are usually excluded or erased; it needs to open up to the dynamic, the energetic, the libidinal, the unrepresentable.

This is Lyotard's position. His criticism of representation makes him reverse the usual terms, favoring (and invoking) disorder instead of order, waste instead of functionality, intransitivity instead of transitivity, the dynamic instead of the inert. Barthes found the unrepresentable within representation, in a series of details that could help redefine its overall design. Lyotard, instead, found it outside representation, in a series of measures that upset the laws that have apparently been defined. These two paths diverge, but both are useful for understanding the terrain and the directions of the development of a ferocious attack on an apparently tranquil notion.

13.4. The Blind Spots of Filmic Representation

Barthes and Lyotard mark two fundamental moments of the debate, although their work on cinema is only episodic.[5] To complete this picture of "philosophical" reflections on the cinema, we should move on to the work of Marie-Claire Ropars, a scholar who focuses primarily on this field (often in conjunction with literature).

Her contribution to the debate is great and varied, articulated in a series of works culminating in *Le texts divisé* (and later followed by *Ecraniques*). In the 1980s her essays found their ideal complement in the journal *Hors Cadre,* which she directed, together with Michèle Lagny and Pierre Sorlin. Her work is articulated at various levels. First, it invites us to liberate ourselves from such traditional concepts as sign, meaning, work, etc., which are corollary to the idea of representation and which tend to turn a film (or a book) into a unitary, functional, and stable space. Instead, it is necessary to change perspective. Like books, films are *texts,* that is, an open combination of elements that are not endowed with a predefined place or role, but which are engaged in weaving and reweaving configurations of a variable order. Even better, it is the place of a *writing,* of a game dominated by the tensions and conflicts that both preside over and precede the mere making of sense.

Ropars carefully analyzes the notion of *writing,* which dates back to Derrida (but which is also present in Barthes and, under a different name and with a different focus, in Lyotard). She shows how such an idea defines a field dominated by pure differentiality (each element is what it is because it "diverges" from the others) and by perennial movement (every element is what it is because it "drifts" elsewhere). Hence, it is possible to return to Eisenstein's notion of *editing*. In both cases we are dealing with ongoing processes, rather than stable results; with agreements that are the result of a clash, rather than a mutual adjustment; with pictures that change before our eyes, rather than finding a point of equilibrium. In this respect, both writing and editing mark the liberation from logocentrism, which is obsessed with the identifiable and the meaningful. They allow us to perceive the making and the unmaking of the text, more than the recognizability of its various components. They refer us to the "constitution of a signifying chain that is reversible and open" more than to the "production of meaning, which should imply stopping, blocking, and fixing the process" (Ropars 1981:49).

Ropars tests this new conceptual horizon in a series of exemplary "readings." We should point out that "reading" a film or a book does not mean giving back what is already there, but entering an often latent dynamic and making it explode with all its productivity. Indeed, it is the "reading" itself that allows a film or a book to appear as the site of writing. The shrewd "reader" will realize that any balance is only apparent, that structures collapse, that differentiality and movement find their place once again. Hence some strategic moves: Ropars relies on elements that seem marginal at first sight; she overcomes the linearity of plots; she uncovers a network of references that go beyond the literal; she analyzes films as if they were novels, and vice versa; above all, she "provokes" the theoretical elements of the text. Thus, *La règle du jeu, M, India Song,* etc., reveal unsuspected sides. They point out that images may now only survive in the form of expectation and absence,[6] thus clearly referring to the many trends that focused on the critique of representation.

Ropars' method is highly personal, unlike her ideas, which were instead widespread in these years. Echoes of them can also be found at the level of criticism in Pascal Bonitzer's essays (many of them originally published in *Cahiers du Cinéma*). He focuses on a series of phenomena that seem to reveal the mechanisms of cinematographic representation, in particular on its relationship with reality. One of these phenomena is the offscreen: in every film, next to the space represented on the screen, there is one that we only imagine, but the existence of which we perceive as equally certain. Classic cinema worked hard to establish the complete homogeneity of the offscreen and on-screen worlds. Consider the game of "announcements" and "confirmations" constituted by the characters' side glances and a subsequent shot of the object they see. An irreducible offscreen space is still there: the space where the camera is situated. This is an "other scene" with respect to the space of the action, a scene that refers to the "material, heterogeneous, and discontinuous reality of the *production* of the fiction" (Bonitzer 1976:17). Every offscreen area, no matter how hard we try to tame it, presents the problem of this "other scene," thus reminding us that representation always gravitates around an invisible point, to which all that is seen on the screen is indebted.

Bonitzer makes similar observations about the extreme close-up. A face or an object loses any relationship with the space around it when enlarged on the screen. Its representation, freed from the obligation of the extension and the depth of the scene, "becomes then pure surface" (1982:37). This does not prevent us from experiencing emotions. That very face and object may elicit our wonder or our horror (as Hitchcock shows), and yet we perceive them as pure images. As a result, representation is in a crisis not because it tends toward an "other scene," but because it reveals all its materiality. Bonitzer continued his work with a successful book (1985) on "nonframing," that is, that very modern way to compose images, playing on the decentralized, the empty, the fragmentary, etc. He analyzes representation starting from one of its "anomalous" moments, contending that only in this way is it possible to grasp its real nature.

13.5. Toward a Representation That Is Other

In the 1970s the need to go beyond the notion of representation often re-sulted in the valorization of experiments that diverged from the usual modes of cinema and that tried new solutions, styles, and formulas. Hence the fre-quent praise of the avant-gardes, especially of those that opposed the idea that a film should represent a world or express an emotion, rather than accounting for itself, for the way it is constructed, or for the materials it uses. Films are neither illustrations nor confessions. They are objects, the product of labor.

The general framework of "aesthetic" essays has already emerged from our analysis of the work published by Wollen, Burch, and Dana in *Afterimage* or by Michelson in *Artforum*. The focus is on the breaks with current practices and on the problems that can be posed within a new horizon. The idea of breaking with "official" cinema is at the core of a large volume by Claudine Eizykman (1976), in which the influence of Lyotard can be discerned. Cinema, in the form in which it has established itself, has three characteristics that also constitute its limits. It is devoted to narration, it is produced on an industrial scale, and it obeys the laws of representation. Yet some films distance themselves from at least one of these features. Bertolucci's *La strategia del ragno* and Fellini's *Satyricon* oppose the traditional way of constructing narrative. Events have no "natural" development comparable to that which guides human affairs; instead, the story divorces history. Other films act at different levels. For instance, Robbe-Grillet's *L'homme qui ment* puts both the story and the mise-en-scène in crisis. In this attack against the narrative, industrial, and representative dimension of cinema, it is important to bring out the energy underlying every linguistic art and the dynamism that is present in every text. Underground cinema, such as Anger's, Brakhage's, Snow's, Nekes', etc., allows this, thanks to its indifference to signifieds and its interest in signifiers.

Filmmaker and theorist Peter Gidal is even more radical. He opposes the politics of moving in small steps and approves only of totally new films. His *structural/materialist cinema* rejects every element of illusionism. The constitutive elements of a film present themselves as what they are (a shot is a shot, not a fragment of the world; a color is a color, not an object's quality). Further, this cinema is self-referential. Its constitutive elements are connected to the process of the film's fabrication (the film shows its grain; the image shows the point of view from which it was shot). Finally, this cinema tends to assume a didactic dimension. Its constitutive elements are explored in a systematic way, in order to show its possibilities and limits (what is in focus is compared to what is out of focus; movement with immobility). Thus, we obtain a film which "does not *represent,* or document, anything" (Gidal [ed.] 1976:1), which is merely the record of its own making: it is a body, an object, the locus of a practice.

To complete the picture of the contributions to the debate on the "aesthetic" level (which we have exemplified with works from "inside" cinematographic experimentalism) we should also mention the historical studies that sought to reconstruct the broader activity of the avant-garde, with its various trends and currents. Dominique Noguez's successful *Eloge du cinéma expérimental* (1979) is a good example of this. This book both reconstructs notable episodes and figures and discusses the reasons behind experimentalism. Another example comes from Dana Polan's *The Political Language of Film and the Avant-Garde,* which, in a broad overview centered on the New

American Cinema, defends those films that encourage, or even require, "the intellective involvement, the conscious engagement of the spectator" (Polan 1985:30). Yet another example comes from Maureen Turim's *Abstraction in Avant-Garde Films* (1985), which discusses how experimentalism tries to step beyond both classic narrative and the alternatives suggested by Modernism.

13.6. Representation and Ideology

In the previous chapter we have already encountered many examples of the third main group of works, characterized by a "militant" spirit. In order to complete the picture, we will now focus on two of the main contributors to *Screen,* Colin MacCabe and Stephen Heath. On various occasions MacCabe discusses the problem of realism. Classic realism (both cinematographic and literary), thanks to the adoption of a comprehensive point of view of the events presented, favors the elimination of all contradictions and tensions. What emerges is a subject (the author, the spectator) that is "presumed to know." We have progressive realism, however, when there are some "contradictions between the dominant discourse of the text and the dominant ideological discourses of the time" (MacCabe 1985:44). In other words, this kind of realism emerges when a film displays a conflict between what it says and what it talks about, or what literally makes it talk. We can also go one step further and initiate a subversive strategy. In this case, we need to question the subject's position and turn it into a locus of dispersion and fractures rather than of "presumed knowledge." The subjects will display their multifarious adherences (to the discursive, to the politic), maybe even revealing their uncertain profiles (someone both speaking and spoken); in any case, they will allow us to see clearly the actual conditions and aims of representation.

MacCabe often also works on the methodological aspects of the problem (in this sense, *Screen* is deeply indebted to him). The work we have just mentioned is, however, relevant in that it shows that the idea of representation (and even of realistic representation) is far from uniform and, instead, lends itself to a multiplicity of positions.

Stephen Heath, one of the most prominent theorists of the time, also analyzes the notion of representation in its various accepted meanings and their outcomes. His analyses of the cinematographic space are especially famous. In fact, a film makes its decisive moves at the level of space: a picture becomes a portion of reality; a surface acquires three-dimensionality and ideally expands beyond its borders; a fragment becomes part of the world. In other words, what we have is "the conversion of seen into scene" (Heath 1981:37). This conversion is at the root of cinematographic narration. The onscreen space becomes the container of an action and is ready to expand as much as the development of the events requires. This conversion also relies on the help of some rules that classic cinema carefully developed, at the level of the composition of the image (e.g., the feeling of depth produced in a picture by the disposition of the objects), the shooting techniques (e.g., the way in which the camera movements can order the objects in sight), and the editing (e.g., the way in which the shot/reaction shot connects the various sections). Above all, this conversion places the spectator in a privileged position: this space displays itself, thanks to the gaze; the many fragments make sense together, thanks to the gaze. The spectator emerges as the *unified and unifying subject* of the vision. He "masters" the representation, accompanying and completing its development. Hence Heath's great attention to the mechanisms that allow the subject–spectator both to produce a fictional space and to be its guarantor: in terms of psychoanalytical processes, this happens because of the *suture,* thanks to which an imaginary totality emerges from a series of isolated shots. Hence, too, the interest in the moments in which the film discloses the presence of this subject–spectator: an example of this comes from the signals for the viewer or the presence of jumps or gaps in the vision. Hence, finally, the analysis of the formation processes of the subject, brought about both by the movie and by the cinematographic *apparatus:* the onscreen images force upon the spectator predefined points of view; the forms and places of the projection also generate equally constraining consumption rituals. We can identify the kinds of subjectivity (some transgressive, some liberating) that cinema brings into play in relation to all these factors.

Once again, we are aware that this brief overview cannot do justice to Heath's broad interests. Here we have concentrated on the elements of his thought that deal most closely with the problem of representation. As with MacCabe, his aim is to "dismantle" both the mechanism behind cinema and, more generally, the discourses that aim to represent the world. This clarifies the ideological implications of his position (such a mechanism aims to create an illusory dimension) as well as its roots (this mechanism rests upon a certain way of constructing a text and defining subjectivity) and positive margins (there are liberating texts and subjectivities).

Other scholars deserve to be mentioned, along with MacCabe and Heath.

In *Screen*'s sphere we think of Willemen, who reminds us that behind every representation there is the concrete labor of "fabricating" images and sounds (some of his essays are now included in Willemen 1994); or of Geoffrey Nowell-Smith, who pays attention to the social environment in which representations circulate and pertain to the whole field of mass culture (including TV sports programs).[7] To conclude this section devoted to the "militant" approaches, we would like to mention a book that greatly influenced the German debate, because it also blends Anglo-French ideas with the autochthonous tradition inaugurated by Benjamin and continued, for instance, by Kluge or Enzensberger:[8] Hartmut Bitomsky's *Die Röte des Rots von Technicolor* (1972). The book is characterized by its fragmentary and evocative style, and it touches upon many issues. Its starting point is the contradictory nature of cinema. Cinema is a means of communication, and as such it favors human relationships; at the same time, it is part of the culture industry, and because it involves commodities it favors human alienation. Within capitalist society films develop their communicative potentialities only if they stick to their function as commodities. The constant reappearance of the same stories, a clear sign of the industrial product, does not underscore what films say, but the very fact that they say it. The communicative act and the persons who perform it become the central elements, more than content itself. Thus, cinema is close to the "language of the proletariat," in which talking and interacting count more than the mutually exchanged news. There are no "knowledges" with access reserved for an elite, but a communicative process to which all are invited.

To complicate matters, however, films work through at least two circuits of communication: an external one, between the screen and the audience; and an internal one, between the fictional characters. The spectator establishes a relationship with the movie through the relationships that the characters entertain among themselves. He learns what has happened together with the protagonist, when the latter is informed. He wonders what will happen together with the heroine, who asks herself the same question. Hence his involvement (according to Bitomsky, an affective involvement) in what is presented on the screen: communicating also means "feeling with."

This leads us to the problem of filmic representation. What texture, what truth value, do the things that appear on the screen have? In itself, an image is a mere surrogate. It substitutes appearances for reality; it shows as present objects that are actually absent. In this sense, it is true that representation is the locus of an illusion. It is also true, however, that this mechanism has by now revealed its underlying logic. The critical efforts made at both the theoretical and the artistic level make it impossible for us to believe fully in this illusion. This means that the more a film tries to provide us with reality, the more it gives away the inanity of its gesture. Indeed, it is useful in this respect, because it signals a mistake without trying to replace it with a "correct version" (see the totally self-reflexive films supported by *Cinéthique* or Gidal). In other words, a representative film is like a midterm exam where a line has been marked in red by the professor. "The red line does not represent the correction of the mistake, but its underscoring: this red is the red of technicolor" (Bitomsky 1972: 133). This line explains the book's title and the idea that representation does not need dismantling as much as it needs to function while making us aware of how it functions.

13.7. Positions

The debate we have tried to reconstruct in broad terms shows the plurality of the positions at play. Some scholars attack films' pretense of giving us back the world in the name of a new philosophy, which is no longer connected to the myth of presence, fullness, and functionality. Others do the same in the name of liberation from bourgeois ideology. Some counterpose current representations to film that only talks about itself, but in so doing says everything about itself. Others aim for a small but significant increase in meaning. Some wish for a language that effects systematic "estrangements." Others dream of corrections made in red. Some underscore the problem of the subject; others insist on formal procedures.

Such a variety of positions does not imply confusion. Attempting to merge the explorer's and the cartographer's attitudes, we have tried to uncover the debate's own articulation. We will complete this picture that we have started to define around the polarity of first cinema and politics and then cinema and representation by adding feminist studies of film, for which a possible polarity could be cinema and gender. Significantly, this new area often confronts and reintroduces with great originality the issues we have been dealing with. With feminists the great work of the 1970s found its ideal completion, and with them many of the choices leading to the 1980s achieved maturation.

14 IMAGE, GENDER, DIFFERENCE

14.1. Feminist Film Theory

Three major factors contributed to the birth and development of feminist film theory, which acquired most of its relevance in the Anglo-American environment. First, the women's movement, which took shape in the beginning of the 1970s and engaged both in analyses at all levels and in an open struggle against the social structures dominated by men. It illuminated such themes as the marginality of female roles, the existence of a repressed creativity, and the separation between what is said and what is experienced. It emphasized women's need to overcome their condition and win new spaces and roles. The second factor was the diffusion of independent cinema and the increasing presence of women among filmmakers. By the mid-1970s about 240 movies had been made by women: testimonials, documentaries, and biographies that were to be used in "consciousness-raising" groups, as well as fictional films, which were to be shown at festivals and specialized exhibitions. The third factor was the study of representation. The attention to the ways in which discourse defines visions of the world and assigns a place to their sender or receiver allowed women to understand both the images in which they were forced to reflect themselves and their confinement in spaces assigned to them by the circuit of social communication. This was simultaneously a form of political work, of filmic practice, and of academic research. Feminist film theory openly referred to these experiences and to some extent provoked their confluence.

Within this framework, the study of cinema was merely a tile in a larger mosaic. Along with it, there were other zones of social activity, other experimentations on languages, and other objects subjected to ideological criticism. Yet cinema was not just *any* tile. Constance Penley observes that film's modes of procedure provide "a model for the construction of subject positions in ideology"; its stories, which develop around Oedipal situations, underscore "the unconscious mechanism of sexual difference in our culture"; its placement among both the products of mass culture and works of art allows us "to examine the question of audience and reception in all its complexity" (Penley 1988:3). With respect to the interests of feminism, in short, film seems to be an almost "perfect object of study." Feminist theory, however, is not just another stage of film theory. From a historical point of view, a number of themes that would later be widely circulated first appeared here (e.g., the problem of visual pleasure). Here, too, some of the concepts already in use found new dimensions (e.g., the idea of subject); also, some new approaches found an application for the first time (e.g., *cultural studies*). Its ability to take up, relaunch, and renew the issues of the debate (even if counterbalanced by a tendency to close in on itself) made feminist film theory a major force between the 1970s and 1980s.[1]

14.2. Patriarchal Cinema, Women's Cinema

The first half of the 1970s witnessed the release of the first documentary films made by women on the universe of women, the birth of trend-setting journals like *Women and Film,* an increase in the number of Women's Film Festivals, and the beginning of periodic meetings among female scholars. In these same years many feminist works denounced the partial and distorted way in which current cinema portrayed women. Three names should be mentioned, among others: Marjorie Rosen (1973), Joan Mellen (1973), and Molly Haskell (1974). Films, whether American or European, commercial or authorial, tended to portray female characters according to stereotypes. Very few actresses managed to present well-rounded characters, perhaps only Mae West and Katharine Hepburn. Thus, it was necessary to fight in order to force cinema to acknowledge what women are and have managed to become inside society.

This polemic really hit home, but its tools diminished its effectiveness. The juxtaposition of stereotypes and reality does not take us very far. We need to ask ourselves why cinema keeps presenting fixed characters, to what extent some portrayals of women are more banal than others, how factual truth may be translated on the screen, and to what extent a film is always a reelaboration of the existent. In other words, we need to ask ourselves what function stereotypes have, before we attack them. Similarly, we need to ask ourselves under which conditions reality can display itself, before we invoke it. This is what Pam Cook and Claire Johnston did, in a wide-ranging series of essays that dealt with the avant-garde, with classic American cinema as embodied by Walsh or Ford, and with the work of female directors like Dorothy Arzner. These essays established the basic coordinates of the debate.

"Woman's Cinema as Counter Cinema" (in Johnston 1973) already defines the framework of feminist film theory. Johnston's starting point is the idea of stereotype that seems to confine women. A stereotype is not merely a banal image, but also a tool for representing reality's typical traits, so as to make it immediately recognizable. It is not by chance that iconography (e.g., the portraits of saints) relies on stereotypes. The question we need to ask, therefore, is: why are female characters more monotonous in classic cinema than male ones? It seems that while the latter refer to narrative iconography, which is attentive to the individuality of each character, the former recall the world of *myth,* where we find only unnuanced presences. This allows myths to fulfill their function. Through "fixed and eternal" figures, they provide the same explanation for events that are always different (all our misfortunes depend on the gods' envy . . .). But this same characteristic gives myths a certain fragility, too. These "fixed and eternal" figures in the end reveal themselves as pure inventions (the gods are only masks . . .). The artifice is uncovered and opens a space for critique.

This premise improves our understanding of classic cinema's portrayal of women. Sexist ideology does not manifest itself by "impoverishing" the feminine presence, but rather by relating it to a timeless universe, peopled by absolute and abstract entities. Unlike man, woman is placed outside history and thus both glorified and marginalized. On the other hand, this "mythologizing" can acquire different meanings. What seems to be innovative is often regressive. Mae West does not portray a liberated woman; on the contrary, her character is an accomplice in the construction of the fetishized woman. Similarly, what seems flat is often much more articulated. While Hawks relates his female characters to the male–nonmale opposition and asks them to put on men's clothes if they wish to play a positive role, Ford connects his female characters to the opposition wish-to-wander–wish-to-settle-down and gives them an active and autonomous role with respect to this choice. In the last analysis, we need to acknowledge the diffused and widespread existence of a *patriarchal cinema,* which is based on giving women a mythical role. But if we want to grasp the intentions and articulations of such cinema, we need to examine its structures in detail.

Changing perspective, it is useless to try to escape this framework by appealing to factual reality. A film never presents the world as it is. It can only *represent* it, that is, provide its symbolic portrayal. On the screen it is not a question of things, but of signs. Appealing to the immediacy or neutrality of the gaze, dreaming that reality presents itself to our sight in an autonomous and direct way, is totally distracting, for it makes us forget that the only way to attack patriarchal cinema is to emphasize its linguistic nature. This was accomplished at the very heart of classic Hollywood cinema by women directors like Dorothy Arzner and Ida Lupino. The former (in particular in *Dance, Girl, Dance*) relies on the stereotypes of the vamp and the innocent and shows their inherent contradictions, by opposing women's desire to be liked and their desire to express themselves. The latter (for instance, in *Not Wanted*) reuses classic iconography and opposes it to the female point of view. The effect of this operation is the creation of distortions and uneasiness inside the story. Both directors work on myths and show their artificiality. What emerges then, at least in its fundamental traits, is a true *countercinema,* which will develop fully when the strong points of the dominant structures have been exposed, interrogated as to their function, and replaced by new structures and orientations.

The core of Claire Johnston's and Pam Cook's thought lies both in the recognition and analysis of *the patriarchal system* and in the valorization and support of *countercinema.* This double objective sustains almost all of their work. For instance, patriarchal ideology is illustrated even more clearly in the work of Raoul Walsh (Cook and Johnston 1974). In his films woman is never an individual with a personality of her own, but a mere object to be exchanged, a token whose value and circulation are determined by men, like the value and circulation of currency. Within this logic any true subversion is unthinkable. When a woman attempts to revolt (*Mamie Stover*), she has to surrender and go back to the old system. Hence the idea that a woman's fate is to "be spoken to," never to "speak." With respect to this kind of cinema, the only possibility that Johnston and Cook identify is the development of a *feminist reading* that "denaturalizes" what films take for granted, showing all the inherent contradictions and emphasizing their untenability. On the other hand, their study of Dorothy Arzner's work (Johnston 1975; Cook 1975) clarifies the possibilities of countercinema. Her films develop the theme of transgression and desire. This theme is already subversive, given the need for order and the invitation to renunciation that we find in patriarchal cinema. Above all, this theme manifests itself in the work of the director through a systematic rupture with the procedures used by patriarchal cinema. This explains the presence of significant moments that embody what is otherwise repressed and the ironic reversals of situations that are canonical elsewhere. This also explains why Arzner plays with and dismantles stereotypes. The two scholars conclude that Arzner literally rewrites patriarchal cinema, making it shed its skin. She exposes the contradictions of the dominant system of representation and entrusts women's discourse with the task of reinterpreting situations. She approaches the foundation of a new language. Future feminist cinema would greatly value her example.

14.3. The Dynamics of Pleasure

The basis for discussion provided by Johnston and Cook was decisively enriched by an equally successful essay by Laura Mulvey, "Visual Pleasure and Narrative Cinema."[2] Mulvey performs a double shift: on the one hand, she devotes her attention not only to the way women are portrayed in films, but also to the role of women as spectators; on the other hand, she parallels her textual analysis with a reflection conducted with the instruments of psychoanalysis. Thus, we move from the characters that take shape on the screen to the dynamics that connect the screen to the audience and from a system of representation to the apparatus that regulates its appearance and consumption.

Her point of departure concerns the *pleasures* afforded by cinema. These take two primary forms: scopophilia, which is connected to the presence of an object as source of excitement; and narcissism, which is connected to the presence of an object as source of identification. Their structures are divergent: the former requires separation from the desired reality (the spectator wants something that is and remains on the screen); the latter requires fusion with the reality through identification (the spectator projects himself onto the screen). Between them there is a commonality and complementarity, however. Both pleasures derive from vision, and the drive to possess the other is reinforced by and reinforces the drive to recognize ourselves on the screen. It is not by chance, then, that classic cinema established a close connection between scopophilia and narcissism. Thanks to the appearance of an imaginary world, the desire to possess (what appears in the film) works in tandem with the processes of identification (with the people in the film).

How does the distinction between the genders operate, with respect to this mechanism? In classic cinema it is the male gaze that continually traverses the scene, while the woman is the object of the gaze; the former looks, the latter is looked at. At the same time, the man acts, is in control of the events, makes things happen; the woman is a passive presence, a decorative element, a mere icon. The former moves the diegesis, the latter remains outside of it. This double situation causes the spectator to choose the hero as the object of identification and the heroine as the object of pleasure. The looking and acting man functions as an alter ego, while the woman, who appears and remains passive, is the source of excitement and the prey. This means that the spectator necessarily goes through the male character to take possession of what he desires, the female character. Consequently, cinema is made for a male audience. If we want to have access to the enjoyment of what appears on the screen, we need to wear men's clothes. The female spectator can only be a male spectator.

The woman who appears on the screen also presents another problem. Her lack of a penis unleashes the fear of castration. Therefore, if, on the one hand, she is a fascinating presence, an icon displayed for man's gaze and enjoyment, on the other hand, she is a threatening presence, a possible source of anxiety. Man can escape this anxiety in two ways: he can choose to confront the reactivation of the trauma represented by the fear of castration and explore, devalue, and demystify the woman. This is the path of voyeurism and sadism, which Hitchcock thoroughly explored. Or he can deny this fear and transform the threatening object into an object of devotion, to be preserved and cultivated. This is the path of fetishism, followed by Sternberg. In both cases, man reemerges as the master of the scene, the source of desire, the motor of the action. The woman plays a passive and subordinate role.

These are the essential ideas developed by Mulvey in her essay, at the core of which we find the *gaze*. The gaze is the instrument of the double pleasure that cinema activates. It is the feature that defines the characters of the story. It is the axis that connects the screen to the audience. Classic cinema makes man (both as character and as spectator) the bearer of the gaze, thus devaluing woman, who becomes a mere icon to be contemplated. This way of viewing things needs to be radically changed. First, we need to emphasize the material presence of the camera by showing how it works, who it works for, and who it works against. Then we need to broaden the range of the spectator's possibilities, not orienting his identification in only one way, but leaving more options open. Finally, and above all, we need to break the mechanism of fascination, both the one that leads to voyeurism and sadism and the one that relies on fetishism. We need to construct a filmic "displeasure," if this may help to reverse the habits that derive from the wish to perpetuate a strict sexual hierarchy.

Mulvey's essay profoundly influenced the debate. Her accent on the gaze and her analysis of it, with the help of psychoanalysis and with an eye to the relationship between screen and audience, were choices that determined the course of the debate. *Gaze, look, pleasure,* etc., became keywords in feminist film theory. But two issues were further debated: the first was whether female audiences are always forced to wear men's clothes if they want to follow a film well. The second was: what happened to the films in which the active character, the bearer of the desire, is a woman? Mulvey (who also engaged in filmmaking with Peter Wollen, with works like *The Riddle of the Sphinx*) returned to these questions.[3] The process of the formation of a woman's sexual identity, starting from infancy, is marked by the emergence of "masculine" traits that are gradually erased. This explains why the "transvestitism" that dominant cinema forces the female spectator to undergo is not a betrayal, but "second nature," submerged and yet easy to assume again. Woman's "transexuality" is legitimated by her psychic history. The same ideas can apply to those heroines, such as Pearl in *Duel in the Sun,* who appear torn between the obligation to bend to the law and the will to free their desire. In this case, too, there is a memory of an "active phase," which showed itself during the process of identity construction and which returns as a fantasy. Female spectators and heroines "become masculine" not only because they are forced to do so or because they dream in vain. Their constitution as "gendered" subjects allows them to do so.

14.4. Difference and Identity

In the second half of the 1970s the debate exploded. First, there were many more opportunities for discussion. Annual meetings were established, such as the Edinburgh Film Festival, where filmic production and theoretical elaboration confronted one another. New journals were established, such as *Camera Obscura,* which aimed to connect feminist investigations with the most advanced positions in the field of symbolic sciences. Anthologies were published that gave a clear picture of the theoretical framework, such as *Women in the Cinema,* edited by K. Kay and G. Peary; *Women in Film Noir,* edited by E. A. Kaplan; and *Sexual Stratagems,* edited by P. Erens.[4] Positions for film teachers opened at universities, in departments of Women's Studies. Systematic attention to films developed in feminist journals such as *m/f,* etc. Two major lines of research also converged. One, present mostly in the United States, was characterized by a sociological approach and was centered around the promotion of a "true" image of woman through the mass media. The other developed in England and relied on the tools of semiotics and psychoanalysis. It was convinced that a discourse could be "true" only if it brought into play its own tools before attempting to mirror reality. Finally, there was a reprise and broadening of the themes focused upon by the first essays. In particular, four great areas of study were established, and they often overlapped.

The first area had a methodological slant: in the name of a "feminist reading" of cinema, it studied the tools of semiotics and the key notions of the psychoanalytical approach. Studying meant correcting, integrating, reorienting. The notion of the subject of the enunciation, which is asexual in linguistics, was connected with gender. The Freudian apparatus, which is centered on male psychic life, was compared to the female experience. Within this framework, Julia Lesage attacked *Screen* for its "orthodox Freudianism" and invited the journal to consider fetishism in other than phallocentric terms. Similarly, Ruby Rich attacked the use of many concepts borrowed from previous theories without considering their value in terms of sexual difference.[5] But studying also means enriching with new applications. This explains the relaunching of the notion of *text* that was conducted by *Camera Obscura* through a study of both classic and avant-garde cinema; or the interest in the *apparatus* that was promoted by Teresa de Lauretis with respect to both the psychic processes and the material conditions behind cinema.[6]

The second area of study was more militant: it valorized women's cinema, both by reexamining the work done by the (few) women directors working between the 1920s and the 1950s and by systematically supporting contemporary women filmmakers. There was no lack of films to analyze. Scholars who chose a retrospective approach worked on Germaine Dulac or Elvira Notaryi as well as Dorothy Arzner and Ida Lupino;[7] others instead focused on contemporary film and studied Yvonne Rainer, Michelle Citron, Laura Mulvey, Marguerite Duras, or Sally Potter.[8]

The third area of study had a historical slant. Scholars attempted a systematic rereading of classic cinema ("patriarchal cinema" par excellence) in order to shed light on its internal contradictions. A contradiction is a zone of darkness where the dominant value system, in particular the hierarchy of the sexes, is subject to a disturbance. In Hawks' *Rio Bravo,* the female roles are given to Angie Dickinson, the protagonist's object of attraction, and to Walter Brennan, the sheriff's helper, who takes care of his office. A contradiction is, however, also an exasperated mise-en-scène of a value system, revealing the latter's lack of naturalness and untenability. The way musicals transform women into a "spectacle" for men ultimately spells out clearly what it means to reduce someone to a mere object of the gaze. A contradiction also emerges when we affirm a value system, at the same time denying its assumptions and consequences. Film noir is certainly not nice to women; yet a feminist reading of it uncovers its powerful critique of the traditional notion of the family, namely, of the institution that some scholars believe to be mainly responsible for killing women's potential.[9]

The fourth area of study focused on the more general problem of female *identity.* There was an attempt to avoid essentialist definitions (such as "the eternal feminine") and to view identity instead as a cultural construct, in particular as the product of the series of discourses that circulate within a society. It is what we say about women, the way we talk to them, that makes them what they are. This perspective allows us, among other things, to understand how the *difference* that marks female identity (woman as "other" from man) involves not only anatomical difference, but also and above all positions and roles that differ. Within our social space, the only model in this sense seems to be exclusion. Woman is confined to the margins of the verbal circuit. Her desire to express herself is suffocated. She is reduced to the mere object of masculine discourses (and desires). And at the same time, she is considered empty, bizarre, extraneous (even to the Oedipal trajectories, which, however, find in her their starting point). To end this situation, we need to consider all the aspects of this *difference,* beyond the opposition between dominant and dominated (which is exemplified by the distinction between the bearer of the gaze—man—and the object of the gaze—woman). In this way, we can grasp the complexity of the mechanisms through which a subject acquires a gendered identity. And at the same time, we can discover the peculiarities and potential available to women because of the attitudes and positions they are forced to assume.[10]

In this context we should reread some of the essays devoted to the narrative roles played by female characters, to the identification processes initiated by films, and to the attitudes and behaviors of female spectators.

We will start with an essay by Jacqueline Rose (1977). Replying to Bellour, the author denies that in *The Birds* Mitch—and through him Hitchcock—is the only source of aggressivity against Melanie. Instead, this aggressivity is a consequence of the film's structure. *The Birds* is constructed, on the one hand, around contrasts and divisions and, on the other hand, around juxtapositions and fusions to the extent that its distinctive trait is the shot/reverse shot, that is, a writing (editing) procedure leading to both the opposition and the overlapping of an "in" and an "out" space: it reveals who stands on one side and who on the other, who looks and who is looked at. Such filmic structure mimes that psychic phase known as the "dialectic of the imaginary relation," in which we confront—even aggressively—the people around us, and which is fundamentally paranoid. This analogy allows the film to reactivate a stage that is fundamental to the formation of the subject (the "ego" defines itself by contrast and incorporation of the "other"). Similarly, film reactivates a stage that is fundamental to the definition of the cinematographic spectacle (the world on the screen always emerges by contrast and incorporation of the "here" and the "elsewhere," of "reality" and the "image"). What is the place and role of woman in this game? Our perception of her as a dangerous object (to be attacked) depends on her privileged relationship with the imaginary, which in turn depends on the pre-Oedipal bonds between mother and daughter. In this respect, woman is closer to the moment when subjectivity emerges, while at the same time she has a more complex identity. Therefore, she can be silenced (like Melanie at the end of the film), but she always remains a point of resistance, perhaps unstable, but more open, too.

Janet Bergstrom (1979) also goes back to Bellour, but she concentrates mainly on the problem of point of view. It is a fact that Hitchcock's female characters never have a point of view of their own (they do not look, they are looked at; in the best of cases, they are looked at while looking). It is also true, however, that his heroines desire (to see and to possess), so much so that often the films indirectly try to muffle the threat caused by this feminine initiative. Hitchcock's main preoccupation seems to be a secret commitment to the reduction of woman's active role, of her desire, of sexual difference.

But he also moves along unforeseen paths. If it is true that the spectators' identification is oriented toward the person who acts (toward the man), it is also true that woman's active role (which is denied to her and yet remains latent), together with the presence of feminine gazes (even when reappropriated by the masculine gaze), allows a *multiple identification*. The female spectator (and the male spectator) can therefore refer to many presences. In this way, the female spectator's profile is defined by her psychological itineraries, rather than by the immediate adherence to the hero or the heroine. In other words, a complex mechanism contributes to the construction of her identity. No equivalence or reflection takes place at once; gender difference (male/female) is not confused with sexual difference (man/woman); the female spectator constructs her subjectivity by borrowing from all sides. This happens with Hitchcock, but the lesson can be extended to all films. Hence, new maneuvering room can be derived for women who, endowed with a non-monolithic identity and ready to cross multiple differences, will no longer be forced to remain silent and inactive.

Other scholars, too, highlight the weight and effects of the feminine presence on the screen. Jacqueline Suter (1979) analyzes Dorothy Arzner's *Christopher Strong* and observes that woman's desire plays a crucial role in the structure of the story. Linda Williams (1981) is interested in such anomalous fields as the horror movie, pornography, and surrealist films. Her hypothesis is that the more the representation of the female body is charged with aesthetic values, the more it helps to celebrate fetishism and to deny sexual differences. Lea Jacobs (1981) studies Irving Rapper's *Now, Voyager* and observes that the desire to live expressed by the heroine (Bette Davis) generates in this case a positive identification, that is, our desire to live as well (narration). Ann Kaplan (1983) analyzes films' enactment of the relationship between mother and daughter and links it with the evocation of a moment that only women can experience. Annette Kuhn (1985) analyzes *The Big Sleep* and explains the obscurities of the story as the result of unconscious male censorship.[11] In these essays, just as in Bergstrom's, there is, however, also a tendency to shift the attention from the film's textual system to the fate of the female spectator, and the debate will continue in this direction.

Mary Ann Doane (1987) considers the "women's movies" that were fashionable in the 1940s. Her thesis is that these films, in tune with the dominant culture and perfectly in parallel with Freud's theory of the drives, tend to deny feminine desire. On the one hand, they present it in the guise of a heroine who intends to guide the events; on the other hand, they circumscribe, counterbalance, and deprive it of its force. This inhibits and neutralizes identification with the woman at the center of the story. Like her twin on the screen, the female spectator can only *desire to desire*. Her aspirations remain, but they are either left without an object or forced to fold in on themselves. The four great genres into which "women's movies" are subdivided confirm this diagnosis. The films that center on illness assimilate woman's desire for the institutional relationship between patient and doctor. In family melodramas desire is sublimated into maternity. Romantic comedies bring desire back to a narcissistic structure: it is not by chance that there are mirrors everywhere, in which a conjunction between (the gaze of) subject and object is realized. Gothic films pair desire with anxiety, such as the fear of dying at the hand of the husband, so that desire is disarmed. In all these cases, woman faces a path that is both open to and denied to her.

Tania Modleski returns to Hitchcock, whose work seems to "provide the perfect testing ground for theories of female spectatorship" (Modleski 1988:8). The fundamental idea of her book is that Hitchcock displays a deep ambivalence toward woman. On the one hand, he turns her into the object of aggression, thus taking sides to an extreme degree with the values of patriarchy. On the other hand, he is fascinated by her presence, although he perceives it as disturbing. This ambivalence also summarizes the two poles of the male response to femininity: identification and terror. We should also note that Hitchcock's attitude toward men is also ambivalent. His presentation of ambiguous sexuality (Norman Bates come to mind) risks destabilizing the gendered identity of both the protagonists and the spectators. There is an evident connection between men's fascination with women, male inability to achieve full masculinity, and men's consequent aggression against anyone who threatens their autonomy and strength. It is, however, more important to underscore that, vis-à-vis this male attitude, which is a clear sign of an identity crisis, Hitchcock's female spectators may answer with resistance. Like their onscreen counterparts, that is, the film heroines (e.g., Charlie's niece in *The Shadow of a Doubt*), they can uncover men's secrets and the blind spots of the patriarchy. At the same time, they can discover "the kinds of pleasure unique to women's relationship with other women" (13). Women's goal is knowing what men do not know (echoing Hitchcock's double movie, Modleski called her book *The Women Who Knew Too Much*), knowing in order to be able to be themselves.

14.5. The Female Experience

Along with the shift of focus from films to their female spectators, the 1980s witnessed the emergence of another exigency, namely, integrating the study of the representations of and for women with the study of the social space where women operate.

Claire Johnston was the first to treat this question, at the beginning of the decade. The textual analyses made with the tools afforded by semiotics and psychoanalysis had a double consequence: they showed that films define the spectator and they emphasized that the shift in the relationship between the two poles is the prerequisite of every essay on cinema as an institution. The spectator that emerges from such studies is a purely abstract construct, however. He has little to do with those who really attend the cinema. Instead, we need to take into account that spectators are "subjects in history, rather than mere subjects of a single text" (Johnston 1980:30). A number of discursive, economic, and political practices define their profiles. "Textual strategies have thus to be posed in conjunctural terms" (31). The suggestions a film makes need to be compared to the specific situation of which they are a product. The structures of representation need to be analyzed in their connections with social processes. There is also "an outside of discourse which has an effectivity and which must be taken into consideration if a productive strategy for ideological struggle in relation to feminist film theory and practice is to be developed" (34).

At the level of theory, the best interpreter of this problem is Teresa de Lauretis. In a book that greatly influenced the debate (de Lauretis 1984), she posits the question of gendered identity at two levels. On the one hand, she examines the ways in which subjectivity is constituted, in and through discourse. This leads her to a complex analysis of how semiotics and psychoanalysis elaborated the notion of the subject; how texts provide not only meanings that hold for everyone, but also suggestions for the individual imagination; how interpellation is decisive in positioning the spectator; how the narrative structures initiate identification processes and provide an opening for desire; and so on. This wide-ranging exploration not only examines many filmic and literary examples; it also discusses the positions of Lacan, Foucault, and Eco, in light of feminist theory. On the other hand, however, de Lauretis also believes that the subject engenders itself (in the double meaning of the term *en-gender:* to generate oneself and to acquire a gender) beyond the discourses that ensnare it. A woman recognizes herself as such, the "I" becomes feminine, so to speak, at the level of *experience,* more than at the level of language.

De Lauretis works a great deal on this final notion, which has a key role in her thought. *Experience* is for her something more than establishing a relationship with events, registering facts, and acquiring competence. It is an interplay of interferences and overlappings between the "internal" and the "external" world, thanks to which we make sense of what happens to us and at the same time define our personality. *Experience* allows us to understand both things and ourselves; or, better put, it allows us to understand things in relation to ourselves and vice versa. In this respect, it is a process through which individuals find their place (or are placed) inside social and historical reality and make it their own. Clearly, *experience* plays a crucial role in the formation of subjectivity. Indeed, the main features that define feminine subjectivity can be traced to this very sphere: a woman has a direct experience of her body, affectivity, exclusion, etc., which are the basis of her gendered identity.

The reference to experience allows de Lauretis to connect the idea of *woman* as it circulates within our culture with the reality of *women* (in the plural) as they live in society and in history. Her project becomes even clearer in a later book (de Lauretis 1987), whose main theme is the complex "social technologies" that a culture deploys in order to model individuals, to assign them places, functions, genders, and so on. Then she analyzes not only representations (films, novels, etc.), but also institutions (cinema, family, university), relations (economic, political, or sexual), and processes (the formation of the "self" and of the "other"). In her view, the more closely an identity is observed, the more complex it appears; an ego tirelessly tends to construct itself only to be undone.

14.6. New Research Trends

The growing attention to the world of women's experience was further enhanced by the growing success of cultural studies, from the mid-1980s onward. Their aim is both to focus on the existence in our societies of a broad range of subcultures (e.g., youth or ethnic) and to study cultures distant from ours. Feminist film theory makes an original contribution to this branch of inquiry. In particular, it tries to connect gendered identity with other kinds of identity, such as racial or national. The shift from language to society is completed by the study of the whole range of determinations that are at play in the latter.[12]

Another element leading to the study of the worlds of women's experience comes from historical studies, in particular from the histories of film reception. Their aim is to understand the audience's composition and its changes over the years. In this case, too, feminist scholars make original contributions, especially in terms of women's role in defining certain forms of vision and the importance of certain iconographic motifs in initiating women's participation.[13]

An interesting work by Miriam Hansen (1991) lies at the intersection of cultural studies and social history. At its core, we find a study both of the behaviors and attitudes of a mostly feminine audience during the 1910s and 1920s in America and of the effects that women's growing tendency to go to cinemas had on the public sphere. An excellent example of this comes from Valentino's films: Hansen emphasizes, on the one hand, how the actor constructed a sexually ambiguous character, although one intended for a female audience; on the other hand, she notices how such a character presents itself through a range of highly ritualized behaviors, which both mediate and reinvigorate the impact of this new figure.

Finally, the idea of investigating the world of women in its concrete and complex aspects comes from the scholars' increasing interest in other mass media, in particular television, a "domestic" device with a largely female or family audience. Once again, we find a number of feminist works in this area.[14]

Toward the end of the 1980s feminist film theory actively participated in the most lively research currents. At the same time, however, it was also dispersed in many directions, often far apart. After all, the discourse on cinema increasingly blended with broader interests: references to specific films appeared in essays on literature, sexuality, or reverie; recuperating a theoretical issue could serve memorial, political, or other aims. This translates the spirit of the times. As far as feminist film theory is concerned, the effect of this attitude (which some scholars perceive as positive, others as problematic) is, on the one hand, its development into simply feminist theory and, on the other hand, its convergence with film theory.[15]

15 TEXT, MIND, SOCIETY

15.1. The Death and Rebirth of Representation

The 1970s witnessed fierce criticism of both the dominant forms and the very concept of representation. The portrayal of the world on the silver screen revealed itself as a form of deception: it tries to show things as they are (though to reproduce something is always to change it); it hides the mechanisms at play (the presence of the camera, ideological bias); it may trigger perverse pleasures (reducing women to objects), etc. In the 1980s representation offered material for discussion as well, but the spirit of the debate changed. Certainly, the "dismantling" carried out during the previous decade provided the basis for discussion. Yet the awareness that representation is a trap was supplemented by the desire to study its current purpose. And to the unmasking of its suppositions and implications was added an interest in its forms. This led to the never answered questions: How does a film work? On what? What is a film's starting point? A direct answer may not be possible, but one must attempt to reply.

An essay by Aumont that was published at the beginning of the decade may help us to define the new spirit of debate (Aumont 1980). His point of departure is precisely the *system of representation* that underlies film images. This system governs the portrayal of the world on the screen and, in particular, the construction of the space in which action takes place. Through it, however, we may access two further dimensions: that which is "within" the representation and that which is "beyond" the representation. The former is constituted by the materials used (colors, lighting, shape, etc.); the latter is constituted by the spectator's involvement in what is portrayed onscreen. Film analysis must take into account all three dimensions and their mutual interplay. It is not enough to reconstruct the world and the space displayed by a film; but neither is it correct to discuss only the "within" or the "beyond" of the representation.

Aumont makes his argument concrete by analyzing the first four sequences of *La règle du jeu*. First and foremost, he deals with the space delineated by the film. This is a space that reproduces "reality," whether by designing the space of an event (referential space), by showing the space as decor (theatrical space), or by using procedures like shot/reverse shot (cinematic space). Space is presented as perfectly recognizable, traversable, inhabitable. It is in this traditional model of representation that the "within" and the "beyond" of the representation come into play. Let us analyze the "within." In depicting space, the film's components (use of black and white, camera movements, framing) reveal their material nature, to the point that we see something concrete and touchable: basically, a pure play of signifiers. Now let us analyze the "beyond." In traversing a space depicted in such a way, the spectator lives "a kind of sensual enjoyment of the image" and is exposed to an "evocative reading" (Aumont 1980:20). The lesson in this is that one can study what is portrayed on the screen (in this film, in all films) only if one knows how to exit and enter continually. The representation is crisscrossed by lines of flight, but it is also a place in which all the elements brought into play by the cinematic "writing" and by the filmic "effects" reconverge.

This seemingly paradoxical exercise in mixing lines of flight and lines of convergence with the delineation and the undoing or prolongation of a world was effectively pursued near the end of the 1980s by Vernet (Vernet 1988). Here the author studies in a provocative and systematic way the *invisibility* that manifests itself at the very heart of the representation. Often (always?) what a film shows revolves around something that is never brought into view: the spectator looks over a portrait of reality and at the same time encounters blind spots in any given portrayal. The challenge, then, consists in gleaning from what actually appears onscreen the decisive symptoms of a scene that came "before" or occurred "elsewhere."

Vernet analyzes five major "figures of absence." With a glance at the camera, the character, looking at the spectator in the theater, seems to make direct contact with him. In reality this does nothing so much as emphasize the complete separation of what is taking place on the screen from the viewer. In the

subjective shot the character, by making himself the source of vision or outlook, seems to represent all that is shown to us. Yet it is while he absents
himself from sight, to a place beyond the frame, to an outside shot, that he
carries weight. In a double exposure, we see at the same moment more than
one level of reality; but a world so portrayed loses its depth, its proportion, its
contours, and often we don't even understand which level of the frame is
foreground and which is background. In portraits, often feminine, hanging
on the walls of the set, heroines seem to "double" their presence. In reality, their role as objects seen by others, prey to masculine desire, and as subjects with undefined identity is confirmed. Finally, the characters presented
as ideals of other characters do not become role models, but usually figures
whom the film denies or obscures or eclipses. They serve as testimony to the
impossibility of embodying perfection.

These five major "figures of absence" clearly demonstrate how the representation is affected by a constant internal fragility and at the same time how
it may succeed in transforming its own weak points into moments of great
strength. It is, then, in its fadings that we can find its strengths. One needs
only to unite centrifugal and centripetal movements and to read the positive
in the negative and vice versa. The only analysis that reaches the heart of the
film is one that knows how to run risks.

15.2. Image and Sound

Vernet and Aumont help us to grasp the attitude that gained currency in the
1980s. The focus is on the ways in which representation works as much as on
the points at which it fades, on the ground it covers as much as on its boundaries. Sound prompts a similar attitude. Perhaps this is because of its inherent
nature: it is an essential component of film, even if it tends to hold a marginal
position. It has fixed rules of use, even though these are often reinvented.
And it is tied to the story, even though it is not exclusively tied to it.

It was not a coincidence that studies of cinema's acoustic dimension pro-
liferated during the 1980s.[1] Michel Chion's three volumes on this theme have
an important place among them. In particular, volume one, devoted to voice
in cinema, is most original. The voice is viewed beyond its function as the
vehicle for words, that is, beyond the contents that it transmits. Instead, it is
seen as an element of cinematographic representation. In this sense, we can
connect it to the construction of scenic space: there are voices that inhabit

such space (onscreen voices), voices that come from its margins (voice-overs), voices that seem directed toward the set (commentary voices), etc. These kinds of voices are, at least partially, a heritage from other media: the dialogues come from the theater, musical accompaniment from melodrama, commentary from the magic lantern. There is, however, a voice through which cinema manifests its peculiar expressive force, the voice that is neither inside nor outside the scenic space and "wanders, totally free, along the surface of the screen" (Chion 1982:15). We intuit its source, without seeing it; and it attracts our attention because it seems to dictate the importance of what appears on the screen. There are numerous examples: Mabuse in *Das Testament des Dr. Mabuse*, Norman in *Psycho*, Elisabeth in *Persona*, Joe in *Sunset Boulevard* offer us moments in which their bodies are out of sight or their lips remain closed even though the sound of their words pervades the representation and defines its tempo and measure. Chion speaks of *acusmatic presences*, using an old term (taken from Scheffer) that indicates a sound whose origin is undetermined. The *acusmatic voice* introduces an element of ubiquitousness, of omniscience, of omnipotence into film; but it also decentralizes the image, opening it to the outside world and upsetting its structure. It broadens the character's sphere of action, but it also disembodies the character. It dominates an entire scene and yet comes from outside it. It reverberates with all the elements in view and yet does not appeal to the responsibility of any element. It incites our curiosity, but at the same time does not offer us unambiguous answers. "The *acusmatic voice* is an element of imbalance, of tension; it is an invitation *to come to see*, perhaps an invitation *to lose oneself*" (Chion 1982:29). For the rest, the acusmatic voice serves as a kind of umbilical cord: it ties us to something we have lost, it puts us on the trail of a presence that has been taken away. Representation then closes in on itself while at the same time it leans toward something other than itself. Centrifugal and centripetal forces overlap; and the difference between functioning and undoing disappears.

Besides this topic,[2] Chion confirms for us how the research of the 1980s was driven by a particular spirit. We find this spirit at the base of several recurrent points. In a film what role should be given to omissions with respect to what is shown? How do we associate the detail with the whole, components with the sum of things? What kind of gaze should we activate? And how do we reconcile the desire to explain with the awareness that there is in the representation something that cannot be evaluated? We find this same spirit, perhaps in the background, in three major lines of inquiry that deal with representation in what appears to be a more positive way. These are three directions of research that do not hesitate to bring principles of explanation into play. The first calls on the constitutive mechanisms of the cinematic text: to understand what the (or a) representation is, one needs to examine how images and sounds are literally formed. The second focuses on the cognitive activity of the viewer: to understand what the (or a) representation is, one needs to penetrate the mind of those who actually (re)construct the representation. The third accentuates the social processes of meaning production: to understand what the (or a) representation is, one must see how a society gives significance(s) to the products that circulate in it. Along parallel lines, the three directions of inquiry assemble various disciplines in support of their work. The first allies itself with semiotics and that field's interest in the text. The second uses cognitive psychology and its attention to the mechanisms used in the perception and comprehension of film. The third is aligned with pragmatics and its attempt to explore the relation of the text to social space. Notwithstanding the offering of an explanatory principle, each group does not hesitate to concentrate on a single element. Nor does their recourse to a discipline imply that these approaches are bound by methodologies. Even here we find (I repeat, in the background) the preoccupation with intersecting itineraries and the desire to grasp the reasons for the successes as well as the points of disintegration of representation.

Let us treat these three main areas, each with its own preoccupations and its own answers.

15.3. The Textual Dimension: The Mechanisms of Enunciation

Within the framework of the "second semiotics" (or is it already the third . . .) the suggestion emerges to approach representation on the basis of its internal mechanisms. The interest is focused mainly on *enunciation,* that is, the group of linguistic operations that literally give birth to a text. The term generally refers to the "act" by which a person uses the possibilities of a language in order to realize a discourse, or the shift from virtuality to manifestation. In our case, starting from cinema's inherent potentialities, it defines what allows a film to take form and to manifest itself, to present itself as a *text,* as a *specific* text, and as that very text in a specific *situation.*

Let us now look more closely at the elements at play. First, enunciation applies to the relationship between a set of expressive possibilities and the choices that lead to every single realization of a film. Therefore, it emphasizes how language is transformed into a text or, we might say, how cinema turns into a film. Enunciation also marks the appearance of elements that do not exist in the virtual dimension. A text that is shown is a text which implies an agency, is addressed to a spectator, and belongs to a specific time and place, etc. Therefore, it underscores the limits that allow a text (a film) to take root in a given situation or to adapt itself to its surroundings. Finally, enunciation can make itself perceptible or disappear: in the first case, it engenders a text that, in representing something, also represents the fact of representing it; in the second case, it originates a text that represents the world directly, without representing its own act of representation. Thus, it underscores the film's ability to inscribe the gesture that gave birth to it in itself, in a way that can be either secret or obvious. There are thus three main elements that the idea of enunciation touches upon: constitution, situation, and possible self-referentiality of the filmic text.

These three issues keep reappearing in much scholarly work, as is shown by the essays collected in issue 38 of the journal *Communications,* devoted to "Enonciation et cinéma." Aumont (1983) focuses on what most makes a film a film, namely, the point of view. Simon (coeditor, with Vernet, of the issue) also asks himself, "Who looks, who speaks in a film?" This question is the starting point for the discovery of narrators who stand either "inside" or "outside," "above" or "next to" the story that is being narrated (Simon 1983). Marie and Vanoye (1983) analyze verbal enunciation in dialogues and study its relationship to visual enunciation. Chateau (1983) wonders how the fictional world is constituted and explores the effects of enunciation on diegesis. Jost (1983) concentrates on the figure of the narrator, focusing mainly on its function as a "filter" with respect to onscreen events.

Although this issue of *Communications* legitimated and relaunched the debate, this kind of study had already been going on for some time. Among the first works we find Jean-Paul Simon's book (1979) on comic cinema and, in particular, the Marx Brothers. Simon does not locate the origin of comedy— as many do—in the simple transgression of social mores, but in the ways in which the filmic text organizes its basic development. In particular, comedy relies on the irruption of the enunciation into the enunciated: the film's constitutive process surfaces and mixes with the represented. Such an insertion serves a double purpose. On the one hand, it allows us to take the onscreen world for what it is, that is, not a real given, but something the text constructs. This implies a critique of the assumed "naturalness" of filmic representation. Comic film dismantles its own mechanisms, while it allows the action to move on. Instead, in a genre that is parallel to comic film, the *film-esprit* or witty comedy, such a dismantling would block the continuation of the discourse. On the other hand, the insertion of the enunciation in the enunciated shows the spectators their fundamental absence from the screen and makes them appreciate their place. The spectators, thus, participate in the game, but at a safe distance (with *film-esprit* this participation implies total involvement instead). Hence a precise definition: "Comic films are a fundamentally duplicitous and ambivalent genre: they are a laboratory for deconstruction and the latter's official limit, a space reserved between the pleasure of the text and enjoyment" (Simon 1979:90).

Simon's investigation is not limited to comic films. He carefully analyzes the enunciation device, in particular the way in which an "I" and a "you" can relate to each other, both in cinema and in such allied fields as painting, TV, or comics. Other scholars also approached the problem of the "subjects" of the filmic discourse, however. Collins' work on the films of Fred Astaire and Ginger Rogers (Collins 1979) comes to mind. Their musical segments show how a "direct link" between the screen and the audience can develop. The lyrics explicitly refer to an "I" (the singer) and a "you" (the listener). The singer looks straight ahead, singing not only to the audience represented within the film, but also to the public watching the film. And the shots that show the audience within the film watching the performance are often followed by subjective shots in which the public in the theater sees through the eyes of an onscreen spectator. As a result, a link is established between the situation presented by the film, at the center of which there are a stage and an audience, and the cinematic situation, characterized by a screen and an auditorium. The latter both is an extension of the former and is reflected by it, so that the film constantly turns in on itself.

Gianfranco Bettetini (1984) both broadens and better defines the field. In reality, every film moves between two poles. On the one hand, there is an ordering principle that holds the whole film together; on the other hand, there is an ideal target, an immanent destination. These two poles, respectively, the "source" and the "addressee" of the enunciation, do not function simply as the traces of the birth of a filmic text and its consequent availability for completion. They also offer both the actual author and the spectator a depicted prolongation, a true symbolic prosthesis. Along this line we should notice that these two poles face each other in the text just as two real–life partners do in a dialogue. Hence the idea that simulated conversations take place in films: the elements of the conversation are organized just as in any everyday chat, with the same questions and answers, etc. Ordinary and filmic communication deeply mirror each other.

Francesco Casetti (1986) focuses his attention on the spectator instead. He opens his work by explaining why the spectator should be thought of within the framework of the enunciation. Before being seen, a film shows itself; and the way in which it displays itself depends on the logic of its construction. We follow the onscreen events, systematically comparing ourselves with a point of view that we are invited to adopt. This point of view is the other side and the complement of the point of view that organized the events. Starting from this premise, Casetti defines his field of investigation. A first step is the analysis of the "presence" of the spectator in the film. In emphasizing their own con-struction, some filmic texts also emphasize their address. Other texts are less defined in this respect and construct more mediated destinations (for instance, by introducing a detective, the spectator's alter ego, as well as a totally fictional character). Therefore, it is possible to distinguish between strong presences (pure observers) and narrative presences (diegetic observers). A second step is the exploration of the spectator's "position." Filmic enunciation gives rise to four main textual configurations, which imply an equal number of positions for the spectator. The objective shots turn the spectator into a neutral witness; the subjective shots turn him/her into a character that is directly involved in the story; the interpellations (such as looking straight into the camera) turn him/her into an interlocutor at the margins of the scene; unreal objective shots (for instance, the *plongées* or "dip" shots) turn him/her instead into a free, bodiless eye, like that of the camera. A third step is the investigation of the spectator's "path." Films contain plenty of direct and indirect "reading instructions." They arouse curiosity, define points that deserve attention, sug-gest possible completions for what they say, and so on. In this sense, it is possible to trace real trajectories, which range from assigning a task to the spectator to opinions expressed by the film about the various hypotheses that the spectator gradually develops. The result of this triple study (of presence, position, and path) is a focus on the wide range of *roles* that a film assigns to its ideal spectator.

Christian Metz (1991) rethinks and systematizes the debate. He observes that one should not equate cinematic and verbal enunciation, which differ in many ways. Whereas a dialogue presents specific signs defining who is implied in the production or the reception of the text (deictics like "I," "you"), a film has no equivalent terms. Similarly, while a dialogue involves real people (the "I" and "you" define them), a film can only refer to generic and biased figures (the spectator reacting to a look into the camera is a typical, not an actual, spectator). Finally, while the sender and the receiver of a dialogue can trade places (so that the "I" becomes "you" and vice versa), a film is a predefined text, where no such exchange can take place. Hence, Metz suggests that cinematic enunciation should be seen not as the creation of one person for another person, but as the simple fact of the film's manifestation of itself (here enunciation is in fact *impersonal*). He also encourages us to perceive film not as a device that connects the text with its context, but as a moment of general self-reflection (here the enunciation involves above all the *reflexive* dimension).

This does not mean that the term *cinematic enunciation* is either incorrect or useless; on the contrary, it allows a useful exploration of the main filmic procedures. Metz gives an overview of them, dividing them into eleven groups. He isolates various "appeals" to the spectator (looking into the camera, a comment made by a character who appears on the scene, a comment made by an invisible spectator, written words that provide extra information, beginning and end titles, etc.). He also speaks of "internal references," such as a screen inside the screen, the presence of symptomatic objects such as mirrors, references to other films, close copies, etc. Metz mentions the display of the "device": in this case, cameras, microphones, and other objects connected (perhaps metaphorically) with production and reception appear on the scene; the introduction of surreptitious "sources," such as characters who see or speak in subjective shots; the falsely neutral images, which make clear that they are constructs precisely by virtue of the way in which they are constructed, and so on. In all these cases, a film "bends" toward itself, sheds light on the principles that organize it, and makes of its self-presentation a term of comparison.

The debate on enunciation does not end with Metz, but he clearly shows how this research area is organized. Representation is connected with the gesture that gave it a body and a shape and does not necessarily involve either individuals (a real "I" and a real "you") or an actual situation (a unique "here and now"). Yet it guides images and sounds, defining their functions and meaning.

Now we will move on to another group of works, in order to complete our picture of the approaches that connect representation with the dynamics of the text, those contributions that center on narrative phenomena.

15.4. The Textual Dimension: The Dynamics of Narration

We have already discussed narratology, in the chapter on the "second semiotics." In particular, we have focused on Chatman's and Browne's contributions, which concentrated on how a story marks the act of storytelling that originates it. François Jost and André Gaudreault, two scholars who were extremely active in the 1980s, further developed this theme. They connected Genette's ideas (fundamental in Chatman and Browne) with a reference to the problems of enunciation.

Gaudreault's starting point is that if films as such are products of enunciation, films as stories are the product of narrations, so that there are at least two organizing principles for sounds and images. But what are the conditions and position of the narration? A written story can always count on a "voice" that organizes and supports it. We can always identify traces of an "author's" presence, albeit through an adjective or an adverb. At the theater, instead, the events seem to unfold on their own. On the stage actions, rather than accounts, take place, and the facts are shown, rather than reconstructed. Cinema combines these two procedures. It shows events and openly determines their flux. *It shows and tells,* providing us with a direct vision of things, and it also reorganizes them for us.[3]

Cinema's ability to merge two fundamental modes of existence of narrative (which Plato had already singled out, speaking of *diegesis*—a story consisting of words—and *mimesis*—a story consisting of facts) has an important consequence. We end up positing the existence, behind the filmic story, of a *mega-narrator,* whose functions include those of both the theatrical and the novelistic narrator. He has both the former's discretion and the latter's effectiveness, the former's neutrality and the latter's mediating ability. Let us add that this mega-narrator emerges during the history of cinema from its very beginnings, when he had a less important role. Early films tended to "reproduce" or "re-present" a preexisting reality, rather than constructing a new one that takes form through the flux of images. The mega-narrator, who is capable of clearly articulating his narration, appears only in the later phases of the history of cinema, when it has achieved a certain maturity. Thus, images presented by an impassive "shower" coexist with written, commenting voices, which give away the presence of a "narrator" who is in control of the game. Or a main narrator, who is responsible for the whole film, coexists with some "delegated narrators" who are in charge of specific parts of the story. Beyond such cases, it is, however, a fact that in cinema we find a presence that "is responsible for the communication of the filmic narrative" (Gaudreault 1988:107): the mega-narrator, who both works on recording and reorganizing the events and controls the stories that appear on the screen.

Gaudreault analyzes the emergence in films of a presence that guides the presentation of the events. Jost focuses instead on how this presence acts. At the movies "the story consists of an *over there* (the transparency, the absolute mimesis) and an *over here* (the gaze)" (Jost 1987:17). On the one hand, there is a world that seems to exist by itself; on the other hand, there is perception without content. Now, neither of these poles can exist without the other. The world that appears on the screen exists insofar as it is the object of a gaze; in turn, if the latter looks around, it does so in order to grasp segments of reality. It is therefore impossible for the two sides not to merge. In so doing, they underscore a clash of some kind between the person who, by having a look at things, tells the story (the narrator), and the person who, by being at the center of this gaze, acts (the character). A story needs both someone who filters and presents it and someone who is part of it and substantiates it. Indeed, these two presences often overlap. In many stories the narrator is embodied in a character, so that the "source" of the narration appears on the scene. The meaning of the story (but Jost seems to imply the meaning of the entire film) emerges from this interplay of comparisons and overlappings.

With this premise, Jost carefully explores the ways of organizing filmic narration. First, the relation between the organizer of the events (the narrator) and those who act in them (the characters) needs to be extended to those who receive them (the spectators), to whom the film is addressed. Second, the organization of the narration works on at least three levels: it involves looking (at things, characters, etc.), listening (films have an acoustic dimension), and knowing what is seen and heard, a knowledge that often surpasses the mere facts of perception. Hence the possibility of relating the narration to three processes: *ocularization,* which concerns the visual data (who is seeing and how?); *auricularization,* which concerns the auditory data (who speaks and who listens, and how?); and *focalization,* which concerns the cognitive dimension (who knows what? what kind of knowledge is it?). If narration is an exercise consisting in the presentation of the world through the "filter" of perception (this is the dialectic of mimesis and gaze), this perception works at all three levels, with the eyes, the ears, the mind.

We will not linger on Jost's detailed typology of the phenomena of ocularization, auricularization, and focalization, distinguishing among "internal" processes (entrusted to a character), "zero" processes (based on a narrator who tends toward anonymity), and "spectatorial" processes (created by the viewer's reelaboration of the film), etc.[4] Let us say that distinguishing these three levels and the existence in each of various "types" of organization allows a comprehensive range of complex combinations. Jost introduces it almost at the end of his work, together with many examples taken both from cinema and from literature. He clearly manages to refine the analytical categories he uses as well as to show that behind the richness of the solutions adopted there are recurrent formulas and standards.

The range of narratological studies is broader than we have been able to show here. Gaudreault and Jost represent only a part (although a highly relevant part) of these studies. Their merit lies in the analysis of the relation between the narrated story and the act of narration, as well as in the discovery—in the encounter of these two components—of the various forms a story can have. Cinematic representation is then connected with the dynamics behind films, thus deepening and broadening the framework of the studies on enunciation.

15.5. Between Text and Mind: The Generative Models

Another way of treating this problem was offered by contributions that were oriented to the teachings of generative linguistics. We are still within the field of the "second semiotics," but the center of attention has shifted. These studies tried to individuate the syntactic and semantic mechanisms that allow the production of "well-formed" filmic sentences. They emphasized the rules followed (perhaps unconsciously) by the author, in order to produce a meaningful, structured discourse, so that the spectator can (still unconsciously) reactivate these mechanisms in order to decode the same discourse. Here lies the difference between the models of enunciation theory and the models of generative theory. The interest no longer lies in the constitution of the film through enunciation, but in the author's and the spectator's ability to realize and understand a film, or in their *competence*. Similarly, the interest no longer lies in the form of the film, as reflected by images and sounds, but in the rules that the author and spectator put to use, or the *grammar* that dictates their behavior.

We are, of course, far from the attempts to construct "filmic grammars," which were typical of the 1930s and 1940. Whereas such studies were prescriptive (showing what should be done), these are explanatory (trying to account for expertise).[5] Instead, we are close to Chomsky and his generative-transformational grammar. All of the authors engaged in this research follow his basic approach. Let us look, for instance, at John M. Carroll's work, one of the first attempts in this direction (Carroll 1980). He retains the idea of a generative process through successive levels that are governed by transformational rules. He only changes the names of the various levels and the kind of rules implied. His hypothesis is, thus, that the starting point of each film is a *meaning,* which is organized in an *event structure* (which orders the main events that shape the world portrayed by a film). This event structure generates a *sequence structure,* which constitutes a trellis for the film's content. The sequence structure is manifested through images and sounds, which form the film that appears on the screen. The construction of any work follows this suggested order, from meaning to manifestation, and the viewer's decoding goes the other way, from manifestation to meaning. Along this two-way path the shift from event structure (which corresponds to Chomsky's deep structure) to sequence structure (which corresponds to the surface structure) is of course fundamental. The transformational rules apply to this transformation. Carroll lists them, and his list accounts for the passage from a situation (which consists of Nominals—agents and environments—and of a Sequence of Actions) to the form of its exposition (which introduces a Character, focuses on his Action, and presents the consequences of this Action, etc.). These rules, which take us back to the traditional "cinematic work" (shooting, choosing a shot, linking various shots, offscreen action, etc.), explain how a film can give different "versions" of the same situation, just as we can formulate different sentences in order to say the same thing.

Dominique Chateau (1986) moves along this same line. In particular, he seeks to account for the various forms a sequence can assume (alternating, linear, etc.). In order to do so, he first formulates the rules that correlate a narrative structure (consisting of subjects and predicates) and a formal structure (which prescribes the order of appearance of the various elements of the narration: for alternation, *ABAB;* for linear sequence, *ABC;* and so on). Then he formulates the rules that transform the formal structure into an action that conforms to the world that is being represented on the screen (*AB* becomes "John flees/Jim chases").

The *ABAB* alternation was carefully studied by Karl D. Möller, who relates various formal structures to this case: parallel editing, clip editing, repeated cut-ins, cut-aways, etc. (Möller 1986).

The most relevant contribution, however, came from Michel Colin. His basic idea is that there is no substantial difference between the mechanisms of film and those that govern a natural language. An audiovisual representation is constructed and decoded in the same way as a verbal sentence. Consequently, the use of the models of generative-transformational grammar (and of two of its extensions, generative semantics and textual grammar of the FPS [Functional Sentence Perspective] kind) does not imply applying categories to cinema that are alien to it, but a correct attempt to explain how a film works, because the latter, "as a discourse," can "be analyzed just like a verbal discourse, with the help of linguistic concepts" (Colin 1985:223). If language and cinema share a deep kinship and a common domain, the same instruments must be used to analyze them.

Obviously, working in this direction leads to the construction of a filmic grammar that, in principle, has the same basis and extension as the grammar of natural languages.[6] Colin analyzes three of its main components. First, the *ideational component,* which refers to the existence of a semantic structure underlying images and sounds. This semantic structure accounts for the "content" of a film or, better, for the logical relations among the elements at play in the "world" portrayed by the film. An example of this is "Agent-Predicate-Patient," which can account for a situation in which a character does something to someone else. Colin realizes that it is difficult to identify such a structure in a film. Yet he believes that the verbal sentences that "interpret" what happens on the screen shed light on it (in short, the proposition "John kills Jim," which explains what I am seeing, uncovers the structure "Agent-Predicate-Patient" behind the current sequence). What matters, however, is the applicability of transformational rules, which make the semantic structure the basis for the organization of images and sounds. Colin shows that the classic rules of deletion, permutation, substitution, and addition (see Colin 1985:100) may also be applied to cinema and that thanks to them it is possible to generate surface structures that account for the sequence in which things appear on the screen. Let us add that such surface structures may be "clothed" with images and sounds, as happens with films. In the case of novels, instead, they are "clothed" with words, thus giving rise to a different manifestation, while remaining the same.

The second component that Colin studies is the *interpersonal* component, which determines the modal structures of a filmic proposition. It concerns the relations between a speaker (in this case, a director) and his own discourse. The modalities in which the events are presented on the screen tell us what kinds of relations are established (if they imply involvement or distancing, diffuse attention or emphasis on a segment, etc.). Focalization belongs here: focusing on an element or giving it nuance already implies a specific attitude toward it.

The third component is the *textual* component, which brings us back to the communicative dynamics developed by the film. The center of attention here is the way in which discourse (in our case, filmic discourse) concretely proceeds, introducing new information along the way and using older information as a presupposed context for newer information. Colin carefully analyzes this process, which he believes exploits the two sides of the frame: to the left, the new data; to the right, the already acquired ones. This follows our alphabetic writing, which in fact adds to the left and preserves to the right. The camera movements or the shot/reverse shot seem, in any case, to confirm this tendency.

Colin's work is richer and more complex than we have been able to show here. His guidelines are clear, however, and they confirm that the contributions we have just discussed may function as a zone of encounter between semiotic and psychological approaches. On the one hand, they attempt to construct a true *filmic grammar,* modeled on the one Chomsky developed for natural languages; on the other hand (still following Chomsky), they display the belief that the linguistic structures and processes uncovered correspond to mental structures and processes.

This mental dimension is at the core of another line of research, which connects filmic representation with the spectator's cognitive processes.

15.6. The Mental Dimension: Cognitive Processes

The recourse to the models of cognitive psychology was one of the most relevant trends of the 1980s. This success was due to many factors. First, there was a desire to gain an empirical base, referring to "effective" processes initiated by the spectator, instead of "symbolic" processes initiated by the text.

Second, there was the possibility of seeing film as a "construct" of both recursive and flexible processes, rather than as something "given" once and for all, as happens in certain semiological approaches. Finally, there was a desire to appeal to a "rational" subject, whose behaviors are linear and verifiable, rather than to a "complex," and in the last analysis "indecipherable," subject, like the subject proposed by psychoanalysis. Other more contingent factors were also responsible for this success. Instead of referring to "imported" problematics, many American scholars liked being able to refer to the framework of cognitive psychology because it was developed, for the most part, in the United States.[7]

David Bordwell initiated this kind of research. His book on filmic narration (1985) led the way for many others. He treats narration as a *process* in which a film suggests steps to the spectator that will help him to reconstruct a story. We have, therefore, three elements: the film, with its ability to provide instructions (above all at the level of plot and style); the spectator, with his ability to perceive and understand (mainly thanks to a series of interpretive schemata); and the story told by the film, which the spectator must reconstruct in his mind. Within this picture, the viewer plays a central role. He collects directions and *reconstructs* the narrated story. Indeed, he *constructs* the film, turning a mixture of shadows, lights, and sounds into an ordered world, endowed with profiles and rhythms of its own.

After briefly recapitulating the terms of the debate, Bordwell focuses his attention on the cognitive activity of the spectator. The latter must first of all grasp what he is shown and told or organize visual and auditory stimuli into precise configurations. In a narrative film, however, it is not enough to "construe images and sounds as if presenting a three-dimensional world, and understand oral or written language. The viewer must take as central cognitive goal the construction of a more or less intelligible story" (Bordwell 1985:33). After all, when they enter a theater, the spectators are ready to address their energy toward this aim and "to apply sets of schemata derived from context and prior experience" (34) in order to achieve it. These schemata are divided into various types. *Prototype schemata,* for instance, allow us to single out the various components of the story, "identifying individual agents, actions, goals, and locales" (34). *Template schemata,* instead, permit the comparison of what is narrated with a prototypical drama, as follows: "introduction of sets and characters/explanation of a state of affairs/complicating action/ensuing events/outcome/ending" (35); they also allow the reorganization, on this basis, of what is being presented. *Procedural schemata,* "operational protocols which dynamically acquire and organize information" (36), allow us to provide the various elements on the screen with a "motivation," both on the basis of compositional reasons and on the basis of intertextual references, realistic elements, or artistic reasons. Finally, *stylistic schemata* allow the spectator to identify and appreciate the way in which the expressive dimension is treated.

These different schemata, real *schemata of film comprehension,* are used by the spectator in order to extract a story from what appears on the screen.

In the course of constructing the story the perceiver uses schemata and incoming cues to make assumptions, draw inferences about current story events, and frame and test hypotheses about prior and upcoming events. Often some inferences must be revised and some hypotheses will have to be suspended while the narrative delays payoff. While hypotheses undergo constant modification, we can isolate critical moments when some are clearly confirmed, disconfirmed, or left open. In any empirical case, this whole process takes place within the terms set by the narrative itself, the spectator's perceptual–cognitive abilities, the circumstances of reception, and prior experiences. (39)

The spectator's activity, therefore, consists in seeing, listening, remembering, assuming, inferring, making hypotheses, and eventually deleting all that appears on the screen. He conducts it, on the one hand, by relying on his own mental resources and on the set of the interpretive schemata that he can manage; on the other hand, as we will see shortly, by trusting the indications provided by the environment of the viewing, and above all by the object of the viewing.

Let us now move on to the second element at play: the film. Film channels the spectator's activity through a series of instructions. A film operates at two levels. The first is the plot, the actual form in which the events are presented. Bordwell calls it *syuzhet,* using a term dear to the Russian formalists. In general, the plot can shape our perception of the story by offering us more or less *plentiful* information (some plots are rarefied, some are overloaded), more or less *pertinent* information (some plots are essential, some are digressive), and information that *corresponds* more or less to the information that structures the fictional world (some plots are linear and complete, others contain permanent or temporary lacunae, others tend toward delays that are remedied only at the end, and still others tend toward redundancy or repetition of the facts presented). In short, the plot controls the amount, appropriateness, and functionality of the information, thus cuing and guiding "the spectators' narrative activity" (57).

The plot, however, obeys precise principles of construction. It connects events on the basis of causal relationships (or, more rarely, of parallelisms); it gives them a temporal order and situates them in space. In other words, "our schematizing and hypothesizing activities are guided by the *syuzhet*'s cues about causality, time, and space" (51). Bordwell devotes two chapters to the way in which the plot works on *time* and *space*. For time it is relevant, for instance, to analyze the *order* of the presentation of the events, with respect to their placement in the fictional world. They may be presented in a succession and perceived as simultaneous or vice versa. Similarly, it is relevant to observe the *frequency* of the events. They may appear in the plot once or many times, and yet function at times as unique events in the fictional world (even if they are presented repeatedly), at times as series of events (even if summarized by a single occurrence). Finally, it is relevant to observe the *duration* of the events. Usually the plot reduces what supposedly happens in the fictional world through ellipses of varying dimensions or compresses it with devices such as acceleration; but the plot may also respect the temporal extension of the events, or even expand them with insertions, or dilate them by slowing them down. As far as space is concerned, after mentioning the function of Renaissance perspective in cinema, Bordwell reminds us that the onscreen scene contains three kinds of cues. The first kind comes from the shooting and concerns such elements as the gradient of depth, the movement of the figures on the scene, the varying intensity of the colors, and so on. Thanks to them, we transform a flat surface into a three-dimensional space. The second kind of cues comes from the editing and concerns the possibility of connecting the isolated spaces of every shot into a whole. The third kind, finally, concerns sound. We should also take into account that these three orders of cues interconnect in order to organize the most delicate and decisive of filmic spaces, the offscreen.

Bordwell devotes very little space to the other level on which films operate: style. This dimension is less essential than that of the plot, because style concerns the technical-linguistic processes that render the plot as cinematography. He does, however, provide many examples of the divergence between fictional events and their mise-en-scène. This occurs when images "exceed" the mere exposition of facts.

Let us now move on to the last element at play: the story that the film suggests and that the spectator is asked to reconstruct (Bordwell uses the formalist term *fabula*). The *fabula* is, obviously, a hypothetical or ideal entity. The story is in fact the plot that has been reordered both logically and chronologically, integrated where a piece was missing, purged of its repetitions, etc. It is, indeed, the "fictional world" that results from the filtering of the film's suggestions through our comprehension schemata. Its features are therefore merely formal: unity, coherence, texture, relevance, etc.

Bordwell devotes the last part of his complex book to the various modes of narration that cinema has relied on over time. We will not linger on the periodization and typology that he presents (classic narration, art-cinema narration, the Russians' historical-materialist narration, parametric narration, and so on). We will only note that style returns to the foreground in this overview. The various forms of storytelling define an equal number of stylistic options (Bordwell, especially in his historical works, sees himself as a scholar of film stylistics). This section confirms the overall framework of the research, which proves its usefulness.

Bordwell made other contributions in this direction: in particular, his successful work on film criticism and on its ways of "watching" a film (Bordwell 1989). Above all, however, he was the guide of a group of scholars who applied cognitive psychology to the study of genres (Carroll on horror films) and of narration (Branigan).[8]

15.7. The Social Dimension: Pragmatics

The third main way to approach film representation is the *pragmatic approach*. Film is connected with the social environment where it appears; with the needs, habits, expectations, attitudes that characterize it; with the time and place where it is produced and projected; with the action of its promoters and beneficiaries, with their respective orientations, intentions, abilities; with the complex of the texts that accompany it, sometimes materially (as complements to the program: fliers, short films, etc.). In a word, the (filmic) *text* is related to its *context,* that is, the "surroundings" where it operates, or at least intends to.

Focusing on the relations between text and context means strictly correlating these two poles until they blend into a somewhat unified reality. It is also impossible to avoid approaching this reality from one side or from the other, however. It is possible to start from the text, to see how it makes hypotheses about its range of action, organizes, and even constructs it; or it is possible to start from the context, to see to what extent it affects, determines, and perhaps even defines what it contains. As much as pragmatics intends to avoid the division of the field (its object is in fact the "communicative situation," the union of text and context), these paths diverge. Hence, there are two kinds of investigation: one moves from text to context, believing that a discourse has great weight in the delineation of the surroundings where it is placed; the other goes from context to text, believing that the circumstances where a discourse appears directly influence its shape and organization. In the first case, the motto seems to be "Tell me what you say, and I will tell you in which situation you intend to or will eventually speak." In the second case, "Tell me in which situation you speak, and I will tell you what you say."

The pragmatics of cinema has had its biggest successes along the first path. A relevant contribution comes from the studies of enunciation. The presence in a film of deictics (that is, of signs that correspond to "I," "here," "now") is perceived as a reference both to the act that gave body and form to the text and to the elements of the context in which this same text finds its place. To give an example: the voice-over underscores the progressive development of the film while it reminds us of the exchange of information taking place between a sender and a receiver, of the fact that both are entitled to a certain knowledge and that this knowledge concerns the real world (if the film is a documentary) or a fictional world (if the film is a fictional account), and so on.

Francesco Casetti (1986) pursues the idea of a connection between enunciation markers and context features. He studies the way in which a film, by manifesting itself, calls upon and delineates the spectator. He points out the various *roles* that are predefined for the receiver. But a film's manifestation is also connected with the concrete viewing of someone in the theater; the textual roles must encounter *bodies,* which function both as their "supports," as places where these roles may take root (this is the spectator's "biological" reality), and as their "reservation," as places where these roles recover their background (this is the cultural dimension, where the spectator lives). In this face-to-face encounter, the implied spectator envisioned by a film is "adjusted" to the actual spectators in the theater, while it offers them a kind of model with which they can compare themselves and to which they are invited to conform. The result is that the hypotheses that developed with the shaping of the text project themselves on the context and prefigure its functioning.

Daniel Dayan (1983) also starts from the text to move on to the context. His idea (which recalls many of the narratological works of the time) is that fictional films always enact, together with the events they narrate, some sort of "theater of communication" where the ways in which the story is constructed and how it should be deciphered are portrayed. The problem, then, is to discern the forms taken by the "theater of communication" (for instance, in Fellini it tends toward mime, in Antonioni toward cerebral "vaudeville," and so on), as well as to grasp the *effects* of its staging. "These effects manifest themselves when we move from the 'immanent' receiver (on the screen) to the 'transcendent' receiver (in the theater)" (Dayan 1983:244). A complex bond is established between these two receivers: the first, more than asking the second to mirror himself in him, gives him a series of instructions that "program" his behavior. That is, the film, rather than defining models of ideal spectators, suggests the behaviors they should have or the operations they should perform. Rather than providing pictures, drawn to scale, of its concrete receiver, it opens new paths that the latter will have to follow. Dayan's key word becomes, therefore, *performance,* that is, making the public in the theater act or, better still, making it react.

But how can a filmic proposition program a reaction? Dayan finds an answer to this question in Austin's "theory of speech acts," which he tries to apply to the field of cinema. (His work was legitimated, after all, by the British philosopher himself, who had already connected verbal situations and behavioral or iconic situations.) His analysis centers on the film *Stagecoach*. Dayan, first of all, notices a strong presence of "behavitives," which consist mainly in "associating (or experiencing solidarity) with someone." In the film they are rendered by a recurrent ritual: more characters observe the same scene, during which they exchange a look of mutual understanding. This creates a "community of observers" for which the event represented becomes a spectacle, and its meaning becomes an exchangeable message; a community that recalls the audience in the theater, which is invited, in turn (also directly by the film), to associate or experience solidarity with the characters on the screen. The other linguistic acts that appear in *Stagecoach* are the verdictives, which consist in "judging someone." An example of this is the reiterated negative evaluation of Dallas, Ringo Kid, and Doc Boone coming from the other travelers. But these verdictives are, on the one hand, bound to be reformulated (Dallas, Ringo Kid, and Doc Boone are the final winners in the story); on the other hand, they are often contradicted by the behavitives (which voice a game of inclusion and exclusion that is stronger than any verdict). The spectator, therefore, in the name of a mainly affective solidarity, may avoid judging them on the basis of a purely formal law and absolve "in the Supreme Court" the characters that played the role of the villain.

Beyond this example, what counts is Dayan's gesture. His approach goes back to the most relevant area of linguistic pragmatics, the "theory of speech acts." In this frame, the passage from text to receiver takes place thanks to the presence in the former of "performatives" that guide the latter's reactions. Following this path Dayan introduces a first typology of the kinds of participation in representation: he distinguishes among *"spectacles for a public,* which rely on the spectator's performance as member of an audience, and *spectacles for a spectator,* which view the disappearance of this performance, which is taken on, and simulated, by the text itself" (1984 : 149). On the one hand, we have moments with a collective reaction; on the other hand, moments in which the reaction is totally enclosed by the linguistic act behind it.

Roger Odin elaborated the most wide-ranging project for a pragmatics of cinema in a series of contributions published during the 1980s.[9] His basic assumption is that film has no meaning in itself. Rather, the sender and the receiver "give it a meaning" through a series of procedures at their disposal in the social space where they operate. This means that there is no real communication between the author and the spectator. Both, however, can rely on the same procedures (and in this case they make the film say the same things; thus they understand each other); or they may enact different procedures (thus each constructing a different film). But what are the procedures that "give meaning" to a film? And what causes their agreement or provokes their disagreement?

Odin analyzes various *modes of production of meaning* in use in our society (indeed, he studies the modes of production of meanings and feelings: a film asks to be both understood and experienced). He characterizes them through the effects they try to achieve. The *spectacular mode* seeks to distract through the vision of a spectacle (it usually applies to escapist films); the *fictional mode* seeks to make the spectator vibrate with the rhythm of the events that are being narrated (it is at work in those films that demand "participation" in the events of their characters); the *energetic mode* seeks to make the spectator vibrate to the rhythm of images and sounds, without regard for the films' actual content (this happens, for instance, with musicals); the *private mode* seeks to make the spectator go back to his own experiences (it applies to home movies); the *documentary mode* seeks to inform about reality (it can be seen in documentary films); the *argumentative mode* seeks to persuade through a lesson of some sort (it applies to didactic films); the *artistic mode* seeks to shed light on an author's production (this happens with art films and films *d'essai*); the *aesthetic mode* seeks to create an interest in the "work" of both images and sounds (it is found in experimental films). These modes are known and practiced by both filmmaker and spectators. Both "intervene" in the film to give it body and depth. And these modes allow us to define or redefine the images and sounds that the film contains, to order or reorder its various elements, to weave or reweave a plot, to designate or recognize a character as having a leading role, to manifest oneself as "I" or recognize oneself as "you," and so on. In so doing, they give meaning to what lies before our eyes. Together, these modes shape a subject's "communicative competence."

The second question was: what creates agreement or disagreement among the modes activated by those who make and those who see the film? It is the *institution* to which the two belong, the social frame that they refer to. In the case of commercial cinema, for instance, the filmmaker tends to tell stories that belong to fictional worlds, with characters that elicit the participation of those who sit in the theater; along parallel lines, the spectator tends to see a story in the film, to traverse this fictional world, and to participate in the characters' experiences. The institution is therefore a social space that dictates behavioral rules: it tells us which procedures need to be applied, and what kind of sense we should make of the film. The institution of "commercial cinema," which—as we have seen—tends toward the spectacular, fictional, and energetic modes, is not alone. There are also the "research" institution, which promotes the artistic and aesthetic modes; the "family" institution, which relies on the private mode (one thinks of home movies); the "didactic" institution, which tends to apply the documentary or argumentative mode (one thinks of the use of films in schools); and so on.

It should be clear that the institution is endowed with materiality. The definition "commercial cinema" implies certain types of machines for the fabrication of film and a certain kind of theater for its consumption. Furthermore, individuals internalize it: directors and spectators of "commercial cinema" know very well what they need to do in order to construct and enjoy a film appropriately. Finally, this institution goes beyond the cinematic world. The term *show business* also applies to other media, just as *family* and *school* also deal with other things. Its most evident feature, however, is its very ability to initiate procedures and operations: in our case, the modes of production of meaning.

The institution ensures the agreement of sender and receiver, but it also regulates their disagreements. The latter derive from the presence of divergent references. Let us think of a film that is made for "commercial cinema" and watched as a "didactic aid": the object is transformed (a spectacular fiction becomes food for thought) because it is worked upon in two different social spaces (respectively, show business and school). Better still: the same object becomes two films, each coherent within "its" institution. Odin adds that in our society films always tend to be presented and consumed as spectacular fiction. There must be truly special conditions for them to become didactic aids (the teacher must destroy our "visual pleasure"), or works of art (critics need to "adopt" them; their enjoyment needs to take place within a festival or a theater *d'essai;* and so on), or historical evidence, etc. There are dominant and subordinate institutions.

Within this framework, what roles can a film play? Every film signals, especially at its beginning, whether it is fictional or documentary. It also contains themes that make it into an escapist story or an engaged work. Let us say, more generally, that every film orients whatever trajectories we may apply to it. It gives mainly "negative" signals, however. Rather than giving instructions, it *blocks* the use of procedures that do not suit it; it prevents the audience from taking it as fiction if it is a documentary film or as an engaged work if it is an escapist story. Its actual role is therefore to resist inadequate productions of meaning, while the institution's role is to promote one procedure or another. Therefore, each subject's moves depend mostly on the social space to which he belongs; better still, it is the communicative community that moves and guides its members. The institution is therefore the true protagonist.

Odin seems to remove all real importance from the text and decisively shift it toward the context. His pragmatics, thus, would seem to go in the opposite direction from the others that we have examined. In reality, if it is true that Odin makes the context responsible for determining the application of one or another mode of production of meaning, it is also true that Odin does not study these modes of production as social practices, but as the preconditions of the text's intelligibility. Before being a concrete action performed on a film, a procedure is an operation that the film needs in order to have meaning; before being an activity undertaken by subjects, it is something required by an object if it is to acquire its own identity. Odin's attention is, thus, devoted more to the linguistic than to the social dimension. Let us repeat that what is at stake is the presupposition of the meaningfulness of a text, rather than actual behavior. It is not by chance that Odin calls his pragmatics a *semio-pragmatics*.

This has two consequences. On the one hand, the text recovers all its weight: it is the beginning and end of the analysis; it is a rebus that asks to be deciphered. On the other hand, the context retains its role: it gives the text its own profile, which allows us to decipher the rebus. In short, it is the text that prompts the exploration of the context, but it is the context that makes the text what it is. The opening toward the social dimension can thus be transformed from a good omen, as with the first pragmatics, into a structurally necessary reference. This opening allows an understanding of the origin of the game: where film acquires its meaning, where it finds its own identity. It also allows us to answer the question of filmic representation: if cinema exists, it exists in the world of everyday life.

15.8. The Textual, the Mental, and the Social

With pragmatics we conclude our overview of the works that, in the 1980s, questioned the way in which filmic representation works. A significant place in them can be assigned to the new disciplinary approaches: semiotics, cognitive psychology, and pragmatics. Their convergences and rivalries were one of the key motifs of the research in this decade.

Each approach singles out a different key element. For semiotics the way in which representation works relies on the dynamics that are internal to the text. These dynamics raise the issues of enunciation (that is, the gesture that gives film its body and shape), narration (that is, the act that sustains a story), and realization (that is, the passage from underlying structure to manifestation). The risk implicit in such a framework (besides forcibly applying to cinema categories that were originally developed for verbal language) [10] is that the text is turned into a self-sufficient and self-explanatory reality. The film is in front of us, with its identity already fully developed, which we can only acknowledge. What appears on the screen not only makes sense in itself, but also has its own roots, and the rules of its functioning, in itself. Hence the latent "ontology of the text" of this approach. Yet this essentialism is avoided most of the time thanks to the awareness that this approach relies on interpretation, that is, on a tension—both open and regulated—between an object and a subject, both of which are indispensable to the game.

For cognitive psychology, filmic representation relies instead on the spectator's mental activity: he (re)formulates what he is seeing and hearing. A film is not a given. It is a construct. If this approach is subtended by a desire to avoid the "ontology of the text," it still runs the risk of completely "empty-ing" the text, turning it not into a weaving of signs, but into a field of stimuli whose only role is to initiate the cognitive processes enacted by the spectator. Film would then be reduced to a set of luminous traces of auditory masses, to which we give meaning through the application of mental processes, some innate and some acquired. Thus, we would be obligated to stop talking about a film as if it were a work identifiable in itself and only to point out what a spectator is capable of doing with this or that film. *Citizen Kane* does not exist; what exists is only a mental construct that is called *Citizen Kane,* before which we need mainly to ask ourselves what perceptive and intellectual processes formed it. The scholars of the cognitive approach are well aware of this para-dox and do not intend to throw away the texts in order to study the minds. Despite this, they risk being deprived of film.

Pragmatics views filmic representation within the social context that de-fines and selects the procedures that "give meaning" to the film. The assump-tion is that the text is such only inasmuch as (and only when) it fits into a context. There is, however, an obvious effort to correlate these two terms: if there is no text without a context, there is no context without a text. This attempt at integrating the two poles has the effect of strongly emphasizing the necessity of both distinguishing and correlating "internal" and "external" ap-proaches (if this spatial metaphor accounts for the terms of the question).

There are many reasons for disagreement. Let us consider, for instance, the perplexity about the "immanent" study of the text. Some suggest that film, unlike verbal discourse, neither "says" nor "communicates"; it only "shows." It is therefore unavoidable to attribute meaning to images and sounds only *a posteriori.* Still, some complain in particular that the studies of enunciation split the spectator, giving the "ideal" one the characteristics of the "real" one and acting as though the former were the latter; it would then be better to face the spectator in flesh and blood, the only "true" spectator.[11] Such per-plexities, however, can be counterbalanced by reasonable answers. First, it is not clear why an image, unlike a word, should be considered semantically empty. Even if it contains simple instructions, it provides some information, at least about actions to be performed; therefore, it has a meaning. Second, it is not clear why we should give up the "simulacrum" of the spectator in the text: people sitting in the theater confront the "mask" that their alter ego wears on the screen, either to wear it or reject it (spectatorial identifications confirm this). More generally, the viewers find in this mask one of the elements that structure their subjectivity (if nothing else, they recognize themselves as receivers, because images and sounds "address" them).

Accusations and justifications may multiply on either front. It is wrong, however, to use them in order to establish a hierarchy of approaches. Their confrontation emphasizes in fact that the disagreement lies in the various ways of approaching the problem of representation. Each sheds light on one aspect of the phenomenon, favoring some of its connections over others and presenting its own explanation of the facts. None of these approaches, however, can boast of working at a "deeper" level than the others. Each aspect (the functioning of the text itself, the mental processes of recognition and comprehension, the social procedures of meaning attribution) is either a presupposition or a background for the others. It is true that we need to go back from the text to the mental processes; but if we want to find out what lies at the core of the mental processes, we need to go back to the text. It is true that we need to relate the spectator's cognitive activity to the social dynamics. But if we want to understand what initiates these social dynamics, we also need to work on the psychological processes.

In short, no approach has exclusive rights to the elements of representation. Each presents only one model of its functioning. It is therefore necessary that these studies, while emphasizing their differences, get ready to engage in dialogue with one another. This is what happens in the best contributions: behind a façade of confrontation there is a wish to "translate" more general preoccupations into the work's own language and to make the answers that it is trying to provide "translatable" into the language of the others. The textual, the mental, and the social are therefore merely branches of the same research. They are different trails in the same territory, streets that converge and diverge, as the case may be. Adventuresome paths.

16 CULTURE, ART, THOUGHT

16.1. The Relevance of Cinema

The 1980s witnessed not only an interrogation of the functioning of representation. A bit more in the background another question circulated: the relevance of cinema to cultural, artistic, and intellectual processes. A film, rather than being just a machine powered by linguistic, psychological, and social mechanisms, appears instead as evidence of elaborations occurring at the intellectual, aesthetic, and philosophical levels. Evidence with an uncertain status: some think of it as clear and direct proof, others think that it only provides clues. But it is in any case crucial evidence, given that it reveals long-lived dynamics and tendencies.

As it is easy to see, the research strategy used here consists of placing cinema in a specific field of phenomena and illuminating its function through the retrieval and comparison of what is in the foreground and what serves as a base. This is not the first time that such a strategy has been used. It appears in all the inquiries that deal with "cinema and literature" or "cinema and contemporary society" that were in favor during the 1920s and 1930s. With respect to the prewar period, however (or the late 1940s and 1950s), there were some important differences. First, there was no longer a need to legitimize cinema (or interest in cinema). By then it was understood that cinema had an equal standing with other cultural products. If anything, there was a preoccupation with recuperating the "popular" aspects of the phenomenon in order to show their complementarity with "high" values. Second, research no longer concentrated on elucidating the "nature" of cinema. Rather, it asked what reverberations its presence had in the bigger picture, whose voices it embodied, which echoes returned to it. Third, the research no longer exhibited an immediate relation with the phenomena studied. The scholar's vision was already "educated," determined by a series of research techniques in the service of a basic problem. In this sense, film was often seen as a *text*, not so much in the sense of structure or process (two definitions we have already encountered), but as an *event*. An event in this sense means a fully realized linguistic product; a happening that takes place in communicative, cultural, intellectual space; a presence aligned with other presences. This event is an object that, besides having a function, has its own *existence* and *texture*, depth, life.

It should be added, however, that the approach that we are trying to reconstruct shows few other patterns of uniformity. More than sharing common traits, it followed personal paths. If we have insisted on the presence of recurrent motifs, and in particular on the idea of film as *evidence* or *event*, it is because throughout this book we have insisted on showing the frame of reference, often unconscious, of the debate. Not that we intend to lose sight of specific ideas: they tell us the roads so far taken. We can organize this territory into three distinct regions, each of which can in turn be divided into smaller provinces. One examines films on the basis of their cultural significance; another views films on the basis of their aesthetic value; and the last treats films as though they were *sui generis* philosophical thought. Let us begin our exploration.

16.2. Cinema and Culture: Stylistic Choices, Exchanges among Arts, Revival of Archetypes, and References to Society

When one sets cinema against a background of cultural processes and investigates it from this position, comfortable or uncomfortable though it may be, the questions that arise are numerous. To what extent does cinema bring into play borrowed means of expression or, on the contrary, give rise to other valuable forms? To what degree does cinema inherit the functions of classic narrative or, on the contrary, forge new paths? To what degree does cinema illustrate social reality on the screen, if somewhat removed, or, on the contrary, impose its own images to the point that they are taken for real?

We find these questions in the research that became dominant after the mid-1970s, above all in departments of Comparative Literature and American

Studies or French Studies in U.S. universities. Several factors contributed to the growth of such research: there was a crisis in the critical tradition personified by Wellek and Warren or New Criticism; research such as Northrop Frye's (through Hayden White) became progressively dominant; new forms, like structuralism, a European import, emerged, as did new teachings, like those of Fredric Jameson or Jonathan Culler; and, finally, there was the feeling that cinema, always capable of carrying on timely dialogue, might know how to furnish information that no other "art" can. This set of impulses led to studies that were obviously literary in nature, but also rich with insights and open to varied approaches. Let us examine some of these studies in order to define more precisely the contours of the area we are discussing.

We can begin with a book by Leo Braudy (1976). In the face of the separation of elite and popular art at the beginning of this century, cinema seemed to offer some sort of common ground. It is thus useful to analyze cinema at the level of staged worlds, of compositional rules, of forms of acting. Braudy dedicates a chapter to each theme. First and foremost, he distinguishes two types of worlds that can appear on the screen. The "open" film suggests a reality that exists before its portrayal, which extends beyond the borders of the frame and invites further exploration. The "closed" film, meanwhile, offers an intentionally constructed reality, one that exhausts itself with its showing and that calls up nothing beyond what it depicts. Renoir and Rossellini typify the open, Lang and Hitchcock the closed film. The director of the open film believes in possibility and literally "finds" a world and treats the viewer as a guest therein. The director of the "closed" film is an autocrat who "creates" a world and treats the viewer as a victim. It would take the arrival of modern cinema for the mixing of these two types of film to occur. We find the same polarity, though, when we examine the rules that support films: genre cinema implies a certain "closedness" at the level of expository formulas, while experimental cinema is more "open." In this case, too, the 1960s witnessed a mixing of openness and closedness. Finally, this polarity is reflected in forms of acting. "The open film emphasizes the continuity and the surprises of a character; the closed film considers character to be only another element in the visual pattern of the film" (Braudy 1976:219). In one case, we have actors who must express potential and varied states of mind; in the other, we have actors who must limit and repress themselves.

Braudy's book (which enjoyed a certain success) clearly indicates the way to proceed. Attention is concentrated on the formal choices a film faces rather than on its ways of functioning. This brings to light cinema's ability to gather and reuse preexistent expressive means (something also visible in literature, theater, and painting), which on the screen acquire new depth and relevance. An analogous discourse is seen in a study by Keith Cohen dedicated to the relation between cinema and literature (Cohen 1979). His research style is somewhat different, being more attentive to the historical dimension, but he maintains the same overall orientation.

Cohen first analyzes the cultural context of cinema's birth. He recalls, for example, the interest on the part of the artistic avant-garde during the second half of the 1800s in light and movement, in fragmentation and multiplicity of points of view. He likewise emphasizes the emergence during the same years of a favorable tendency to synthesize naturalism and impressionism, the recovery of secondary aesthetic forms, and the incorporation of technology into art. On this basis, Cohen goes on to explore the "dynamics of exchange" that were established between filmic and literary narrative. There are three main points of contact. Both in the twentieth-century novel and in cinema (especially the latter), the statuses of objects and subjects are reversed. Objects are animated and subjects petrified. There are temporal distortions—the prolonged present, nonchronological story lines, and simultaneity. And point of view is relativized, by multiplying perspectives and mixing participation and detachment.

Besides treating cinema through its formal structures, Cohen shows extremely clearly how these structures depend on the dialogue and on the continual interchanges that this new medium establishes with the entire field of culture. The studies of Frank McConnell further expand the picture. The object of his inquiry is always narrative, whether cinematic or literary. But his focus shifts from the expressive means with which we transcribe reality to the forms with which we interpret our life (McConnell 1975 and especially 1979).

The didactic nature of all narration is McConnell's point of departure. The story seems to lead its readers or viewers to escape from the world, while in fact it helps them to form an idea of themselves and their surroundings. Through the construction of a fictitious universe, they are supplied with facts that can be utilized in the real world. This is because the story activates "archetypes." "Archetypes" always constitute an interpretive key to phenomena. The contrast between good and evil tells us that conflict between humans is inevitable and that it has moral roots. Flight and return show that for all forms of personal maturation it is necessary to pass through moments of detachment and reconciliation, etc. Because of these archetypal roots, stories are able to offer explanations and to suggest ways of behaving.

All this holds true for the cinematic story, too. Film has in fact taken over the position previously held by literary narrative—and before that by oral traditions. The content remains the same: in its most "basic form," it deals with "the story of an individual's relation to his or her social, political or cultural ambience" (1979). Naturally, we need to see what narrative structures generate such an "elementary form of the story." McConnell (who rereads Frye by way of Rousseau) suggests that there exist in literature and cinema four "fundamental myths," each characterized by a heroic type, a certain ambience, and some sort of transgression that the hero must confront. In the "epic," the hero is a sovereign, the ambience is a city to be founded, and the transgression is against the gods. The *Aeneid* and *Ivan Groznij* follow this pattern. In the "romance," the hero is a knight, his mission is to maintain order, and the sin is committed against other men. *The Song of Roland* and *My Darling Clementine* both have this fundamental narrative core. In "melodrama," the hero is an "agent" (a detective, a lawyer, a reporter) who in the face of the conflict between ostensible morality and the secret violation of the law seeks somehow to recover the precepts on which the city was founded. The examples analyzed by McConnell are *The Secret Agent* and *North by Northwest*. In "satire" the hero is either a Messiah or a lunatic who lives in a city where the distinction between the law and its infraction, between good and evil, has been lost, where life has become intolerable. The examples discussed are *Die Verwandlung* and *Taxi Driver*.

The delineation of four archetypal structures not only allows McConnell to collect the transplants from literature to cinema and from cinema to literature. It also enables him to show the functions carried out by the cinematic story. Narrations through images and sounds, not unlike those transmitted through words, help us to decipher the world and to find solutions to the dilemmas we face. The functions of film are at the center of another group of studies that pay particular attention to the social implications of every expressive choice. In these works, the artistic dynamics are related to the dynamics present in any community.

The first example, from the 1950s, is offered by Robert Warshow. His analysis of the gangster, seen as the negative underside of the modern entrepreneur, and of the man of the West, seen as a carryover of the romantic hero, tends to show how cinema, like popular literature, "reads" and "transcribes" the world through interpretive keys (Warshow 1962). This idea is taken up again in the work of Michael Wood. "Classic" Hollywood production is characterized by genre (the musical, the western), by actors (Gene Kelly, Rita Hayworth), and by situations (falling in love, solitude) that take aim at the basic traits of American culture and the way it thinks of the individual, the couple, sexuality, fate, etc. The idea is basically that films may be capable of giving substance to the typical worries and problems of each society, in addition to the great myths: worries and problems that on the screen are translated into stories that constitute moments of self-awareness and, at the same time, escapist outlets. Thus, it is possible to treat every Hollywood product as a text that allows "the study of what might be called the back of the American mind" (Wood 1975:117). Cinema tells us how we see ourselves and what we think of ourselves and the world.

Another seminal work within this area of inquiry is Robert Stam's *Reflexivity in Film and Literature,* in which he explores all the valences of the process by which films refer to themselves, to their own making, to their intertext, their textual structure, their authorship, their mode of addressing the spectator, and their reception. The paradoxical nature of reflexivity, Stam seems to claim, resides in the fact that the reflexive film fulfills itself to the extent in which it refers to nothing but itself. However, it is in this very same act that, paradoxically, it discovers the "other." In other words, reflexivity points to the cultural artifact's nature as a mask of reality and at the same time, it is precisely this unmasking that reveals a possible access if not to reality itself, at least to the reality of the text.

We could mention other works.[1] But those we have discussed allow us to define the area of study: an interest in the stylistic options that characterize a system of representation (Braudy); or in expressive forms used by cinema and other fields (Cohen); or in the great myths that cinema inherits and reuses (McConnell); or in the outlines that allow us to reconstruct a mentality (Warshow, Wood). In all four cases, cinema is tied to the cultural dynamics that both pervade and nourish it: a film is itself to the extent that it leads to something else.

16.3. Cinema and Culture: Formal Structures and Social Functions, Constant Elements and Contingent Factors

This type of study, which flourished above all in the American academic environment, was also present in the European environment. It is enough to cite three highly diverse works, each of which is equally capable of serving as an example of the major directions of this research.

The first is an extremely successful essay by Thomas Elsaesser on melodrama (1972). First, he retraces the origins of the genre, from the medieval morality play to the Romantic theater of postrevolutionary France. Then he explains the social function of melodrama: the events narrated, though extreme and schematic, allow the translation of ordinary themes (e.g., the contrast between desire and law, responsibility and freedom, emergent and established classes) into situations that refer to common experiences. In this way the spectator (or reader) can arrive at an explanation of the dynamics that in part escape his understanding through the narrative's reference to his life. Along the same lines, Elsaesser brings the structures of melodrama to light. He emphasizes the role of "counterpoint" (between character and decor or principal and marginal events) and the presence of real "condensations" (the psychological states of characters are reflected in the objects around them). Finally, he analyzes the way in which the genre faces the worries that pervaded American society in the 1950s. The stories focus on the conflict between generations or between the sexes, reveal a claustrophobic atmosphere, deal with panic and hysteria.

The second contribution also takes as its object of study a cinematographic genre. Maurizio Grande treats comedy "Italian style" in his work (1986). His point of departure is the opposition (read in light of Frye's work) between the tragic and the comic. While the tragic highlights "social schism, the difference between the individual and the group, the estrangement of leaders and community" (Grande 1986:42), the comic shows the daily conflict between the individual and society and the "adaptation" of the former to the latter. This is the source of comedy's interest in the hero (a common character) who wavers between integration into or rejection of society and who ends up opting for a pacifying solution. Hence the centrality in comedy "Italian style" of four major myths that also characterize four currents within the genre: the myth of entrance into society (developed, for example, in *Le ragazze di Piazza di Spagna* or *Due soldi di speranza*); the myth of forced adaptation to social norms (present in *Il segno di Venere* or *I soliti ignoti*); the myth of fraud and travesty (an "excess of adaptation that inevitably results in an imbalance": *Una vita difficile* or *Divorzio all'italiana*); and the myth of lost innocence (*Pane, amore e fantasia* or *Poveri ma belli,* in which the danger of "misunderstanding as a way of life" is confronted and in which the solutions offered by the comic turn into crises).

The third exemplary contribution to this field of study is a far-reaching and very personal work by Jacques Aumont on the relations between cinema and painting (1989). The guiding idea here is that the encounter between the two media—cinema and painting—exchanged more problems than formal procedures. From this point of view, Aumont, for example, proposes seeing the Lumières as the last impressionist painters. Their films in fact revolve around two questions posed by impressionism: the problem of "reconstituting" reality through its impalpable elements (light and air) and the problem of defining by means of the "cut" or shape of an image a visual field and a distance between object and observer. In the same way, Aumont links the construction of filmic space and time to the painting of the last two centuries. In particular, he recalls the attempts of painting to represent "common moments" (scenes of daily life) rather than "meaningful moments" and at the same time to give a sense of the future (the series) or of comings and goings (collage). Likewise, he recalls attempts to link that which is represented on the surface of the canvas to what remains beyond its borders. The borders of a painting in turn become a valuable object (gilt frames) and simultaneously an inevitable and often problematic limit to the representation. Cinema, art of the ephemeral, of the progressive, of the ordinary, is also the art of balancing between what is seen and what is only intuited. It carries on this search and gives it new depth. Finally, Aumont links cinema's "variable eye," certainly its most valuable conquest, with a more complex itinerary: the road that traverses the taste for sketches and the interest in life's daily scenes expressed by nineteenth-century painting, which is also affected by the different perceptions of the world brought about by train travel or the sense of staging created by the "panoramas" in vogue during the last century and which culminates in the mobility of the movie camera, the multiplicity of its perspectives, and the permutation of frames allowed by editing, etc. In all this, cinema is not just the "heir" of an investigation already under way. On the contrary, it leads to the discovery of what was often implicit, and it restores to other ideas something it has made more profound. In other words, "the relation between cinema and painting does not rest in correspondences or affiliations dear to classical aesthetes" (Aumont 1989:253). The two poles constantly interact, exchange questions and experiments, blur their respective borders, and make the goals that the other has achieved into their starting point. Rather than involving analogies or transplants, at play here is a movement that may lie underground, but that remains decisive: the confluence and separation of two fields, their fragmentation and recomposition.

Once again the works that could be cited are very numerous. I am thinking, for example, of the studies interested in "intertextuality" and the way in which certain themes or certain procedures "pass" from one text to another, of those works interested in "intermediation" or the way in which different mediums exchange roles and experiences. These two focal points often produced noteworthy results in the 1980s.[2] Moreover, in Europe we also find, perhaps with different motivations or tones, a research atmosphere that relates cinema to cultural dynamics.

This line of research, from either side of the Atlantic, is marked by a double polarity. When attention falls on a film's stylistic choices or on its expressive means shared with other media, at the center of the analysis are *formal structures*. When instead one talks of film's capacity to bring new life to myths or to make itself witness to a way of thinking, then one questions above all *social functions*. Similarly, when one speaks of great choices of mythic roots, in some ways one is *proceeding from history*. When one talks about stylistic procedures or symptoms or traces, then one is documenting *circumscribed and precise dynamics*. Therefore, *formal structures* and *social functions* can be paired with *universal constants* and *contingent elements*. Cinema carries on a dialogue with culture because it brings all these references into play. Each aspect, however, can lead to different emphases. The debate over cinematographic genres furnishes proof of this.

16.4. Cinema and Culture: Between Archetypes and Rituals

In the last twenty years genre research has enjoyed growing success. Not that this area had been poorly or infrequently studied. It is enough to cite the works of Bazin on the evolution of the western or those of Warshow on the westerner and the gangster to demonstrate quite the opposite.[3] Still, it was a territory left in large part in the hands of passionate critics and unrepentant cinephiles. At the beginning of the 1970s genre's strategic importance began to be understood. Genre allows us to go beyond the film/director concept dear to the "authorial" approach and to grasp more inclusive dynamics. In fact, research brings to light how much precedes (or exceeds) the choice of this or that expressive solution. We discover the importance of habits that ask to be satisfied, the convenience of proceeding by imitation and repetition, the intervention of recurrent narrative schemes, the efficacy of a cliché communication, the predisposition to read the new in terms of the already known. The result is that we no longer think of genre as a mechanism of banalization, unless it is revived as such by the work of an author with his own poetics. On the contrary, it is an essential device for understanding what makes cinema an art that is both "industrial" and "popular."[4]

Here we discover the existence of a fundamental agreement that ties the person who makes a film to the viewer. Genre is a collection of shared rules that allows the filmmaker to use established communicative formulas and the viewer to organize his own system of expectations. There is, in short, an agreement between the filmmaker and his audience (McArthur 1972:20), a tacit "convention" that allows the participants to understand one another (Kitses 1970:24). But what is such an agreement based on? Buscombe (1970) and McArthur (1972) praise the role of iconography: genre results from the presence of recurrent figures, be they characters or atmosphere. Kitses (1970) also speaks of historical references (one cannot define the western without referring to the conquest of the West or the Civil War), fixed themes (there is no western without the contrast between the gun and the law or between sheep and cattle), and models that derive from theater or literature. Other scholars add new elements: the use of an established style, the appearance of the same actors, the resurgence of period styles. The list could be expanded. The fact remains that formal elements (characters, themes, procedures) come into play and that they are *also* tied to a social function (the need to recognize what is being shown to us; the usefulness of recurrent solutions; the impulse to translate history into stories, etc.). One is not limited to formal elements, as was the case for those who reduced genre to a collection of typical features; on the contrary, one must always try to keep genre's social functions in mind.[5]

Now, precisely from this confluence, we see another division emerge. What is the range of action of genre? Does it have a universal appeal, such that it touches human life everywhere and always, or is its reach more circumscribed, operating within precise periods and contexts? Does it therefore draw its sources from something that is represented in all times and places, like a fable or a proverb, or does it create them from specific facts pertaining to a single community?

Stuart Kaminsky, to whom we owe one of the most successful studies of genre (1974), insists above all on its universality. Genre, like other forms of popular narrative, has universal roots. It is perfectly true that to understand the western it is necessary to keep in mind some of the stereotypes formed over the last two hundred years, but the true roots of these stereotypes are to be found in the heart of ancient myths. Genre films reelaborate the themes and problems that constitute myth: the contrast between good and evil, individual and community, freedom and law, and the need to find a point of equilibrium between the two terms of a dilemma. Each genre film reuses a myth: the "dirty" hero of detective films shows us a resurrected Perseus; in the western's villain we recognize the person tossed out of earthly paradise; and so forth. This means that genre films are nothing more than the latest version of something permanent. They embody *archetypes* to which we have never ceased to refer. A simple glance at their substance and their roots allows us to grasp their outlines and functions.

If Kaminsky tends toward a "global" interpretation of genre films, others insist instead on the possibility of circumscribing their reach. For Pye (1975), genre takes up fixed forms, but gives them a particular shape. In this sense, it is useful to keep in mind the narrative models behind each genre (models that recall Frye's "modes": romance, tragedy, comedy, etc.; and that provide a text with its infrastructure). But it is even more useful to focus on the levels of style, the forms of plot, or the character typologies that give substance to such narrative models. Pye applies his theory to the western, and he discovers that the presence or absence of a realistic treatment completely determines the definition of the genre.

Along these lines, John Cawelti's reflections are particularly important. For him, rather than speaking of genre, it is better to speak of *formula*. The term makes at least two things clear. On the one hand, it emphasizes the fact that we are faced with anonymous and repetitive structures rather than with individual and unpredictable acts. A culture needs not only "inventions" that assure change, but "conventions" that guarantee stability. On the other hand, he emphasizes the fact that we are faced with structures tied to precise ends rather than with models that can be adapted to all ends. A culture needs not only major frames of reference, but also representations that concentrate on the worries of a given age. This second point is decisive: formulas are notations of configurations operative in specific epochs and contexts rather than eternal and universal truths (as genres seem to be if one thinks of them as simple reworkings of myths; see Cawelti 1971:7). Still, the difference is also interpreted as follows: formulas, more than discarding the great narrative models, "translate" them into richer and more concrete and thus more effective structures. In fact, thanks to formulas, "specific cultural themes and stereotypes become embodied in more universal story archetypes" (Cawelti

1976:6). A critical event in the community, like the conflict between the sheriff and bandits in the West, can be related to the internal struggle between good and evil and in this way acquire additional depth of meaning. At the same time, thanks to formulas, these same archetypes materialize in characters, settings, and situations that have significance for the culture that brings them into being. The struggle between good and evil is in and of itself an abstraction. Only when it takes the form of a conflict between the sheriff and bandits does it acquire a precise meaning for all members of a community. The result is not to stop speaking to Man (as myths did and still do); but at the same time to speak to men (who live in a given time and place).

Will Wright proceeds in the same direction. One can only speak of the mythic roots of genre if the terminology can be agreed on. Myth has always represented an attempt "to read" the world. Even before being a canonical story to reuse and renew, it is "a structure with social meaning" (Wright 1976: 17), thanks to which a community can find explanations for events. Genres do not work any differently. They offer explanatory keys to phenomena. They speak to us of the disruptive force of desire, of the inevitability of destiny, etc. They do so while keeping in mind the themes and problems that characterize each community. They are, therefore, "on top of" the dynamics at work at that moment. Thus, one can say that a society has the genres that it deserves: those that best reflect its obsessions and also its good omens, its wounds and its potential points of equilibrium.

The insistence that genre films portray a circumscribed and timely reality has more than one consequence. Above all, more elements are brought into play. Genres no longer have to do only with archetypes, but also with historical, social, and linguistic factors. Rick Altman concentrates on the linguistic factors. A genre presents either recurrent content (the same character, action, atmosphere) or a fixed form of exposition (the same type of plot, which in detective films controls the unfolding of the investigation, in musicals decides which parts are sung and which are spoken, etc.). Thus, genre can be defined semantically and syntactically. Altman's idea is that "some of the most important questions of genre studies can be asked only when they are combined." The best approach is a "semantic/syntactic approach to genre study" (Altman 1984a: 11). A similar point of view helps us to understand, for example, why genre is better expressed in some films than in others. These films reproduce a universe that is as typical as its plot is canonical. Above all, Altman's perspective helps us to understand how a genre evolves. We can have stable semantic content and changes at the syntactical level (this is the case with musicals, which renew themselves by appropriating melodramatic plots); we can also have stable syntax and changes in content (as in the case of the western, set in different times and places but continuing to tell the same story). Altman adds that this mechanism allows a real negotiation between Hollywood and its public. New proposals or requests can be introduced gradually, put to the test, and succeed only if they prove themselves worthy. In this way, the genre film can change its skin and at the same time remain the same.

Thomas Schatz (1981) offers some parallel and complementary observations. With respect to the individual films that constitute it, genre is a little like a "grammar" with respect to individual discourses. It is a system of shared and internalized rules that lends itself to diverse applications, but applications that all conform to the canon. Schatz attempts to limn out this "grammar." In particular, he brings to light the role of its narrative components or characters, settings, conflicts, and resolutions. Likewise, he emphasizes the existence of two major models: one tied to themes of order that is at work in western, gangster, and detective movies; the other tied to themes of integration and visible in musicals, screwball comedies, and melodramas. Schatz further suggests that the linguistic rules fundamental to genre films have their counterpart in the rules of the industry: the "narrative economy" that films obey is the flip side of the "material economy" that regulates the studios. Hence the usefulness of integrating a study of forms and representation with an analysis of modes of production, two contiguous and interactive realities.

The second consequence of a more circumscribed examination of genre films emphasizes their functions. By linking them more closely to social reality, one can see more clearly what they respond to. In Cawelti, for example, we find a list of "cultural functions." Genre (for him, formula) offers first and foremost a synthesis and reaffirmation of the values practiced by a society. From this point of view, genre fulfills a function similar to that fulfilled by ritual. Second, genre constitutes "entertainment with rules known to everyone" (Cawelti 1971 : 32), and in this sense it assumes the same role as games. Finally, genres "seem to be one way in which the individuals in a culture act out certain unconscious or repressed needs, or express in an overt and symbolic fashion certain latent motives which they must give expression to but cannot face openly" (Cawelti 1971 : 33). In this sense, genre resembles dreams. The list is expanded by Cawelti himself and by other scholars. But these three dimensions, the ritual, the ludic, and the oneiric, constitute the basis of every list.

Of the three, *ritual* is certainly the most interesting (and, not incidentally, the most discussed). Genre allows everyone to recognize himself as a member of a community, with the same points of reference and values. Genre helps to mitigate conflict and to find ways of mediation, if only at a symbolic level. Finally, genre gives rise to a predetermined consumption, almost ritualistic. In this sense, it contributes directly to the processes on which a society is built. It not only reflects how a group of individuals thinks or believes or sees; it also triggers behaviors that keep this group together. The function of genre could not be more greatly praised: when its ritual value is brought to light, it becomes one of the tools of sociability.

Let us conclude our discussion of genre. Anyone who wants a broader picture of the debate has at his disposition an excellent anthology (Grant 1986). We started with the pact that links the filmmaker and the viewer, and we have pointed out a series of factors that ideally proceed from the presence of *archetypes* common to mankind to the presence of *rituals* that hold a specific community together. Along the way we have confirmed the two great polarities that accompany the study of cinema as a cultural fact. On the one hand, we have seen the equal importance of formal elements and social functions. In defining genre, sometimes one appeals to procedures or canonical themes, sometimes to needs to be satisfied or goals to be pursued. On the other hand, we have seen the equal importance of universal factors and more circumscribed factors. In studying genre there is emphasis on the intervention of perennial models as well as on elements that pertain to a specific area or age. Furthermore, our review of genre in film has allowed us to understand the takeoff of an exploration that pays attention above all to *popular culture* (and not just the "culture industry"). The action of an author or experimentation of a group is not foregrounded here; what is foregrounded is a presence that is widespread among and shared by all the members of a community. This presence, moreover, is something that supports the community by enabling it to share themes, values, and behaviors. Hence, we have an interrogation of the cultural identity of different communities as expressed in films, novels, speeches, etc., that circulate. This is the central theme of "cultural studies," a research trend that enjoyed great success near the end of the 1980s. Though not specifically occupied with cinema, it skirted research like that on genres.

16.5. Cinema and Society: Representation and Identity

The term "cultural studies" designates an interdisciplinary approach born in Britain around the activity of the Birmingham Centre for Contemporary Cultural Studies which, during the 1980s, spread out in all the Anglophone countries.[6] Within this perspective, culture (taken as a whole, with no distinctions between high and low culture, but rather as a "whole way of life") is the site in which different forces compete to gain control over meanings; and since meanings and representations are the bricks by which identity is formed, cultural studies tends to analyze cultural products to seek how subjectivity is socially constructed. Cultural studies was born within the field of Marxist literary theory, represented in late 1950s and 1960s England by the work of theorists such as William Haggar, Raymond Williams, and E. P. Thompson, and it has reached the most accomplished formulation of its ethical-political-pedagogical project through the reflection of Stuart Hall. In its mature phase, cultural studies gathers the contributions of different critical approaches such as the Gramscian conceptualization of the relationship between politics and culture, the structuralist and poststructuralist critiques of ideology, the Foucauldian equation of knowledge and power, the attention to the politics of gender brought about by feminist film theory, and the race studies contribution to the formulation of the notion of cultural identity.

Cultural studies' main concern is to design the geography of power relations within the cultural realm by tracing down the sites, the ways, the authorship of meanings. In relation to this, one of its fundamental tenets is that the subject is defined in terms of a constant negotiation between the ideological framework that permeates cultural products, the subject's material conditions of existence, social and anthropological components (such as gender, class, race or ethnicity, sex), and interpretive freedom. Cultural studies' ethical-political thrust can be thought of as a struggle over meanings and is two-directional: on the one side—the side of the production of meanings—there is an effort to assure authenticity to representations, to give voice to marginalized subjects, to foster competing world-visions; on the other side, the theorization of a certain amount of freedom, on the part of the subject, in the reception of those meanings, in the evaluation of experiences, representations, events. In other words, on the one hand, cultural studies engages in the politics of representation; on the other hand, it works for a re-conceptualization of spectatorship.

Cultural studies' influence on film studies is expressed in the analysis of the presence and circulation of cultural meanings, and thus in the effort to measure the authenticity of representations within film texts; in addition, cultural studies has encouraged research into the processes of identity formation within the spectatorial situation with reference to the spectator's negotiation of textual meanings. Furthermore, as a consequence of cultural studies' refusal of structuralist ahistoricism and its insistence on a diachronic conception of the subject, it has offered a meaningful contribution to the opening up of a dialogue between historiographical theory and practice, and it has produced a new object of inquiry: the relationship between modes of production, distribution, and reception of films and the process of subject formation (in personal as well as political and social terms) of spectators in a given historical moment.

Cultural studies has fueled and animated particularly the field of reception studies, which deserves closer attention. Since the early 1980s a new and growing interest has animated cinema studies: the historical study of the reception of cinema. The concern with audiences and the analysis of the meanings they take from film can be described as the result of a number of factors. First, the discovery of the political nature of all representations and the critique of ideology (fostered, for example, by the *Screen* group) bring attention not only to the individual responses to cultural products, but also to the social construction of meaning and the way in which identities are socially constructed through the consumption of the film. Second, the growing interrogation of the relationship between cinema and society, text and context, gives way to a conception of cinema as an institution, a regime of belief to which individuals are exposed. Third, within cinema studies there is the need to historicize the communicative models employed to understand the role of cinema within society, accompanied by the realization that film history is not only and simply the history of films but also the history of cinema audiences. Thus historians (see Allen 1990) start to research exhibition practices and audience composition (in terms of class, gender, race, etc.) in the attempt to understand what meanings historical spectators took from certain films and what role cinema-going played in their lives. A strong influence on the turn to the study of spectatorship was also exerted by the dissemination of cultural studies programs in the American academy: cultural studies' concern with popular culture and processes of identity formation fostered the turn to the ethnography of consumption. Although cultural studies' early work had been focused on television audiences, there are some seminal works that attempt to apply its theoretical framework and methodologies of inquiry to the analysis of cinema audiences. Janet Staiger's *Interpreting Films* (1992) offers a good overview of the existing reception theories—which she describes as either text-activated, reader-activated, or context-activated—and calls for a historical materialist approach, that is, the consideration of what readings of a certain text were available to the historical spectators. In other words, the historical materialist approach seeks the "historical explanation of the event of interpreting a text" and it does so by looking at the intertext of the literature on the film but also, and mainly, at the discursive formations that inform a film's reading in relation to the specific historical situation. Staiger then demonstrates the application of this approach in a number of case studies of audience responses throughout American film history, from *Uncle Tom's Cabin* to *Zelig*. Judith Mayne's *Cinema and Spectatorship* focuses primarily on how film contexts address their spectator (thus not rejecting altogether the tools of textual analysis) by exploring at the same time the paradoxical, dynamic relation between "subject" and "viewer." In other words, Mayne's effort is directed toward the conceptualization of spectatorship between determinism and voluntarism. She claims her concern is with "the play and variation that exist at particular junctures between the competing claims of film spectatorship—as the function of an apparatus, as a means of ideological control, on the one hand, and as a series of discontinuous, heterogeneous, and sometimes empowering responses, on the other" (Mayne 1993 : 102).[7]

Parallel to this concern with spectatorship and partly indebted to it is a strain of studies centered on the conceptualization of the viewing subject and the analysis of how it came into being historically. Here I will briefly mention only Jonathan Crary's work on the pre-cinematic observer, based on the assumption that problems of vision have always been linked to questions of the body and of social power; Ann Friedberg's *Window Shopping,* centered on the historical construction of the film spectator's mobile virtual gaze; and Linda Williams' collection of essays, *Viewing Positions,* which gathers various contributions exploring different aspects of the viewing subject in relation to issues of public versus private sphere, technologies of vision, the way in which film texts address and construct different subject positions, and the role of the viewing body vis à vis the film body.

16.6. Cinema and Art: The Return of Aesthetics

To this point, in speaking of the significance of cinema, we have insisted on its cultural relevance. But film also has aesthetic relevance. One of the research trends of the 1980s led to a reconsideration of the artistic dimension of film. This exigency reemerged after a decade that was mainly attentive to ideological and social values. This return to the discussion of the quality of a work was almost a "countertendency." But many paths led to this end.

Dudley Andrew, in a volume programmatically entitled *Film in the Aura of the Art*, connects aesthetics and differentiation. A work, he says, owes its quality to the fact that it stands out from an indistinct background. "The art cinema promises something no other group of films can: to question, change, or disregard standard film making, in seeking to convey or discover the utterly new or the formerly hidden. It is under this promise that these films claim a right to perpetual interest and existence" (Andrew 1984:5–6). A series of analyses provides examples of this: Griffith's *Broken Blossoms* and the search for a new "narrative ethos"; Murnau's *Sunrise* and a kind of framing that creates "reverential awe"; Vigo's *L'Atalante* with its antiacademic attitude; Capra's *Meet John Doe* and its use of experimental montage; etc.

For Andrew, the differences regard either language or modes of production, the themes dealt with or forms of consumption. We are on terrain that is broader than that designated by the romantic concept of "exceptionality," which even here works from a model. Kristin Thompson instead focuses on linguistic differences. The important thing is that a film brings in procedures that "break" with those currently in use. Her examples range from *Ivan Groznij* (Thompson 1981) to *Stage Fright* to *Laura* to *Lancelot du Lac* or *Sauve qui peut (la vie)* (Thompson 1988). Her carefully explained methodology takes us back to the Russian formalists, for whom art originated with the use of language not tied to practical ends and the employment of the process of estrangement. For Thompson, too, "rupture" serves to suspend functionality and to revitalize old standards. The reference is for the rest explicit: her approach is labeled neoformalist.

A second major way of understanding aesthetics, besides an appeal to difference, is to link it to the tension between what exists and what is possible. A work owes its quality to the fact that it broadens the horizons of the territory where it inscribes itself. Thus, infraction of the rules of the current canon is unimportant. What matters is that the rules of the canon are put into perspective and reveal either their limits or their potential.

Giorgio Tinazzi (1983) notes that the equipment and procedures used by cinema seem to make it a simple copy of reality. In numerous films, a nontraditional use of traditional tools obstructs this perception and leads to a sort of short-circuiting. At the same moment in which a technique is applied, it is

charged with the task of showing itself (Spielberg), questioning itself (Eisenstein), propounding old experiences in a new way (*Fedora*), or becoming the
true protagonist (*Il mistero di Oberwald*). The film continues to work, but at
the same time it undergoes a kind of transformation.

This mechanism functions in even the most refractory areas. This is the
case with remakes, sequels, serials, or films that seem to obey only the logic
of the film industry. In reality, repetition and seriality trigger more than a
reference. They send cinema back to its origins, to an atmosphere of fascination with the working of machines, with the spectacle of the commodity,
with the metropolitan setting. Likewise, they remind cinema of its narrative
dimension through recourse to stories that are always different and always
the same. They thus bring into play the roots and the branches of the medium. They attract our attention to what is behind and alongside a film. They
help us to outline its field of action better, with its boundaries and eventual
readjustments. Even works apparently lacking any depth thus become more
meaningful.

Tinazzi's thoughts are interesting because they link art and technique.
Cinema must take into account its own conditions of existence. To be open
to what is possible, it should not design a remote horizon (art as prophecy).
Neither should it evoke another place (art as utopia). Rather, it should multiply its levels and play on its self-reflexivity. A third major zone of interest
relates aesthetics to the intensity of the reactions it elicits. In this case, a work
owes its quality to its ability to make the viewer live a special experience.

It is precisely with the term "experience" that a noted work by Gerald
Mast concludes. His underlying idea is that a work of art is a harmonious and
self-sufficient universe (Mast 1977). A film is above all a microcosm that reproduces, reorders, and to some degree idealizes the world around us. This
reorganization of existence into an independent world makes use of successive images and sounds. Their use obeys certain precise aesthetic laws, like
balance, economy of means, logical development, and so forth. Such a composition, however, is supposed "to strike" the viewer; that is, both to provide
him with sensations and to elicit his participation. This means that along with
a "mimetic" component (reconstruction of a world) there is also a "cinematic" component (creation of a feeling): one must trigger the other. This is
the source of the final appeal to the experience of the viewer. He "lives" the
microcosm unfolding before his eyes. And the more perfect such a microcosm is, the more intensely the viewer can live in it. The result will be a

greater nearness to reality, be it internal or external (Mast 1977), and a bringing to light of the dilemmas that characterize human existence.

The idea of experience also dominates the pages of an Italian scholar, Edoardo Bruno (if Mast is tied to a neoclassical idea of art, in Bruno the references, even if nuanced, are to phenomenological thought). The experience invited by cinema is at least threefold. It is a visual experience: the spectator is an active accomplice, ready to participate in what he sees and to recognize himself as a seeing subject. It is an experience of signification: "to read" a film means to grasp its obvious meanings, but also to be ready to understand its imperceptible details, its recondite themes, its elusive meaning, its anomalies, and so on. Finally, it is an experience of another reality: the world that appears onscreen differs from the world of everyday life. It is a "planned" reality, open to utopia and fantasy. After all, "art does not reproduce, it proposes" (Bruno 1986:87). The moment of experience, therefore, is a moment in which the film and the viewer are indissolubly linked. This union creates a situation that enriches both the viewer and the film. And by this linking a situation is created by which the viewer or the film or both are expanded. A film is lived and lived intensely.[8]

The notion of experience is central also to Vivian Sobchack's *The Address of the Eye* (1992), in which she attempts a phenomenological foundation of the film experience based on the homology between "the structure of consciousness as the correlation of intentional act and intentional object and the . . . structure of vision as the correlation of viewing view and viewed view" (p. 55). The film, as much as the human subject, is both an object viewed and a viewing subject. By employing two technological devices (the camera and its projector), the film reproduces the same commutation between perception and expression which is the essential connotation of the human existential experience, that is, being-in-the-world as an international body. In other words, the spectator and the film exist as both subject and object of vision. This allows Sobchack to claim that the film experience is best expressed as the "address of the eye": "address, as noun and verb, both denotes a location where one resides and the activity of transcending the body's location," thus opening up a possibility of human choice and freedom vis-à-vis the determinism of the text and of the historical and cultural situation. This theoretical framework results in a critique of classical film theories that she describes as informed by three metaphors: the frame, the window, and the mirror. The frame expresses the transcendental idealist position based on the assumption that the filmic object is expression-in-itself. The metaphor of the window is emblematic of the theories of realism based on the idea that the filmic object is perception-in-itself. Phenomenology rejects the former as "subjective psychologism" and the latter as "objective empiricism." Finally, the mirror is the metaphor for those theories (Marxism, cultural studies, and feminist film theory) which insist on the ideological, tautological nature of cinema: these theories lose their political strength because they are unable to conceive of a strong and (to a certain extent) free subject. The main benefit of semiotic phenomenology is its claim that the situation of the subject, its material conditions of existence, and its body do not represent limitations to its liberty or determinations of its will; rather, they are its fundamental starting point, the immanence that it constantly transcends through intentionality.

These, then, were the roads taken, starting in the mid-1970s, toward the *recuperation of the aesthetic.* Sometimes art was associated with the creation of difference (with respect to the ordinary). Sometimes it was associated with the creation of tension between the real and the possible or with work that reflects on itself and its own being. At times it was associated with the evocation of an experience, which leads the viewer "to live" what is seen. There were also more tangential paths, but the explorers made use of these three above all to penetrate now the forest, now the desert.

16.7. Cinema and Thought: Philosophers before the Silver Screen

After cultural and aesthetic relevance, the last way of understanding the significance of cinema is to investigate its philosophical import. To what extent does film lend itself to reflection on truly philosophical themes? And to what extent does film itself reflect on these themes?

This double question, which during the 1960s would have scandalized many,[9] began to seem more justified in the 1970s. Philosophical reflection can use cinema as one of its comparative terms; and cinema can in turn be considered a place of reflection. Thus, one needs to allow space for the *thought of cinema,* in the sense of both thought *on* cinema and thought *in* cinema.

The American philosopher Stanley Cavell devotes great attention to cinema. His contributions (especially Cavell 1971) have given rise to interest and polemic on the other side of the ocean. Cavell explicitly poses the problem of the relation between cinema and philosophical thinking. With what legitimacy can the first become the object of the second and in some way add to it? How can the second deal with the first, or perhaps even settle into its territory?

From the point of view of cinema, the convergence of the two is justified above all by the self-reflexive nature of film. Any film contains some speculative motifs. Any film responds to the questions it has raised with its own positions and proceedings. Thus, a film thinks and offers itself up as its own testimony. This is probably typical of any art; it is certainly typical of any medium. All the tools invented to put us in contact with the world first put us in contact with themselves. All the devices called upon to broaden our perceptive and mental faculties propose themselves as objects of perception and thought.

From the philosophical point of view, convergence with cinema is harder to explain. That the first deals with and overlaps the second may seem outrageous. But there are in fact three reasons that justify it. Above all, philosophy is outrageous all by itself: "It seeks to disquiet the foundations of our lives and to offer us in recompense nothing better than itself" (Cavell 1981:9). Second, philosophy, through cinema, can pose the problem of the *cultural inheritance* on which all thought is based. Cavell obviously refers to the American intellectual ambience, with respect to which he advances a kind of paradoxical dilemma. Between Kant and Capra, who constitutes the more relevant and explicit common reference? Cavell leaves both the question and its answer open. On the one hand, the problem is not deciding what belongs to a common cultural inheritance, but the appropriateness and value of this inheritance. On the other, appropriateness and value are not defined *a priori* but in the course of inquiry. Thus, Kant and Capra are placed side by side (as in one of Cavell's essays, 1981). This juxtaposition allows verification of both the needs of the research and its validity. Third, the convergence of the two worlds serves to define better the *field* of philosophical research. To this end, Cavell cites Emerson and Thoreau as the first representatives of a tendency, which was revitalized by Austin and Wittgenstein, to abstain from references to the great, the high, and the remote and instead to find inspiration in what is common, quotidian, current—or, in a word, in what pertains to our ordinary experience. Cinema (and genre or generic cinema more than authorial cinema; Cavell openly takes issue with the "Philistines" who watch Welles rather than Hawks, or Eisenstein rather than Capra [Cavell 1981:40]) constitutes just such an ordinary experience, and an important part of it. It is the object of interest and conversation, of pleasure and rejection, of personal elaboration and collective memory. In short, it is something that demarcates our life's horizon. To reflect on cinema, on the way in which it gives itself to experience and in which we experience it, becomes, rather than an outrageous gesture, a necessity.

This placing of cinema on the horizon of life is definitely the strongest reason why Cavell, as a philosopher, occupied himself with cinema. He suffers, however, a kind of relapse in the definition that he himself gives of cinema, as his most famous work shows (Cavell 1971). Briefly, cinema is not so much a medium for Cavell, not so much an instrument for perceiving the world, as it is the "world seen," or the real as it assaults our senses. The image on the screen restores reality to us in its fullness, as we would perceive it through a wide-open window. In short, as an object of ordinary experience, cinema becomes an ordinary way of experiencing objects. Through cinema, reality becomes familiar again, becomes closer—in and of itself, in its concrete outlines, in its effective manifestations. Cinema is real: it is a moment of experience, either when we go to see it or for what it shows us.

Cavell's thought is naturally much more articulated. Cinema and reality are not indistinguishable; but cinema cannot be reduced to simple "recording" of reality; reality is never shown in and of itself, but in our experience of it. Showing reality through and in cinema makes it possible for a film to show reality to us. In other words, it is clear that on the screen we see shadow and light; nevertheless we interpret what we see "as though" it dealt with life. Effectively, on the screen life is presented to us, not in itself, but as a means by which we can grasp it.

The case of Gilles Deleuze and his singularly influential volumes on cinema (1983, 1985) is more complex.[10] For Deleuze philosophy is not an inquiry that preexists its field of investigation. On the contrary, it is an activity that takes form and develops through contact with its objects of study. In this sense it is "a practice of concepts" that "must be judged in the light of the other practices with which it interferes" (Deleuze 1985 [1989]: 280). Furthermore, art and science are also practices. Rather than concepts, art creates perceptual clusters and science creates functions. But concepts, perceptual clusters, and functions are all unstable and always revocable actualizations of the infinite movement of thought.

This premise clarifies the terms of the encounter between philosophy and cinema. Both are sites of thought, each in its own way. For example, film shows an idea of space or time as much as a philosophical essay does (or a tract on physics), even though it may be through the play of light and shadow rather than through general categories or the diagrams that are the result of an experiment. Philosophy therefore cannot pretend to intervene in cinema from the outside, imposing on it its own standards. It can only establish a kind of active alliance, made up of intersection and reciprocity. It behooves it to do this in part because of its propensity to be "nomadic," in the sense that it tends to question the approaches of other disciplines and to restudy and to revive their experience; in part because other fields perhaps come closer to the heart of philosophy than philosophy itself does, at least when they express the development of thought in a more complete and advanced way than does philosophy; in part because cinema itself needs philosophy in order to give conceptual form to its reflection. As much as cinema is part of thought, it is not cinema's job to construct concepts. "Cinema's concepts are not given in cinema." On the other hand, "no technical determination, whether applied (psychoanalysis, linguistics) or reflexive, is sufficient to constitute the concepts of cinema itself." Therefore, "cinema itself is a new practice of images and signs whose theory philosophy must produce as conceptual practice" (Deleuze 1985 [1989]: 280).

It is precisely to this conceptual practice that Deleuze dedicates himself. His tool is a classification of filmic forms, a broad and accurate taxonomy of the ways in which cinema presents itself. His inspiration comes from Charles S. Peirce, an American logician who, during the second half of the 1800s, tried to construct a summary table of the different modes of self-expression and signification. Yet this descriptive ambition is still useful for highlighting the innate possibilities of cinema and for defining its nature. We have already explained why cinema is part of thought. It should also be said, however, that thought is never "thought about something." If anything, it is instead the experience of the essence of things. In this sense, if cinema "thinks," it is not because "it tells" (Deleuze, as we will see, firmly denies the assimilation of film to discourse), but because it tests essences or, if you wish, presents (and presents itself as) a type of being. In this way, the form of thought that film incarnates is the same thing as the form of reality that it expresses in its images and sounds and in which it is identified. For cinema, thinking, presenting, and being are the same thing.

It is here (but not only here) that Deleuze is able to recapture Bergson's insights. Here Deleuze rediscovers the idea of a continuity between thought and existence (consciousness is not *of* something, but *is* something, and it is in the essence of things). An articulation of the forms of reality also returns here, to be juxtaposed with the taxonomy of sign forms (or logical forms) derived from Peirce. For Bergson (reread by Deleuze) there are three states or levels of what is real: the *all,* reality in eternal becoming, which expresses the complex of virtual relations between objects; *movement,* which can be "absolute" (as the differentiation and actualization of the all in objects and, vice versa, as the reunion of objects with the all) or "relative" (the movement established between individual objects, thanks to action-reaction); and individual *objects,* which are determinations made from the totality of things. So how do these three levels of reality relate to cinema?

First, cinema is able to restore them all. Bergson, as is well known, absolutely condemned the new medium, because he saw in its constituent element, that is, in the frame, an "immobile shape" capable of giving only an illusory sense of movement. Deleuze, on the contrary, points out how, thanks to montage, camera movement, depth of field, etc., film can develop not just single poses, but also effective movement. He further notes that in many contemporary works, through linking shots, systematic offscreen shots, perverse and obsessive framing, and so on, the sense of pure virtuality, of the whole, is even affirmed. Therefore, cinema possesses three types of images, which correspond to the three real states: the *instantaneous image,* which works only in the present and expresses the single objects; the *movement-image,* which expresses the distance between the present and the virtual and the steps taken to close the distance between them; and the *time-image,* which expresses the unbreakable unity of the present and the virtual, pure duration.

Second, it is confirmed that cinema does not trace or portray what is real; it *restores* it. On the screen we do not see a copy of the world; we see reality as it appears in one or another of its guises or reality as it offers itself in one of its manifestations. We can perhaps say that there is a "perceived reality"; we should remember, however, that every perception is only a circumscribed, framed, determined reality—and therefore nothing more than a specific instance of the real. Hence the idea of a reality-image. Like the idea of a thought-image, this last (we repeat) is not detached from things, but "inside" their becoming, "inside" their expression of themselves.

Thus, we have cinema as thought and reality at all its levels. The presuppositions on which the wide-ranging work of Deleuze rests can be summarized in these two statements. We should add that the French philosopher fully exploits these directives. On the one hand, in fact, they serve to attack, for example, those who think of the image as a linguistic structure. The latter, instead, "even with its verbal elements, is neither a language system nor a language. It is a plastic mass, an a-signifying and a-syntaxic material, a material not formed linguistically. . . . It is not an enunciation, and these are not utterances. It is an '*utterable*'" (*enunciable*) (Deleuze 1985 [1989]: 29). Exactly so— it is both reality and thought, and not speech. And in this sense it is more than something expressed or said. It is the horizon of every expression, the condition of every speech.

On the other hand, Deleuze uses his basic points to illustrate the passage from classic to modern cinema. This passage shows up in a crisis of the movement-image and especially in its most representative variant, the action-image; and in the increase of the time-image; above all, at its emblematic moment, the crystal-image. This means that recent cinema looks at reality more than it actualizes reality. Recent cinema tries to give us reality that is open to possibility, that is in tension with totality. Along parallel lines, modernity is characterized by a play of repetitions, excesses, and parodies and by a progressive increase in density and its consequent fullness. If there is a future for cinema, as for the other arts, this leads (Bazin?) to the heart of life.

For our part, we will not try to reconstruct the broad design laid out by Deleuze. We will not go over his itinerary, which runs from genre to authorial cinema, from cinema based on certainty to that which stages doubts and falseness, from cinema based on montage to that based on shots, from Eisenstein to Welles, from Griffith to Godard. Neither will we take up once again his overviews, some of which, like the one dedicated to montage, are extremely effective, and some of which, like that on narrative cinema, reduced to a variable combination of actions and situations, are less convincing. And, finally, we will not discuss his complex typology, in which his three types of image generate numerous variants. In the field of movement-images alone we have the variants of percept-image, affect-image, drive-image, action-image, reflection-image, and relation-image.

Here we wish to limit ourselves to the principles that support Deleuze's discourse. For this reason, we have emphasized above all the reasons that led him as a philosopher to become interested in cinema and his characterization of it. In particular, the direct connection between cinema and reality allows us to conclude with an indication of a kind of duplicity that controls his work (no less than Cavell's). On the one hand, philosophy's turning to cinema and discovering its realistic basis can be seen as symptoms of strength. If in fact the state of philosophy today is nomadic, or somewhat outside its usual territory, cinema (which is not different from reality, but a different reality) offers philosophy a decidedly productive area of work. But, on the other hand, philosophy's turning to cinema and discovering its basis in reality are also symptoms of weakness. It is as though philosophical thought found itself incapable of working with existent forms and remade itself, using cinema as its representative, its emblem. In short, it is as though philosophy, orphan of the world, availed itself of cinema for its world. It is thus perhaps a loss (the deterioration of the relation with actual facts) more than a desire for wholeness that leads our philosophers to cinema. And it is perhaps a loss (the impossibility of a major ontology) that leads them to propose a cinematic ontology. The view of things clouds over, wavers, is lost: and on the screen we see suddenly not a semblance of or a substitute for reality, but reality itself, in its entirety, in its fullness. The credits roll: and life begins.

17 HISTORY, HISTORIES, HISTORIOGRAPHY

17.1. A Sense of History

One of the most relevant traits of the research of the 1980s was the strong resurgence of interest in film history. Not that studies of this kind had ever ceased. They did suffer a certain eclipse, however, during the 1960s and 1970s, partly because of the weight given to approaches like the semiotic or the psychoanalytical, approaches hardly inclined to seeing reality-in-the-making in cinema. The resurgence of history was massive, and it contained more than a few novel elements.[1]

In the first place, there was a decided distancing from the traditional histories of cinema. These were accused, often openly, of four serious limitations. One was to have put films at the center of attention. In reality, cinema is a much more complex machine that undergoes the intervention of technological, economic, and social factors—factors not necessarily seen in the works it produces. Then traditional histories used inadequate research tools, like the personal memory of the researcher or the use of stars' testimony. The documentary base should be a great deal more ample and should be evaluated critically. Also, limited categories of analysis were used, like those of school or movement or period; worse, the work was tautological, trying to explain authors through their works and works through their authors. In reality, events are organized in more articulated forms, in which influences are never unambiguous or direct. Finally, traditional histories adopted elementary forms of exposition, speaking of "birth," "development," "maturity," "decadence." Facts are not disposed to follow a linear chronology that imitates human life, but rather to follow more controversial and sinuous paths.

Thus, traditional film histories—from Ramsaye's in the late 1920s to that (decidedly more complex) of Sadoul in the 1940s[2]—were mistaken in their choice of object of study, their method, their "slant" or shape, their writing. They were too close to the histories of literature and art to grasp the outlines of the new phenomenon. They were too tied to threadbare interpretive "frames" (the moral myth, with the figures of Justice, Persecution, Triumph, reminding us of the never-ending fight between Good and Evil, or the political myth, with its themes of Commitment, Sacrifice, and Liberty, reminding us of the battles for personal and national freedom) to discover the logic that underlies the development of cinema.

Second, there was a series of favorable circumstances. The availability of filmic texts was increasing, because of the systematic recovery of lost films, the restoration or reissuing of works long unavailable, and the transfer to tape of a growing portion of the filmic patrimony. The mass of available (and accessible) documentary materials was increasing, in part because they were turned over to American universities by studio archives, in part because of the accessibility of papers belonging to private companies and governments that previously had been reserved. Finally, national and international research projects were beginning to be delineated, and they were receiving more financial aid than in the past. Often they were supported by film libraries that wanted to go beyond the mere conservation of films and were interested in the emergence of new areas of study, like film philology.

Third, there was a growing awareness of the problems inherent in "doing history" in general. Film scholars, too, were beginning to make contact with the rethinking of the framework of historical research. In fact, they occasionally found themselves participating as protagonists in the debate. Take, for example, the critique of the concept of the event. Changes occur not just as the result of facts of epic proportions (and thus the sensational film or the work that breaks with tradition), but also as the result of quotidian events. Another example is the broadening of the idea of chronology. Development through time is not based just on cause-effect, but also on accumulation, direct or distant influences, cycles, and so on. Likewise, there is no single tempo, but there are differentiated advances, faster when the substitution of one theme or another is at play, slower when dealing with the destiny of a style, and slower still when dealing with the ordering of a genre. Or, again, take the redefinition of the idea of documentation. The things tracked down by the historian are never clear proofs but objects ("monuments") to be questioned (or reevaluated) with specific methods, using semiotics in the case of film texts, sociology in the case of consumerism, economics in the case of industrial organizations, etc. Finally, I am thinking of the changes in the expository techniques of history. Accounts are not required to be "stories," but "statements," rich in diverse materials—that is, statistics and textual analyses, biographical notes and legal extracts. These accounts need not be only written, but may avail themselves of other supports, like the video or cinema itself.

The end result was the emergence of new frames of reference. Having left aside the examples furnished by literary and art histories, film scholars were beginning to set store by the experiences of political history (to understand how cinema is a frequent instrument of propaganda and always a field of controversy), of business history (to analyze both the economic–industrial "machine" behind the making of films and the ways of making the most of a film), of social history (to understand how cinema determines behaviors and orientations and at the same time how it reveals the worries and certainties of a community), and so on. After all, generalist historians themselves were beginning to discover in cinema a source of great richness and utility. They appreciated cinema's ability to record events and also to show how a society perceives events. They likewise appreciated cinema's ability to let reality speak for itself, as well as its ability to give substance to dreams and fantasies. They appreciated cinema's capacity to be "prophetic," perhaps in a marginal work, and also to build "public" images, common to all layers of society. In this sense, there was a twofold exchange: the more one perceived that film history should work in the field of history in general, the more history saw in film history possibilities for exchange.

The end point of this series of steps and countersteps was the delineation, also for cinema, of what Lagny efficiently defines as the "problem history" (1992:41, 47). This kind of history does not hide the work of the researcher behind a presumed objectivity, but makes explicit the researcher's choices and procedures. It adopts a multiplicity of tools, yet never pretends to put forth a definitive view. Above all, such history realizes that the meaning of things depends on the way in which they are approached and thus, rather than "restoring" reality, it "rebuilds" it—or, better yet, "constructs" it as the object of its discourse.

Sometimes in radical ways, at other times in more measured ways, it was truly this *problem history* that characterized the research of the 1980s. Let us examine this research in a bit more detail, isolating three main areas, each characterized by a series of "questions" or points of departure: economic-industrial histories, social histories, and aesthetic-linguistic histories.

17.2. Economic-Industrial Histories

Perhaps the most unified area of film history is that of the works on the economic, industrial, technological realities of cinema. This includes studies that, long considered "ancillary," had come into their own by the late 1960s. The research was motivated by the belief that focusing exclusively on works and authors cannot explain either the origin of the former or the situations in which the latter work. Many turning points and many phases of stability are, in fact, the result of financial, production, and technological factors. Financial factors: consider the proprietary attitude of the major and minor companies, the system of tracking down capital for productions, the relation between investments and revenues, the role of national and foreign markets, and so on. Production factors: there are recurrent forms of labor organization, professionals ready to conquer or defend their own arenas, more or less fixed teams and routines, criteria on which decisions are based and made, internal hierarchies in the studios or on the sets, etc. Technological factors: each period uses equipment in its own way; it favors some innovations and stifles others; it has at its disposal a limited set of available means (specific kinds of films, formats, cameras, and so forth). Thus, a film is also the final result of the conditions of its existence.

Some fundamental questions arise. How important to the destiny of cinema is the fact that it is also a "machine"? To what extent do change and resistance to change, with respect to mode of production, kind of product, and proprietary attitudes, determine more general changes or lack of the same? And at the same time, to what extent are the reasons behind each of these sectors common to other areas of entertainment, of the culture industry, and of leisure activities? What becomes obvious is that the history of cinema is an integral part of the "industries of the imaginary." The resultant research associated with the history of cinema, so far considered marginal, appears to be decisive for the delineation of the main scenarios that cinema uses to organize its own development.

But let us get to the concrete articulation of the researches. We will not linger over the studies that initiated this field of research, from the work of Bächlin (1945) to that of Mercillon (1953) or Bizzarri and Solaroli (1958).

These were by and large pioneering works, useful because they drew with broad strokes the outlines for research. But they took more care in recognizing recurrent typologies than in reconstructing the ways in which one moves from one typology to another. In any case, we have already discussed them in the chapter on the sociology of cinema.

Among the more recent historically oriented works are those that concern themselves above all with *economic-financial factors*. This is the case of a contribution by Janet Wasko (1982), which covers the ups and downs of Wall Street's interest in the film industry, the role of banks in change, including technological change (with the advent of the talkies), the succession of various ways of financing films, etc. The guiding idea is that capital represents the true protagonist of film's destiny: in some ways it is outside the studios, in New York financial circles, that the decisions that count are made. Other researchers, like Douglas Gomery (1984), show instead how Hollywood, that is, the place where movies are produced, has more than a little say in the matter.

Studies dealing with the industrial organization of cinema are more numerous. One of the seminal works in this area is Michael Conant's 1960 study of the battle over antitrust laws that took place from 1938 to 1948 between the U.S. government and the big movie companies. Conant examines the means by which the major companies formed an oligopoly, based above all on exclusive distribution rights. He traces the reasons why the Justice Department sued Paramount and the other companies. He examines the consequences, which he considers positive, of the Supreme Court's ruling in favor of the government.

Thomas Guback (1969), instead, analyzes the relations between the European and American movie industries after World War II. This was an unequal relationship because of the profound differences in economic funding, in production organization, and in company policy. The stronger American industry attempted to take over and dismantle the weaker European industry. There was consistent aid from the U.S. government, especially from the Department of Defense, which used cinema as an ideological weapon. The result, however, was a change in the profiles of national cultures, a removal of every peculiarity, a homogenization of cultures, in the name of providing products with universal appeal.

Robert Allen and Douglas Gomery, while valuing Guback's work, criticize the excessive rapidity of his jump from economic to cultural processes.

One cannot presume that economic processes determine cultural processes in such a direct way. To Guback's Marxist stance, Allen and Gomery counterpose an "industrial analysis," which gives a great deal of weight to three factors. The first consists of the profits of each company, thanks to efficient production and distribution and also to a series of political-social conditions: this is the sphere of *performance*. The second factor involves each company's pricing policy, marketing strategies, the company's involvement in research, innovation, etc., all with an eye to the attainment of exemplary results: this is the sphere of *conduct*. The third factor consists of the degree of product differentiation, integration of the various sectors, and, above all, cooperation between the various companies (with periods of monopoly, oligopoly, and open competition): i.e., the sphere of *market structures*. In the background we have a series of *basic conditions:* the state of technology, the availability of raw materials, the flexibility of prices, the rate of growth, the purchase methods, and so on (Allen and Gomery 1985 : 138ff.). The two authors apply their model to the birth of the American film industry, showing the complex of factors at play and defining the reasons for the positive results of some solutions and the failure of others.

The most representative scholar of this line of research is Tino Balio. His history of the American film industry (Balio 1976) is interesting in at least two respects. First, broad retrospective vistas are supplemented by extremely varied material, ranging from the remembrances of stars to business records, from major studios' promotional inserts to the critiques that appeared in the magazines of the time. Thus, we are able to grasp not just the logic that drives the film industry, but also the way in which the industry represents itself to consumers. Second, Balio's reconstruction lays out the entire series of elements at play, even though he tends to dwell on those elements that most decisively affect each period. During the origins of the industry, for example, one such element was the conquest of a new public. Between the years 1908 and 1930 we have the dispute between the first trust (MPPC)[3] and the independents. During Hollywood's golden age we have the production organization of the major studios, etc. In this way, we discover how the film industry is a *complex system,* in which all elements are interdependent and tend toward equilibrium. Every change puts a sector in crisis, which is often dramatic (one thinks of the introduction of sound, which forced studios to seek out new stars, or of the antitrust laws, which necessitated the separation of production and management). Change affects the entire industry, which is forced to make readjustments; the industry finds a solution, however, in new organizations, new synergies, new products, without ever "stalling out."

Besides the financial and industrial analyses, we should mention some works on *film technology*. Frequently, they merely point out the "first time" a certain piece of machinery was used or praise the "great personalities" who introduced this or that innovation. Such studies lack an awareness of the complexity of the factors at play. There are exceptions: for instance, Deslandes' work traces the birth and first steps of cinema with accuracy and depth (Deslandes 1966; Deslandes and Richard 1968).[4] But the most interesting contributions link technology to other aspects of the film "machine." The most famous example is a series of articles by Jean-Luis Comolli (1971–1972) dedicated to the study of "technology and ideology." He deals with two areas: the birth of cinema and the death and resurrection of the depth of field. The first is seen not as the result of a series of personal inventions, but as the response to an ideological demand (to see life as it is) and to an economic demand (to find a source of profit). This represents the terminal point of a collective and anonymous search in the second half of the 1800s, which investigated both the reproduction of reality and the forms of the mise-en-scène. In the case of the depth of field, too, we encounter more than just technological processes. The disappearance of the depth of field in the 1920s is often attributed to the introduction of panchromatic film, associated with the use of incandescent light, which made it necessary to open or widen the lenses of cameras and thus to reduce the range of focus. In reality, what came about was a new idea of "true vision," no longer guaranteed by the presence of space conceived of as depth, but linked to the capacity to reproduce the world with all its shadings (which panchromatic film made possible). Thus, the need for a response to an ideological demand guided the development of film technology. Inventions alone are meaningless.

Rick Altman (1984b, 1985, 1986, 1989) connects technology and different forms of representation. Soundtracks provide him with an optimum testing ground for his theory. There are two principles at play here: perspective, which leads to the differentiation of sound intensity with respect to the nearness or distance of the camera; and intelligibility, or rendering all sound, regardless of source, equally perceptible. In the first half of the 1930s perspective triumphed; by the end of the 1930s the need for intelligibility had become predominant. This cinema, rather than "tuning in" scenic space, gave precedence to the role of speech and to the story line (see Altman 1989:129). It seems unnecessary to mention that all sound technology adapted itself to this new direction of things.

Allen and Gomery (1985) take another tack. Film technology, they contend, depends on economics. The example they use is the introduction of the soundtrack. Soundtracks had been possible for some time. Yet, because the bankers who controlled Warner Bros. decided to oppose Paramount and Loew's on a new front, Warner Bros. was the first to reach an agreement with Western Electric and to use a system set up by that company, to risk enormous investments, and to avail itself of a resource that outmaneuvered the competition.

Other scholars deal with the technological dimension of cinema. We will discuss some of them later. Let us close this brief review with a more general observation. Economic-industrial histories often tend to isolate their object from its context: notwithstanding the exceptions just considered, technology is usually seen as a separate sector, with its own autonomous logic. It was against this tendency that, during the 1980s, concepts like *mode of production* gained ground. Mode of production refers to both the "order" used by the cinematic machine and the "philosophy" that rules its functioning. Thus, basic economic categories like the organization of labor, professional skills, the financial system, and the technological apparatus are supplemented with elements like the idea of film shared by the members of a group (means of expression or a mere commodity?), the meaning one attaches to the actual activity (a creation or just a job?), the classification of films (culture or spectacle?), film models (author film or series? a high-level product or B movie?—naturally, none of these should be taken as alternatives). The procedure can be risky, as is the case with too direct an analogy between economics and semiotics or between the industrial and the ideological. But it can also produce useful gains.

Another way of contesting the "autonomy" of economic-industrial histories is to write histories that place economic-industrial facts in a larger frame of reference. One can use comparisons, as, for example, Bordwell, Staiger, and Thompson did in their wide-ranging work on classic American cinema (1985). They relate the dimension of production and the stylistic dimension in such a way as to show a tie of reciprocal functionality between the two (for that matter, how could this kind of cinema have "held together" for forty years if the work processes and forms of representations had not been linked to one another?). Or one can demonstrate how all the elements fit together, as does Brunetta in his history of Italian film (1979, 1982): financial production and technological aspects alternate with political-cultural and aesthetic-linguistic ones. This approach yields an overview that is at once broad and varied, and the idea that each element has its own role but in turn depends on another.

We will come back to this research. For the moment it is left to us to examine the other areas where historical research is concentrated.

17.3. Sociocultural Histories

From the 1970s onward, the works that consider the social implications of the development of cinema kept multiplying. Such studies are prompted by a double set of interests. On the one hand, they stress the medium's ability to reflect the behaviors and attitudes of a society. Films are considered a valuable testimony to the ways of acting and thinking in a community; they are thought of as a *mirror* (perhaps idealized, perhaps deformed, but no less faithful for that) of the acts, customs, aspirations, beliefs, and values that constitute a culture.[5] On the other hand, scholars stress the ability of cinema to intervene in social processes. As evidence they cite the medium's ability to reinforce or destroy widespread beliefs, its furnishing of inspiring models, its exposure of repressed desires, its bringing together of individuals with the same tastes and opinions, its nourishing of styles, its creation of jobs and of close-knit professional groups. In short, film's function as a social *agent* is highlighted.

A series of questions arises from all this. How does cinema relate to other social realities? Under what constraints does it labor? What purposes does it serve? To whom does it give a voice, and to whom does it deny a voice? What depth and weight do films' themes carry? With which other media does cinema collaborate in order to create public opinion? What influence does the viewer have on film proposals? How are film people organized? At bottom, there are two key questions. How much is cinema able to amplify the changes in the ways of living and feeling? And how much does it contribute to such changes? It is precisely a mirror of life and a social agent; a reflection and an instigator of cultural mores. It is both of these, often at the same time.

Let us try to be more explicit. The first, more traditional area of study establishes the *relation between cinema and politics*. Such studies examine the position cinema held in a given time and place, as well as the interventions in the field by government, political parties, economic powers, and secular and religious groups. These works are often simplistic, based as they are on the fight between freedom and oppression (a classic story: Cinderella and her stepmother). There is no lack, though, of rich and more considered approaches, often supported by a vast array of documentation (i.e., laws, parliamentary debates and public actions, as well as workers' depositions, discussions in trade journals, contracts, the filmmakers' social role, etc.). One example of this kind of work is the two-volume study of the films of Vichy France by Paul Leglise (1969, 1977). He covers the means of control and protection of cinema on the part of public authorities as well as the formation of a professional and business organization. Another example is Mino Argentieri's book on Italian cinema under Fascism (1979). He shows the Fascist regime's increasing control of production and its developing interest in the use of film (especially news footage) as propaganda. This line of research is present in more comprehensive works, like those by Jeancolas (1979, 1983) on French cinema or those, already mentioned, by Brunetta (1979, 1982) on Italian cinema. This same line of research also serves as a model for more circumscribed investigations, dealing, for example, with legislation or censorship (Jacobs 1991).

A second focus is found in those studies that concentrate on the *representations of social reality* that films bear, be it directly, through works with a documentary flavor, or indirectly, in works that are more or less current or probable, but that, in any case, lend substance to the way in which we perceive or imagine the world around us. A great deal of attention is paid to the images of individuals, communities, widespread behaviors, aspirations and collective fears, shared knowledge, ambiences, and idiosyncratic attitudes that cinema offers. We have already discussed (in the chapter on cinema and sociology) the more or less seminal research on these lines: Kracauer's volume (1947) on the films of the Weimar Republic. There one sees how films produced during that period vacillate between a futile rebelliousness and a kind of consoling conformism, between an appeal to tyranny and the fear of chaos. There is a certain evident hesitation that clearly demonstrates the unhappiness of the German people following defeat and that anticipates the authoritarian solution of Nazism.

Marc Ferro and especially Pierre Sorlin take up and relaunch this kind of research, and with greater historical competence (Kracauer is more of a sociologist). For Ferro (1977), cinema reflects reality at all levels: it tells stories that play up certain of life's aspects and downplay others; it uses a language that betrays the way in which directors and their social group adhere to their themes; it triggers reactions that clarify the ideological substrata of a given society. This allows for an overall analysis. Ferro uses as evidence not just what a film says, but what it does not say, its style, the way in which it is read, and so on. He reconstructs Nazi obsessions through the editing of *Jud Süss.* He considers the change in social climate in pre- and postwar France by showing the different receptions of *La grande illusion.* For Sorlin the idea of mirroring needs to be not only broadened, but also surpassed. A film, before showing us the interests and orientations of a society, shows us the horizon of thought along which it travels. Before telling us what a given society chooses to portray, a film tells us what is considered portrayable. Thus, Sorlin posits the idea of the *visible,* by which he designates what filmmakers consider easily presentable and what viewers can easily perceive. The result is to bring into focus both the kind of "image" a culture uses to portray reality and the idea of the "image of reality" a culture possesses. In an early work (1977), Sorlin applies this concept to Italian film and society in the post–World War II period. He shows which concerns seem to have obsessed both film and society and also which ideas determined the way in which the world was portrayed. In a subsequent work (1991), Sorlin broadens his research to include all of postwar Europe. He lays out a series of recurrent themes, correlates them with each national culture, places them in broader frameworks of thought, and compares them to trends in cinematic consumption.

We can include in the same group of studies research that shows the ways in which a society *represents itself* in order to create a sense of belonging among its members, who share common themes of discussion and models of reference. America's representation of itself in the 1940s is at the center of a work by Dana Polan (1986): contrary to what one might think, films from the period do not give a consolatory image; neither do they promulgate a "family" ideology. Instead they record symbolically all the disquiet and uneasiness present in a community-in-the-making. Other studies we might mention include those concerned with the ways in which subcultures (the young), or emergent cultures (Afro-American), or oppressed cultures (women's) represent themselves. On the horizon are, naturally, the "histories of mentality," which through an analysis of the texts that circulate in a society bring out that society's ideological orientations, conceptions of life, and perceptions of the world.

A third group of studies concentrates on the social *structures* and *dynamics* that originate with cinema. Here, again, the film-as-social-agent comes into play more than the film-as-mirror, though many of these works (like those already mentioned) tend to blur the lines of this distinction. An interesting investigative area studies the "cinematic ambience." Works in this field discuss the life and work of those people who "make films": actors, directors, producers, technicians, agents, and so on. It is, unfortunately, a lightly traveled line of thought, even though one can acknowledge the merit of two classic essays (Rosten and Powdermaker).[6] Also, Sklar (1975) follows this path in his analysis of the economic and production factors of the studios in an effort to reconstruct the character of the "Hollywood community."

Research on the distribution and consumption of films is more common. This brings to light the impact, be it cultural or contextual, of cinema. Analyses of the environmental impact focus on the location of theaters in an urban context, their architecture, their furnishings, and their changes over time.[7] The cultural impact is studied in order to see what kinds of audiences frequent theaters. What are their demographic composition (young/adult, men/women), their social standing (subproletariat, immigrant, middle-class), their tastes (musicals rather than detective stories), their focus of attention (stars, story lines), their inclination to be concerned with cinema beyond films (buying magazines, gadgets, etc.)? The early film-going public is most interesting. It was more diverse than one might think. In the 1910s there was a larger middle-class presence. After World War I the public was characterized by a growing disenchantment with cinema. Much of this research can be classified as dealing with "local histories," with cities like Milwaukee, Perpignan, or Montpellier chosen for study.[8] Other works analyze consumption along with production in an effort to demonstrate reciprocal adjustments (see especially Sklar 1975). Still others broaden their view to encompass phenomena like star worship in an effort to get a better grasp of the social processes engendered by going to the movies (see Hansen 1991 on Valentino's fans). At least four such works come to mind. First we have Bernardini's research (1980–1982) on the organization of cinema in Italy from its origins to the end of the 1920s and Yuri Tsivian's (1991) on the consumption of films in Russia during the same period. Both, though different in approach, constitute a valuable attempt at reconstructing the history of the audience of a national cinema. There is also a monographic issue of *Iris* on "Early Cinema Audiences" (11, 1990) that discusses problems like initial audiences' class and status affiliations (Janet Staiger); how the processes of urbanization and social stratification augment the numbers of the film-going public (Richard Abel); and the makeup of a cinematic "imagination" (Elena Dagrada). Finally, and most importantly, we have Gian Piero Brunetta's book (1989), which traces the history of film consumption to the present. This work avails itself of an extremely rich array of documentation, from the arts pages of newspapers to sociological reports, from memoirs to censorship tracts, with the result that the author grasps the phenomenon in both its collectively ritualistic and personal, experiential aspects. Brunetta has written one of the most important chapters of the research on what he himself calls "popular vision." We have certainly not exhausted examples of this kind of work. It must be said that, on the contrary, the studies about behavior and the orientations of consumption, along with those about theaters, are ever more numerous. In the background we can glimpse a "history of customs," which finds in the study of modern film both fertile documentary terrain and a useful point of departure for reflection.

Besides the preceding investigations, there are others that are interested in the "social discourses" that accompany and orient consumption. These are works on film criticism and, more generally, on the way in which cinema is discussed in popular magazines; on the image of the whole phenomenon provided by film scholars (this book aspires to this category); on cultural movements, like the movie clubs in which the showing of a film is accompanied by a discussion of it; and so forth.[9] Here the frame of reference is rather a "history of public opinion," which parallels and complements the already mentioned "history of custom."

The last field of study has as its object the diffusion not just in cinema but in other media of recurrent motifs, like travel, money, the Passion of Christ. The aim of these studies is twofold. First, they want to show how film serves as both a point of transition and a resonating chamber for themes and figures that are typical of both cultivated tradition and popular culture. Cinematic screens receive and toss back the entire patrimony of our imagination. This is followed by "intertextual" research, which compares diverse works in order to show the diffusion of a myth (Kirby on trains), or the permanence of an icon (Uricchio on the Passion of Christ), or, in a more problematic key, the effects of "rewriting" (Ropars on the film adaptation of a series of novels).[10] Then there is research that seeks to show how cinema may entertain relationships with other media that are characterized by both conflict and collaboration: cinema's arrival on the scene implies eclipse for some instruments of communication, revival for others, and restructuring for all of them. From this derives an "intermediary" research that compares the functions and problems of each communicative sphere in order to discover the role of cinema and the restructurings that it brings to the entire field.[11] Behind both kinds of investigation (which are frequently mixed) is the desire to outline the "background" against which cinema works and at the same time to define the "connective tissue" of a culture: this is research on "text and context," capable of bringing into focus the action of the first, the depth of the second. The idea of a "history of representation" is perhaps the best way to give a sense of the framework in which these studies are inscribed.

These are, in broad strokes, the outlines of sociocultural history. Here too, as with economic-industrial histories, we observe the risk of a lack of integration into cinema's general context and the attempt to blend with other approaches. We might well repeat things we have already said. But let us proceed directly to the third major area of study, the aesthetic-linguistic.

17.4. Aesthetic-Linguistic Histories

This appears to be the most traditional sector, heir to the "sacred histories" that dealt solely with masterpieces and personalities. In reality, this is the area of study that, precisely in order to free itself from the "sacred" models, has undergone the most profound internal changes. Now it asks extremely different questions from those previously asked (when we asked, with Snow White, "Who is the fairest of them all?"). It is useful to understand what formal procedures cinema favored over time, the kinds of materials it used, to what degree cinema influenced the field of artistic phenomena, what cultural or ideological implications it carried, how it linked means of production and forms of representation, and, finally, the ties it established between each work and the context from which it sprang. Rather than evaluating single films, the focus here is on determining the procedures and construction of films; rather than giving a pantheon of names (perhaps unexpected and eccentric: each "sacred history" has a "counterhistory" that accompanies it), it is of interest to reconstruct the processes that make film a form of expression and communication.

The first means of confronting such questions is to reconstruct the path that led to a work or group of works: we are dealing with "a history of artistic creation," carried on with philological tools. One example is the wide-ranging and extremely accurate work by Lino Miccichè on Visconti (1990).

He focuses above all on the cultural environment in which each film was conceptualized, giving particular attention to the intellectual alignments characteristic of its era and to the network of personal and professional relations that formed around its author. He then traces the work behind each film: source materials are examined (be they novels that were adapted, as was the case with *Ossessione* and *La terra trema,* or original screenplays like *Bellissima*); the various stages of the production of a screenplay are compared; the multitude of references in each film are reexplained; the influence of the effects of each technical or production decision is evaluated; and so on. Finally, the films themselves are analyzed. For each one a particular approach is chosen (the narrative structure in *Ossessione,* the typology of the sequences in *La terra trema,* the system of the characters in *Bellissima*). The author shows the role of formal procedures (for example, the visual punctuation in *La terra trema*). Regularities and anomalies are pointed out (the weight of di- and trichotomies, again in *La terra trema*). The principles that govern Viscontian "film writing" are uncovered, and, in a sort of aftermath, this writing is analyzed from the point of view of its origins (to stress the faithfulness to the original source of the writing: fidelity to Verga, for example, is maintained not by carefully mimicking the plot but in the way the narration unfolds) or in conjunction with other contemporary stylistic lines.

In his work Miccichè carefully avoids the old vice of determinism, which consists in positing a necessary accord between premises and their result. On the contrary, each stage of artistic creation is seen as the reformulation of an open-ended idea that is firmed up only in the finished work. This allows him to clarify two things at the same time: on the one hand, each film's *conditions of existence* or that which made it what it is; on the other hand, the *virtual text* that unfolds around each film or the possibilities that perhaps only came close to realization, but that nonetheless are still present between the lines as more or less distant echoes.[12]

Other scholars also attempt to link work on sources with textual analysis. Charles Musser, in his book on Porter (1991), reconstructs the passage from early cinema to the narrative-industrial film in its numerous aspects, from linguistic refinements to technological breakthroughs, from transformations in the means of production to changes in the cultural models used. The result is an overview in which texts are linked with the motivations that guided their execution. We should also mention the essays by Bouvier and Leutrat on *Nosferatu* (1981), by Bertetto on *Metropolis* (1990), those on the origins of cinema collected in *Ce que je vois de mon ciné* (Gaudreault 1988b), and so on. It remains to be said that film philology still found it difficult, at the threshold of the 1990s, to leave behind its merely archival dimension and to embark on a path that connects reconstruction and interpretation.[13]

The other road along which aesthetic-linguistic histories were moving is better delineated and more used. The goal of this group of histories is to bring into focus the stylistic procedures, the narrative structures, or the models of representation that dominated the films of a given period. We are moving within the horizon of a "history of form." The conversion of quite a few semiologists to diachronic studies contributed to its fortunes during these years.

The weakest version (I could say dreariest) of such work is that proposed by Barry Salt (1983) under the rubric of "statistical style analysis." He systematically reviews the procedures present in films from a given period and calculates the frequency of their appearance. Thus, one can learn the percentage of camera movements in the 1930s as compared to the 1940s; how often close shots are used in the 1920s as compared to the 1930s; the average length of the shots in the 1950s as compared to those from the 1960s; etc. Salt justifies his endeavor as the only one that is scientific. He does not discuss, however, crucial problems like the criteria he used to determine his time periods or the role of each procedure with regard to filmic signification as a whole.

The suggestion made by David Bordwell, Janet Staiger, and Kristin Thompson is considerably more sound, though still in the school of "historical stylistics." Their broad study (1985) covers the outlines of classic American cinema from 1917 to 1960. Here the attention is given not so much to individual technological-linguistic elements (like the cut of a shot, mobility of the camera, ways of editing), but to the way in which such elements become part of a coherent *stylistic system,* which correlates their functions and disciplines their use. One means of transition from scene to scene (for example, a fade-out) is interesting because it plays a specific role (indicating, for example, a time-lapse); because it establishes a link with other elements (for example, it can interact with a musical interval); and because it conforms to a norm (for instance, it indicates a break in the action). There are three stylistic systems that interest these scholars: narration, based, in classical cinema, on the sequentiality and parallelism of the events being represented; the representation of time, based on linearity and continuity; and the representation of space, linked to shots that give preference to centering, balance, and front views and to a sense of continuity among the places slowly brought into view. The analysis of each system is extremely detailed. In particular, Bordwell and Thompson examine the various elements at play, define their complex role, and relate the action of these elements to recurrent laws. In this way they show the great principles that govern classic cinema (e.g., continuity, balance, instant recognition, etc.). They also show, however, that there are changes in function (e.g., the passing of time is shown by a dissolve; but more recently, by a direct cut); readjustments of the rules in use (e.g., at the end of the 1910s films still allowed "holes" in the construction of space, though shortly thereafter this was much more carefully controlled). Their work generates either a picture of a "style" that remained basically unchanged during the period under study or a more finely defined periodization, corresponding to significant changes in the organization of each system. We might add that their design is reinforced by continual comparison between the stylistic norms used in films and the modes of production current in Hollywood studios (analyzed by Staiger). These scholars are not simply extending their analysis to include economic, industrial, and technological aspects; they are showing how each "structured film practice" (and classic cinema is the most famous "mode of film practice") makes linguistic and production norms two sides of the same coin.

Beyond its intrinsic merit, *The Classical Hollywood Cinema* is indicative of an entire research tendency. At the methodological level, it promotes the idea of making "laws of style" evident and linking them to the modes of production.[14] At the level of content it is fascinated by the idea of approaching a "mode of film practice" such as classic cinema. Noël Burch's important contribution can be situated against this background. He, too, is attentive to the stylistic dimension (in fact, he was a forerunner in this kind of inquiry); he is most interested in the "margins" of classicism and especially in their formation in the mid-1910s and their undoing during the 1960s.

The stated goal of *Praxis du cinéma* (Burch 1969) is to delineate some of the criteria for *composition* of a film. Burch seeks to see the way in which available expressive means are combined and used. Almost immediately, however, the author superimposes another objective: Burch is more fascinated by cases that show tension, discord, and imbalance than by the moments of accord between the basic elements of film. He is more interested in the *dialectics* that run through a film than in neutral and functional composition. He isolates various kinds of *dialectics:* in terms of photography, between focused and blurred; in terms of the running of the film, between regular speed and changes in speed, or direction, or stops; in terms of time, between normal and abnormal duration; in terms of space, between what is in the shot and what lies outside of it; in terms of shooting, between strict control of the set and an openness to serendipitous events; etc. The range of these dialectics varies, from mere juxtapositions, to conflicts among homogeneous elements, to conflicts among different levels, and so on. In any case, these dialectics "illuminate" film writing, carry the writing beyond usual paths, and make all of its internal problems perceptible. Modern cinema, which would build on the ashes of classic cinema in the 1950s, is fundamentally characterized by similar dialectics. Thus, Burch dedicates long and accurate analyses to "exemplary" films, like *Cronaca di un amore* (Antonioni, 1950) and *Une simple histoire* (Hanoun, 1959), and to top-of-the-line directors, like Godard and Rouch (as well as to films that anticipated future trends, like Renoir's *Nana*).

Praxis du cinéma is not presented as historical research in the strictest sense, even though today it can be read as such. *Life to Those Shadows* (Burch 1990) is, however, explicit historical research. Here the reverse tack is taken: Burch studies the development of classic cinema from the jumble of experiments that we call primitive cinema. The shift, which took place between 1905 and 1915, followed some general principles. First, simple juxtaposition of shots was gradually replaced by rigorous linkages. Instead of scenes that are self-sufficient or "autarchical," we have scenes linked by mutual ties. Instead of bipolar structures (beginning/end), we have tripolar ones (beginning/continuation/end). Instead of a mass of data to "grasp," we have a design that allows for a "guided" reading. A process of filmic *linearization* emerges. In particular, films about the Passion and chase films contributed to this linearization.

Second, "tangible" space replaces "flat" space. Painted backdrops gradually give way to alternating interiors and exteriors; uniform lighting is replaced by a "play" of light that exploits chiaroscuro; the use of frontal shots only gives way to a rich diversity of points of view, often located in the very center of the action. This constitutes a building of "aptic" space, which is perceived in all its depth and seems like a continuation of the space we live in. Third, a story that leaves the viewer "outside" its unfolding comes to be replaced by a diegetic universe that "absorbs" the viewer. The use of direct appeals ceases (e.g., looking into the camera eye, which actually represents a moment at which the theater and the screen are most put in contrast), replaced by more subtle complicities based on the audience's identification with the hero of the piece. There is no longer a need for background knowledge in order to understand what is being shown (like an awareness of the Holy Scriptures for films about the Passion of Christ). It is replaced by a story that contains its own explanatory principles. The constant sensation of "being at the movies," often reinforced by the presence of a lecturer in the theater, disappears. Instead, one feels oneself to be at the center of the story, in the place where it is happening, and in the best possible place to watch it. These processes of *internalization* and of *becoming ubiquitous* make it possible for the viewer always to be tuned into the film. Therefore, the radical changes realized in the 1910s led to a new sense of time, space, and story. They correlate with equally radical transformations on the level of production and on the level of spectatorship.

In referring to the formal characteristics of both the earliest cinema and classical cinema, Burch speaks, respectively, of "primitive" and "institutional" modes of representation. The term *mode of representation* refers to a group of principles, norms, and orientations that in some ways encompass Bordwell's individual *stylistic systems*. We find ourselves in the same area (Bordwell, after all, speaks of the integration of systems): Burch's examination, however, stresses global designs and is more comprehensive. We would add that the *modes of representation,* combined with the *modes of production,* are concepts at the center of many investigations. It is sufficient to mention two anthologies here, both dedicated to the earliest cinema. One is edited by André Gaudreault (1988b) and deals with point of view; the other, edited by Thomas Elsaesser (1990), treats shot composition and story construction. Both exemplify the intensity and the modalities of a research concerned with both modes of representation and modes of production.

Still in the area of "history of form" there is another approach that should be mentioned. After Salt's "enumerative" study (with its statistical stylistics) and Bordwell's and Burch's "structural" works (with their interest in stylistic systems and modes of representation) comes the "transversal" approach, which isolates a theme or a figure, follows it through a text or group of texts, brings out all its aspects and functions, sees the effects it has on signification, and investigates its reverberations in other events, including those outside the original framework of the investigation.

One example of this kind of research is the work of the trio Lagny, Ropars, and Sorlin. These scholars (whom we have already met individually) have done several collective studies. For example, in two volumes dedicated to Eisenstein's *October* (Sorlin and Ropars 1976 and Lagny, Ropars, and Sorlin 1979) the theme of revolution organizes the inquiry. They show how a film "on" and "for" the revolution is divided between the illustration of the event, the desire to discuss its meaning, and the desire to problematize the means of its depiction. This gesture is common to other avant-garde works, which are suspended between the telling (of a story) and the discourse (on history and the artistic practice that mirrors it).

Their analysis of popular French cinema of the 1930s (Lagny, Ropars, and Sorlin 1986) is more complex (and more adventuresome). Here their themes are the attitudes of the French toward their colonies, the prefiguration of future conflicts, the relation between individual and society, and the roles of the principal actors. The themes, distant though they may be, show continual overlapping: their examination leads the authors to determine the strong points on which the films rely (e.g., the complementarity of fragile but brilliant female characters and protective but uncertain male characters) and the blank spaces, the insignificant moments that are woven into the films.

Jean-Louis Leutrat emphasizes the play of intertextual references. Analyzing the earliest westerns (Leutrat 1985, 1987), he notes how the genre is shaped by a series of discourses that traverse and exceed the discourse of the films. Thus, he examines the genre's relations to burlesque, melodrama, and vaudeville, whose procedures and whose audience the western appropriates (only to later break these ties: *l'alliance brisée*). He studies the strategies used to promote the films: press books, ads, flyers, but also the very decorations in the theaters, window displays, and the "numbers" recited in the street that explain and anticipate what will be shown on the screen. He reconstructs the way in which the public received films and began to recognize them as "genre pieces." He studies the shooting techniques that were being established and the styles that were spreading. Finally, he gathers journalistic accounts of the world of movies, which identify the "western's audience" as a particular group (the notice of the burial of an extra who died during filming is moving . . .). Leutrat's research, constructed from a fascinating montage of theatrical blurbs, production diaries, newspaper articles, critical pieces, etc., lays out completely the workings of a *spectacular machine* and shows how not just the western, but all cinema functions inside a closely woven *net of social discourses,* which give it meaning and order.

The third area of aesthetic-linguistic histories witnesses a shift of attention toward the problems and orientations that over time have characterized artistic research in the movies. Here we are within the horizon of a "history of the idea and practice of art." We have already seen works of this kind: Andrew (1984) on aesthetic forms; Tinazzi (1983) on self-reflexive processes; Thompson (1981, 1988) on the breaking of current codes; etc. We should mention, once again, the contribution of Aumont (1989), who works on the relation between cinema and painting, considering a broad panorama of questions from the end of the 1800s until today that have dealt with artistic practices, and above all those questions that concerned the notion of image. We should also mention a completely different but complementary area, research on "popular art" and on the way in which cinema actually fits into it.[15]

17.5. Erudite History, Global History

The three large areas into which we have subdivided historical research (economic-industrial, sociocultural, and aesthetic-linguistic) do not cover the entire field. There are two zones of investigation, which are identifiable more for their research style than for their subject matter, of which we should speak.

The first is composed of what we might call *erudite histories*. These include research that is characterized by an extreme wealth of data, by a visible cinemaphilic vocation, and by a pronounced taste for documentation, but also by open resistance to the use of research tools that are too complex, like those used in economics, sociology, and semiotics. Erudite histories make contributions that are useful (because they are extremely rich in facts), passionate (because they are motivated by a love of cinema), delightful and amusing (because they are accompanied by precious materials), but also timid (because they are reluctant to problematize the phenomena under investigation or to generalize from collected data).

Many investigations of early cinema fall into this grouping. Animated by the spirit of discovery, erudite history finds ever new evidence. Its lack of preconceptions leads it to be interested in situations that have long been undervalued. At the same time, its desire to stick to facts keeps it from grasping either the broader or the more recondite sense of things. Specialized journals often offer studies of this type. Most of them were founded late in the 1970s as a way to publish the work of a group of scholars or a film library. In Italy *Griffithiana* and *Immagine* often publish studies of this kind.

Another mainstay of this area is the catalogue-history. Such histories re-view films worthy of attention, be they recognized masterpieces or eccentric works. Scholars comment on them according to criteria of taste. They also supply facts about the filmmakers, the production, and public reactions. They place films under rubrics of trend or school or style. They tie films to their age. And, finally, they call on some authority as proof of their own affirma-tions. It is sufficient to mention the elegant works of Claude Beylie;[16] but every country has its own "cinemaphile historian."

One final example comes from biographical accounts. One takes a direc-tor or an actor or a producer and reconstructs his artistic and personal life, demonstrates his contribution to the evolution of cinema, and brings out his role in the events of the age. These works are often excellent, like Gianni Rondolino's two books on Visconti (1981) and Rossellini (1989), in which the vast mass of documentation is used to construct an effective picture of the subject. In these works, private lives and collective history are mixed, as are social changes and new ways to make movies, political events and artistic debates—all in an effort to understand how individuals move in their envi-ronment and era.

In some ways, *global histories* are the opposite of erudite histories. Global histories are based on research that is equally rich in facts, but that is aware of the variety of factors at play. They are also aware of the necessity of confront-ing each factor with adequate research tools and of the importance of pro-ceeding by systematic comparisons. Greater attention is therefore given to both methodology and the organization of the research.

The goal of these histories already surfaces in "panoptic" histories, in which all the elements are put forth in a sort of composite picture (rather like those medieval frescoes that show all the exploits of a saint on one wall). It also shows up in the "stratigraphic" histories, which highlight the depth and the composition of the ground in which cinema takes root (rather like those archaeological excavations that show the layering of civilizations). Many "lo-cal histories," in the shape of "the movies in . . . ," follow this kind of design, but there is some indulgence toward erudition, when the pieces do not quite come together.

This goal is attained above all in "multidimensional" histories, in which each individual factor is studied and then regularly associated with other fac-tors. This is the case with Bordwell, Staiger, and Thompson's work on clas-sic American cinema (1985), which revolves around the parallelism between stylistic systems and modes of production. And it is especially the case with Brunetta's work on Italian cinema (1979, 1982), based as it is on an even greater number of elements. His research in fact covers financial, production, and technological aspects; political, legislative, and institutional participation; linguistic, stylistic, narratological elements; the films produced and their authors; forms of consumption; and cultural backgrounds. The data are classified in homogeneous groupings and at the same time compared (though from a distance) with those from neighboring areas. Brunetta, on more than one occasion, justifies this way of proceeding. For example, he suggests that the object of his work is "to show at every step how the history of cinema is not just a history of films, but the result of multiple processes and the interaction of a variety of forces" (Brunetta 1979 : 10). Likewise, he comments that "for the film historian, historiographic truth does not consist so much in the ability to produce a *history,* but rather in his ability to keep in mind that there are *many histories,* and in knowing how to bring them to light in a net of new, unforeseen relations" (1982 : 13). Thus, the business of following more threads and being able to tie them together is basic for Brunetta. History is an interweaving of facts or, better put, an interweaving of many histories, and it should be investigated as such. The result of this approach is to bring to light a panoramic view that shows all its complexities and articulation. In particular, it becomes clear how in Italian cinema (but the same can also be said for other national forms of cinema) the determining factors are both numerous and subject to change. Sometimes it is a film that changes the overall picture (who could think of Neorealism without *Roma città aperta*?); sometimes it is a law; at other times changes in the audiences. The developmental rhythms of events are likewise numerous and changeable: the maturation of a production procedure takes a long time, an author's work less time, the evolution of customs a very long time, and so on. Therefore, we see a multiplicity of both determining factors and chronologies. After all, as we saw in the beginning of the chapter, it is precisely with matters like these that contemporary historiography concerns itself.

17.6. History/Theory

As a coda to this review, it behooves us to return to problems of a general nature. The most immediate is the relation between the history of cinema and history in general. We have already acknowledged that the former values the rethinkings that characterize the latter, and the latter takes more and more into consideration the data brought out by the former. We would add that an awareness of moving within the same *horizon* is penetrating both sides. Likewise, the concept of films as a *historical source* has scholars in both fields, who often work side by side.[17]

The second problem involves the main options confronting film historians. Again, we have already discussed some of the options, like the choice between history that is solely concerned with filmic works and history that takes into consideration the cinematic "machine." Or between history that subdivides its subject into distinct sections and history that brings all the sections together to compose a comprehensive subject. Other options should also be recalled. There is history made with words alone and multimedia history, which is expressed through media that are more closely related to what is being studied. There is history that takes the form of a report and that privileges plain facts and history that takes the form of a story, which inserts data into a narrative. Other options affect the very principles of research. For example, there is history that photographs successive "states" (giving us a portrait of an era, the norms to which a style conforms, the balances that govern a means of production) and history that stresses the "development" of things (and that thinks of an era, a style, a means of production as an unstable, changing reality). There is empirical history, which stops at a recitation of facts, and hermeneutical history, which operates at all levels on conjectures. There is history that is open to the intervention of other disciplines, even though they are not interested in diachronic development, and history that thinks of itself as a kind of autonomous science, as the only one capable of working with time and thus having its own methods. We need to keep in mind all these alternatives in order to grasp the meaning and orientation of the different research methods.

A third problem, and perhaps the most delicate, is that of the relations between film history and film theory. In the course of the 1980s history was often thought of as "outside" or "against" theory, as a discourse on things rather than on ideas. In truth, relations between history and theory are closer than we might think.

First, each history has its own theory, a theory of just what history is and what cinema is. In this respect, all historical reconstructions are more or less tributaries of the dominant theoretical orientations. This is true for the past. It was the necessity of showing cinema's artistry, typical of an era disposed to aesthetic-cultural approaches, that led Sadoul to give precedence to master-pieces, innovations, and derivations. It was the conviction that the medium has its own intrinsic nature, tied to an essentialist approach, that led Bazin to interpret every change as a step toward a complete reproduction of reality. It was the linguistic method that, in a time characterized by disciplinary approaches, permitted Metz to view cinematic modernity as a change in narrative codes. And this is also true for the present. All the inquiries reviewed in this chapter, and the differences between them, are possible because today we think of cinema as an open field, to be freely questioned, whose borders can be crossed again and again. Thus, there is no history without theory: all history is the confirmation of a theory.

Second, theory is also part of history. If the latter wishes to explain all the aspects of the path followed by cinema, then it should concern itself with the three "machines" that drive films: the industrial machine, which regulates the production and distribution of films; the psychological machine, which regulates the understanding and consumption of films; and the discursive machine, which regulates the social perception of films. Theory, together with criticism, is at the center of the discursive "machine." It helps to define the society's idea of cinema and thus the attitudes, expectations, and criteria for judgment that concern it. In this sense, the reconstruction of the way in which the phenomenon has in time been defined, analyzed, and questioned over time can—indeed, must—constitute an important chapter in the history of cinema. Theory, then, is not just the presupposition of each history, but also one of its possible contents. Once again, there is no history without theory; and every history is also the history of theories.

We need history, but it is always pervaded by theory.

18 CINEMA AND THEORY: BY WAY OF A CONCLUSION

18.1. Theorizing

In today's far-reaching revision of film theories, which includes this contribution, some recurring tendencies are emerging. There is a revisiting of the classics in an attempt to show their modernity, as in Marie-Claire Ropars' rereading of Eisenstein. There is a recovery of minor traditions still partially unexplored, as seen in Dudley Andrew's reuse of phenomenology. There is a desire to find in the past the roots of some recent experiences, as in the case of Roger Odin's attempts to show continuity between structural and pragmatic semiotics. There is an attempt to merge the old and the new, as seen in Bordwell's mixing of formalism and cognitive psychology. There is a desire to eliminate completely some previous models in the name of establishing a more rigorous epistemology, as seen in Noël Carroll's revisiting of both classic and modern theories.[1]

The panorama that this work has tried to portray points up other aspects: the richness of debate that has never ceased to accompany the production and reception of films; the sometimes radical transformations that at times marked the research; the causes and effects of various theoretical positions; the cultural climates in which the proposals came to fruition. Theory has emerged as the device by means of which one tries to understand cinema, to define it, to analyze it, to reconsider it. It is a device that is not necessarily scientifically rational (as those who reserve the label *theory* for a highly formalized construct would like; these are the same people who do not realize that even scientific theories are no longer required by epistemology to fit such a model). Rather, theory is a device that is used to acquire knowledge. Theory cannot be reduced to an abstract form of knowledge; it is more nuanced, just like metaphor, analogy, parallelism, which provide a basis for equally efficient explication. Theory does not respond only to formal internal criteria, but also to a practical dimension—like the need to vanquish the unknown, to respond to timely questions, to find consensus.

We do not wish to say with all this that film theories are devoid of rationality: they often appeal to it, and explicitly. We only wish to make the point that reason is not the primary characteristic of a theory. The primary characteristic of a theory is its *cognitive* capacity, in the broadest sense of the word. In particular, it is the ability to present itself as *institutionalized, social, and historical knowledge*. In the preceding pages, we have seen this at every step. Theory is a device that focuses and at the same time charts thoughtful content, means of observation, attitudes toward the world at large. It focuses them in the sense that it gives them a more or less fixed form; it charts them in that through them it evaluates the work of scholars. From this point of view, it "institutionalizes" knowledge; theory defines both its limits and its utility. Furthermore, a theory is knowledge that circulates among those working in a given field and through them reaches broader audiences, producing discussion, loyalties, and dissent. In this respect, it is a social device, something that is diffused and shared within a community. Finally, a theory is also a historical event: it is a discourse that comes on the scene at a given time, in a given place, and by its very presence it is capable of defining the ambience in which it appears. In this sense, it is a historical reality, something that reflects the path (or even the error) of thought.

Institutionalization, socialization, and historicity are the traits of film theories that we have (or at least would like to have) emphasized. These are the traits that most tenaciously accompany the life of theory.

18.2. Beyond Cinema

On the threshold of the centenary of cinema's birth we ask what will become of film theories. We have no wish to act the prophet: predictions by scholars are all too often given the lie by facts. We only want to try to point out some possible directions for theory.

If there is one feature of the most recent theories that should make us beware, it is that the questions asked of cinema often transcend the phenomenon they wish to discuss. They come from "out there" and head toward "the beyond." It is cinema itself that invites this practice—from the moment at which it denies its separate identity and defines itself as a crossroads of diverse experience. For a long time cinema has not been identified with one kind of film: it is a fictional full-length movie, but also an experimental work, an amateur's 8-millimeter production, an ethnographic documentary, a teaching tool, an author's test-run. Now cinema is not even identified exclusively with movies: it is a product of and for television, a news video; it integrates theatrical works; and it is, moreover, a model of literary writing, a depiction of customs, a document for historians, a revealer of cultural tendencies, the material for literary articles, the object of parody, material for study. Furthermore, it is a museum piece, a video collection, cultural property, the object of a cinemaphile's passion. This is nothing new, though it is particularly notable today.

Cinema no longer has its own place, if it ever did have one. The works it has given us survive as memory in glossy books, as publicity quotes, as models for television serials. Experiences that cinema made known return in the form of exotic mass-vacations, in video clips, in the special effects of business conventions. The language that cinema developed serves as a model for the layout of illustrated magazines, for the organization of party games, for journalistic reports. Further, cinema in turn follows publicity, magazines, games, television. It no longer has its own place, because it is everywhere, or at least everywhere where we are dealing with aesthetics and communication.

It is for this reason that the research questions about cinema often come from "out there" and head toward "the beyond." It is because cinema extends to and is dispersed in many other spheres. And it is also for this reason that theory can no longer offer unequivocal, direct, definitive answers. Its only chance is to offer a *research network* that both pursues and envelops the object under study. Theory must be a fragmented and dispersed form of knowledge, knowledge *about* cinema as well as *beyond* cinema. In this way, at least for a while, we can keep cinema in our midst.

NOTES

Introduction

1. Film theories have received increasing attention lately. After Guido Aristarco's pioneering work (published in 1951, with a second edition in 1963), many histories, anthologies, and collections of essays have appeared. Among the histories, we should mention Andrew Tudor's ground-breaking work (1974), a less broad, but also more profound book by Brian Henderson (1980), two polemic contributions by Noël Carroll (1988a, 1988b), and above all two overviews offered by Dudley Andrew, the first devoted to "classic" film theory (1976b), the second to more recent theories (1976a). Neither should one forget the very personal and effective compendium put together by Jacques Aumont, Alain Bergala, Michel Marie, and Marc Vernet (1984). Among the anthologies, many should be mentioned: one by Richard Dyer MacCann (1966); the especially successful works by Gerald Mast and Marshall Cohen (1974, second and third editions in 1979 and 1985); two volumes by Bill Nichols (1976, 1985); and the more focused work by Philip Rosen (1986). There are a great many collections that synthesize the work of a journal (Screen 1977 and 1982 come to mind) or that reconstruct specific areas of the debate (see the collections of feminist essays edited by Doane, Mellencamp, and Williams in 1984, by Penley in 1988, and by Bruno and Nadotti in 1991). Finally, among the collections of essays, two special issues of *Iris* (1 and 2) should be mentioned since they mark the birth of the journal in 1983 and define the state of the art of theoretical studies. Issue 8 of *Hors Cadre* clarifies the situation of semiotic, psychoanalytical, and historical approaches to cinema. This is only a tentative list. An exhaustive one would be far too long. Its aim is to show how film theory has always attracted researchers, and now more than ever.

2. It is necessary to add that both in epistemological research and in colloquial language the term *theory* is more and more often used along a scale of progressive situations. At a minimal level, a theory is a common opinion, belief, or terminology through which it is possible to observe and talk about reality. At a higher level, a theory is a scientific project. Finally, but only in the last analysis, it is a coherent, axiomatic consideration capable of explaining and foreseeing a series of events. In the course of

this work we will see how film "theories" usually fit the first meaning of the word, often the second, and sometimes even the third. This opposes those who (like Carroll 1988a) think that a (scientific) theory can only be of the third kind and who try to destroy some film theories because they do not match such a model.

3. This work contains many controversial cases, which should have been amended: Bresson's and Tarkovskij's observations come to mind.

4. This aspect of film theory is especially emphasized by Grignaffini (1989).

5. It is Metz (1977b) who speaks of three "mechanisms."

1.   Postwar Film Theories

1. B. Croce, "Una lettera," *Bianco e Nero* 10 (1948). Within Italy we should recall how the acknowledgment of cinema's role was helped by such books as the anthology *L'arte del film,* ed. G. Aristarco (Milan: Bompiani, 1950).

2. Cinema will fully begin to be viewed as an autonomous subject for university research only later, namely, around the mid-1960s in Italy and during the 1970s in France, the United States, and England. The importance of the Institut de Filmologie lies, however, in the fact that it made official the interest in cinema (sanctioning its "acceptance") on the part of scholars who came from "strong" disciplines such as psychology and sociology.

3. *Solaria,* unnumbered (1927); *L'Italiano* 17–18 (1933). The birth of a "cultivated criticism" should also be mentioned. It took place in literary journals such as, besides *Solaria* itself, *Il Baretti* and *La Fiera Letteraria.* Above all, it is necessary to mention the contributions that systematically appeared in *Convegno* and its supplement, *Cineconvegno.* Some theorists also published in cinema magazines, such as *Cinematografo* or, later, *Cinema.* Most of these magazines and journals, however, either had a merely divulgatory or propagandistic aim or tended to provide specialized professional information.

4. It should be noted that, in turn, there was also a split within criticism itself: on the one hand, we have a kind of criticism that refuses all contacts with theory (or that stands as a theory itself) and that highlights its initiatory and specialist characteristics, to the point of reviewing films that are literally invisible; on the other hand, popular criticism gradually loses all content, so that it becomes impossible to distinguish it from advertising or newspaper articles.

5. Incommunicability can be defined as the inability of humans to understand either implied or inferred meanings of quotidian discourse. The last two moments in which we find a strong understanding between production and theory are Neorealism and the Nouvelle Vague. The avant-garde cinema of the 1970s is too often used by theory more as a pretext or as a fetish than as an interlocutor.

6. Of course, the consequences of this practice can be observed too: during the second half of the 1980s, for instance, America reacted to all "imported" theories and attempted to elaborate an "American" film theory (especially on the basis of cognitive psychology).

7. C. Metz, "Une étape dans la réflexion sur le cinéma," *Critique* 214. Reprinted in Metz (1972).

8. Andrew (1984), pp. 4ff.

9. For the idea of the three components of a scientific theory, to be analyzed both synchronically and diachronically, see G. Buchdahl, "Styles of Scientific Thinking," in F. Bevilacqua, ed., *Using History of Physics in Innovatory Physics Education* (Pavia: CSD, 1983). See also Buchdahl, *Metaphysics and Philosophy of Science: Descartes to Kant* (Cambridge: Cambridge University Press, 1969).

10. For the concept of the "scientific paradigm," see T. Kuhn, *The Structure of Scientific Revolutions* (Chicago: University of Chicago Press, 1962); for a clarification of the concept, see M. Masterman, "The Nature of a Paradigm," in I. Lakatos and A. Musgrave, *Criticism and the Growth of Knowledge* (Cambridge: Cambridge University Press, 1970).

11. The title of the essay is "Ontologie de l'image photographique," and the subtitle of the volume is "Ontologie et langage" (Bazin 1958).

12. This is the title of the four volumes containing Bazin's major essays (1958–1962).

13. It may be interesting to note that, even if there is no exact correspondence between theory elaboration and film production, the three paradigms are somewhat influenced by the transformations of the object of their study. Ontological theory is oriented toward classic cinema, which is highly codified even in its anomalies. Methodological theory responds, instead, to modern cinema; that is, a cinema that takes advantage of its institutionalization either to further reflect on it or to play against it; if the approach poses the problem of point of view, it is also because the identity of its object now depends on the kind of operation for which it serves as a theater. Finally, field theory faces a deeply changed landscape, dominated by dispersion, rupture, and the isolated occasion. It is the typical situation of contemporary cinema; as if to account for this condition, field theory constructs its path like an adventure.

2.   Cinema and Reality

1. I am thinking in particular of such theorists as Antonello Gerbi and Alberto Consiglio. More complex than the former are the positions of Luigi Chiarini (whose thought relies on Gentile more than on Croce) and Umberto Barbaro (where the idealistic elements are more blurred).

2. For a statement on Neorealism and a description of how theory finds its place in it, see Miccichè (1975) and Brunetta (1982).

3. Two preliminary observations are necessary. First, Italian films are always a source of interest and discussion, even abroad, and the interest manifested, for example, by the journal *L'Ecran Français* comes to mind. Second, the rebirth of the theoretical debate is paralleled by a growing interest in cinema at all levels, as witnessed by the prestigious collection Biblioteca Cinematografica (edited by G. Viazzi and A. Buzzi and published by Poligono), the illustrated screenplays of the Cineteca Domus (published by Domus), the rebirth of the journal *Cinema,* the circulation of the Vitagliano magazines, and so on.

4. See the critical overview of the contemporary debate in *Bianco e Nero* 1 (1947);

in the same issue (the first after an interruption of the journal's publication), see also
U. Barbaro's "Ancora della terza fase ovverossia del film."

5. See the debate initiated by L. Chiarini with "L'immagine filmica," *Bianco e
Nero* 6 (1948), followed up by C. L. Ragghianti's "Croce e il cinema come arte," *Bianco
e Nero* 8, and finished by B. Croce himself in "Una lettera," *Bianco e Nero* 10 (1948).

6. Giovanni Verga is the father of the nineteenth-century Italian literary movement of *verismo* (realism).

7. The work of the group writing for *Cinema* is generally directly connected with
the birth of Neorealism. The two follow paths that are only partially parallel, however
(despite Luchino Visconti's crucial role). The wish for a recuperation of Verga's lesson
is expressed by M. Alicata and G. De Santis in "Verità poesia: Verga e il Cinema
italiano," *Cinema* 127 (1941), and in "Ancora di Verga e del cinema italiano," *Cinema*
130 (1941). The idea of a more direct cinema is supported by M. Antonioni in "Per
un film sul fiume Po," *Cinema* 68 (1939). For an analysis of the group's contribution
to Neorealist thought, see Miccichè (1990).

8. A reconstruction of the relationship between politics and culture at the time is
found in Brunetta (1982). He emphasizes how, among many appeals and open letters,
the manifesto published in *L'Unità* (Feb. 22, 1948) was especially important (Brunetta
1982:144). Also stimulating is A. Abruzzese's "Il rapporto politica-cultura durante il
neorealismo," in *Politica e cultura nel dopoguerra* (Pesaro: Quaderno della Mostra Internazionale di Pesaro, 1974). The proceedings of the convention in Perugia can be read
in U. Barbaro, ed., *Il cinema e l'uomo moderno* (n.p.: Le edizioni sociali, 1950).

9. For a clear definition of Zavattini's theoretical reflection, see G. Moneti, ed.,
Lessico zavattiniano (Venice: Marsilio, 1992). See also Zavattini's collected essays on
Neorealism in Argentieri (1979).

10. All quotations, originally in Italian, were translated by Francesca Chiostri and
Elizabeth Gard Bartolini-Salimbeni.

11. Aristarco's opinions on Neorealism, expressed mostly through the reviews he
published first in *Cinema* and then in *Cinema Nuovo,* also emerge from his systematic
critique of the condition of theoretical discourse. See his "Urgenza di una revisione
dell'attuale indagine critica" and his work leading up to *Storia delle teoriche del film.*

12. We speak of general value not only from a theoretical but also from a "political" point of view. Zavattini somehow represents the "utopian" side of Neorealism,
whereas Aristarco develops a "path" that he tries to make "practicable."

13. Among Chiarini's work it is necessary to mention his direction of the journal
Rivista del Cinema Italiano in the mid-1950s. Among Barbaro's achievements is his official role within the PCI [Italian Communist Party].

14. Among the many other scholars participating in the debate, it is perhaps worth
mentioning Father Félix Morlion. He was a controversial figure, accused of having connections with the conservatives and of attempting to "break" the left front. His position,
however, is interesting in that, on the one hand, he views Neorealism through the filter
of neoscholastic aesthetics; on the other hand, he emphasizes the Neorealist ability to
represent not only the visible universe, but also "the movements of the invisible soul"
(F. Morlion, "Le basi filosofiche del neorealismo italiano," *Bianco e Nero* 4 [1948]),
initiating a path that will be continued by such post-Bazin scholars as Agel.

15. This triple dimension of Bazin's realism is clearly presented by G. Grignaffini

in the introduction to her edited volume *La pelle e l'anima: Intorno alla Nouvelle Vague* (Florence: La Casa Usher, 1984).

16. There is no need to underscore Bazin's splendid "perversity"; for him death is obscure if it is made into spectacle, but sublime if it helps to reveal the world.

17. See mainly the text of Merleau-Ponty's lecture "Le cinéma et la nouvelle psychologie," which is contemporary with the opening essay of Bazin's collection (later included in Merleau-Ponty 1948). He believes that modern psychology and philosophy have taught us that there is no "I" as opposed to the concrete universe, but a consciousness pervading every situation, confronting other consciousnesses. It is on this basis that cinema's realism can be fully understood. On the one hand, a film has a meaning like any other thing, for both "appeal to our ability to tacitly decipher the world or the people, and to coexist with them" (Merleau-Ponty 1948). On the other hand, a film translates any emotion into a behavior, so as to objectify it, yet without making it into an independent action and without reducing the possibility of participation.

18. For a comprehensive study of Bazin's life and work, see D. Andrew, *André Bazin* (Oxford: Oxford University Press, 1978).

19. After studying cinema from the early 1920s to the beginning of Nazism when he worked as a critic for *Frankfurter Zeitung,* Kracauer returned to cinema in the second half of the 1940s, mostly as a historian and a sociologist. We will deal with a part of his activity in a later chapter, emphasizing his contributions to film analysis from a sociological point of view. *Theory of Film* is instead an attempt to define the "nature" of the medium. It is clear, however, that there is a connection between Kracauer as an "essentialist" and as a "disciplinary" theorist (as there is a connection with Kracauer as a critic). Our choice to separate these two aspects is only an attempt to underscore the double nature of his thought. On Kracauer and *Theory of Film,* see the very useful introduction by Miriam Hansen to the reprint of the book for Princeton University Press, 1997.

20. On this topic, see, for instance, B. De Marchi, "Realismo socialista e religione della verità," *Comunicazioni Sociali* 2–3 (1982).

21. On this phenomenon, see, for instance, L. Marcorelles, *Eléments pour un nouveau cinéma* (Paris: Unesco, 1970).

3.   Cinema and the Imaginary

1. See the successful definition of cinema as the *dream factory,* which insistently reappears in the 1920s and 1930s and which constitutes the title of I. Ehrenburg's book *Die Traumfabrik* (Berlin: Malik, 1931).

2. This statement echoes one of the opening sentences of the book: "Cinema is essentially surrealist" (Kirou 1953 : 7).

3. It is not by chance, after all, that Kirou not only directed such magazines as *La Vie Cinématographique* but also worked for the above-mentioned *Positif.*

4. Another book that describes equally well the "theories of the fantastic" is R. Prédal's *Le cinéma fantastique* (Paris: Sechers, 1970).

5. Besides Breton's direct influence, we find in this area also an echo of the ideas of such early postwar theorists as L'Herbier, Epstein, etc.

6. Two references could be useful here, totally different in origin and weight: G.

Mammuccari's clearly anti-Neorealist book *La soggettivazione nel film* (Roma: Smeriglio, 1951); and S. Brakhage's *Metaphors on Vision* (New York: Film Culture, 1963), the manifesto of a filmmaker advocating a totally unrealistic practice.

7. See the essay "Le cinéma ou l'homme imaginaire," *Revue Internationale de Filmologie* 22–24 (1955), which presents and anticipates the homonymous book of the following year.

4.   Cinema and Language

1. Among the works published during the 1950s and early 1960s (we will mention only those in Italian and French, for this bibliography is meant only as an indication of a trend of study) are G. Calendoli, ed., *Cinema e teatro* (Rome: Edizioni dell Ateneo, 1957); E. Fuzelier, "Théâtre et cinéma," *Etudes Cinématographiques* 6–7 (1960); *Le belle arti e il film* (Rome: Bianco e Nero, 1950); H. Lemaître, *Beaux arts et cinéma* (Paris: Ed. du Cerf, 1956); A. Bertolucci, ed., "Letterato al cinema," *Sequenze* 9 (1950); M. Fuzelier, *Cinéma et literature* (Paris: Ed. du Cerf, 1964); M. D'Avack, *Cinema e letteratura* (Rome: Canesi, 1964); P. Baldelli, *Film e opera letteraria* (Padua: Marsilio, 1964); A. Napolitano, *Cinema e narrativa* (Naples: Genovese, 1965); *Cinema e TV* (Venice: Mostra Internazionale d'Arte Cinematografica, 1953). For a more complete bibliography, see, for instance, H. Ross, *Film as Literature, Literature as Film* (Westport: Greenwood Press, 1987).

2. It should be noted, however, that Ragghianti had a strong influence on the prewar studies on cinema and that his influence continued after 1945. The core of his work is his definition of cinema as a "figurative art," with special attention to such themes as the nature of the image, spatiality, and temporality.

3. For a complete reconstruction of the debate, with reference to later contributions, see Miccichè (1979), especially the chapter on "Cinema e letteratura."

4. R. Bataille, *Grammaire cinématographique* (n.p.: Taffin Lefort, 1947); A. Berthomieu, *Essai de grammaire cinématographique* (Paris: La Nouvelle Edition, 1946); J. Roger, *Grammaire du cinéma* (Brussels/Paris: Editions Universitaires, 1953).

5. See, in particular, Taddei (1963). Here, on the one hand, the author emphasizes in an even more convincing and lucid way the difference between represented and representation; on the other hand, he analyzes the consequences of considering films linguistic facts (however, he does so in a rather strict way; for instance, he distinguishes between essential and accessory components of the image as sign).

6. For a survey of the many attempts—from the postwar years to the advent of semiotics—to build "grammars of cinema," see Odin (1978b).

7. A good example of this trend comes from A. Casty, *The Dramatic Art of the Film* (New York: Harper and Row, 1971). More interesting in its originality is S. Sharff, *The Elements of Cinema: Towards a Theory of Cinematic Impact* (New York: Columbia University Press, 1982). The latter identifies eight great models of linguistic structure: separation, parallel action, slow disclosure, familiar image, moving camera, multiangularity, master shot discipline, orchestration.

8. See Carroll (1980), Chapter 3.

9. Among Della Volpe's later work on cinema, it is worth mentioning in particu-

lar his presentation at the convention "Linguaggio e ideologia nel film" held in Pesaro within the Mostra del Nuovo Cinema in 1967 (and published as proceedings in 1989), where he openly displays an interest in the emerging semiotics.

10. See Metz's review of the first volume of *Esthétique,* significantly entitled "Une étape dans la réflexion sur le cinéma" and published in Metz (1972), together with his review of Mitry's second volume.

11. See Mitry's own definition of his work: a study of the "conditions of filmic expression, evidently based upon the psychology of perceptions and the phenomenon of conscience" (1965: 179). But aesthetics and psychology also work as the "epistemological background" of his research. In fact, Mitry believes that even the simplest knowledge of the cinematic phenomenon cannot but consider the latter an aesthetic object and itself a form of knowledge, namely, the cognitive reelaboration of external data, in themselves unrelated to the subject. Thus, the intervention of these two sciences derives both from the specificity of what is under investigation—an artistic object—and from what research implies—a work of knowledge.

12. See in particular Mitry (1965: 10ff.), where he criticizes Bazin's idea of the sequence shot.

13. Mitry uses the word "néantification" (1963 : 178).

14. To borrow some terms Mitry does not use, we can say that what is at play here is not simply a greater or lesser similarity to the world, but the dawning of a presence standing for an absence and the ability of what appears on the screen to recall what is not physically there. Thus, we are dealing with a representation that is to be understood not just as *Vorstellung,* but as *Darstellung.* The tension between these two moments is the foundation of any signifying device. As soon as cinema acknowledges this tension, it can help explain to what extent and why cinema has a fully linguistic nature.

15. See, for instance, his statement that although they represent a specific moment, filmic images "suggest all other moments similar to this, namely, all the 'possible' ones of the same kind. With them and through them, the representation of a single aspect, of a single moment, penetrates the 'essence' of the things represented, of their eidetic 'in themselves'" (Mitry 1963 : 178). Thus, an image gives the represented an exemplary and absolute dimension, making it different from reality, while also making it the latter's full representative. Alterity becomes identity, and the symbolic order completely explains its structure.

16. On Della Volpe's polemic against ontologism, see for instance "Problemi di un'estetica scientifica," in Della Volpe (1954).

17. Mitry continues his polemic against semiotics even in his last book, one year before this death, *La sémiologie en question* (Paris: Ed. du Cerf, 1987). Thus, he keeps his position to the very end, even though it is completely outdated. An attempt to view Mitry as a "modern" thinker (an interpretation that differs from our own) is found in E. Dagrada, "Jean Mitry, un 'sémiologue malgré lui,'" *Cinégrafie* 1 : 2 (1989).

5.   An Interlude

1. We need to mention other movements, besides the ones quoted above: the Polish cinema of October (since 1956), the Nova Vlna in Prague (since 1962), the

Hungarian Cinema of the Rebirth (after 1963), the Spanish Nuevo Cine (in the 1960s), the Italian Giovane Cinema (mid-1960s), the Mexican Nueva Ola (1960s), the Japanese Nouvelle Vague (1960s), the newly born African cinema, and later the Chilean cinema of Unidad Popular.

2. There is a vast bibliography on the "new cinema" of the 1950s and 1960s. The first attempt to assemble one can be found in Miccichè (1972), where the "Introduzione a una conclusione" also frames the phenomenon very well. An essential collection of essays by various authors is *Poetiche delle nouvelles vagues* (Venice: Marsilio, 1989). See also, with reference to the "historical avant-garde," P. A. Sitney, ed., *The Avant-Garde Film* (New York: New York University Press, 1978). For each isolated movement, see R. Turigliatto, ed., *Nouvelle Vague* (Turin: Cinema Giovani, 1995); E. Martini, ed., *Free Cinema e dintorni* (Turin: Cinema Giovani, 1991); S. Renan, *The American Underground Film* (New York: Dutton, 1967); L. Marcorelles, *Living Cinema* (London: Allen, 1973); and so on. Finally, the volumes on each national cinema published yearly by the Mostra Internazionale del Nuovo Cinema and the publisher Marsilio in the collection Nuovocinema/Pesaro are of capital value.

3. Miccichè (1972) deals with the problem of the continuity and discontinuity between the "new cinema" of the 1960s and that of the following decades. He does so both at an ideological level (the idea of a "mediated" break with the "cinema de papa" is replaced by the idea of an absolute alternative with respect to current cinema) and at the aesthetic level (the "subjectivity" of the first is replaced by an "objectivity" no longer bound to mirroring reality, but to critical analysis of the latter).

4. Miccichè (1972) insists on the awareness of an "expressive responsibility" as the unifying factor (maybe the only one) of the many *new cinemas*. He defines this awareness as an "ethics" or—even better—as an "ethics of aesthetics" (18).

5. The idea of the *author* had already been introduced in the 1930s in Italy by such Crocean theorists as Alberto Consiglio.

6. In the introduction to *La pelle e l'anima* (Florence: La casa Usher, 1984), Grignaffini carefully reconstructs the concept of the *auteur* as it appears within the Nouvelle Vague and relates it to the need for realism insisted on by Bazin.

7. In his thorough reconstruction of the activities of the *Cahiers du Cinéma*, G. De Vincenti (1980) suggests a division of the "politique des auteurs" into four periods: the first, 1951–1953, gravitates around the idea that the style of a film expresses its author's poetics. The second, 1954–1959, introduces the search for a more precise "idea of cinema." The third, 1959–1962, is connected to the "MacMahon school" (from the name of the cinema that cinephilic critics frequented). The fourth, 1962–1965, revises the notion of "politique," while trying to remain faithful to it. Our reconstruction will of necessity be less detailed.

8. A. Bazin, "Comment peut-on être Hitchcocko-hawksien?" *Cahiers du Cinéma* 44 (1955), and "De la politique des auteurs," *Cahiers du Cinéma* 70 (1957). In particular, Bazin refuses to share the admiration shown by the young journalists of the journal for Hawks, Preminger, and many other American directors. His is a paradoxical search for authorship and for personal poetics within a commercial and industrialized cinema. On the other hand, Bazin praises the "politique" for at least two reasons. This trend forces the critics to give up a superficial knowledge of the medium to acquire a "specialized erudition" (thus constantly stimulating the renewal of cinema). He also helps

to understand that reducing films to their content overlooks cinema's own peculiarity, its ability to express itself through images. "Every technique sends us back to a metaphysics." Only if we pay the greatest attention to cinema's expressive techniques (as the "politique" does) will we grasp the real meaning of a film, both as an author's work and as a cinematic work. Bazin insists, finally, on the ethical-moral dimension of the work of art: "The true seriousness of a work is not necessarily proportional either to the seriousness of its topic or to the apparent solemnity of its style. What counts is not the topics and the explicit way they are treated, but their ability, in so doing, to approach even indirectly implicitly moral or social values" ("Comment peut-on être Hitchcocko-hawksien?").

9. For a complete analysis (with an anthology of writings) of this, see J. Caughie, ed., *Theories of Authorship* (London: Routledge and Kegan Paul, 1981).

10. "Interior meaning is extrapolated from the tension between a director's personality and his material" (Sarris 1962).

11. In this sense, see what the Manifesto of the Free Cinema states, apparently contradicting itself: "No film can be too personal. . . . Implicit in our attitude is a belief in freedom, in the importance of people and in the significance of the everyday"; but the manifesto also stresses the idea that any attitude implies a stylistic choice. The partial text of the manifesto is found in R. Manvell, *New Cinema in Britain* (London: Studio Vista, 1969), p. 51.

12. In this sense, we should also mention the distinction made by Espinosa between *popular art* and *mass art*. "The former has nothing to do with the latter. Popular art needs the people's personal, individual taste, which it tends to develop. On the contrary, mass art—or art for the masses—needs the lack of popular taste. Truly, mass art will be such only when the masses themselves will produce art. Instead, these days mass art is the art produced by some for the masses" (Espinosa 1973).

13. S. Alvarez, "El cine como uno de los medios masivos de comunicación," *Cine Cubano* 49–51 (1967); O. Getino, "Hacia una cinematografía legalizada por el pueblo," *Cine y Liberación* 1 (1972).

14. This is the "ethics of aesthetics" discussed by Miccichè (1972).

6.   Methodological Theories

1. For an overview of filmology, see E. Lowry's wide-ranging volume *The Filmology Movement and Film Study in France* (Ann Arbor: UMI Research Press, 1985), where the idea of a true continuity of attitudes between filmology and semiology is introduced (see the chapter "The Legacy of Filmology"). The same hypothesis is sustained by G. De Vincenti, "Alle origini della semiotica cinematografica: Cohen-Séat," *Biblioteca Teatrale* 10–11 (1974). A much more synthetic reconstruction is made by Z. Gawrack, "La filmologie: Bilan des la naissance jusqu'à 1958," *Ikon* 65–66 (1968).

7.   Psychology of Cinema

1. H. Münsterberg, *The Photoplay: A Psychological Study* (New York: Appleton and Co., 1916). For the contributions from the 1930s, see, for instance, R. Allendy,

"La valeur psychologique de l'image," *L'Art Cinématographique* 1 (1926); and C. Musatti, *Elementi di psicologia della testimonianza* (Padua: Cedam, 1931).

2. Filmology also deals with the exploration of the physiological basis of vision. See the bibliography compiled by G. Marinato, "La ricerca elettroencefalografica in filmologia," *Ikon* 51 (1965).

3. This volume is also commendable for the broad bibliographic discussion on the studies of a psycho-physiological nature. It is, however, evident that the artificial environment where the experiments are conducted takes us far away from the "real" cinema.

4. There are, however, some notable exceptions, such as Michotte.

5. We should not forget to mention two typical confluences of the 1960s and 1970s, respectively: that between psychology and semiology and that between psychology and psychoanalysis. Here the idea of *cinematic situation* is reintroduced, and its appearance changes. In the first case, it is reconnected to a *communicative situation* where a major role is played by factors such as the kind of information provided by the various channels, the presence of specific technico-linguistic competences, the ways in which a message is lineally organized, etc. In the second case, it is slowly replaced by an *apparatus,* indicating a relationship between the spectator and film modeled on that between a subject and its psychic apparatus. We will return to these points later.

8.   Sociology of Cinema

1. In Italy these oppositions found their formulation during the 1930s in the slogan "Films are art, cinema is an industry," introduced by L. Chiarini in *Cinque capitoli sul film* (Rome: E. Italiane, 1941).

2. A (critical) analysis of the attempt to merge the symbolic and economic aspects can be found in P. Ortoleva, "Sulla categoria modo di produzione: Note sullo stato attuale dei rapporti tra storiografia e ricerca sul cinema," in V. Zagarrio, ed., *Dietro lo schermo* (Venice: Marsilio, 1988).

3. We refer, in particular, to Herbert Blumer's work, published in the 1930s by Macmillan.

4. The word is used in its etymological meaning, with no reference to the homonymous theory.

5. Morin (1954) summarizes the core of his interest, which can be viewed, ideally, as many chapters of his research: (a) the discovery of the archaic and magical dimension of cinematic language; (b) the identification function of the star, which is a true collective archetype presenting itself as a behavioral model; (c) the awareness of the specific civilizing role acquired by Hollywood cinema, which is both supporter of and vehicle for a specific culture that attacks markets, different artistic and cultural regions, managing to disturb and install itself in them.

6. See, for instance, F. Alberoni, *L'elite senza potere* (Milan: Vita e Pensiero, 1963); G. Huaco, *The Sociology of Film Art* (New York: Basic Books, 1965); G. P. Prandstraller, *Professione regista* (Cosenza: Lerici, 1977).

7. An important precursor of this view, before the war, was W. Benjamin, whose

essay "Das Kunstwerk im Zeitalter seiner technischen Reproduzierbarkeit" was published in Paris in 1936, in *Zeitschrift für Sozialforschung*. The circulation of Benjamin's ideas in the postwar years, it should be noted, in parallel with and beyond Adorno's, made "The Work of Art in the Age of Mechanical Reproduction" an important point of reference.

8. Further suggestions for the definition of Kracauer's attitude toward cinema come from his *Das Ornament der Masse* (Frankfurt: Suhrkamp, 1963), translated into English as *The Mass Ornament* (Cambridge, Mass.: Harvard University Press, 1995).

9. Galli and Rositi ascribe two fundamental characteristics to cinema. First, while reflecting society, films privilege certain aspects and leave out others; American cinema pays more attention to the values introduced by mass culture, such as "conflictual optimism, personal engagement, and affective positivity" (Galli and Rositi 1967:259). Second, films not only reflect society, but also orient it; and American cinema finds some real "antibodies" to the general uneasiness in the values introduced by the mass media. These two points are a starting point for the understanding of cinema's "influence" on a country's sociopolitical destiny.

10. Sorlin (1977:15) separates mentality and ideology, which we instead join.

11. A third, historical interest characterizes Sorlin's work besides these two. It emerges, however, mostly in other works, and we will analyze them elsewhere.

9.   Semiotics of Cinema

1. Or, as they used to say, following the then dominant dictates of structuralist linguistics, especially De Saussure's, "semiology."

2. The acts of these two conferences, published respectively in 1966 ("Per una nuova coscienza critica del linguaggio cinematografico," *Nuovi Argomenti* 2) and in 1968 (*Linguaggio e ideologia nel film* [Novara: Cafieri]), were reprinted in *Per una nuova critica* 1989.

3. There are also systems with no zero articulation or with mobile articulations. See Eco (1968:138ff.).

4. For a complete picture, see two anthologies: Urrutia (1976) and Termine (1979). See also Odin's excellent and complete review (1990), which broadens the period under investigation.

5. We have intentionally left out Pasolini's analysis of "prosaic cinema" and "poetic cinema" ("cinema di prosa," "cinema di poesia"), included in Pasolini (1972). It is of great interest, but it is not directly related to semiotics.

6. This chapter was first published, in a somewhat different version, in *New Left Review* 49 (1968), under the title "Cinema: Code and Image" and signed with the pseudonym Lee Russel.

7. In a later, revised edition of his book, Wollen criticizes uniformity in favor of dispersion, the former being a *trompe-l'oeil*, the latter sending us back to the material basis of filmic signification. While rediscovering Peirce, Wollen here displays a "political" fear that we will examine in a later chapter.

8. See *Semiotica* 1:3 (1969), later reprinted in Worth's posthumously published *Studying Visual Communication* (1981).

9. A proof of this connection comes from the essay "Cognitive Aspects of Sequence in Visual Communication," *Audio Visual Review* 16:2 (1968).

10. Metz pursues this line of thought in his next work, where he deals with the problem of a semio-psychoanalytic approach (Metz 1977b).

11. Marie and Brunetta complain about the often unwarranted multiplication of the various research fields: the former compares semiotics to a hydra ("L'enseignement du cinéma et l'hydre sémiologique," *Ça Cinéma* 18 [1979]); the latter speaks of "theoretical consumerism" (in the preface to P. Madron, ed., *L'analisi del film* [Parma: Pratiche, 1984]).

12. Barthes openly speaks of the "second semiotics" in "Le troisième sens," *Cahiers du Cinéma* 222 (1970). Among others, F. Casetti and S. Ghislotti use this work in "Lo scenario francese," *Bianco e Nero* 4 (1985).

13. We have chosen to mention only a few of the many important attempts to define the filmic text. See, for instance, K. Asanuma, "Films: Oeuvres ou textes?" *Ça Cinéma* 7–8 (1975), insisting both on the presence of the work of writing [*écriture*] and on the film's ability to represent a world and to communicate it to us.

14. Bellour also approaches the theme of filmic analysis in "Le texte introuvable," in Bellour (1979), where he analyzes the problem of the texture and quotability of films, and in "L'analisi alla fiamma," *Carte Semiotiche* 1 (1985), where he criticizes the idea of analysis as a "separate practice." Of course, many authors conducted textural analyses with theoretical intent: besides the names already introduced, we should mention D. Andrew, D. Bordwell, D. Chateau, T. Kuntzel, F. Jost, S. Heath, A. Gardies, J.-P. Simon, P. Willemen, etc. We will return to their work later in this book. Also, the collective works by Bailblé, Marie, Ropars, Sorlin, and Lagny deserve to be mentioned. An excellent collection of textual analyses has been edited by R. Bellour, *Le cinéma américain* (Paris: Flammarion, 1980); another collection, devoted to more recent currents of study, has been edited by F. Casetti and R. Odin, "L'analisis del film, oggi," *Carte Semiotiche* 1 (1985).

15. Metz's interest in the narrative dimension of cinema also emerges in other essays included in the same volume, above all in "Remarques pour une phénoménologie du narratif" and "Le cinéma moderne et sa narrativité" (1968).

16. Chatman's main lines are common to other scholars. See, for instance, R. Campari's works on the genres of cinematographic narrative (*I modelli narrativi: Cinema americano, 1945–1973* [Parma: Quaderni di Storia dell'Arte, 1974] and *Il racconto del film* [Bari: Laterza, 1983]). In F. Vanoye's *Récit écrit, récit filmique* (Paris: Cedic, 1979) we find a good introduction to narratology.

17. It should be noted that it is not by chance that the transitions in classic cinema were made on the basis of movements and perceptions.

18. Works that deal with nonnarrative cinema, with the help of semio-narratological concepts, also are part of this picture. Among many, we will mention a work on didactic films: J. Jacquinot, *Cinéma et pédagogie* (Paris: Puf, 1977).

19. We should mention at least M. Nash's "*Vampyr* and the Fantastic," *Screen* 17:3 (1976); and P. Willemen's "The Fugitive Subject," in P. Hardy, ed., *Raoul Walsh* (Edinburgh: Edinburgh Film Festival, 1974).

20. E. Dagrada, "Strategia testuale e soggettiva in *Spellbound*," *Carte Semiotiche* 1

(1985); "The Diegetic Look: Pragmatics of the POV Shot," *Iris* 7 (1986); J. Fontanille, *Les espaces subjectifs: Introduction à la sémiotique de l'observateur* (Paris: Hachette, 1989); and, finally, Jost (1987). The thematics of the gaze is applied to a single author by L. Cuccu, in *Antonioni: Il discorso dello sguardo* (Pisa: ETS, 1990).

10.   Psychoanalysis of Cinema

1. An exhaustive bibliography of the psychoanalytical studies on cinema can be found in S. Ferrari, *Psicoanalisi: Arte e letteratura, Bibliografia generale 1900–1983* (Parma: Pratiche, 1985).

2. Among Musatti's many works on cinema, see at least the pages included in *Psicoanalisi e vita contemporanea* (Turin: Boringhieri, 1960). Still in the field of filmology, see Y. Deprun's "Cinéma et transfert," *Revue International de Filmologie* 2 (1947).

3. See, in particular, J. Chasseguet-Smirgel, *Pour un psychanalyse de l'art et de la créativité* (Paris: Payot, 1971).

4. See, for instance, R. T. Eberwein, *Film and the Dream Screen* (Princeton: Princeton University Press, 1984). Eberwein reintroduces the analogy between cinematographic and oneiric situation from a—so to speak—"genetic" point of view. Our first dreams, as shown by Lewin's work on the "dream screen," derive from a material support on which they are projected (the mother's breast or its substitute) and from the baby's increasing self-awareness; cinema only reactivates this psychic structure, placing a screen and spectator face to face. In this light, it is possible to study once again all the film passages that evoke, either explicitly or implicitly, the dreamer's experience.

5. In order to understand fully Baudry's discourse on cinema, we should not forget his work on literature, especially "Ecriture, fiction, idéologie" and "Freud et la 'création littéraire,'" in *Tel Quel, Théorie d'ensemble* (Paris: Seuil, 1968).

6. Our translation of the French *dispositif* leaves room for both "device" and "apparatus" (the latter, as in English, more openly refers to psychology, but also defines an economic-industrial complex).

7. Once again, we need to go back to the French in order to retain the original pun: "avoir un (sa)voir divin."

8. Bellour explicitly speaks of "narcissistic doubling" (1979: 22).

11.   Field Theories

1. For a careful study of the role of hermeneutics in the reorientation of film theory, see Andrew (1984).

2. See Odin (1988) and Aumont and Marie (1988) on textual analysis and its role in theory.

3. At this level, we can identify some personal attitudes: Ropars' "deconstruction," Lyotard's "energetism," Thompson's "neoformalism," Andrew's "recuperation of phenomenology," Mast's "neoclassicism," etc.

12.   Politics, Ideology, and Alternatives

1. For a general picture of the debate on cinema and politics from 1968 on, with special reference to the French/Anglo-American situation, see S. Harvey, *May '68 and Film Culture* (London: BFI, 1979); and D. N. Rodowick's broad *The Crisis of Political Modernism* (Urbana: University of Illinois Press, 1988).

2. The section that followed this one in the Italian text has been deleted at the author's request. The remaining sections and notes have been renumbered accordingly.

3. See two of Althusser's classic definitions of ideology: "Ideology is a system (with a logic and rigor of its own) of representations (images, myths, ideas, or concepts) that exist and have a given role inside a given society" (*Pour Marx*); and "Ideology is a representation of the imaginary relationship that individuals have with their actual life conditions" (*Idéologie et appareils*).

4. Fargier refers to Althusser's notions of "dominant structure."

5. These ongoing and more profound investigations allow *Cinéthique* to apply to cinema a group of concepts developed in a broader context by Kristeva, Sollers, Derrida, and others, besides Althusser.

6. P. Bonitzer, "Film/Politique," *Cahiers du Cinéma* 222 (1970); S. Daney and J. P. Oudart, "Travail, lecture, jouissance," *Cahiers du Cinéma* 222 (1970); J.-L. Comolli, "Film/Politique (2): L'aveu: 15 propositions," *Cahiers du Cinéma* 224 (1970); J. Narboni, "La vicariance du pouvoir," *Cahiers du Cinéma* 224 (1970); and so on.

7. Besides *Cahiers du Cinéma* (1970a and 1970b), see Bonitzer et al., " 'La vie est à nous,' film militant," *Cahiers du Cinéma* 218 (1970); and later J.-L. Comolli and F. Gere's analysis of *Hangmen Also Die* and *To Be or Not to Be,* in *Cahiers du Cinéma* 286, 288, 290/291 (1978).

8. This principle of reading recalls Althusser once again: the relationship between *vu* and *bévue* guiding the study of *Lire le Capital.*

9. The opposition between these different positions is also affected by the fact that *La Nouvelle Critique* belongs to the official left (that of the PCF [French Communist Party]), while *Cinéthique* and *Cahiers* are close to the new left (that of the Marxist-Leninist and Maoist groups).

10. Comolli also notes, still at the level of ideological effects, that the presence of speaking subject-authors reassures the subject-spectators of their ability to be the "masters" of the game (masters of both words and images).

11. Two "insiders" reconstructed the journal's life: C. MacCabe, "Class of '68: Elements of an Intellectual Autobiography," in MacCabe (1985); P. Wollen, "Semiotic Counter-Strategies: Retrospect 1982," in Wollen (1982).

12. At its birth, *Screen* was the organ of the SEFT (Society for Education in Film and Television) and was connected with the BFI (British Film Institute). The need to define the meaning of its educational policy detached *Screen* from the BFI in 1971; similarly, the increasingly smaller financial aid provided by the SEFT, which initially helped the journal's development, led to its death. See MacCabe (1985).

13. In particular, see the studies by Heath (*Touch of Evil,* issues 1 and 2, 1975; *Suspicion,* issue 3, 1976; and so on). See also Nash, "*Vampyr* and the Fantastic," issue 3,

1976; Rosen, "Difference and Displacement in *Seventh Heaven,*" issue 2, 1977; Drummond, "Textual Space in *Un chien andalou,*" issue 3, 1977; and so on.

14. See Willemen and Heath's opening essay in issues 1–2 (1973); Heath's and MacCabe's essays in issue 3 (1974); "Film and System: Terms of Analysis," *Screen* 1 : 2 (1975).

15. This project was realized, for instance, in issues 2 (1974) and 4 (1975) on Brecht and 3 and 4 (1974) on the Russian formalists, as well as elsewhere.

16. See, for instance, issue 2 (1975), which opens with Metz's "The Imaginary Signifier," followed by J. Lesage's "The Human Subject: You, He, or Me?"; see also issue 3 (1975) with L. Mulvey's "Visual Pleasure"; and issue 4 (1977), entirely devoted to the notion of suture. Previously, however, S. Heath had already found himself demanding the development of a theory of the subject, if only to dismiss the empiricism of the author theory.

17. See, besides L. Mulvey's essay mentioned in note 16, S. Heath's important essay "Difference," in issue 3 (1978).

18. Already in the editorial in issue 2 (1974), Brewster and MacCabe juxtaposed the "militant" and the "avant-garde" artists and encouraged discussion of their opposition.

19. The journal's first issue, published in 1970, was devoted to "Film and Politics"; the second to "Avant-Garde Films"; the sixth (1976) to "Perspectives on English Independent Cinema"; the eighth and ninth (1980, 1981) to primitive cinema and the contemporary avant-garde; and so on.

20. The essay was later included in Wollen (1982).

21. Also, "The Two Avant-Gardes" was published in Wollen (1982), together with other essays on the same theme, some of which were published in *Screen.*

22. Among the journals we should have discussed, let us mention *Cinéaste* (interested in filmmakers' activity and in documentaries), *Jump Cut* (more militant), and *Octobre* (aesthetic debate).

13.   Representation, Unrepresented, Unrepresentable

1. See in particular J. Derrida's influential essay "Le théâtre de la cruauté et la clôture de la représentation," in *L'écriture et la différence* (Paris: Seuil, 1967).

2. "Eléments de sémiologie," *Communications* 4 (1964); "Rhétorique de l'image," *Communications* 4 (1964) and "Introduction à l'analyse structurale des récits," *Communications* 8 (1966) (both in Barthes 1977); *Système de la mode* (Paris: Seuil, 1967); etc.

3. References to Barthes' "theory of the image" can be found in S. Ungar, "Persistence of the Image: Barthes, Photography and the Resistance to Film," in S. Ungar and B. McGraw, eds., *Signs in Culture: Roland Barthes Today* (Iowa City: University of Iowa Press, 1989).

4. This background is described in *Discours, figure* (Paris: Klincksieck, 1971); see also the collection of essays called *Des dispositifs pulsionnels* (Paris: UGE, n.d.), which includes "L'a-cinéma" as well as such essays as "Capitalisme énergumène" and "La

peinture comme dispositif libidinal." For Lyotard, a device is what transforms forces into representation.

5. This is not so true in Barthes' case. He also wrote other essays on cinema, among which is the fascinating "En sortant du cinéma," *Communications* 23 (1975).

6. For this beautiful formulation, see Ropars (1990).

7. Outside the *Screen* group, scholars such as Philip Rosen and David Rodowick are worth mentioning, as well as a large group belonging to the school of Anglo-American feminism, which we will discuss later.

8. On Kluge's theory, see A. Kluge and O. Negt, *Kritische Theorie und Marxismus* (n.p.: Gravenhage, 1974). On Enzensberger's ideas, see H. M. Enzensberger, "Constituents of a Theory of the Media," *New Left Review* 64 (1970).

14.   Image, Gender, Difference

1. For a reconstruction of the feminist debate from the insider's perspective, see, for instance, the introductions by Doane et al. (1984), by Penley (1988), and by Bruno and Nadotti (1991); see also C. Gledhill's "Recent Developments in Feminist Criticism," *Quarterly Review of Film Studies* 5:4 (1978); and J. Mayne's "Feminist Film Theory and Criticism," *Sign* 11:1 (1985).

2. The essay was published in *Screen* 16:3 (1975) and later included in Mulvey (1989).

3. See in particular "Afterthoughts on 'Visual Pleasure and Narrative Cinema' inspired by *Duel in the Sun*," *Framework* 6:15–17 (1981).

4. K. Kay and G. Peary, eds., *Women in the Cinema* (New York: Dutton, 1977); E. A. Kaplan, ed., *Women in Film Noir* (London: BFI, 1978); P. Erens, ed., *Sexual Stratagems* (New York: Horizon Press, 1979).

5. J. Lesage, "The Human Subject: You, He or Me?, or, The Case of the Missing Penis," *Screen* 16:2 (1975); R. Rich, "The Crisis of Naming in Feminist Film Criticism," *Jump Cut* 19 (1978).

6. See in particular Bergstrom (1979) and De Lauretis and Heath (1980).

7. See, for instance, S. Flitterman, "Montage/Discourse: Germaine Dulac's *The Smiling Madame*," *Wide Angle* 4:3 (1980); W. Dozoretz, "Madame Beudet's Smile: Feminine or Feminist?" *Film Reader* 5 (1982); etc.

8. S. Flitterman and J. Suter, "Textual Riddles: An Interview with Laura Mulvey," *Discourse* 1 (1979); B. Ruby Rich and L. Williams, "The Right of Re-vision: Michelle Citron's *Daughter's Rite*," *Film Quarterly* 1 (1971); "Yvonne Rainer: An Introduction," *Camera Obscura* 1 (1976); E. Lyon, "The Cinema of Lol V. Stein," *Camera Obscura* 6 (1980); J. Copjec, "*India Song/Son nom de Venise dans Calcutta désert*: The Compulsion to Repeat," *October* 17 (1981); etc.

9. For an effective summary of these positions, with a bibliography, see J. Mayne, "Feminist Film Theory and Criticism," *Sign* 11:1 (1985).

10. Within this debate between identity and difference, a few texts are most frequently cited; among them, besides such classics as Freud, Lacan, Metz, Althusser, etc., we should mention K. Silverman's effective and personal compendium, *The Subject of Semiotics* (New York: Oxford University Press, 1983).

11. See A. Kuhn's *Women's Pictures: Feminism and Cinema* (London: Routledge, 1982), which summarizes the meaning of this debate well.

12. On the relationship between feminist film theory and cultural studies, see T. Modleski, "Some Functions of Feminist Criticism, or the Scandal of the Mute Body," *October* 49 (1989).

13. For this kind of study, see, for instance, M. B. Haralovich, "Film and Social History: Reproducing Social Relationship," *Wide Angle* 8:2 (1986); L. Rabinovitz, "Temptations of Pleasure: Nickelodeons, Amusement Parks and the Sigh of Female Sexuality," *Camera Obscura* 23 (1990); etc.

14. See, for instance, the special issue of *Camera Obscura,* 16 (1988); L. Mulvey's "Melodrama in and out of the Home," in C. MacCabe, ed., *High Theory/Low Culture: Analyzing Popular Television and Film* (Manchester: Manchester University Press, 1986).

15. A sign of this "dispersion" of feminist film theory (and, in the background, of the transformations that feminist film theory itself undergoes) is the shift from women's studies to gender studies, theorized by feminists themselves. Within this frame, an interesting debate is the one on "Men in Feminism," an example of which is found in A. Jardine and P. Smith, eds., *Men in Feminism* (New York: Methuen, 1978). T. Modleski takes a polemic stand in *Feminism without Women: Culture and Criticism in the "Post-Feminist" Age* (New York: Routledge, 1991).

15.   Text, Mind, Society

1. Besides Chion's books, to which we will return, there is a wide range of special issues of journals: *Yale French Studies* 60 (1980; R. Altman, ed., "Cinema Sound"); *Iris* 3:1 (1985; F. Vanoye, ed., "La parole au cinéma"); *Hors Cadre* 3 (1985; "Voix off"); *Protée* 13:2 (1985; "Sons et narrations au cinéma"); *Vibration* 4 (1987; "Les musiques des films"). Within this picture, we should not forget the historical approach, which is exemplified by G. Rondolino, *Cinema e musica* (Turin: Utet, 1991).

2. Chion continued his study in *Le son au cinéma* (Paris: Ed. de l'Etoile, 1985), on music and the mise-en-scène of sounds; and in *La toile trouée* (1988), on words.

3. In particular, a film works on *showing* at the level of the mise-en-scène, when decisions are made about the events that should be filmed, and at the level of the recording of these events, when the camera observes what lies in front of the camera eye; it works instead on *narration* at the level of editing, when the events are organized sequentially, thus uncovering the "logic" that drives them.

4. *Ocularization* may be "internal," that is, entrusted directly to a character (in the case of the subjective shot) or "zero," that is, unrelated to any observer on the scene (in the case of the objective shot). Internal ocularization, in turn, may be "secondary" (when it emerges from the juxtaposition of seer and seen) or "primary" (when the seer is merely suggested by the modes of the filming). There is also "modalized" ocularization (some explicit features tell us that the image is a character's thought) and "hallucinated" ocularization (here we cannot easily decide if the image is the result of a character's thoughts or if it is presented objectively and, therefore, we must infer its nature from its content). Finally, "spectatorial" ocularization is activated when the image shows something that the character clearly does not notice. *Auricularization,* too,

may be "internal" (if it takes place through a character) or "zero" (if it is independent of the character on the screen). Similarly, the internal one may be "secondary" (a "talking" subjective shot, obtained thanks to an editing procedure) or "primary" (a "talking" subjective shot, obtained through a simple alteration of the sound). The intermediate cases are also relevant: "disconnected" auricularization, shifting from the subjective to the objective dimension, and "captured" auricularization, shifting from the objective to the subjective dimension. Finally, there are "free occurrences," for which the sender of the enunciation is directly responsible (one thinks of the music that accompanies the scenes). As far as *focalization* is concerned, it may be "internal" (the character is the explicit source of the knowledge), "external" (the opposite), or "spectatorial" (the knowledge is the product of the viewer's complete or partial re-elaboration). For a discussion of Jost's categories, which he derives from Genette, and a rereading of Genette, see G. Cremonini, *L'autore, il narratore, lo spettatore* (Turin: Loescher, 1988).

5. On the difference between these two kinds of grammar, and on the characteristics and situation of the second, see Metz's essay "Sémiologie audio-visuelle et linguistique générative" (1977a) and Odin's careful overview, "Modèle grammatical, modèles linguistiques et étude du langage cinématographique" (1978b).

6. Or, rather, it leads to the construction of a filmic grammar that, in principle, *coincides* with the grammar of natural languages, because films and verbal speech have "similar functions, therefore also identical structures." See Colin (1985:97).

7. One of the factors in favor of cognitive psychology is its ability to play a leading role in many fields, including the study of language, mostly thanks to its contributions in the field of artificial intelligence.

8. N. Carroll, *The Philosophy of Horror or Paradoxes of the Hearth* (New York: Routledge, 1990); E. Branigan, *Narrative Comprehension and Film* (London: Routledge, 1992). On this trend in film studies, the special issue of *Iris* 5:2 (1989), on "Cinema and Cognitive Psychology," is especially significant.

9. For an overall picture, see in particular Odin (1983). On fictional films, see also "L'entrée du spectateur dans la fiction," in J. Aumont and J. L. Leutrat (1980); and "Mise en phase, déphasage, performativité," *Communications* 38 (1983); on family films, see "Rhétorique du film de famille," *Revue d'Esthétique* 1–2 (1979); on documentary films, see "Film documentaire, lecture documentarisante," in *Cinémas et réalités* (St. Etienne: Cierec, 1984); on fable-films, "*Neighbours* di Norman MacLaren: Un film favola," *Carte Semiotiche* 1 (1985); on musical films, "Du spectateur fictionnalisant au nouveau spectateur: Approche sémiopragmatique," *Iris* 5:1 (1988).

10. We find this critique in Bordwell (1985), among others.

11. This critique is found in Bordwell (1985) and Odin (1983), among others.

16.   Culture, Art, Thought

1. For example, those of Beverle Houston and Marsha Kinder, who, using a method of their own called "transformalist," focus on the procedures used by a film in relation to current rules and demonstrate the significance of individual choices. See

B. Houston and M. Kinder, *Self and Cinema: A Transformalist Perspective* (Pleasantville: Redgrave, 1980).

2. The essays in J. E. Muller, ed., "Texte et médialité," *Mana* 7 (1987), are examples of this line of study. A separate chapter would be necessary to consider the use of new tools in the traditional exploration of the relations between cinema and literature. See especially J. Paech, *Literatur und Film* (Stuttgart: Metzler, 1988), and his idea of the "Literarisierung" of cinema.

3. A. Bazin and J.-L. Rieupeyrout, *Le western ou le cinéma américain par excellence* (Paris: Ed. du Cerf, 1953); Bazin (1962); Warshow (1962).

4. Naturally the reservations of those who followed Adorno and the Frankfurt School did not disappear entirely. They continued to see in genre simply a "serial product," functional in the cultural industry. Interest was growing, however, in what led a large audience to support this kind of movie and in its legacies.

5. Here we are comparing *structural* and *functional* definitions of genres. It should not be forgotten that even before this contrast, other, much more radical ones are at work. Is genre a reality with its own consistency, recognizable by itself, or the fruit of some scholar's observations, or a comfortable label of little value for a group of texts? And again: is genre defined deductively, through the construction of an abstract typology and the control of whatever pigeonholes are filled in the course of time, or is it defined inductively, through the study of diverse experiences and the resultant generalizations? Finally, does genre have an existence that crosses history, remaining the same in all eras and cultures, or is it dependent on the contexts in which it appears, ready to change its own meaning with changes in time and place? On these questions, which, in literary studies, have given rise to an imposing bibliography, see G. Genette, ed., *Théorie des genres* (Paris: Seuil, 1986); as regards cinema, see Buscombe (1970) and Altman (1984a); for observations of methodology, see F. Casetti, "Les genres cinématographiques: Quelques problèmes de méthode," *Ça Cinéma* 18 (1979).

6. An extremely useful anthology on cultural studies is L. Grossberg et al., eds., *Cultural Studies* (New York: Routledge, 1992). See also T. Bennet, ed., *Culture, Ideology and Social Process: A Reader* (London: Batsford, 1981); and C. MacCabe (1986).

7. The bibliography on this subject is extremely wide. I will mention only a few essays that interrogate the role of audience studies within cinema studies such as Allor's "Relocating the Site of the Audience," *Critical Studies in Mass Communication* 5, no. 3 (1988): 217–254; Robert C. Allen's "From Exhibition to Reception: Reflections on the Audience in Film History," *Screen* 31, no. 4 (1990): 347-356; and *Camera Obscura's* special issue on "The Female Spectator," edited by Janet Bergstrom and Mary Anne Doane, no. 20–21 (1989)—especially relevant because it manifests the feminist film theory investment in the issue of spectatorship and its important contribution to the exploration of the field.

8. See also Bruno (1978).

9. There is no lack of exceptions: other than the works we have already mentioned in the course of this book, there are those by Gentile, who in 1935 wrote the preface to Luigi Chiarini's first book, *Cinematografo;* and by Munier, who in 1967 published an essay in the *Revue d'Esthétique,* "Le chant second," in which he treats the problems of cinema.

10. Deleuze's interest in cinema goes beyond the two volumes dedicated specifically to it. It is enough to remember the note in the Italian edition of *Logica del senso,* in which Deleuze defines himself and Guattari as the Laurel and Hardy of philosophy and his thought as a "cinema-philosophy" (Milan: Feltrinelli, 1975). On the reasons for Deleuze's interest in cinema, we should cite the interviews edited by G. Cabasso and F. Revault d'Allonnes and those edited by R. Bellour and F. Ewald, published respectively in 1985 and 1988 and found in G. Deleuze, *Pourparlers* (Paris: Minuit, 1990).

17.   History, Histories, Historiography

1. Lagny (1992) provides an excellent picture of the "new" film historiography. Also, Allen and Gomery (1985) is an important point of reference: the work by these two authors contains a rich collection of studies and research examples. Important evidence of the ongoing debated can be seen in *Iris* 2:2 (1984; issue on "Pour une théorie de l'histoire du cinéma") and *Hors Cadre* 7 (1989; the section entitled "Quelle histoire et pourquoi"), as well as in Aumont et al. (1989); see also Rosen (1984); Sklar (1988); Elsaesser (1986).

2. T. Ramsaye, *A Million and One Nights* (New York: Simon and Schuster, 1926); G. Sadoul, *Histoire du cinéma mondial* (Paris: Flammarion, 1949), and *Histoire générale du cinéma* (Paris: Denoël, 1947–), in six volumes.

3. Motion Picture Patents Company.

4. See also J. Limbacher's good survey, *Four Aspects of the Film* (New York: Brussel and Brussel, 1968).

5. The term *culture* defines here the set of activities that take place in a society, considered for their symbolic value; the representations of the self, the world, other people, etc., that circulate in that society; finally, the artistic and intellectual production that take place in a society.

6. L. Rosten, *Hollywood: The Movie Colony, The Movie Makers* (New York: Harcourt Brace, 1941); H. Powdermaker, *Hollywood: The Dream Factory* (Boston: Little-Brown, 1950).

7. An example of such works is C. Herzog, "The Movie Palace and the Theatrical Sources of Its Architectural Style," *Cinema Journal* 20:2 (1981); see also the issue of *Iris* 12 (1991) devoted to "Cinema and Architecture" and edited by P. Cherchi Usai and F. Kessler.

8. See, for instance, L. Wilden, *Milwaukee Movie Palaces* (Milwaukee: Milwaukee County Historical Society, 1986); J. André and M. André, *Une saison Lumière à Montpellier* (Perpignan: Institut Vigo, 1984); R. Noëll, "Le spectacle cinématographique à Perpignan entre 1896 et 1944," *Cahiers de la Cinématique,* special issue (1973).

9. See, for example, H. Diederichs, *Anfänge Deutscher Filmkritik* (Stuttgart: n.p., 1986), on the birth of criticism in Germany, in particular through the journal *Bild und Film.*

10. W. Uricchio and R. E. Pearson, "What Is Miracle? The Competing Discourses of the Natural and the Supernatural in *The Life of Moses,*" *RSSI* 11:2–3 (1991); L.

Kirby, *Parallel Tracks: The Railroad and Silent Cinema* (Durham, N.C.: Duke University Press, 1997).

11. See for example, S. Hayward and G. Vincendeau, *French Film, Text and Context* (London: Routledge, 1990).

12. The idea of *virtual text* is also introduced by J. Tsivian (to define the set of a film's intertextual references) and by P. Cherchi Usai (to define the hypothetical version of a film, which includes all its variants).

13. The German journal *Diskurs Film* is devoted totally to film philology: see in particular issue 2 (1988), entitled "Konstruktion und Rekonstruktion." It includes essays by H. Bath (who suggests reconstructing silent movies on the basis of their "rhetorical" base), by L. Bauer (who defends the "hermeneutical" approach), and by H. Birett (who focuses on the use of "statistical" methods). See also issue 4 (1991), entitled "Einführung in die Filmphilologie," edited by K. Kanzog. It presents itself as a manual for the recognition, reconstruction, and description of original versions. Another effective book is that by P. Cherchi Usai, *Una passione infiammabile* (Turin: Utet, 1991). The same scholar edited a special issue of *Comunicazioni di Massa* 4:3, on film philology and restoration.

14. Bordwell himself returned to the structure of the investigation, at least in part, in his analysis of Ozu's poetics (*Ozu and the Poetics of Cinema* [London: BFI, 1988]). Its echoes can also be found, for example, in V. Sánchez Biosca's beautiful *Sombras de Weimar* (Madrid: Verdoux, 1990), which gives an overview of German cinema in the years after World War I and shows how three stylistic models clash in it: the hermeneutical-metaphorical (characterized by the hypertrophy of the figurative dimension), the narrative (characterized by the transparence of the diegesis), and the analytical-constructive (characterized by the presence of a declared filmic enunciation).

15. In this respect, A. Costa's work is of interest. It is about visual spectacles and their influence, especially on early cinema. See Costa (1983).

16. C. Beylie, *Les film-clés du cinéma* (Paris: Bordas, 1987). To this kind of work we should also add *filmographies,* such as Chirat's in France, Martinelli and Bernardini's in Italy, and so on.

17. In this field we should emphasize the increasing number of studies on historic films (that both "write" history and "accumulate" sources): historical representation is at the core of G. Schmid's *Die Figuren des Kaleidoskops* (Salzburg: Neugebauer Verlag, 1983) and is part of P. Ortoleva's *Scene dal passato* (Turin: Loescher, 1991).

18.   Cinema and Theory

1. See Ropars (1981), Andrew (1978), Odin (1990), Bordwell (1985), Carroll (1988a, 1988b), etc.

BIBLIOGRAPHY

The bibliography contains the texts expressly presented and discussed. It does not include texts that are merely cited. Information on those works can be obtained from the notes.

Abruzzese, A.
1973   *Forme estetiche e società di massa.* Venice: Marsilio.
1974   *L'immagine filmica.* Rome: Bulzoni.
1977   "Lavoro astratto e lavoro concreto nei processi di produzione artistica: Hollywood." *Sociologia della letteratura* 1.
1979   *La grande scimmia.* Rome: Napoleone.

Allen, R. C.
1990   "From Exhibition to Reception: Reflections on the Audience in Film History." *Screen* 31, no. 4.

Allen, R. C., and D. Gomery
1985   *Film History: Theory and Practice.* New York: Knopf.

Altman, R.
1984a   "A Semantic/Syntactic Approach to Film Genre." *Cinema Journal* 23 : 3.
1984b   "Toward a Theory of the History of Representational Technology." *Iris* 2 : 2.
1985   "The Technology of the Voice." *Iris* 3 : 1.
1986   "The Technology of the Voice." *Iris* 4 : 1.
1987   *The American Film Musical.* Bloomington and Indianapolis: Indiana University Press.
1989   "Technologie et répresentation: L'espace sonore." In Aumont, Gaudreault, and Marie 1989.

Ancona, L.
1963   "Il film come elemento nella dinamica dell'aggressività." *Ikon* 46.
1967   "Il comico nello spettacolo (interpretazione psicologica)." *Ikon* 63.

Anderson, L.

1957a   "Free Cinema." *Universities and Left Review* 2.

1957b   "Get Out and Push." In T. Maschler (ed.), *Declaration*. London: Mac-
         Gibbon and Kee.

Andrew, D.

1976a   *Concepts in Film Theory*. New York and Oxford: Oxford University Press.

1976b   *The Major Film Theories*. New York and Oxford: Oxford University Press.

1978   "The Neglected Tradition of Phenomenology in Film Theory." *Wide
         Angle* 2 : 2.

1984   *Film in the Aura of the Art*. Princeton: Princeton University Press.

Argentieri, M.

1979   *L'occhio del regime*. Florence: Vallecchi.

Aristarco, G.

1950   "La terra trema." *Cinema* 32.

1951   *Storia delle teoriche del film*. Turin: Einaudi.

1955a   "Dal neorealismo al realismo." *Cinema Nuovo* 53.

1955b   "È realismo." *Cinema Nuovo* 55.

1965   *Il dissolvimento della ragione*. Milan: Feltrinelli.

Astruc, A.

1948   "Naissance d'une nouvelle avant-garde: La caméra-stylo." *Ecran Français*
         144.

Aumont, J.

1980   "L'espace et la matière." In Aumont and Leutrat 1980.

1983   "Le point de vue." *Communications* 38.

1989   *L'oeil interminable*. Paris: Librairie Séguier.

1990   *L'image*. Paris: Nathan.

Aumont, J., A. Bergala, M. Marie, and M. Vernet

1984   *Esthétique du cinéma*. Paris: Nathan. (English translation: *Aesthetics of Film*.
         Austin: University of Texas Press, 1992.)

Aumont, J., A. Gaudreault, and M. Marie (eds.)

1989   *Histoire du cinéma: Nouvelles approches*. Paris: Publications de la Sorbonne.

Aumont, J., and J.-L. Leutrat (eds.)

1980   *Théorie du film*. Paris: Albatros.

Aumont, J., and M. Marie

1988   *L'analyse des films*. Paris: Nathan.

Bächlin, P.

1945   *Der Film als Ware*. Basel: Burg Verlag.

Bailblé, C., M. Marie, and M.-C. Ropars

1975   *Muriel: Histoire d'une recherche*. Paris: Galilee.

Balio, T. (ed.)

1976   *The American Film Industry.* Madison: University of Wisconsin Press.

Barbaro, U.

1953   "Il cinema di fronte alla realtà." In *Poesia del film.* Rome: Filmcritica.

Baroni, M. R., et al.

1989   *Emozioni in celluloide.* Milan: Raffaello Cortina.

Barthes, R.

1970   "Le troisième sens." *Cahiers du Cinéma* 222. (English translation: "The Third Meaning." In *Image, Music, Text.* New York: Hill and Wang, 1977.)

1977   *Image, Music, Text.* New York: Hill and Wang.

Baudry, J. L.

1978   *L'effet cinéma.* Paris: Albatros. (Partial English translation: "Ideological Effects of the Basic Cinematographic Apparatus." In T. Hak Kyung Cha [ed.], *Apparatus: Cinematic Apparatus, Selected Writings.* New York: Tanam Press, 1980.)

Bazin, A.

1958   *Qu'est-ce que le cinéma? I, Ontologie et langage.* Paris: Editions du Cerf. (Partial English translation: *What Is Cinema?* Berkeley and Los Angeles: University of California Press, 1967.)

1959   *Qu'est-ce que le cinéma? II, Le cinéma et les autres arts.* Paris: Editions du Cerf. (Partial English translation: *What Is Cinema?* Berkeley and Los Angeles: University of California Press, 1967.)

1961   *Qu'est-ce que le cinéma? III, Cinéma et sociologie.* Paris: Editions du Cerf. (Partial English translation: *What Is Cinema?* vol. 2. Berkeley and Los Angeles: University of California Press, 1971.)

1962   *Qu'est-ce que le cinéma? IV, Une esthétique de la réalité: le néorealisme.* Paris: Editions du Cerf. (Partial English translation: *What Is Cinema?* vol. 2. Berkeley and Los Angeles: University of California Press, 1971.)

Bellour, R.

1979   *L'analyse du film.* Paris: Albatros.

1980   "A batons rompus." In Aumont and Leutrat 1980.

Bergstrom, J.

1979   "Enunciation and Sexual Difference." *Camera Obscura* 3–4.

Bernardini, A.

1980–

1982   *Cinema muto italiano.* 3 vols. Bari: Laterza.

Bertetto, P.

1990   *Fritz Lang: Metropolis.* Turin: Lindau.

Bettetini, G.

1968   *Cinema: Lingua e scrittura.* Milan: Bompiani. (English translation: *The Language and Technique of the Film.* The Hague: Mouton, 1973.)

1971   *L'indice del realismo*. Milan: Bompiani.
1975   *Produzione del senso e messa in scena*. Milan: Bompiani.
1979   *Tempo del senso*. Milan: Bompiani.
1984   *La conversazione audiovisiva*. Milan: Bompiani.

Bitomsky, H.
1972   *Die Röte des Rots von Technicolor*. Neuwied and Darmstat: Luchterhand.

Bizzarri, L., and L. Solaroli
1958   *L'industria cinematografica italiana*. Florence: Parenti.

Bluestone, G.
1957   *Novels into Film*. Berkeley: University of California Press.

Bonitzer, P.
1976   *Le regard et la voix*. Paris: UGE.
1982   *Le champ aveugle*. Paris: Cahiers du Cinéma/Gallimard.
1985   *Décadrages: Cinéma et peinture*. Paris: Editions de l'Etoile.

Bonnel, R.
1978   *Le cinéma exploité*. Paris: Seuil.

Bordwell, D.
1985   *Narration in Fiction Film*. Madison: University of Wisconsin Press.
1989   *Making Meaning: Inference and Rhetoric in the Interpretation of Cinema*. Cambridge: Harvard University Press.

Bordwell, D., J. Staiger, and K. Thompson
1985   *The Classical Hollywood Cinema: Film Style and Mode of Production to 1960*. New York: Columbia University Press.

Bouvier, M., and J.-L. Leutrat
1981   *Nosferatu*. Paris: Gallimard.

Brakhage, S.
1963   *Metaphors on Vision*. New York: Film Culture.

Branigan, E.
1984   *Point of View in the Cinema*. Berlin, New York, and Amsterdam: Mouton.

Braudy, L.
1976   *The World in a Frame*. New York: Anchor Press–Doubleday.

Brewster, B., and C. MacCabe
1974   "Editorial." *Screen* 15, no. 1.

Brooks, V.
1985   "Film, Perception and Cognitive Psychology." *Millennium Film Journal* 14–15.
1989   "Restoring the Meaning in Cinematic Movement: What Is the Text in a Dance Film?" *Iris* 9.

Browne, N.
1982   *The Rhetoric of Filmic Narration.* Ann Arbor: UMI Research Press.

Bruce, D. J.
1953   "Remémoration du matériel filmique." *Revue Internationale de Filmologie* 4:12.

Brunetta, G. P.
1970   *Forma e parola nel cinema.* Padua: Liviana.
1974   *Nascita del racconto cinematografico.* Padua: Patron.
1979   *Storia del cinema italiano: 1895–1945.* Rome: Editori Riuniti.
1982   *Storia del cinema italiano: Dal 1945 agli anni '80.* Rome: Editori Riuniti.
1989   *Buio in sala.* Venice: Marsilio.

Bruno, E.
1978   *Film altro reale.* Milan: Il Formichiere.
1986   *Film come esperienza.* Rome: Bulzoni.

Bruno, G., and M. Nadotti (eds.)
1991   *Immagini allo schermo.* Turin: Rosenberg and Sellier.

Burch, N.
1969   *Praxis du cinéma.* Paris: Gallimard. (English translation: *Theory of Film Practice.* New York: Praeger, 1973.)
1990   *Life to Those Shadows.* Berkeley and Los Angeles: University of California Press.

Burch, N., and J. Dana
1974   "Propositions." *Afterimage* 5.

Buscombe, E.
1970   "The Idea of Genre in the American Cinema." *Screen* 11:2.

Cahiers du Cinéma
1970a   "Morocco de Joseph von Sternberg." *Cahiers du Cinéma* 225.
1970b   "Young Mr. Lincoln de John Ford." *Cahiers du Cinéma* 223. (English translation: "John Ford's Young Mister Lincoln." In Rosen [ed.] 1986.)

Carroll, J. M.
1980   *Towards a Structural Psychology of Cinema.* The Hague: Mouton.

Carroll, N.
1988a   *Mystifying Movies: Fads and Fallacies in Contemporary Film Theory.* New York: Columbia University Press.
1988b   *Philosophical Problems of Classical Film Theory.* Princeton: Princeton University Press.

Casetti, F.
1980   "Le texte du film." In Aumont and Leutrat 1980.
1986   *Dentro lo sguardo.* Milan: Bompiani. (English translation: *Inside the Gaze.* Bloomington: Indiana University Press, 1986.)

Cavell, S.
1971   *The World Viewed.* Cambridge: Harvard University Press.
1981   *Pursuits of Happiness.* Cambridge and London: Harvard University Press.

Cawelti, J.
1971   *The Six-gun Mystique.* Bowling Green: Bowling Green University Popular Press.
1976   *Adventure, Mystery and Romance: Formula Stories as Art and Popular Culture.* Chicago: University of Chicago Press.

Chateau, D.
1983   "Diégèse et énonciation." *Communications* 38.
1986   *Le cinéma comme langage.* Paris: AISS–IASPA.

Chateau, D., A. Gardies, and F. Jost (eds.)
1981   *Cinémas de la modernité.* Paris: Klincksieck.

Chateau, D., and F. Jost
1979   *Nouveau cinéma, nouvelle sémiologie.* Paris: UGE.

Chatman, S.
1978   *Story and Discourse.* Ithaca and London: Cornell University Press.

Chevassu, F.
1963   *Langage cinématographique.* Paris: Cahiers de l'Education Permanente.

Chiarini, L.
1951   "Discorso sul neorealismo." *Bianco e Nero* 7. Also in L. Chiarini, *Il film nella battaglia delle idee.* Milan and Rome: Bocca, 1954.
1952   "Spettacolo e film." In *Belfagor.* Also in Chiarini 1962.
1962   *Arte e tecnica del film.* Bari: Laterza.

Chion, M.
1982   *La voix au cinéma.* Paris: Editions de l'Etoile. (English translation: *The Voice in Cinema.* New York: Columbia University Press, 1998.)

Cinéthique
1969   "Economique-idéologique-formel: Entretien avec Marcellin Pleynet et Jean Thibaudeau." *Cinéthique* 3.
1971   "Texte collectif." *Cinéthique* 9–11.

Cohen, K.
1979   *Film and Fiction: The Dynamics of Exchange.* New Haven: Yale University Press.

Cohen-Séat, G.
1946   *Essai sur les principes d'une philosophie du cinéma: I, Introduction générale.* Paris: PUF.

Colin, M.
1985   *Langue, film, discours.* Paris: Klincksieck.

Collet, Jean, et al.
1975   *Lectures du film*. Paris: Albatros.

Collins, J.
1979   "Vers la définition d'une matrice de la comédie musicale: La place du spectateur dans la machine textuelle." *Ça Cinéma* 16.

Comolli, J.-L.
1971–
1972   "Technique et idéologie." *Cahiers du Cinéma* 229 (1971), 230 (1971), 231 (1971), 233 (1971), 234–235 (1971–1972), 241 (1972). (Partial English translation: "Technique and Ideology: Camera, Perspective, Depth of Field." In Rosen [ed.] 1986.)

Comolli, J.-L., and J. Narboni
1969a   "Cinéma/Idéologie/Critique." *Cahiers du Cinéma* 216. (English translation: "Cinema/Ideology/Criticism." In G. Mast, M. Cohen, and L. Braudy [eds.], *Film Theory and Criticism*. New York and Oxford: Oxford University Press, 1992.)
1969b   "Cinéma/Idéologie/Critique." *Cahiers du Cinéma* 217.

Conant, M.
1960   *Antitrust in the Motion Picture Industry: Economic and Legal Analysis*. Berkeley and Los Angeles: University of California Press.

Cook, P.
1975   "Approaching the Work of Dorothy Arzner." In *The Work of Dorothy Arzner*. London: BFI.

Cook, P., and C. Johnston
1974   "The Place of Woman in the Cinema of Raoul Walsh." In *Raoul Walsh*. Edinburgh: Edinburgh Film Festival.

Costa, A. (ed.)
1983   *La meccanica del visibile*. Florence: La Casa Usher, 1983.

Crary, J.
1990   *Techniques of the Observer*. Cambridge, Mass.: MIT Press.

Dayan, D.
1983   *Western Graffiti*. Paris: Clancier Guénaud.
1984   "Le spectateur performé." *Hors Cadre* 2.

Degand, C.
1972   *Le cinéma, cette industrie*. Paris: Editions Techniques et Economiques.

De Lauretis, T.
1984   *Alice Doesn't*. Bloomington: Indiana University Press.
1987   *Technologies of Gender*. Bloomington: Indiana University Press.

De Lauretis, T., and S. Heath (eds.)
1980   *The Cinematic Apparatus*. London: Macmillan.

Deleuze, G.
1983   *L'image-mouvement*. Paris: Minuit. (English translation: *The Movement-Image*. London: Athlone Press, 1986.)
1985   *L'image-temps*. Paris: Minuit. (English translation: *Time Image*. London: Athlone Press, 1989.)

Della Volpe, G.
1954   *Il verosimile filmico e altri scritti di estetica*. Rome: Edizioni di Filmcritica.

Deslandes, J.
1966   *Histoire comparée du cinéma*. Paris: Castermann.

Deslandes, J., and J. Richards
1968   *Histoire comparée du cinéma*, vol. 2. Paris: Castermann.

Detassis, P., and G. Grignaffini
1981   *Sequenza segreta*. Milan: Feltrinelli.

De Vincenti, G.
1980   *Il cinema e i film: I, Cahiers du cinéma 1951–1969*. Venice: Marsilio.

Di Giammatteo, F.
1950   "Significato e conseguenze del linguaggio cinematografico." *Bianco e Nero* 3.

Doane, M. A.
1987   *The Desire to Desire: The Woman's Film of the 1940's*. Bloomington: Indiana University Press.

Doane, M. A., P. Mellencamp, and L. Williams (eds.)
1984   *Re-vision: Essays in Feminist Film Criticism*. Los Angeles: American Film Institute–University Publications of America.

Durand, J.
1958   *Le cinéma et son public*. Toulouse: Sirey.

Eco, U.
1968   *La struttura assente*. Milan: Bompiani. (An earlier version of the section on cinema is translated as "Articulation of the Cinematic Code." In Nichols [ed.] 1976.)

Eizykman, C.
1976   *La jouissance-cinéma*. Paris: UGE.

Elsaesser, T.
1972   "Tales of Sound and Fury." *Monogram* 4.
1986   "The New Film History." *Sight and Sound* (Autumn).

Elsaesser, T. (ed.)
1990   *Early Cinema: Space, Frame, Narrative*. London: BFI.

Espinosa, J. G.
1973   *Por un cine imperfecto*. Caracas: Rociane–Fondo Editorial Salvador de la Plaza.

Fargier, J. P.
1969   "La parenthèse et le détour." *Cinéthique* 5.
1970a   "Le processus de production de film." *Cinéthique* 6.
1970b   "Vers le récit rouge." *Cinéthique* 7–8.

Feldmann, E.
1956   "Considérations sur la situation du spectateur au cinéma." *Revue Internationale de Filmologie* 26.

Fernandez, D.
1975   *Eisenstein*. Paris: Grasset.

Ferro, M.
1975   *Analyse de film, analyse de sociétés*. Paris: Hachette.
1977   *Cinéma et histoire*. Paris: Denoël-Gonthier. (English translation: *Cinema and History*. Detroit: Wayne State University Press, 1988.)

Film Culture
1961   "The First Statement of the New American Cinema Group." *Film Culture* 22–23.

Fofi, G.
1969   "Alla ricerca del positivo." *Ombre Rosse* 8.

Fraisse, P., and G. de Montmollin
1952   "Sur la mémoire des films." *Revue Internationale de Filmologie* 9.

Friedberg, A.
1993   *Window Shopping: Cinema and the Postmodern*. Berkeley and Los Angeles: University of California Press.

Friedmann, G., and E. Morin
1952   "Sociologie du cinéma." *Revue Internationale de Filmologie* 3 : 10.
1955   "De la méthode en sociologie du cinéma." In *Actes du II Congrès Internationale de Filmologie*. Paris: Sorbonne.

Galli, G., and F. Rositi
1967   *Cultura di massa e comportamento collettivo*. Bologna: Il Mulino.

Gardies, A.
1980   *Approche du récit filmique*. Paris: Albatros.

Garroni, E.
1968   *Semiotica ed estetica*. Bari: Laterza.
1972   *Progetto di semiotica*. Bari: Laterza.

Gaudreault, A.
1988a   *Du littéraire au filmique*. Paris: Méridiens Klincksieck.

Gaudreault, A. (ed.)
1988b   *Ce que je vois de mon ciné*. Paris: Méridiens Klincksieck.

Getino, O., and F. Solanas
1973   "Hacia un tercer cine: Apuntes y experiencias para el desarrollo de un cine
         de liberación en el tercer mundo." In *Cine, cultura y descolonización*. Buenos
         Aires: Siglo XXI. (Partial English translation: "Toward a Third Cinema."
         In Nichols [ed.] 1976.)

Gheude, M.
1970   "Les photogrammes comme signifiant." *Cinéthique* 7/8.

Gibson, J. J.
1979,
1986   "Motion Pictures and Visual Awareness." In *The Ecological Approach to
         Visual Perception*. Boston: Houghton Mifflin; Hillsdale, N.J.: Lawrence
         Erlbaum Associates.

Gidal, P.
1975   "Theory and Definition of Structural/Materialist Film." *Studio Interna-
         tional* 190:978.

Gidal, P. (ed.)
1976   *Structural Film Anthology*. London: BFI.

Gomery, D.
1984   "Film Culture and Industry: Recent Formulation in Economic History."
         Iris 2:2.

Grande, M.
1974   "Semiotica e cinema: Dal processo al sistema." *Filmcritica*, 249/250.
1986   *Abiti nuziali e biglietti di banca*. Rome: Bulzoni.

Grant, B. K. (ed.)
1986   *Film Genre Reader*. Austin: University of Texas Press.

Grignaffini, G.
1989   *Sapere e teorie del cinema: Il periodo del muto*. Bologna: CLUEB.

Guback, T.
1969   *The International Film Industry*. Bloomington: Indiana University Press.

Hagemann, W.
1952   *Der Film: Wesen und Gestalt*. Heidelberg: Kurt Vowinkel Verlag.

Hansen, M.
1991   *Babel and Babylon: Spectatorship in American Silent Film*. Cambridge and
         London: Harvard University Press.

Haskell, M.
1974   *From Reverence to Rape*. New York: Holt, Rinehart and Winston.

Heath, S.
1981   *Questions of Cinema*. London: Macmillan.

Helman, A.
1970   *O dziele filmowym: Material, technika, struktura.* Cracow: Wydawnictwo Literackie.

Henderson, B.
1980   *A Critique of Film Theory.* New York: Dutton.

Hochberg, J.
1989   "The Perception of Moving Images." *Iris* 9.

Hochberg, J., and V. Brooks
1978   "The Perception of Motion Pictures." In E. C. Carterette and M. P. Friedman (eds.), *Handbook of Perception,* vol. 10. New York: Academic Press.

Hoensch, J.
1976   "Fragen an die Filmsemiologie." *Semiosis* 3.

Horkheimer, M., and T. W. Adorno
1947   *Dialektik der Aufklärung.* Amsterdam: Querido Verlag. (English translation: *Dialectic of Enlightenment.* New York: Herder and Herder, 1972.)

Ivanov, V.
1975   "Funkcii i kategorii jazyka kino." *Semeiotike* 7.

Jacobs, L.
1981   "*Now, Voyager:* Some Problems of Enunciation and Sexual Difference." *Camera Obscura* 7.
1991   *The Wages of Sin: Censorship and the Fallen Woman Film, 1928–1942.* Madison: University of Wisconsin Press.

Jarvie, I.
1970   *Toward a Sociology of Cinema.* London: Routledge and Kegan Paul.

Jeancolas, J.-P.
1979   *Le cinéma des Français: La V République.* Paris: Stock.
1983   *Quinze ans d'années trente: Le cinéma des Français, 1929–1944.* Paris: Stock.

Johnston, C.
1975   "Dorothy Arzner: Critical Strategies." In *The Work of Dorothy Arzner.* London: BFI.
1976   "Toward a Feminist Film Practice: Some Theses." *Edinburgh Magazine* 1.
1980   "The Subject of Feminist Film Theory/Practice." *Screen* 21:2.

Johnston, C. (ed.)
1973   *Notes on Woman's Cinema.* London: SEFT 1975.

Jost, F.
1983   "Narration(s): En deça et au-delà." *Communications* 38.
1987   *L'oeil-caméra.* Lyon: Pul.

Kaminsky, S.
1974   *American Film Genres*. Dayton: Pfaum.

Kaplan, A.
1983   *Women and Film: Both Sides of the Camera*. New York: Methuen.

Kawin, B. F.
1978   *Mindscreen*. Princeton: Princeton University Press.

Kirou, A.
1953   *Le surréalisme au cinéma*. Paris: Arcanes.

Kitses, J.
1970   *Horizons West*. Bloomington: Indiana University Press.

Knilli, F. (ed.)
1971   *Semiotik des Films*. Munich: Hanser.

Knilli, F., and E. Reiss
1971   *Einfürung in die Film- und Fernsehanalyse*. Steinback-Giessen: Anabas.

Koch, A. W.
1971   *Varia semiotica*. Hildesheim: Olms.

Kracauer, S.
1947   *From Caligari to Hitler*. Princeton: Princeton University Press.
1960   *Theory of Film*. New York: Oxford University Press.

Kuhn, A.
1985   *The Power of the Image*. London: Routledge and Kegan Paul.

Kuntzel, T.
1972   "Le travail du film." *Communications* 19.
1973   "Le défilement." *Revue d'Esthétique* 2–4.
1975a   "Le travail du film 2." *Communications* 23. (English translation: "The Film-Work, 2." *Camera Obscura* 5 [1980].)
1975b   "Savoir, pouvoir, voir." *Ça Cinéma* 7–8.

Laffay, A.
1964   *Logique du cinéma*. Paris: Masson et Cie.

Lagny, M.
1992   *De l'histoire du cinéma: Méthode historique et histoire du cinéma*. Paris: Colin.

Lagny, M., M. C. Ropars, and P. Sorlin
1979   *La révolution figurée: Film, histoire, politique*. Paris: Albatros.
1986   *Générique des années 30*. Paris: PUV.

Lambert, G.
1959   "Free Cinema." *Sight and Sound* (Spring).

Lebel, J. P.
1971   *Cinéma et idéologie*. Paris: Editions Sociales.

Leblanc, G.
1969   "Direction." *Cinéthique* 5.

Lebovici, S.
1949   "Psychanalise et cinéma." *Revue Internationale de Filmologie* 5.

Leglise, P.
1969   *Histoire de la politique du cinema français: Le cinéma et la Troisième République.* Paris: Lherminier.
1977   *Histoire de la politique du cinéma française: Le cinéma entre deux républiques.* Paris: Lherminier.

Lenne, G.
1970   *Le cinéma "fantastique" et ses mythologies.* Paris: Editions du Cerf.

Leutrat, J.-L.
1985   *L'alliance brisée: Le Western des années 1920.* Lyon: PUL.
1987   *Le Western: Archéologie d'un genre.* Lyon: PUL.

Lotman, J.
1973   *Semiotika kino i problemy kinoestetiki.* Tallin.

Lukács, G.
1963   *Ästhetik I: Die Eigenart des Ästhetischen.* Berlin-Spandau: Hermann Luchterhand.

Lumbelli, L.
1974   *La comunicazione filmica.* Florence: La Nuova Italia.

Lyotard, J.-F.
1973   "L'a-cinéma." *Revue d'Esthétique* 2–4. (English translation: "Acinema." In Rosen [ed.] 1986.)

MacCabe, C.
1978   "The Discursive and the Ideological in Film: Notes on the Condition of Political Intervention." *Screen* 19, no. 4.
1985   *Tracking the Signifier.* Minneapolis: University of Minnesota Press.
1986   *High Theory/Low Culture: Analysing Popular Television and Culture.* Manchester: Manchester University Press.

MacCann, R. D. (ed.)
1966   *Film: A Montage of Theories.* New York: Dutton.

Marie, M., and F. Vanoye
1983   "Comment parler la bouche pleine?" *Communications* 38.

Martin, M.
1955   *Le langage cinématographique.* Paris: Editions du Cerf.

Mast, G.
1977   *Film/Cinema/Movie: A Theory of Experience.* New York: Harper and Row.

Mast, G., and M. Cohen (eds.)
1974   *Film Theory and Criticism.* New York and Oxford: Oxford University Press.

May, R.
1947   *Il linguaggio del film.* Milan: Il Poligono.

Mayne, J.
1993   *Cinema and Spectatorship.* London and New York: Routledge.

McArthur, C.
1972   *Underworld USA.* London: Secker and Warburg.

McConnell, F.
1975   *The Spoken Seen: Film and Romantic Imagination.* Baltimore: John Hopkins
        University Press.
1979   *Storytelling and Mythmaking: Images from Film and Literature.* New York: Ox-
        ford University Press.

Mekas, J.
1959   "A Call for a Generation of Film-Makers." *Film Culture* 19. (Also in P. A.
        Sitney [ed.], *Film Culture Reader.* New York and Washington: Praeger,
        1970.)

Melchiorre, V.
1972   *L'immaginazione simbolica.* Bologna: Il Mulino.

Mellen, J.
1973   *Women and Their Sexuality in the New Film.* New York: Horizon.

Mercillon, H.
1953   *Cinéma et monopoles.* Paris: Colin.

Merleau-Ponty, M.
1948   *Sens et non sens.* Paris. (English translation: *Sense and Non-Sense.* Evanston,
        Ill.: Northwestern University Press, 1964.)

Metz, Ch.
1968   *Essais sur la signification au cinéma.* Paris: Klincksieck. (English translation:
        Film Language: A Semiotics of the Cinema. New York: Oxford University
        Press, 1974.)
1971   *Langage et cinéma.* Paris: Larousse. (English translation: *Language and Ci-
        nema.* The Hague: Mouton, 1974.)
1972   *Essais sur la signification au cinéma: II.* Paris: Klincksieck.
1977a   *Essais sémiotiques.* Paris: Klincksieck.
1977b   *Le signifiant imaginaire.* Paris: UGE. (English translation: *The Imaginary
        Signifier: Psychoanalysis and the Cinema.* Bloomington: Indiana University
        Press, 1982.)
1991   *L'énonciation impersonelle ou le site du film.* Paris: Klincksieck.

Mialaret, G., and M. G. Méliès

1954   "Expériences sur la compréhension du langage cinématographique par l'enfant." *Revue Internationale de Filmologie* 18 – 19.

Miccichè, L.

1972   *Il nuovo cinema delgi anni '6o.* Turin: ERI.
1979   *La ragione e lo sguardo.* Cosenza: Lerici.
1990   *Visconti e il neorealismo.* Venice: Marsilio.

Miccichè, L. (ed.)

1975   *Il neorealismo cinematografico italiano.* Venice: Marsilio.

Michelson, A.

1972a   "The Man with the Movie Camera: From Magician to Epistemologist." *Artforum* (March).
1972b   "Screen/Surface: The Politics of Illusionism." *Artforum* (September).

Michotte, A.

1948   "Le caractère de 'réalité' des projections cinématographiques." *Revue Internationale de Filmologie* 3 – 4.
1953   "La participation émotionelle du spectateur à l'action représentée à l'écran." *Revue Internationale de Filmologie* 13.
1961   "Le réel et l'irréel dans l'image." *Revue Internationale de Filmologie* 39.

Mitry, J.

1963   *Esthétique et psychologie du cinéma: Les structures.* Paris: Editions Universitaires.
1965   *Esthétique et psychologie du cinéma: Les formes.* Paris: Editions Universitaires.

Modleski, T.

1988   *The Women Who Knew Too Much.* New York: Methuen.

Möller, K. D.

1978   "Diagrammatische Syntagme und einfache Formen." In *Die Einstellung als Grösse einer Filmsemiotik.* Münster: Maks.
1986   *Filmsprache: Eine kritische Theoriegeschichte.* Münster: Maks.

Morin, E.

1953a   "Le problème des effets dangereux du cinéma." *Revue Internationale de Filmologie* 14 – 15.
1953b   "Recherches sur le public cinématographique." *Revue Internationale de Filmologie* 12.
1954   "Le cinéma sous l'angle sociologique." In *Eventail de l'histoire vivante: Hommage à Lucien Febvre,* vol. 2. Paris: Colin. Reprinted in "Sociologie du cinéma." In *Sociologie.* Paris: Fayard, 1984.
1956   *Le cinéma ou l'homme imaginaire.* Paris: Minuit. (Italian translation: *Il cinema o l'uomo immaginario* [Milan: Feltrinellil, 1982].)
1957   *Les stars.* Paris: Seuil.
1962   *L'esprit du temps.* Paris: Grasset.

Mulvey, L.
1989   *Visual and Other Pleasures.* Bloomington: Indiana University Press.

Musatti, C.
1949   "Le cinéma et la psychanalyse." *Revue Internationale de Filmologie* 6.

Musser, Ch.
1991   *Before the Nickelodeon: Edwin S. Porter and the Edison Manufacturing Company.* Berkeley and Los Angeles: University of California Press.

Nichols, B. (ed.)
1976   *Movies and Methods.* Berkeley, Los Angeles, and London: University of California Press.
1985   *Movies and Methods II.* Berkeley, Los Angeles, and London: University of California Press.

Noguez, D.
1979   *Eloge du cinéma expérimental.* Paris: Centre Pompidou.

Odin, R.
1977   "Dix années d'analyses textuelles de films." *Linguistique et Sémiologie* 3.
1978a   "La sémiologie du cinéma existe-t-elle?" In *Regards sur la sémiologie contemporaine.* St. Etienne: Cierec.
1978b   "Modèle grammatical, modèles linguistiques et étude du langage cinematographique." *Cahiers du 20e Siècle* 9.
1983   "Pour une sémio-pragmatique du cinéma." *Iris* 1 : 1.
1988   "Semiotica e analisi testuale del film." *Bianco e Nero* 11.
1990   *Cinéma et production de sens.* Paris: Colin.

Ombre Rosse
1968a   "Cultura al servizio della rivoluzione." *Ombre Rosse* 5.
1968b   "Cultura o rivoluzione?" *Ombre Rosse* 4.

Oudart, J.-P.
1969a   "La suture." *Cahiers du Cinéma* 211.
1969b   "La suture, II." *Cahiers du Cinéma* 212.
1971   "L'effet de réel." *Cahiers du Cinéma* 228.

Pasolini, P. P.
1972   *Empirismo eretico.* Milan: Garzanti. (English translation: *Heretical Empiricism.* Bloomington: Indiana University Press, 1988.)

Penley, C. (ed.)
1988   *Feminism and Film Theory.* New York: Routledge.

Perkins, V.
1972   *Film as Film.* Harmondsworth: Penguin.

Per una nuova critica
1989   *Per una nuova critica: I convegni pesaresi, 1965–1967.* Venice: Marsilio.

Peters, J. M.
1981   *Pictorial Signs and the Language of Film.* Amsterdam: Rodopi.

Polan, D. B.
1981,
1985   *The Political Language of Film and the Avant-Garde.* Ann Arbor: UMI Research Press.
1986   *Power and Paranoia: History, Narrative and the American Cinema, 1940–1950.* New York: Columbia University Press.

La production du cinéma
1980   *La production du cinéma.* Grenoble: PUG.

Prokop, D.
1970   *Soziologie des Films.* Berlin: Luchterhand.

Pryluck, C.
1968   "Structural Analysis of Motion Pictures as a Symbol System." *Audio Visual Communication Review* 16:4.

Pryluck, C., and R. E. Snow
1967   "Toward a Psycholinguistics of Cinema." *Audio Visual Communication Review* 15:1.

Pye, D.
1975   "Genre and Movies." *Movie* 20.

Quaglietti, L.
1980   *Storia economico-politica del cinema italiano, 1945–1980.* Rome: Editori Riuniti.

Ragghianti, C. L.
1952   *Cinema arte figurativa.* Turin: Einaudi.

Rey, A.
1954   "La perception d'un ensemble de déplacements." *Revue Internationale de Filmologie* 17.

Rocha, G.
1963   *Revisão critica do cinema brasileiro.* Rio de Janeiro: Editora Civilização Brasileira.
1981   *Revolução do cinema novo.* Rio de Janeiro: Alhambra-Embrafilm.

Rohmer, E.
1954   "A qui la faute?" *Cahiers du Cinéma* 39.
1984   *Le goût de la beauté.* Paris: Editions de l'Etoile. (English translation: *The Taste for Beauty.* New York: Cambridge University Press, 1989.)

Romano, D.
1965   *L'esperienza cinematografica.* Florence: Barbera.

Rondolino, G.
1981   *Luchino Visconti.* Turin: Utet.
1989   *Roberto Rossellini.* Turin: Utet.

Ropars, M. C.
1976   "Le film comme texte." *Le Français Aujourd'hui* 32.
1981   *Le texte divisé*. Paris: PUF.
1990   *Ecraniques: Le film du texte*. Lille: Pul.

Rose, J.
1977   "Paranoia and the Film System." *Screen* 17:4.

Rosen, M.
1973   *Popcorn Venus*. New York: Avon Books.

Rosen, P.
1984   "Securing the Historical: Historiography and the Classical Cinema." In
         P. Mellencamp and P. Rosen (eds.), *Cinema Histories, Cinema Practices*.
         Frederick, Md.: American Film Institute.

Rosen, P. (ed.)
1986   *Narrative, Apparatus, Ideology: A Film Theory Reader*. New York: Columbia
         University Press.

Salt, B.
1983   *Film Style and Technology: History and Analysis*. London: Starword.

Sanjinés, J.
1979   *Teoría y práctica de un cine junto al pueblo*. Mexico City: Siglo XXI.

Sarris, A.
1962   "Notes on the Auteur Theory in 1962." *Film Culture* 27 (Winter).
1968   *The American Cinema: Directors and Directions*. New York: Dutton.
1970   "Notes on the Auteur Theory in 1970." *Film Comment* 6:3.

Schatz, T.
1981   *Hollywood Genres: Formulas, Film-making and the Studio System*. Philadel-
         phia: Temple University Press.

Screen
1977   *Screen Reader 1*. London: SEFT.
1982   *Screen Reader 2*. London: British Film Institute.

Simon, J.-P.
1978   "Réferérence et désignation: Notes sur la déixis cinématographique." In
         Regards sur la sémiologie contemporaine. St. Etienne: Cierec.
1979   *Le filmique et le comique*. Paris: Albatros.
1981   "Notes sur la temporalité cinematographique dans les films diégétiques."
         In Chateau, Gardies, and Jost 1981.
1983   "Enonciation et narration." *Communications* 38.

Sklar, R.
1975   *Movie-Made America*. New York: Vintage Books.
1988   "Oh, Althusser! Historiography and the Rise of Cinema Studies." *Radical
         History Review* 41.

Sobchack, V.
1992   *The Address of the Eye: A Phenomenology of Film Experience*. Princeton: Princeton University Press.

Sorlin, P.
1977   *Sociologie du cinéma*. Paris: Aubier Montaigne.
1991   *European Cinemas, European Societies*. New York and London: Routledge.

Sorlin, P., and M. C. Ropars
1976   *Octobre: Ecriture et idéologie*. Paris: Albatros.

Souriau, E. (ed.)
1953   *L'univers filmique*. Paris: Flammarion.

Spoto, D.
1979   *The Art of Alfred Hitchcock*. New York: Doubleday.

Staiger, J.
1992   *Interpreting Films: Studies in the Historical Reception of American Cinema*. Princeton: Princeton University Press.

Stam, R.
1985   *Reflexivity in Film and Literature*. Ann Arbor, Mich.: UMI Research Press. (Reprinted, New York: Columbia University Press, 1992.)

Suter, J.
1979   "Feminine Discourse in *Christopher Strong*." *Camera Obscura* 3–4.

Taddei, N.
1963   *Trattato di teoria cinematografica: L'immagine*. Milan: I 7.

Talens, J., et al.
1978   *Elementos para una semiótica del texto artístico*. Madrid: Cátedra.

Termine, L.
1969   "L'altra cultura e ipotesi di un'arte nuova." *Cinema Nuovo* 202.

Termine, L. (ed.)
1979   *Dentro l'immagine*. Turin: Tirrenia.

Thompson, K.
1981   *Eisenstein's Ivan the Terrible: A Neoformalist Analysis*. Princeton: Princeton University Press.
1988   *Breaking the Glass Armor: Neoformalist Film Analysis*. Princeton: Princeton University Press.

Tinazzi, G.
1983   *La copia originale*. Venice: Marsilio.

Tinazzi, G. (ed.)
1972   "Strutturalismo e critica del film." *Bianco e Nero* 3/4.

Tomasino, R.
1978   *La forma del cinema*. Lecce: Milella.

Truffaut, F.
1954   "Une certaine tendance du cinéma français." *Cahiers du Cinéma* 31. (English translation: "A Certain Tendency of the French Cinema." In Nichols [ed.] 1976.)
1957   "Le cinéma français crève sous les fausses légendes." *Arts* 619.

Tsivian, J. (J. Ciu'jan)
1991   *Istoričeskaja recepcija kino: Kinematograf v Rossii, 1896–1930*. Riga: Zinatne.

Tudor, A.
1974   *Theories of Film*. London: Secker and Warburg.

Turim, M.
1985   *Abstraction in Avant-Garde Films*. Ann Arbor: UMI Research Press.

Urrutia, J.
1972   *Ensayos de lingüística externa cinematográfica*. Madrid: Colegio Univ. San Pablo.

Urrutia, J. (ed.)
1976   *Contribuciones al análisis semiológico del film*. Valencia: Torres.

Vernet, M.
1988   *Figures de l'absence*. Paris: Editions Cahiers du Cinéma.

Wallon, H.
1953   "L'acte perceptif et le cinéma." *Revue Internationale de Filmologie* 13.

Warshow, R.
1962   *The Immediate Experience*. New York: Doubleday.

Wasko, J.
1982   *Movies and Money: Financing the American Film Industry*. Norwood: Ablex Publishing Corporation.

Willemen, P.
1994   *Looks and Frictions: Essays in Cultural Studies and Film Theory*. Bloomington: Indiana University Press / London: BFI.

Williams, L.
1981   "Film Body: An Implantation of Perversion." *Cine-Tracts* 12.

Wolfenstein, M., and N. Leites
1950   *Movies: A Psychological Study*. Glencoe: Free Press.

Wollen, P.
1969   *Signs and Meaning in the Cinema*. London: Secker and Warburg.
1982   *Readings and Writings*. London: Verso.

Wood, M.
1975   *America in the Movies: Or, "Santa Maria, It Had Slipped My Mind."* New York: Basic Books.

Worth, S.
1969   "The Development of a Semiotic of Film." *Semiotica* 1 : 3.
1981   *Studying Visual Communication*. Philadelphia: University of Pennsylvania Press.

Wright, W.
1976   *Sixguns and Society: A Structural Study of the Western*. Berkeley: University of California Press.

Zavattini, C.
1979   *Neorealismo ecc*. Milan: Bompiani.

Zazzo, B., and R. Zazzo
1949   "Une expérience sur la compréhension du film." *Revue Internationale de Filmologie* 6.

Zazzo, R.
1949   "Niveau mental et compréhension du cinéma." *Revue Internationale de Filmologie* 5.

INDEX OF NAMES